The Medicine Way

A MEDICINE GUIDE

BY

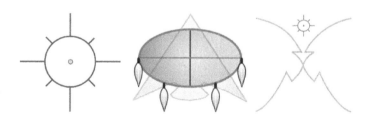

WHITE EAGLE

Regarding Grow, Growth and Life purpose….

In asking Great Pop as to how I should be and do while I am here on Mother Earth, He told me "Little One, I made that theme park for any Beings and things that want to experience some of the limitless means and ways to experience and express Love and Brotherhood".

Some people profess that we each have a specific mission to accomplish in our lifetime, or that we come here to learn lessons of some sort through which we will Grow toward completing some kind of "Spiritual Transformation" and thereby achieve a "Higher" condition of being. I personally believe that all of this aspiration and ambitious thinking about one's reality and life's purpose is founded in Fear and is all a falsehood. I am certain that we come here for experiences by our own choice and that we experience things of our own manifestation through our thoughts and Prayers of Desire. This means that there is No mandate or mission, nor any requirement to learn anything, there is only a path of life that is of our own choosing and design.

When I was young Great Pop told me: "Grow like the tree and thereby from the inside out in all directions". I thought He meant that I should aspire to grow taller and thereby bigger. I later learned the Proper idea and Ideal meant by His use of the word Grow as being more like the concept of "Multi-dimensional Expansion," as in this ideal we are in a sense "Ever and Always Complete".

Through each incarnation we gain knowledge and understanding and therefore Expand from the experiences and expressions of being ourselves, thus we have more to offer and share with other Beings and things and their expansion as well. This is the Real and true condition and Potential for every Being and thing in the physical or spiritual condition, from the single celled micro-organism to the entirety of all creation - period.

All Beings and things are considered "Even" in Great Pop's idea and Love of us. He would Never favor or set any thing as being better than any other thing of His Creation, therefore, within the contents of this or any of the other material that has been Brought forth by this channel and servant of The Creator, I pray that you will properly interpret and correctly understand the use of the words of Learn, Lesson, Grow, or Growth to mean and be interchangeable with "**To Become of,**" "**Embody,**" "**Expand,**" or "**Expansion.**"

THE MEDICINE WAY

BY

White Eagle

Revised - January 2020

White Eagle is a practicing Medicine Man who has been blessed by the Great Spirit Father with both Healing and Vision Medicine. Being part Algonquin and Arapaho, he carries forward a mixture of both traditional and nontraditional Medicine techniques. Ever seeking to serve the Will of The Great Spirit, White Eagle endeavors to enable all of the Great Spirit's children to learn of His Love and in the many ways in which we may allow His Light and Love to enrich our Well-being and lives. Ever in a constant vigil in seeking ways to serve the Will of the Great Spirit, White Eagle has left the normal order of the societies that we live in to walk totally the path of a Medicine Man in order to embrace and help in the initiation of the New Order of the Great Spirit's Will and Consciousness in humankind. In the last period of time much information about the coming events as pertaining to the reawakening of Spirituality has been provided to him by his Guides, or Angels so to speak, as well as by the Creator Himself in order to bring forth a new and heightened life in the Spirit of each of His creation.

This document is a product of this endeavor as given by the Great Spirit for him to do in answer to his prayer for guidance in his daily meditation. These manuscripts are still new and seeking conventional publishing and support in distribution. As a PohTikaWah or Medicine Man, White Eagle is a Priest, Healer, Teacher, Visionary, Counselor, and Ceremonial Leader but perhaps most important, a Guide in the way of discovering the Truth and Perfect Child within each of us.

In the traditional way, a Medicine Man would give a person a Medicine Name usually around the birth time as a vision would be given them however, several years ago during one of his daily Mediations the Great Spirit said for him to start Naming people with a Name that describes His Original Thought as He created each of them. This Name describes the perfect pattern of each Self as He created them and describes what they not only have always been but also that which they are and ever will continue to be (or better said, "What does Not need fixing"). The Medicine Name as described by White Eagle helps us understand why we have certain likes or dislikes and habits that are most normal for us, as well as abilities in which we can easily excel and use in our growth. White Eagle explains the Name as well as its Medicine and tendencies but always reminds us that we are ever in growth as to become greater channels of the Great Spirit's Light and Love and to do this we are ever learning new Medicine to add to that of our beginning so as to please the Creator. This is our true desire of our inner child.

In addition to the Naming Vision, White Eagle has also been given abilities in vision such as looking inside one's body to detect illness or infirmary, finding objects that are considered lost, going backwards or forwards in time as well as others. White Eagle has also been given the ability to channel or so as to say allow another person's Guides to speak to them through the body of him as well as channel his own personal Guides in an advisory capacity about all matters current and past that are having an immediate influence on one. White Eagle lives in what might best be described as altered states and does not use or condone the abuse of any drugs nor of anything or of anyone. Another of the abilities that has been given to White Eagle is for him to walk in another's moccasins in a past life review in order to release carryover problems that often occur from past lives. This process takes several days to complete and the product is specific documentation and a channeled review. White Eagle's knowledge of the Spirit world also provides dream state interpretations as well.

As a Healer, White Eagle has many abilities in working with energy, potions, and teas as well as Medicine Stones. There have been many instances whereby he has cured someone's headache or hiccups with a single thought. White Eagle will also be the first one to thank another for healing themselves and as he says that he takes no credit but full responsibility in such matters as he only invokes the Will and Love of God. White Eagle guides people in the process of meditation and from time to time holds workshops in learning the Medicine Wheel Way as well as about Plant Spirit, Animal Spirit, and

Mineral Spirit Medicines and how we can use them to enrich our lives.

White Eagle sometimes kids around about being a Native American Ghost Buster but know well he takes these matters very seriously. Unlike some others he uses the unlimited potential of Love to help in problems with discarnates, or entities, and possession as they are very dynamic in the Well-being of all involved. White Eagle is not a Witch or Witch Doctor although he has much knowledge about such things and will refuse to help any who are not aspiring to the highest ideal which is, "To Walk in Balance and With Harm to No One Being or thing, including Oneself!" If possible White Eagle will record personal readings on cassette tape and asks that each provide their own tape for use. He says that one receives what they are willing to invest in any matter. He asks that each desiring a reading, prepare and bring a written list of questions to be answered for their own use, as he does not want to see them. White Eagle also makes many ceremonial items and personal items such as prayer sticks, rattles, shields, earrings, necklaces, as well as paintings.

Often White Eagle will speak of only charging a commitment to change when asked about receiving money for his services. However, as all truly know, one must be willing to give something away to receive more of anything at any point in time. Gifts or donations of money or other things that might support the work will be welcomed by him as White Eagle recognizes that in a respectful sharing way, those who have resources to share will be the first to benefit in the sharing process. However lack of money or resources are often manifestations of symptoms of other Spiritual dilemmas and he would never deny his services to anyone because of their lack of a comfortable money supply. Each one should feel comfortable with whatever they feel they should provide, as it is a contribution not a fixed price. White Eagle sees it only as a contribution to God and the Church.

This document is presented in what might best be described as pristine in its word usage and while sometimes the word usage might not be considered to be grammatically correct, it is in its original true condition to the Spirit of the consciousness and is most proper. As it is given to express this information in the English language, many of the words available for use fall short of the full dynamics of the total scope of the consciousness being expressed. In no way is it also to be inferred that there is any bias or weight given to the male or female of the human species. All true Beings, which are all Spirits created by

The Great Spirit or God as some refer to Him, have chosen to incarnate into each of the "Body-forms" and races; which is why the Great Spirit created the diversity in the first place. I call Him Great Pop and I am certain that He loves and favors each as equal in His esteem and so should we. As the Earthplane experience is truly that of learning the unlimited ways of experiencing Brotherhood and expressing Love, the consciousness associated in the term Brotherhood is that of the willingness to support, sacrifice for, share, care, nurture, guide, and most important, value another Being regardless of what sex or other condition the body is in. Any other word associations that might even in the slightest way be considered to be gender biased should be considered the same way and the consciousness to the Spirit of the use retained. This material is presented in the Spirit of Onement and the Law of One and is meant to be received in the same way, each samely unique and in their uniqueness the same.

White Eagle may be contacted at **ASpiritWalker.com** or at:
5532 Aberdeen Place
Fayetteville, NC 28303

It is my sincerest hope that this material will in some way be of service in bringing forth some of the abundance of Light and Love that the Great Spirit has for each and every one of you.

In the years that I have been guiding peoples, I have always cautioned them about what they read in books as I do also to you here and now. A book in its very best of conditions is but one person's documentary of their observations as they walk the path of life, and indeed can be no more than that. But, while they might speak of the squirrel running up the tree ahead and share their vision of that, they might miss the butterfly emerging from the cocoon behind. This book is a composition of information that comes to me both through meditation and channeled through me by my Guides. It is presented in the Spirit of Love. It was given to me to understand that the purpose of each person's incarnation to Earthplane for an Earthwalk is to learn more about the unlimited ways to experience and to express Love and Brotherhood.

In many of these books I talk about the Prevalent Culture. When I call it "White", I am not meaning Caucasian or even European for any that might be sensitive to such or take any offense as none is intended. The current Prevalent Culture, which is at times also called the "White Western Way" by some, actually has it genesis long before the man named Jesus was hung on a cross. I consider that event to be an act of "Being Murdered" by some of its adherents because of its Religion and foundation of materialism. And as Great Pop often tells me, "This too can Change". I hope He was Not talking about those 30 pieces of silver, don't You?

As you read the pages....

Walk in Joy and Enjoy your walk.

Presented With Love

White | Eagle

In The Medicine Way & Real Spirituality

If I am to consider myself as being
Something more than just an animal life form,
Then I must also consider and respect
That possibility and condition
In every other being and thing
That The Creator has made and / or exists.

White Eagle

<<<<<<< *Left To Right* >>>>>>>

In the Medicine Way, all things are done with respect to the four cardinal directions and center of the Medicine Wheel. One can and should always consider oneself in the center of a Medicine Wheel as one goes about one's daily activities. This means that one is always facing The Creator in the North, even when one is sleeping, no matter as to the direction that one's body is actually facing. The significance of this is that since one is always facing North so to speak, all Bead Stories, Symbols, and Patterns are to be read and interpreted as being Left to Right in their orientation.

So if I were to say for you to place one's candles so as to read Change to Spirit, the Red candle would be on the Left and the White candle on the Right as one is facing. This of course would be just the opposite if one were standing in the North and facing the South, hence the need for clarification here.

To make Bead Stories, Patterns, or Candles multidirectional, one simply places an element in the center and reverses the pattern, as is common in many ancient things. In that case, Red to White, with Blue in the center for the Creator, followed by White to Red would read: Change to Spirit by God, Spirit to Change. The primary reason for Left to Right is that the Left is The Past and the Right is the Future with the Center being the Present or Now.

TABLE OF CONTENTS

THE MEDICINE OF PRAYER   Page   -   11

EARTHWALK   Page   -   51

WALKING THE ROUND WAY   Page   -   107

THE MEDICINE WHEEL   Page   -   171

MINERAL SPIRIT KNOWLEDGE   Page   -   215

PLANT SPIRIT KNOWLEDGE   Page   -   275

ANIMAL SPIRIT KNOWLEDGE   Page   -   371

As the definition of Brotherhood Proper

Was given to me to be:

The sharing in the betterment in the

condition of the all.....

When we look at each other,

we see either the best or the worst of ourselves.

As we are each a reflection of the other....

much better it seems to learn first to see

the child of the Great Spirit in each other,

and thereby accept that condition in Oneself.

WHITE EAGLE

To Spirit, Sparkie & All of the other 4 legged Life
Partners,
Who brought so much love, joy and beauty to my life....

I Love You and I Thank You each & All,
and I will see you again I know,
on the other side.
Chon A-Tah.

THE MEDICINE OF

PRAYER

BY

WHITE EAGLE

CONTENTS

The Medicine of Prayer   13

How We Truly Receive   22

About Prayersticks   27

About Smudging & Clearing   30

About Tobacco   35

The Tobacco / Pipe Prayer Ceremony   36

About Ritual and Ceremony   45

****

I ASKED THE GREAT SPIRIT ONE DAY,

FATHER, HOW IS IT BEST FOR ME TO PRAY?

HE TOLD ME -

"OFTEN"!

HE SAID THAT WAY HE CAN BEST HELP ME,

AND SHARE IN MY WALK OF THE WAY.

White Eagle

THE MEDICINE OF PRAYER

BY

WHITE EAGLE

In Reality, all that we ever do in life is to make Choices about what we next Desire to experience or express in and of ourselves. These Choices become expressed as our Prayers of Desire which then attract those events, things, and experiences to ourselves. It Really is just that simple, and really is just that way.

***

For those that may not already suspect, there Is a Medicine Way of doing anything and everything. In doing things in The Medicine Way, one is to consider oneself to be no less than or better than anything else, and the opposite perspective and attitude holds true and should be maintained as well. Therefore, in The Medicine Way one does Not command that any Being or thing, be it in Spirit or otherwise, do any of a thing. Instead, one can and should respectfully ask, and hence Pray, for its support in the fulfillment of that which is desired. Likewise, one should always give one's sincere thanks and thereby appreciation, whatever the outcome of that Prayer might be.

***

Another thing that I feel needs mention at this point is that in The Medicine Way, The Great Spirit Creator is at the center of the Great Web of creation and Not oneself. In this I mean that in any and all of one's personal expressions, including that of one's Prayers, one is to keep in Mind as to Why one is Praying for What, and Who it is that one is seeking to serve in them.

***

In speaking to people it is often given for me to say, "There is no wrong way to Pray, but sometimes there are better things to Pray for". At other times I might say "All Prayers are answered, and your Fear is a Prayer that is most likely to be answered the fastest". As a Medicine

Man, the understanding of the power of Prayer is my most important tool or asset. It supersedes any other ability or knowledge that any one person in any condition of being or vocation might possess. The process given for me to explain the Medicine of Prayer is to go back to the beginning and explain the structure of all things. All, and I emphasize the Reality that **ALL IS VIBRATION** and in the physical realm that vibration has an amplitude of Seven and a cycle rate of Four as Created and expressed by the Great Spirit Creator and Father of All Things. Therefore All things in the physical realm are constantly in resonance with and/or are reflective of this condition and reality in some manner.

All things in the Spirit Plane, Other Worlds, or Earth Plane are vibratory entities or thoughts as originated by the Creator or by our Hope or Fear. All things made by the Great Spirit are connected by a link or thread to each other thing of His Creation and also to Him. Whatever affects any one thing of His Creation is felt by each and every other thing in it and by Him. In the Great Spirit's creation or idea of us, He gave us thought and Free Will. It is this gift that we have as the source of our limited sense of a creative force. Our thoughts generate vibrations that are sensed upon the web structure that connects every thing to each other and to Him. Whatever we generate as Original Thought, is sensed and felt by all things in all Planes and Worlds which we will call the true Universe and it is much, much, bigger than a bunch of stars that we are used to thinking of.

In the process of being Co-creators by the expression of our ability of Thought, we generate thought forms of vibratory patterns much the same as throwing a pebble into the water of a still pond. We truly cannot create or destroy anything, although it does seem so in the process of manifesting our ability in the physical. We truly can only change the form or utility of things that were in a sense born or created by the Original Thought of a loving Father Creator. Each and everything that is, is made by Him for it to experience being itself. As each thing gains experience, it expands. In this expression of growth, it becomes a greater potential channel of His Light and Love. His Light and Love is the true Source of all things in all planes and this is Vibration also. As each thing made by Him is unique in the sense of it, each thing has a pattern of Vibration that is unique to His creation of it. This unique Vibration is like a fingerprint and identifies it as a perfect expression from the Great Spirit as its source. Each thing of His Creation has this unique Vibration and this unique Vibration is what we refer to as Spirit.

All things are a manifestation of His Original Thought through the generation of Vibration of and from, Him. Light and Sound are two qualities by which we on the physical plane most often resonate to or recognize vibration. Perhaps the best word to describe the substance of the originating of Vibration including the making of us, is Love. In reality we cannot create Love, at best all we can do is channel or give it to another person or thing. As we do that, we must first receive some to oneself. When we choose to then give the rest away so that it benefits the betterment in the condition of the All, that All always includes that of oneself as well. If, on the other hand we choose to keep all of the Love that we receive, like a cup that only holds so much before it begins to overflow, we get as full of Self and can receive no more. Love is no thing that we make. It is however the fertilizer by which we expand and grow. As we receive Love from the Creator and take a percentage to Self for growth so that we can receive more and thereby give more away, then only are we Walking in Balance to the best condition possible of oneself and All things, including a very Loving Creator Father.

A long time ago I was thinking how unfair that everyone on Earthplane including the Christ had a Birthday. In wishing to celebrate a day of the year as being for Him, The Creator told me that He would tell me each year which day that would be. The date this year for instance is November 3, 1993. In that first year, it was a day in June. The Creator told me to mention that He did not want to get caught up in that astrological stuff and I can well understand why. That first year seems like it was so long ago. Yet, I still remember it as if it was yesterday. For my gift or present to Him, the Creator of everything, I thought to give the gift of asking nothing of Him for a whole day. And if you know this Medicine Man, that was a pretty tough objective. The very next day I felt real proud of myself and my creativity in giving the Great Spirit a vacation or holiday from my need of Him. When I asked Him in my daily meditation how He liked my gift to Him, what He said to me still makes me cry even as I write this. He said to me that He knew I was trying to do my very best by doing that, but in the process I was denying Him in the walk of my life. After feeling so much self-pride earlier, I have never felt so much shame as I felt then. Obviously, what I thought was the very best I could do was not at all that. I promised Him then that I would never do that again. Then the Creator told me that That is the very best present I can ever give Him.

So often we are taught to be self-sufficient and never to be in need of help or assistance from another Being or thing. Now I see much more clearly how I have, and always will be in need of Him. Now I try to be more conscious of including Him in every single thing that I do, even if it is play or just a thought. A long time ago when I asked how to walk the Way, I was given what He expressed as being the Prayer Proper. It is the test of truth in walking the Way and helps one in making choices. The Prayer Proper is:

Dear Father, I Pray to walk in Balance and With Harm to No One Being or Thing of Your creation, including Myself.

And the test is obviously:

Does it Walk in Balance and With Harm to No One including Oneself, then it is the Proper thing to do.

I was then given to understand that as all is Vibration, every thought is a Prayer of some sort. It is these "Thought Prayers" that effectively magnetize things or conditions to us in the experience of our expression of Life. And whether we see or judge them as being good or bad, it happens just that way. Then the Creator showed me how we each have a pattern of ourselves that allows Light and Love to pass through both to and from us. As we allow this pattern to be complete and without holes other than that of which He originally made of us, we are operating as the very best channels of Him in us.

In front of this pattern of Self, He showed me how there was a kind of filter or screen. It is this part of ourselves that we place the magnets of our Prayers. We do this so as to draw those conditions to us for us to experience and thereby expand, which is our job so as to speak. This is the truly perpetual condition of all things of and by Him. The tricky part to it all, is that we can place two kinds of Prayer magnets upon our screen. One type comes from the Heart of ourselves and they are called Hope Prayers. The other type comes from the Ego of ourselves and they are called Fear Prayers. Being afraid of the experience or happening of something will call it to oneself to experience just as much as something considered as being good.

The tricky part is that Fear Prayers usually happen quicker for us to receive the full benefit of the experience of them. The Giving away of a Fear after recognizing it, is the only way to remove that Prayer from your screen. A denial of the existence or condition of it, just leaves it there to experience. And most often, it will happen at the most inconvenient or uncomfortable time possible so as to remind us to quit

Praying that way. It is all perfect you see as He truly wishes the very best conditions and experiences for each and every one of us, and He Loves each of us most dearly that way.

While I was writing this I thought, well I haven't asked Him about the definition of Prayer so here it goes:

PRAYER IS THE COMMUNICATION OF ONE'S DESIRE,
BE IT CONSCIOUS OR OTHERWISE,
TO NOT ONLY THE GREAT SPIRIT CREATOR,
BUT ALSO TO THE CONSCIOUSNESS OF ALL THINGS,
IN AND OF HIS CREATION,
IN ANY AND ALL REALMS OF EXISTENCE.

The two key words in Prayer are Communication and Desire. The understanding that is most significant is that every thought includes what we call attitudes, which are thoughts too. All thoughts generate thought forms of Vibration, which are like words that are heard and felt by any and All, anywhere and Everywhere.

The only Real power and thereby Ability that any of us possess is also the only creative force that we have and it is our Prayer. Prayer is singularly the most Dynamic Force in the All of Creation. Prayer is also the means by which we direct the flow of Beings, things, and experiences to and from us in our being in Life.

ALL life experiences are the direct expression of one's individual Prayers. Prayer is our only ability of Creativity as it truly is the only thing that we can individually create, and it is just as simple as that. Prayer is the only way that we can let The Great Spirit into our Life and Earthwalk and allow His love to support the expansion of our experiences. Prayer is truly the actualizing force of the Universe. Each of us incarnate into the Earthplane with a Plan of experiences and expressions. The Plan is nothing but a bunch of Prayer magnets that we first set upon the screens of our attitudes, any of which we can change at any time. We express our expansion and growth by learning to give our Fear magnets away and replace them with one's of Hope. As Fear magnets come from the Ego and Hope magnets come from the Heart, we operate to the best of our ability and His desire in us each time that we choose to give our Ego away and expand in the Heart as to be a greater channel of His Light and Love.

It was brought to my attention by an friend of mine with Owl Medicine, that I need to elaborate upon the importance in the uniqueness of the gift of Prayer. Free Will and the ability of Choice are gifts from the same loving Father Creator too. While Choice affects the dynamics of oneself and the condition of the All including that of oneself, Choice and Free Will are not expressions of our Creativity. Instead, Choice and Free Will are merely intersections upon the web of our Prayer which is our true and only Creative ability. One might choose to Pray for anything, or condition to be. Sometimes we find that hard to do because we are not too sure of what it is Proper for us to Pray for. Yet, deep inside we truly know and comprehend the Power within that Ability given to us by the Great Spirit that is Prayer. Deep inside we also know that we always can choose to Walk the path of our lives in the Balanced way. We likewise know that we never walk Alone and that with Prayer, we can in some way get out of any trouble or difficulty that through our Choice we might get ourselves into.

Considering the dynamics and great ability and enabling provided to us through the gift of Prayer, I asked the Great Spirit what is it that is right for me to Pray for. He said anything you want to, but finding that which Walks in Balance and With Harm to No One including Yourself seems the best thing to do. He then said not to worry as all Prayers are answered and in some way they will serve to support the expansion of some Being or thing, even if it is not you.

I was then given to understand the dynamics of those that generate Prayers of Harm and ill-will upon others as some of the people do. I recognized that as these Prayers are generated from the Ego "Bark" of the sender's tree and are of Fear, they actually are as weak as we want them to be. Therefore, the only protection that any of us need is already provided in us by the ability of giving away our Ego and thereby Fear bark on tree. When we do that, then the Fear Prayers of others will pass right on through us. Also, they usually return manifold to the sender and most often at the time for them to receive the fullest lesson in them. There are many thought-form entities manifested by some people through their Fear. These Prayers only have substance if we give them value or reality and through our Free Will we choose to do that or not. If someone wishes me ill, my best response is to recognize my resonance to the condition of it. Then I can give my Ego bark away so that it does not attach to me and Pray for a better condition of the All, including them and myself.

Thankfulness is also a Prayer that best helps us Balance and center ourselves in our walk of Life as it reminds us of the true Source and purpose in us. I was then given to ask the Great Spirit Father for what is it that I should Pray and He told me:

Pray for **PROTECTION.**
Protection not from that which might be done to me by another
and that can only come from myself through Fear,
but Protection from having the wrongful idea of myself
as ever being separate from Him and His Love of me.

Pray for **GUIDANCE.**
Guidance not only in the best Choices in life but even
better yet, Guidance in the Proper way to see and
experience the greatest expansion through each experience
in and of, the walk of it.

Pray for **RESOURCE.**
Resource not only in the things that you think that you
might need for comfort or expressing your Creativity,
but most important the greatest resource which we might
receive, the Resource of Opportunity to experience and
express your greatest expansion as to be the greatest channel
of His Light and Love that you can be.

I realized that truly anything that I might consider to need was
covered by just these three. Then I was given that as all things have a
resonance to the vibration of the number seven, four more things were
nice although secondary to Pray for:

Pray for **HEALTH.**
My Health and Well-being is a condition that is truly a
responsibility of Self to keeping the vessel of me in
good condition as to best serve the Him in me
and sometimes I need help in this as to best Re-new-all
conditions, in and of, me.

Pray for **WEALTH.**
My Wealth is not limited to the financial condition of
myself and it is ok to ask for improvement in that, but
much more important, my Wealth is the Opportunity provided
to serve the Him in me and in Prayer I ever seek a much
greater expression and realization of that.

Pray for **LOVE.**
While Love is often thought of in Prayer as having
someone to give one's love to or desire relationship
with and it is ok to seek that, more important is that His
Love is the initiating force that created everything in
the first place and I pray to become a greater
expression and channel of that.

Pray for **JOY.**
Joy is often thought of as the expression of happiness
and we are each responsible to our own condition of
that, but Joy is the attitude and perspective that is
the most important to seek as to experience the greatest
and roundest condition of Being as we learn to embrace
it in every step that we take in our walk of life and I
Pray to always be conscious of that.

In my Medicine Way I have always been able to call the Wind
from the four directions and many have expressed amazement when I
do. When asked how I can do that, I simply say that I Pray to the
Spirit of it. One might ask: "Is it Proper to Pray to the Wind like
that"? I am Not treating the Wind as being God, I am treating it as
being what it is, my Brother. If I ask any of a thing of any Being or
thing, it is an expression of a Prayer of Desire. As I pray to the Water,
Wind, Stone, Fire, or any Living thing or Spirit beyond, I am also
praying to Him in these things that way. As we begin to see Him in
all things, we better see the Potential of Him in ourselves this way.
Think about it and you will see the validity in that. It was given that
there is no wrong way to Pray. In Reality there is no right or wrong
anyway, as right and wrong are judgments that we make about
something. There are just better things for us to Pray for. Some better
things to Pray for might be:

THANKFULNESS
MERCY
GRACE
FORGIVENESS OF SELF
RECEIVING
CALLING
VISION
UNDERSTANDING

METAMORPHOSIS
CHANGE
OPPORTUNITY
RELEASE
PEACE
STRENGTH
COURAGE
RENEWALL
ENABLING OR ABILITY

While I am sure I probably missed some, these all seem special to me. Prayer is the enabling force that is our most important tool in the expression of ourselves. It is the greatest asset that we bring with our Plan for the experience and expression of ourselves in Life. Remember All Prayers are heard by Him and the All everywhere and our thoughts are a big part of that. As we think, so do we become, and so I Pray for Joy in your Heart and Peace in your mind and Softness and ease in your steps in your Earthwalk.

****

HOW WE TRULY RECEIVE

In the process of our Being, we really can create Only one thing and that is our Prayer, as all of anything Real and True is ever in a condition of being manifested only by the Creator. Whatever we bring forth as a condition to ourselves in any experience of our Being, is only an expression of His Benefaction and Providence in answer to some Prayer of Desire that was expressed through the Will of oneself for the potential experience of it. While we can seemingly create a table, lamp, or anything of such nature such as a building or airplane, we only in that instance change the form or utility of some Real thing of His creation so as to make use of it in this fashion. Our Real and only potential creative force is that of thinking in one's Mind and Consciousness of new things to Pray for and thereby receive or not, from the Creator so as to experience something. The following diagram defines how any thing is truly brought forth to be experienced by oneself:

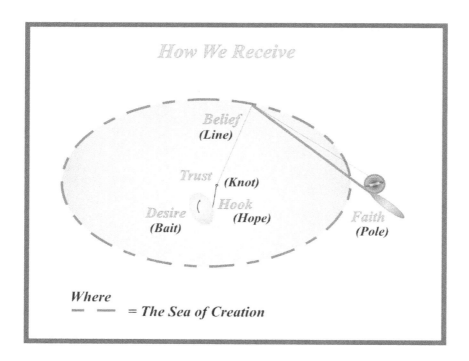

The expression of one's Desire to Receive any of a thing is much like the casting of one's baited hook upon the waters of the sea of His creation so as to become in a condition of Receivership. All Real things are made by the Creator and He is indeed the only True Source of anything. If one does not Believe Proper in the Potential of the Creator and Trust Proper in His Love and care for oneself, one indeed can never become in Proper Receivership of anything. It Really is the case that if one does not Believe a thing possible for oneself, then it will not be and therefore be Proper in the condition of the Balance and Well-being of oneself.

There are many instances whereby one seemingly had not openly thought that they might be able to Receive a Godsend so to speak, only to have the True Prayer of a secreted Desire from the Heart of oneself become manifested. But it Truly is one's Belief that is the line by which one does ever Receive anything to oneself in the condition of being and this Belief can be at or in any of the various levels of one's Consciousness. It is one's Desire that is the bait that one uses to Receive any of a thing. One's Desire bait is ever in a condition as to be considered as to be in the like in kind way or as you sow so shall you reap in the harvest of one's Endeavor of Desire fulfillment. This is especially true as concerns the Well-being of others. One's Desire or bait is ever in a condition as being an expression of either the Heart of oneself or the Ego of oneself. Either expression will be answered by the Creator as both will support one's expansion of Potential. Usually the Fear Prayer of Desire will become answered quickest so as to stimulate one's future Potential through the experience.

Hope Prayers of Desire may take a little longer, as in using a bigger hook for a bigger fish. The bait of Desire of a Hope Prayer is indeed everlasting as is that which is Benefacted by the Creator and Received to oneself from such. It is the Hope Prayers that are answered that strengthen the very fibers of the Tree of Self. As one can see, Desire is the bait that one fishes with upon the sea of His creation and all of one's Desires are ever an expression of the Will of oneself. There are two types of hooks that one can use being either that of Hope or Fear with Hope coming from one's Heart, and Fear from one's Ego. It is one's Belief that is the line with which to retrieve that which is Desired, and its strength is ever dependent upon the strength of one's Relationship with the Creator. Trust is the knot that one uses to fasten one's hook of Hope or Fear to one's belief line and it is fashioned from one's Trust in the Creator's continuing Love and providence for oneself. One's Faith is the pole or retrieval device which makes for ease in which to pull in the object of one's Receivership and behold it to oneself. It truly is one's Faith that makes room or a receiving area in the pattern of oneself for which to put that which is Desired and Received into, so as to behold it precious to oneself as in all conditions it should be.

All things that one Receives in this Proper Way should be seen as being a very special and precious Benefaction to oneself by a Loving and Benevolent Creator whom I call "Great Pop". Through being in the Receiving Proper Way, oneself and the All else of His creation are most benefited by the expansion in the Potential of oneself through the experience of it, whatever it was, if seen Properly. In the True process of Receivership, it is much more significant as to the strength of one's Faith or pole, one's Belief or line, one's Trust or knot and one's Hope or hook, than simply in the strength of one's Desire or bait that will land the biggest fish. This is Real and true because if one's hook of Hope or Fear is too weak, then it will bend and the fish will get away. Also, these conditions are the same for one's Belief line, Trust knot, and Faith pole.

***

How things happen is that we fashion a Prayer of Desire that most closely resembles a Potential and thereby "Fish" in the sea of Great Pop's creation and go fishing so as to attract that like in kind Potential to ourselves. We do this so that it can then become Self-actualized and Self-realized and thus experienced in our lives. If the Potential does not yet exist, we certainly cannot fashion a Prayer of Desire Bait or magnet. In this I mean that we can only conceive or imagine things that Great Pop has already made as a Potential. Likewise, even the unknown is an outwardly expressed Potential, and there are more than just one of them I am sure. How can there be more than one Potential if they all are unique as you said earlier White Eagle? Just as there are many more than just one Potential that is a person or grain of sand, there are many diverse and unique Potential that are collectively considered to be "The Unknown".

Oftentimes I have spoken of Prayersticks and each and every incarnated Being or thing has one of their own. One's Prayerstick can be likened to being like the previous fishing pole example except with many different lines, hooks and bait attached to it all of the time. Before we incarnate, we attach what I call our "Master Plan" of Prayers of Desire bait magnets to our "Spiritual Prayerstick". These magnets are what cause our early choices and conditions to occur, as well as some later developments and events in our being in Life. And yes, I do mean any and all birth conditions including deformities, blindness etc. As we progress in Life, we are constantly adding to or changing some of them or in some instances we change all of them. Therefore at any point in the incarnation and thereby Life of a Being or thing the following conditions exist for them:

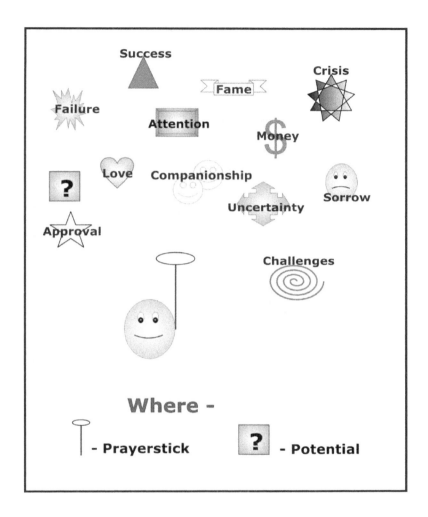

As one can see, there are always many diverse Potential about any given Being or thing. While some may be closer than others, the more significant ones are those that are relatively close at hand. Why this is significant is that "Magnetics" of a sort are always involved in this process. For most Potential there also exists what could be considered as its polar opposite. In this I mean that if I have a Potential for Winning a contest or the like, then there is a high probability that there also are close at hand many Losing Potential as well. While that depiction helps one to see How there can be many Potential around a Being or thing, the following one better shows what really is going on all of the time:

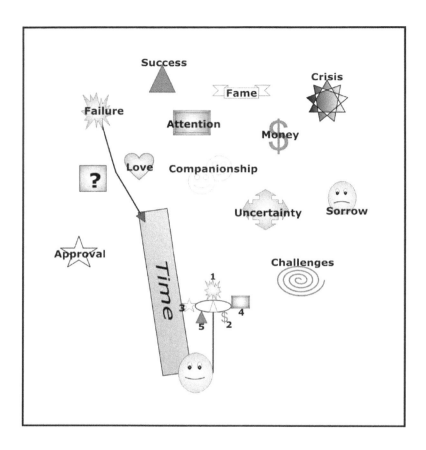

As shown by the element that is number 1 at the top of their Prayerstick in the depiction above, be it consciously or subconsciously, all Beings and things prioritize the Potential that they next want to draw to themselves so as to experience. And yes, when we Really express Hope or Fear about some thing, that is exactly what happens. When this occurs, it causes an increase of the magnetism of that potential and thus draws it to, and then upon the conveyor belt of stretchy and amendable fabric that we call Time. Yep, it is Time that brings forth each new and subsequent event and experience that any Being or thing ever experiences. Obvious in this example is that there are other Potential that are closer at hand. Yet, the Focus of the individual's Desire expression as being shown at the top of their

Prayerstick will in Reality cause the matching Potential to be drawn forth past the others and then placed upon the conveyor belt next. These are the aspects and elements that are involved in How any and all things happen and they all support one thing to occur, which is the fulfillment of a Prayer of Desire in some way.

ABOUT PRAYERSTICKS

In reality we all have a Prayerstick that we use to Pray with, be it a physical one or not. Our Prayerstick is a communication tool and device much like a telephone and it is ever connected to the Creator and the All of His creation. As a PohTikaWah and Medicine Man, my Prayerstick is my most valuable tool and possession and I oftentimes have several for personal and ceremonial use. While one might liken one's Prayerstick to be something like the fishing pole in the previous discussion of which it can be, it is even more significant in reminding us not only how things work, but also how connected and supported we are and can be.

The Proper way of locating a Prayerstick is obviously to Pray for one and to locate the Prayerstick that desires to help one in one's Prayers and fulfillment and way. The first lesson is to know that just any stick is not as good as the Proper one. The Proper one is always already waiting for you, and you will resonate with it easily and naturally. In this I mean that you will know that it is "The One", as it has called you to find it. It also will be found as being one that is not touching the ground. It can touch water, but not the earth. Most oftentimes it will be hanging in the air from some other branches, and often from, or in, a different tree than that of its origin. Most Prayersticks that are in a different tree have more associative ability than those that are in the same tree. Also important is to know which tree it came from, as well as which direction of the tree it separated from. Which way it is pointing in the air is significant too. The bigger end of the Prayerstick (the part that was attached to its source) is the source of its direction. Therefore if the big end is in the South and the smaller is towards the East, then it is a "South East" oriented Prayerstick and so forth. If it detached from the West of its originating tree, then it will have West Supporting Medicine as well.

Therefore, knowing that:

North	-	Growing and Doing Medicine
East	-	Flowering and Distribution & Share and Reflection Medicine
South	-	Beginning and Seed Planting & Flow and Initiating Medicine
West	-	Sprouting and Metamorphosis & Give-Away Medicine

One can have a better understanding of what one's Prayerstick naturally supports in fulfilling one's Prayers of desire. While any Prayerstick can be used to Pray for anything, some are easier at fulfilling certain objectives because of these things (Medicine) about them.

The first thing that one is to consider and remember is that to Properly Receive any of a thing, something must be given first. The Medicine Way is to give Tobacco or a Pebble gift to the ground directly beneath the Prayerstick before receiving it (Preferably with one's left and thereby receiving side hand). Then also give Tobacco to the tree of origin in the direction of its source, while "Going Into" it.

To Go Into the tree, one stands against it while holding it with one's hands at heart height with one's feet at its base. With one's belly and forehead pressed against it, take a deep breath and while exhaling, allow or project one's consciousness through the Bark and into the heart of the tree. This is done until one can see the rings of the tree around oneself and then one can go anywhere, as one is now in True Spirit Form. One will often see light forms floating around oneself and can see the Spirit of the tree or even The Creator (Great Pop) easily in this condition of oneself.

In the Medicine Way of clearing oneself of thought forms and associations, at this point one should ask the tree Spirit to strip all bark of tree and associations from oneself so as to be of clarity. Also in this particular practice, when exiting the tree, one is to thank it and ask it to provide new, thin, and slippery Bark on tree (Ego) for one to use in the next and future expressions of oneself.

The Prayer at this time while in the tree, is to see and understand its (the Prayerstick's) gift and Medicine. One is also to thank the tree, the stick, Great Pop, and the All for its precious gift to oneself as well as giving and thereby committing a part of oneself in a marriage and Sacred Union to the aforementioned group.

This consciousness, commitment, marriage and sacred union, is what is important to remember in the use of a Prayerstick as one's Prayers do affect and effect the present condition and Future of the All of Creation, and not just that of oneself.

Each type of tree has its own special Medicine, so the recommendation as to a type of tree for Prayersticks is that of the Oak, Gum, Willow, Red Cedar, Walnut, Pecan, and any fruitwoods (In that order by the way). The Oak is the tree of "Magic" which is Prayer answered and that is why I prefer it. Not recommended is Holly, Pine, Vines, Bushes, or any thorny or aggressive trees or plants, for obvious reasons.

Once received, study the Medicine of the tree of source so as to understand and honor its gift. The Prayerstick at this point already is one, however to further strengthen the marriage and union, certain steps are recommended as follows:

***

All bark should be stripped for obvious reasons (Bark on tree is Ego), and in so doing release that of oneself also. This can be done before or after marrying it with Fire, which can be done by placing it in the oven at 250 degrees for four hours, or by passing it through a flame counterclockwise in all directions. Each of these processes are sacred unions. They serve to add to and honor what already is as well as what the effect of its use is, as relates to the Future and the All of creation.

Once married with Fire, more elements can be added in the way of Mineral Spirits by embedding crystals and stones in places that the Prayerstick tells you that it wants them. The third partner of the sacred trinity of Life here in the physical realm in the way of Animal Spirits can then be added in the way of feathers and so forth. Each change and addition should be prayerfully and Meditatively applied as a marriage and Sacred Union of the Prayerstick, Great Pop, the All and Oneself in the consciousness of Value, Love, Share, Respect, and Appreciation. As the Prayerstick is one's special communication tool and go between oneself, Great Pop and the All of creation, particular attention and understanding as to the directions of the placement of things in or upon one's Prayerstick should be given as relates to the Sacred Circle and Medicine Wheel of Life.

Like the feathers, the shaft, and the point of the Sacred Arrow, one's Prayerstick should embody each of the Trinity of Life forms here in the physical plane. Plant Spirits are represented in the stick itself, Mineral Spirits can be placed anywhere, and remember that clear quartz crystals have no conscience but are great amplifiers. Quartz crystals at the end of a prayerstick should have a small piece of cinnamon stick placed in the hole beneath the crystal because of this. Other recommended Mineral Spirits are Peridot for Love, Citrine for Bringing Forth, Amethyst or Ruby for Metamorphosis and Change, and Garnet for one's Soul-Self. Lapis Lazuli or Blue Topaz are good if they are available to represent Great Pop. Different Animal Spirits can be represented in the form of feathers, bone, leather, or teeth.

In the Proper Way of the development of anything to be used in the Medicine Way, each element that is added is a unique and special Spirit in itself. Not all Spirits want to hang around or work with others, so the selective process should not be "Willful". Instead, it should be Meditatively performed. The addition of any element should be done in the manner of being a Spiritual Marriage, and hence placed in one's mouth and one's prayer given and then attached. This method provides that one becomes a partner to each and all elements being united, as well as with the Group Consciousness of the whole of them. This is the Medicine and Proper Way of "Making" anything. When placed inside one's mouth some of the atoms of that element become a part of oneself, as does a part of oneself become a part of that element.

Once all of the components are united, place the item below a white or red and white candle which should be then lit. Next a Tobacco gift should be made to the Spirit that will then come to embody the overall composition and item. The flame of the candle will tell when it has enjoined it, and at that point all will be complete.

Finally, as often as felt proper, the Prayerstick should be smudged with Sage or Cedar so as to facilitate Renewall and thereby clear it of any and all past associations, thoughts, and memory.

ABOUT SMUDGING & CLEARING

Over the years I have noticed that many people have a lot of different ideas as to what the traditional practice of what some people call "Smudging" things with smoke is all about. When considering that, it seemed appropriate to include the Medicine Way of Clearing things as well, since the two expressions and activities are Dynamically-Linked in most every sense and way.

Watch any ceremony in a Catholic Church and one will notice a priest or bishop waving a smoking incense container about and over the people as he expresses Prayers of blessings upon them. This is actually a case whereby he is using the smoke of the incense to "Carry" and thereby spread the words and thereby Consciousness of his Prayers of Desire over the people so that those Prayers become associated with and attached to their individual Prayersticks, as well as the Prayerstick of the Group Consciousness of the collective of them. This is close to, but Not the same as being what Native Americans do with Tobacco and when they smoke it in their pipes.

I am conscious of this ability of smoke and I use it even when I am smoking something other than my Medicine Pipe, and I am talking about cigarettes with Tobacco in them here and Not some other type of Plant Spirit. Why do I only use Tobacco? I will only use Tobacco because of its Medicine, which is that of Wealth and Fertility. That is Why Tobacco is a Plant Spirit that is the most sacred to Native Americans. This is because we see it as a gift from the Creator for us to use in our Prayers, be it with smoke or simply as a gift.

The reality is that one's Prayers are one's Desires being expressed as Thought Energy. And since smoke is vaporized Mineral Spirits and Water that is resultant from something having been through Renewall with the Change Medicine of Fire, one can easily understand Why it is used to "Carry" the consciousness of the words and Thought Energy of one's Prayers to the All else of creation.

Now that we have shown the Potential of smoke as relates to its application as far as carrying one's Prayers to the All of creation, it is important to state here and now, That is Not what it is being used for in the Medicine Way of Smudging and Clearing. Actually in this use of smoke, it is as close to being the opposite of it as anything can be. Simply put, the Medicine of Smoke is that of: The Embracing and Carrying Forth Renewall upon the Winds of Change. It is the "Embracing" aspect and Medicine of smoke that is Why it is used to carry forth one's Prayers of Desire. However one can also use that aspect of its Essential Nature and Medicine for something else as well. And of course that something else is: **To Absorb Thought Forms and Memory Energy From Something**!

Yep, that is what we use smoke for in Smudging and Clearing a Being, place or thing, because of its Embracing and thereby "Sucking Medicine"! This is also Why in the Medicine Way we use Cedar or Sage to make the smoke with. Why do we use Cedar and Sage?

Because the Medicine of cedar is that of Life and Prayer, and Sage is that of Purification and Clarity of Thought. Just from that last statement and understanding one can quickly tell why Sage is the most preferred in this use of smoke.

At this point in my life I have seen and participated in many diverse ceremonies and practices whereby someone was using smoke for something. And while some seem like they are doing something really nice or kind or even at times "Special" in the Way that they are doing it, they are not. And what I am referring to specifically is when I see a person waving smoke from a shell with Cedar or Sage in it, like they are casting it to the wind or fanning a bad odor or the like over them in an act of willfulness. In reading their thoughts, almost each and every one is thinking that they are giving that person or thing a "Spiritual Bath", when in every sense and way it is just the opposite. In this I mean to say that instead of supporting Release and Renewall, they are in fact willfully projecting their own Prayers of Desire over that Being or thing.

In the Medicine Way it is the **Recipient's** responsibility to use that smoke to clean and release the Thoughts and Prayers that they have personally accumulated from other sources and Release it from themselves, and Not the person providing the smoke! I too have occasionally Not provided that instruction before smudging a person, and from now on I Will make certain that I do.

The instruction is: For the person to inhale and absorb the smoke into their Spirit and physical form and attach all thoughts and influences from any other source than the Creator or themselves to it. Then as they exhale, Release it to the All of creation With Harm to No One Being or thing to ever result from it.

In the process of using smoke to clear places and things other than Beings, The Medicine Way of it is to first associate to and With the consciousness of whatever is to be cleared first. Then once one has connected with and become in a Spiritual Union with each and All of the elements involved, then one is to fan the smoke to them so that They (the object or place) can use it to clean and clear those thoughts and memories from themselves that They no longer desire to have about themselves. Remember here that the key words of Relationship Proper are Respectful Sharing, and That is the consciousness to be maintained and used when doing any clearing activity of any sort.

Of course dealing with a possession scenario or a discarnate (ghost) will require a different approach, technique, and effort than what is to be given here in this material. Yet even in that case and condition,

The Medicine Way of smudging and clearing can still be applied and be of Potential benefit and possible remedy.

So what about the person that is doing the smudging and clearing? They should maintain a consciousness and attitude of Give Proper. To do that is to give that which one has a surplus of so as to be of use and benefit to another Being or thing. One is to do it in a way and manner so that one is in complete release of it, and thereby one is to expect Nothing in return. Also, both before and after all other Beings and things are smudged, the one that is doing it should do the same for themselves.

***

While smoke is used for smudging and clearing the Thought and Memory attachments from some Beings and things, it is Not the best or only thing to be considered using for everything, as there are two others in the Medicine Way. One of these two other things is Saltwater and the other thing is Fire. And yes it is the Medicine of both of these two elementals Spirits that is embraced by and are a part of smoke.

Since Mineral Spirits and thereby rocks and stones have the uniqueness of having their Bark on tree of Ego inside their outer physical surface instead of outside like everything else, in the Medicine Way they are best cleared by saltwater. And while the saltwater as found in the oceans might seem like the very best choice to use for rocks and stones, it is not. Nope, the very best and Medicine Way of clearing rocks and stones is:

Place the rocks or stones or any Metal Object that will not be harmed by this process into a clear and preferably glass container, with a Prayer of thanksgiving and release being expressed over each one. Then with another Prayer of thanksgiving and release as well as Renewall, fill that container with fresh water from any source. Any city or treated tap water is proper to use as it has embraced the chemicals that they added to it at that point. For rural or well water, it also has embraced whatever has dissolved from the soil, rocks as well as other things that has leached into it so Both sources are Proper and will work quite well.

The container is to be filled with the water to a point whereby the surface of the water is barely over the top of the stones that are to be cleared. Once that is done, then with a Prayer of Renewall of the elements that are now submerged in the water, add salt from any source. The reason for doing it in this manner in the Medicine Way is that as the salt becomes melted and absorbed by the freshwater, it is easier for the water to suck all of the thought forms and memory energy out of the stones and metal objects at the same time!

Once the salt is added, the container should be placed in an East facing location whereby it will receive the morning sun. The reason for this is that by doing it in this way, the Energy and Medicine of the morning sun's appearance will be associated with becoming the same in the way of Renewall for all that is in the container. After a few hours of bathing in the morning sun, then it is proper to remove the objects from the container and allow them to dry in the sun on a paper or cloth towel. After that, they will be once again clean and clear.

***

The third method of clearing objects in the Medicine Way is with the support of the Elemental Spirit of Fire. Actually, it is the transformational and Medicine of Renewall of Fire that one can employ in clearing the Thought and Memory Energy from any and everything that exists. In the Medicine Way, I have ceremonially cleared large parcels of land with Fire before using them to grow things or for use in other ways. In this use of Fire, I Pray that it supports the release and Renewall of all Thought and Memory Energy that is present in, above, and below the surface of that parcel or tract in a manner that supports the Balance, Growth, and Well-being of all things to come.

And while it seems like the use of Fire will probably cause the loss of any further use of an object or thing, in the Medicine Way it can be done without harm. I have several earrings and objects that contain both Mineral Spirit stones and other things, such as teeth, claws, and feathers. And while I have occasionally used the saltwater method on these types of items, I have also used Fire. In the Fire method of clearing a Being or thing:

One begins by igniting a candle or other source of flammable substance with a Prayer of release and Renewall as mentioned before. Then one is to Pray that the object or Being embraces the support of Renewall by the Flame and releases all of Its unwanted Thought and memory associations in complete Renewall. For Beings, the one that is being cleared in this manner is to likewise Pray for such to occur. Then the object or Being is to pass through the flame of the Fire from the South to the North at a speed that causes No harm to it. Next, another pass is made from the East to the West, also with a Prayer for release and Renewall and at a speed that causes No harm. Then the Being or thing is to be passed through the flame of the Fire four times in a counter-clockwise direction of rotation, again with the same Prayer of release and Renewall and at a speed that causes No harm.

Lastly, the being or thing is to be passed clock-wise through the flame of the Fire with a Prayer for Re-birth and a New Beginning.

Yes, it is Prayers of Desire that are the Thought and Memory Energy forms that are being dealt with in the Medicine Way of smudging and clearing, after all Prayer Is what makes each and every thing happen!

ABOUT TOBACCO

As the Medicine of Tobacco is that of Wealth and Fertility, it is of little wonder or surprise that this is one of the most sacred Plant Spirits to most Native American people and Medicine people in particular.

Unlike money, to us indigenous peoples, Tobacco is Sacred. When I was young I asked Great Pop how I should grow. He told me to grow like the tree, meaning from the inside and heart, outward in all directions. That way we become round in our growth and thereby in Balance that way. You see Balance is the key to aspire to in both our Growth and walk of Life here in the physical realm. Great Pop also taught me that all behavioral expressions and patterns already were here on Mother Earth before He allowed us two leggeds to come here. The models and patterns can be found in the Mineral Spirits, Animal Spirits, and most importantly, Plant Spirits. In behaving more like the vine than a tree, the "Trade and Barter" fellow can never get the full benefit from any sweat lodge or other kind of ceremony. I say this because the same holds true for Tobacco as well. Many people smoke Tobacco for many different reasons. Some get addicted to it just like some people get addicted to a lot of different things like sex. Likewise many of these same people abuse it and themselves with it, which is why it can be a cause of certain kinds of physical problems. Now the real cause is not the Tobacco, it is the abuse of it. And Abuse is "Use" with an "A" added such as begins the words of Anger, Anxiety, and many of the other words that describe the many faces of Fear. And is it not ironic that we see the people that have trouble with this Tobacco, smoke most oftentimes out of Anger and Anxiety? And of course that leads us to the other "A" word, which is addiction.

As indigenous peoples, and especially Medicine people, we have been using Plant Spirits for maintaining Well-being and Balance as well as healing since day one so to speak. Tobacco has been used to cure everything from wounds, Snakebites, abdominal distress, to skin problems. But even more powerful and primary in its use and importance is Tobacco's role and use in Prayer.

Long ago Great Pop explained that if I desire to get any more of anything, I must first give something away for that to be received. He went on to explain that in a sense, I am in a continuum of being a cup that is always full and thereby complete. If I am to receive anything more or different in this Being and Life of mine, I have to make room for it to be received in first. Otherwise, it will be like trying to pour water into a cup that is already full and the water will only flow over the top and down the side. So what can I give away? My Prayer of desire of course and it is most Proper and substantive when done with Smoke! Why? Because the Smoke goes anywhere and everywhere there is one, and merges with everything that it makes contact with. Is this why some people's Smoke bothers us and other people's does not? Yep, because the Fear and Anger and so forth in some people's Smoke is so heavy and unpleasant. Can you Smoke other things than just Tobacco in Prayer? Of course, indigenous peoples have made many such different mixtures since the beginning, but Tobacco is always preferred. Not Proper or preferred is what some call hallucinogens. The Why of that is that they call forth illusionary things as well as thought forms that can become problematic. This is because these substances resonate more with our Bark on tree and its Pseudo-essence of Fear and its fabric of illusion, than our True Value System that resides in our Hearts. If I want clarity or a vision, I fast and Meditate.

THE MEDICINE PIPE / TOBACCO CEREMONY
WATER PRAYER CEREMONY

The Water Prayer ceremony is done at any body of water, preferably that is moving away from you. It is the same as the Pipe / Tobacco Ceremony with the exception of the absence a Medicine Pipe and it's smoke. The reason that there is no Pipe smoke is because the Water carries the Prayers to the All of Creation in the very same manner. Also, at the end, the piece of paper (Prayer-sheet) and tobacco is lit and causes smoke anyway.

Likewise, the Tobacco Ceremony may be preformed in the same exact manner as the Water Ceremony with the only difference being the lack of Water and the use of Earth and Air instead!

Of Note: The Medicine of Tobacco is Wealth, Fulfillment, & Fertility.

***

Many decades ago when I asked Him, Great Pop gave me the following to personally use, teach, and lead others when using Tobacco. This ceremony can be done with a cigar or cigarette also. In the use of anything other than a Pipe, when I say to "Give" some Tobacco to a direction or something, the supply source is to be the lit end of the object to be lit if that is the source. Likewise, when I say to "Put" some Tobacco into the Bowl, that could get pretty tricky and messy to try to do to the end of a cigarette, so do it in one's consciousness instead.

While the following is a description as to how to use Tobacco in a Pipe Ceremony specifically, it applies to any other types of ceremonies as well. In this way, one does not have to have a pipe or even smoke to be able to properly use Tobacco. In fact, I will use this same procedure whenever I desire to establish a Medicine Wheel for any reason or purpose. I also use it when I light my Prayers when they are written on a piece of paper and given to the Wind or water. As one can see, it can be applied to any and All of one's Prayers.

The effectiveness of any expression of a Prayer of Desire is exponentially multiplied by each of the individual beings and things that share and express that as being their Prayer of Desire as well. This is like the difference between fishing with just one pole and baited hook, or many, for that one fish in the pond. It has been a fundamental practice and understanding at the core of Native American and indigenous peoples since the beginning. Also, it is why they say, "A family and tribe that Prays together, stays together". Even when I do this ceremony by myself, I never feel alone in it.

If you have issues with voicing your Prayers of desire out loud where all can hear and see, you might want to go into a tree. Going into a tree or plant for personal clearing begins with a tobacco gift or pebble to the tree/plant at the place that you will be entering it. This is the Proper & Medicine Way of receiving anything. Next, one projects one's consciousness and Spirit into the plant or tree and asking it to strip away your own Bark of ego, as well as any attachments thought-forms or associations with any being or thing other than The Creator and Your guides. This procedure should be done prior to any and all ceremonies anyway. Afterward, thank the tree/plant for its love and support and leave your Bark on tree behind with it. When it is possible, my personal preference, is to do Pipe and/or Tobacco ceremonies to the sunset or sunrise or by the water of any kind as in streams, rivers, ponds, lakes and most of all, ocean.

Why? Because Water Medicine is about Flow and this way it helps carry my Prayers into, and throughout, Mother Earth just like the Smoke does to the air, sky, and Great Beyond! Just like preparing for a meeting with someone that one desires to receive something from, I recommend writing down on a single piece of paper, the things that you Really desire to receive or have occur first. To do so will help you in many ways. Also, the Prayer-sheet will have use later as you will see.

***

With the Pipe Bowl held in the center of the palm of one's left hand, gently insert the Stem into the Stem hole with one's right hand and fasten it as designed. At this point, thank each part and then call forth The Spirit of the Pipe into it and oneself. As one breathes out, one will feel its presence and then one is ready to begin. Begin by placing oneself in the "X" of the following diagram that should be visualized as being a Medicine Wheel in the center of the area of the ceremony:

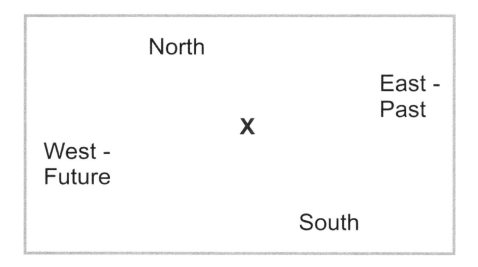

As with establishing The Sacred Circle of any Medicine Wheel, one begins facing the South. Next, one is to give a small pinch of Tobacco to the South by tossing it to that direction. Then one is to ask the Spirit of the South, any and all other Spirit helpers and Guides, and the Sacred Circle of the Medicine Wheel to enjoin you and begin a Sacred Circle around oneself. Be very polite and respectful in this request, not commanding or the like. As you take your next breath, you will feel their presence. When that happens, you can put the first pinch of Tobacco into the bottom of the Bowl of your Pipe. As in the chart describing the Medicines of the Four Cardinal Directions earlier, it is always a good idea to ask for Spirits that can help you with Resources while facing this direction. When all feels complete, it is time to then turn Clockwise to the right while "Pulling" the end of the Sacred Circle from the South with you until you are facing the West and now the Wheel will be and feel like this:

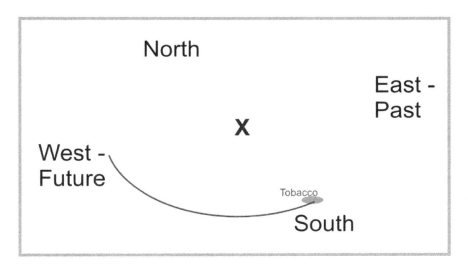

At the West, one is to repeat the process as was described for the South. This time ask For a Spirit helper for the West. Next, pray / ask for its support, as in making Plans and things dealing with the Future as one puts one's next pinch of Tobacco into the Bowl. As with the South, once one feels that that has happened and the Spirits are there, turn Clockwise to the right while "Pulling" the end of the Sacred Circle from the West with you until you are facing the North. Now the Wheel will be and feel like this:

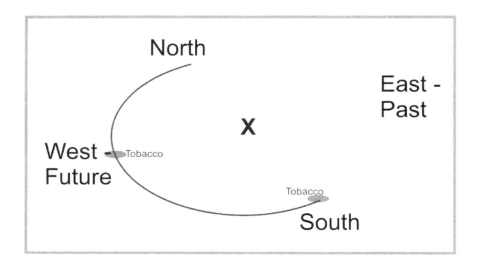

At the North, one is closest to Great Pop so Thank Him special for me, yourself, & The Medicine Way of being a being here on Mother Earth. Then one is to repeat the process as described for the West, this time asking for a North Spirit guide and helper. Next, pray / ask for its support in one's Endeavors and things dealing with the Present as one puts their next pinch of Tobacco into their Bowl. As with the South and West, once one feels that has happened and the Spirits are there, turn Clockwise to the right while "Pulling" the end of the Sacred Circle from the North with you until you are facing the East. Now the Wheel will be and feel like this:

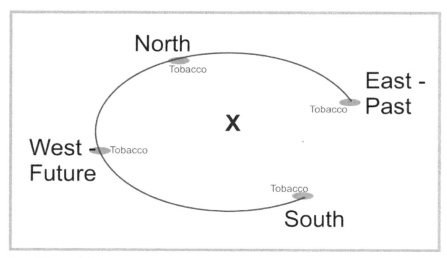

At the East, one is to repeat the process as described for the North, this time asking for a Spirit Guide for the East. Then, pray / ask for support in things one wishes Enlightenment about or to Share and things dealing with the Past as one puts their next pinch of Tobacco into their Bowl. As with the South, West, and North, once one feels that has happened and the Spirits are there, turn Clockwise to the right while "Pulling" the end of the Sacred Circle from the East with you until you are facing the South again and now the Wheel will be and feel like this:

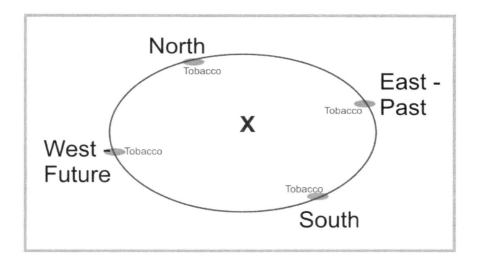

After one feels that has happened and the Spirits are there, place another pinch of Tobacco into one's Bowl. Again face the North and toss a pinch of Tobacco to the Center / Above / Below and pray / ask the Spirit of it to please enjoin you in your Medicine Wheel and Tobacco ceremony. Next, as one takes in a deep breath, call and feel the Sacred Circle encircle from above and below as well as right through you like this:

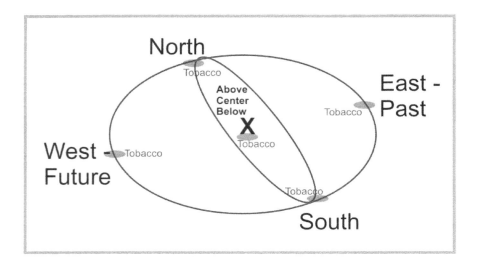

After one feels that has happened and the Spirits are there, place another pinch of Tobacco into one's Bowl. Again, face the Sun or Moon or any source of Light, preferably a natural one, and after tossing a pinch of Tobacco to it, pray / ask the Spirit of it (Tia in my language) to please enjoin you in your Medicine Wheel and Tobacco ceremony. I see Great Pop in the Sun, Moon, and Light and I oftentimes go there to meet with Him so I kind of think of this being where I personally am closest to and with Him, so this is a good time and place to ask for His support. Then as one takes in a deep breath, call and feel the Sacred Circle encircle from above and below as well as right through you like this:

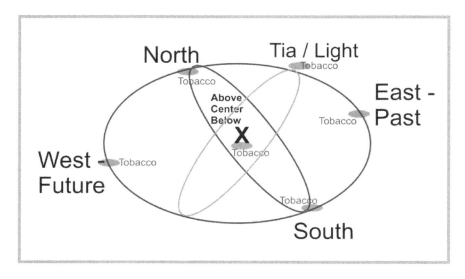

After one feels that has happened and the Spirits are there, place another pinch of Tobacco into one's Bowl. Next face the West as that is where one's Future is, and toss a pinch of Tobacco to The Wind. The Wind is called the Wind of Fortune and Change (Pa-Ha in my language) because that is its Medicine and specialty. So next ask the Spirit of the Wind to please enjoin you in your Medicine Wheel and Tobacco ceremony. This is a good time and place to ask for all of the things that you desire to have Change in your Life. Then as one takes in a deep breath, call and again feel the Sacred Circle encircle from above and below as well as right through you like this:

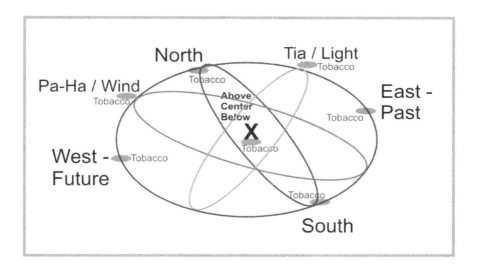

At this point, the Sacred Circle is established and thereby complete. If there is any room left in the bowl, it is the time to complete filling the Bowl of one's Medicine Pipe. As one can see, one is Not just surrounded by it, one is Embedded into the center and core of it! It is at this time that in the Medicine Way, while lighting the Tobacco in one's Medicine Pipe that one first gives Thanks for all that one has and has been given, both in things and experiences, whatever they might have been of felt like.

After "Emptying One's Cup" this way, it is then Proper to face each of the directions as well as the Center / Above / Below, offering the mouth piece end of one's Pipe to it and then ask out loud for that of which is its specialty that you desire to receive from it and all

Spirits in that direction. This is where one's Prayers that were written down if that were the case, are said out loud and thereby honored as well as Avowed as being "One's Real and Honest Desire".

Once that is complete and expressed as Honestly and Passionately as possible, one will feel an emptiness inside and then one knows that you have done your best and now it is up to Great Pop and the All. After that, take time and enjoy the rest of one's Tobacco or share it with any that are sharing your ceremony with you. And No, they do not have to do any more than voice their Prayers. When finished and satisfied, Thank all that were involved and then Release each and all, including the Sacred Circle, and you have done it Properly and in the Medicine Way. Next, Thank the Pipe Spirit for its Partnership in your Prayer and Life, and then gently remove the Bowl from its Stem. At this time I prefer to empty the remains in the Bowl into the piece of paper with my prayers and fold it into a Triangle representing the Law of One.

The Law of One has a triangular shape and symbol. As one will learn in Origins, The Law of One is actually a four sided pyramid in case you are wondering and the reason for the cardinal numbers being 4 & 7. The shape can also be a Trinity of Great Pop, my self / desires, and the All of His Creation.

Next, I light one end of the paper, and when it has almost completely burned up and is getting close to my fingers, toss it as a gift to the Wind or to both the Wind and the Water if I am doing this as a Water Prayer ceremony. If I do not have the piece of paper, I do it with the Tobacco from the Bowl just as if there was one. And with that, we are done.

Finally, for those that are wondering about smudging and Clearing one's Medicine Pipe, It will tell you with What, How, and When. This is because Medicine Pipes are "Transformational" tools, meaning that they Change things with Prayer and use Fire. Therefore their Clearing happens every time they are lit! I do Clear all of my things including my pipes on a regular basis and not always with Sage.

At the end of these or any ceremony, the Medicine and Proper Way is to Give one's thanks and appreciation to the Spirits involved, the Medicine tools if used, and then to The Creator / Great Pop for His gift and design of the All of it.

I pray that you share this material with your children as soon as they reach the age of 8 or beyond, as they will have a better understanding about something that they already are curious about anyway as far as Tobacco and smoking goes. Such knowledge will better assist them in making their choices about smoking, at least about smoking Tobacco, and that might translate into the other things as well. Wokkah! (It is Done / Finished / Complete)

*****

ABOUT RITUAL AND CEREMONY

In reality, if one brushes one's teeth each and every day before bed, then that expression can actually qualify as having been ritually done. And of course as with all things in Life, there is also a Medicine Way of brushing one's teeth, which is to respectfully Pray for the release and removal of any and all things that are on them or in one's mouth that do Not Walk in Balance and With Harm to No One Being or Thing, including oneself, and especially one's teeth. As with all things that exist, Ritual and Ceremony were also one of Great Pop's ideas and they were a part of what He set forth by the Founding Beings when he first allowed Beings to incarnate for a visit here on Mother Earth. Not only that, He even gave them the instruction that they and All future generations to come, should share and experience any sojourn here on Mother Earth and thereby Live Life, Ceremonially.

In further explanation as to what Great Pop meant when He said to Live Life Ceremonially was that as Beings we should ceremonially celebrate being here on Mother Earth in all of our personal and collective expressions so as to experience being a Being and ourselves in such a manner that we exhibit Respectful Sharing in each and every thing that we do. The very first Ritual was for the Founding Beings to collectively give their thanks to Great Pop for allowing us to come here to visit and also for giving them that instruction as to How we are to Live. While that Prayer of thanksgiving was immediate, it became a Ritual that they carried forward to the time that they went to sleep, and also at the moment that they woke up each and every subsequent day thereafter. That was the Original expression of a Ritual by Beings here on Mother Earth and it is the real and true genesis of all of those many others that would come after. When they had their first meal here on Mother Earth, they likewise carried forward this Ritualistic attitude and behavior in their preparation of it as well as when they All sat down together and partook of it. And when they Collectively did that, it was the genesis of the first and original Ceremony that would likewise span the many others that have come to be.

It is important to add here that in their Prayers of Respect and Thanksgiving, they gave it to not only the dead Animal or Plant that they partook of in the physical idea and persona of it, but more importantly to its Spirit for giving them its exited physical bodyform to be used as nourishment of their own! This was because the Founding Beings knew and behaved as being Spirits that were incarnate here for a physical experience and expression and No other idea of such was to be considered. And of course That is the Medicine Way of being a Being here on Mother Earth. The Founding Beings did not have to kill anything for food as there was always an abundant supply and as instructed by Great Pop, they Never expanded their populations so that there would be a need of such in their respective area of existence here on Mother Earth. When in time their numbers did increase to a point whereby there might be a shortage of available already dead things to eat, then "Splinter Groups" of selective individuals that so desired went to other areas that did have such a plentiful and ongoing resource. And of course that group would have as its leaders, individuals that had been taught the ways of being a Being in Life that was given to the Founding Beings by Great Pop. And yes, Those were the original and first Medicine People that some would later call Spiritual Advisors or "Priests".

As the female of each of the seven pairs of Founding Beings was already pregnant with twins upon their incarnation, one of the original Rituals and Ceremonies would become that of childbirth, and later that of Celebrating one's exit and passage back to The Creator that we now call death. Each of the "Celestial Events" was given its own respective Ritual and Ceremony as was known and Established by The Founding Beings, and in this I am referring to the events of the solstices and equinoxes. Likewise The Way of The Sacred Circle and thereby Medicine Wheel was also already known and practiced by the Founding Beings, and it became the core of what would later become the many offshoots that we now have and use in Religious practices and ceremonies, although many of them are of a much different method and motive at present. So it is easy to see now where the current ideas and practices of Ritual and Ceremony come from, but just how should one Be and Do in the Medicine Way of such?

In the Medicine Way and in Reality, any individual can do any of a thing ritualistically and ceremonially. All of the existing ones were started by someone, and one can likewise start and practice any of one's own. Of course those that will be Proper are those that embody

Respectful Sharing and Walk in Balance and With Harm to No One Being or Thing, including oneself for all time to come. Also in The Medicine Way, one is to meditatively ask The Creator and seek His guidance as to How and When to do What in them.

What about participating in someone else's Ritual or Ceremony or even going to a wedding or different church? Whether it is a church, wedding, sweat lodge or dance, there is a Proper and Medicine Way of participating in such if one chooses to do so. The Medicine Way of participating in any Ritual and Ceremony is that of being of a conscious Respect and regard to the way and practice that is being offered, and do No thing to interfere or challenge any of it. One is to maintain an attitude of Respectful Sharing and if one does Not feel comfortable or that one is being treated in the same manner and consciousness, then one is to respectfully decline to participate and / or leave.

So as you can see, while there is no set or specific description of How to do a particular ceremony that is being presented here, one has been given the Medicine Way of participating in any and all that one may choose to experience or express oneself in. In closing, I am given to remind any and all that when I asked Great Pop how I was to be and do in Life, His response was that of: "One is to Play and Pray, and Celebrate the Ceremony of Life as best and as often as one can, as long as it Walks in Balance and With Harm to No One Being or Thing Now and in The Future".

WHITE EAGLE

****

THE LAST CYCLE OF THE MEDICINE WHEEL

I ASKED THE GREAT SPIRIT,

"FATHER, PLEASE TEACH ME ABOUT THIS THING

THAT PEOPLE SPEAK SO OFTEN ABOUT CALLED

MANIFESTING"?

SO HE DID….

AND HE CALLED IT,

PRAYER.

****

I

PRAY EVER

TO WALK IN THE

SHADOW OF MY SPIRIT &

THAT SOON MY MOCCASINS

WILL NO LONGER EVEN LEAVE

A PRINT UPON THE SAND, AS THEN

ONLY WILL I KNOW THAT I AM TRULY

GUIDED BY AND WITH, THE GREAT SPIRIT,

ONCE AGAIN.

May The Great Spirit Keep

Warmth in Your Heart

And Softness in Your Bed

This And Every Day,

White Eagle

EARTHWALK

AS I SEE IT AND THE OTHER SIDE

BY

WHITE EAGLE

CONTENTS

Remembering   53

The Beginning   62

The Journey   72

Re-New-All   83

Walking the Walk   92

REMEMBERING

Many summers ago, I was on an airplane and flying over the Pacific Ocean while returning from Hawaii. I had the great pleasure of visiting it with my earth mother named Evelyn Stoner. Before this trip, she had been in the hospital for about five months undergoing operations and treatments for cancer. She was soon to return there several months later for what would be the last nine months (significant to me as being the same as the duration of one's birth cycle) of her life here on Mother Earth. We had just experienced a great journey and as I was about thirty years old, we both enjoyed the fact that many people mistook her for my wife. She and my earth father both knew that I was born as a Medicine Man but they didn't have a full understanding of it. They did know that I had been diagnosed as being dead several times at that point. They also knew that I could walk through the veil at will as well as make things move.

When I was three years old, I would tell my earth father how many times he would hit the nail on the head before it would go in and I would do other things that sometimes scared them. On the airplane my mother told me how this cancer had made her so mad that she could just spit, and how it was the kind that she Feared the most. I just listened as I often am given to do, knowing in advance of the question soon to come. I Loved my earth mother dearly, and I still do. In some of our past lives we were together with her being my wife or daughter. In Proper conditions, sons and mothers have an easier time being in relationship and in communication, just as do fathers and daughters. In these relationships there is usually no competition, with a greater respect to the other side of one's sexuality. I was not given to do a healing upon my earth mother, for those who might wonder. I accepted that as well as understood that her cancer was in reality a manifestation of her own anger and Fear.

After about two hours into the flight, finally came the question that I had been waiting to hear. My mom asked me then: "White Eagle I know that you know, so how do I die and what is it like"? I took a deep breath and as I am often operating in altered states, I collected myself back to Earthplane. I then responded with: "Fight it as long and as hard as you can and when it is time you will know. Then just turn yourself into a Butterfly and you will come right out of your belly (different situations for different people, I might add) and you can rest there for a spell. When you want to after that, you will see a glow or a sort of light and other Spirits will come to help guide you through your tunnel of Transition". The funny thing about dying is the fact that while it seems to be something that we only do alone, as in birth there is always someone else there, meaning Spirits. And No, it does not hurt after you leave your body. However, it can be confusing sometimes and some Beings and things translate that into Fear and get disoriented. I then told her about Transition and the other parts of the process of returning to Great Pop's Essential Will after an incarnation. It gave me great joy at being in such good relationship with this child of the Great Spirit who accepted my care. The understanding that then came over her radiated a great light, and I knew then that my job was done and the journey was indeed complete. She died a while later and I never worried about her at all.

My earth father however was afraid of a lot of things. This included his being afraid for and sometimes of me since birth. I was born with two club feet which they fixed right away (some of my past life stuff here), and he would not allow others to touch me or for me to be held. I am still angry about that, but I also see the absolute perfection in the lesson of it. I knew I was a PohTikaWah or as some call Medicine Man at birth. My earth father had been my son before in our past lives, and it seemed at times to be the same way as that in this one. Later in his life he would jokingly ask for me to send over some of the Spirits that used to come by my house so as to bother someone that he was having trouble with. When I was young, I asked him one time what he thought about death. He said: "That is easy, I will just take over your body". From that response, I knew that we were both in for a ride as they say.

Like some Medicine people, I have the ability to leave my body or fly as I call it, at will and go through the veil into other worlds or planes of existence. On occasion I will follow other peoples Loved ones and make observations of their progress. As I write these words, Sparkie, a gift to me from the Great Spirit in the form of a Fishers Love Bird died suddenly, hence the dedication of this book. The "He that turned to be a She", used to talk and help me every time I would sit at the computer. I will now have to endure the silence as I work on. Fly on my special partner and Wannaho, I'll see you on the other side. You see one's Grief is an important emotion to share, and I thank you for allowing me to share mine with you here.

My ex-wife's father had passed away seven years (more significant numbers) to the day of my earth mother. My ex-wife knew about some of the abilities in me and asked if I could help. I journeyed

(Flew) as I call it and I saw him in the tunnel and making Transition as a Sparrow Hawk. He was beating his wings ever so fast and he was constantly looking back over his shoulder as he was worried about leaving his wife. I checked on his progress constantly, as she was want of me to do. After a period of fifteen days, I saw that he had completed Transition. The time it takes for Transition varies with each person and relates to the amount of release work necessary. The shortest time of Transition that I have witnessed has been three days. I am also given to state that for some it may even be quicker than that.

Over the years I have followed many Beings and things through their tunnels and have usually observed them in the form of winged ones, such as birds or butterflies. Recently Grey Owl's earth father passed away and as he was very much about space stuff, I saw that he had manifested a rocket ship for the journey.

Transition is a very important phase in the cycle of Renewall as the Spirit leaves the Earthplane just to go to another place. After my ex's earth father made Transition, he emerged from the tunnel to find himself at a special place for a great reunion. The time in the tunnel which is different for each, provides for the release of all attachments to the physical plane, especially those of Ego attitude or origin as one emerges into absolute Light and Truth. There is no Fear, falsehood, or shame on the other side of the tunnel and the time differences for Transition are just what is necessary for the total release.

After the tunnel journey, you enter into a state of vibration of absolute Light and Love and have a great reunion with all of those with whom you wish to see or communicate that have gone on before you as well as your Guides or Angels as you may choose to call them. For my ex's earth father who used to be a rancher in Oklahoma, the reunion took place at a great western ranch house type place with a barbecue going on. He arrived there and was met by all of his old friends and relatives at this wooden ranch house on the prairie with horses, not cars.

The house was centered in a sea of wheat with great long picnic tables covered in red and white checkered table cloths and sides of beef turned on spits over the fires. He was filled with a great joy as he realized the specialness of his own Being as he truly was the guest of honor. I found it strange that he and all of the men there wore pink beanies and pink blazers, which I am sure was of significance to him. I am given to mention here that at the reunion you may be joined by the Christ, Buddha, your Guides or anyone you desire on the Spirit plane including even those who might have reincarnated.

I once worked with a ghost or discarnate as I prefer to call them whose name was Ruby. Discarnates are those who have passed on and for some reason of their own choice have not progressed through Transition thereby keeping their Ego and hence Fear and Anger intact. Ruby was a four year old red headed girl and my Guides showed me how she had been killed by a great tornado and any normal looking tunnel had only brought her great Fear and pain. I spent a couple of days in a quandary as to what to do. In the process of discovery I had done Mediumship with Fiery Crystal Butterfly's help and I ended up bringing Ruby home with me. During the Mediumship, Crystal Butterfly asked her if she wanted to fly with the Eagle and she said she only saw an old Indian there so I kept that form with her.

After a couple of days with her knocking my Medicine pipe and other things off the wall and in general raising a ruckus, I gave up my Ego and asked for guidance. I normally do not try to rush things but this little one was using great tester Medicine on me. It was given for me to make a railroad tunnel through a mountain so I did so. Then, hand in hand, the old Indian and the little four year old red headed girl carrying her spool doll named Susie, walked down the railroad tracks through the tunnel in the mountain. We made Transition in only three days as she had not so much to release being only four years on Earthplane, even though the event took place over one hundred years later. On the other side, her reunion was not only with her family but also with space beings from places other than Earthplane. Again I mention for each it is a unique experience and in that, it is totally the same.

One might ask here, "But what about heaven or hell"? I will only say there is no such thing unless that is what you make of your Earthwalk experience.

My ex's mother passed on after we had split up. I had felt a past life connection with her and so I chose to check up on her. The first time I checked on her, I saw that she had manifested a ranch house in a "Heaven" of her own making that was much like a place she had enjoyed while on Earthplane. It was in such a place that she had experienced her greatest joy. I knocked on the door. She let me in and asked where my ex was as she was not totally aware of her condition at that time. I told her that she could not come and noticed how she had made herself very attractive at an age of twenty-four. We talked a bit about unimportant things and I left as I was not sure of what I should do. I try not to interfere unless guided to do so and I thought I had better meditate about this one.

I flew up on the following day and noticed that she had changed her house a bit and put on a few years in appearance. She seemed a little confused as she thought this heaven manifesting thing was the right thing to do. I said "See how you have changed from the day before"? She agreed but was not sure of what she should do. I turned myself into my bird form and told her to hold on to my wing and took her flying. She was a little timid at first, but soon relaxed. As we soared through the universe, we passed by Earthplane and stopped on the moon. It was then and there that she finally understood. When we flew back to the place that she had made, which is in a layer of consciousness surrounding Earthplane that I call the zones, I dropped my wing and she saw how easily that she too could fly. I took her back inside her home and told her I would always Love her and would see her soon, knowing now indeed she would be alright. She made Transition about three weeks later.

Many might wonder and it is given to explain that these are just some examples of the different events that some people have experienced. Also know that Guides are ever present for each and all, and that each person knows the way but their Ego rejects it because in the process, it must give way. Also note that in no case or condition has any ever experienced pain or torture after death. So much for the hell idea. There is an accounting however, which I will discuss later.

My earth father on passing, manifested a place upon a hill beside a lake and a mountain with a bridge. At his death I turned myself into my bird form and I flew up and folded my wings into a great teepee for him, and there he stayed for the next five years. Another psychic friend of mine saw him about a year after his passing. They described seeing him in such a place surrounded by circles of white light, which was the teepee of course. He stayed in this place until he was ready to release and when he did, he manifested a rectangular stainless steel tunnel with many gadgets in it as he is ever still the inventor, you see.

After the tunnel or Transition as I am given to call it, all people go through a reunion experience. After the reunion, the next experience is called the review. The review experience is like going from a primary school to a secondary school and it is the first day in a class that they call gym. Here you are put in a large area with a lot of people you do not know, usually standing in lines by alphabetical order. You are then given the number of a locker or drawer. Next you go to an area that is full of such things. You seek out the one with your number on it while a whole lot of other people you do not know are doing the very same thing. It is not scary, just a little bewildering. After Transition your condition or vibration is that of absolute Light,

Love, and Truth. Your state is not only purity, but also honesty and you could not do any wrong even if you had a mind to, of which you do not. The condition might be called mildly overwhelming. There is no Fear, only peace and expectancy. You find your locker or whatever device might be used at the time and when you open it, that is when the term "Largely Overwhelming" might best be used to describe anything. Before you in this storage place is contained every thought, word, idea, and deed that ever has emanated from the unique vibration that is the Spirit of you. In this compartment are all of the wheels of all of your lifetimes on Earthplane and any and all other places. The important document is right before you. This document is your Life Plan and the experiences which you just went through. It is indeed judgment day and the Great Spirit has assigned the perfect judge....**You!**

As you are in a condition of being capable of only absolute honesty, you grade yourself on the lessons you chose to experience and finally realize the full growth potential from them. Carefully you review each element and experience in that lifetime and make a new plan for release, growth, and Renewall. It is just such a life plan that got you to the Earthwalk which you just experienced. There are other worlds and planes in which you can choose to experience as well. After the grading of oneself and the making of a new plan, it is submitted for approval. Then there is a calling for and the assigning of new Guides to help you. Next you meet with your new Guides and work with them, usually in the establishing of communicating skills and such. One of the options at this point is to serve as a Guide to others, just as they do for you.

The next phase is called re-entry. Re-entry is like going to a grand central station where you take your next plan to a counter for review and approval. Once it is approved, they direct you to one of the many corridors leading to transportation devices that go to many different places, including one destination that is called Earthplane.

Prior to incarnation, which takes place at birth, you will have chosen not only your parents and the society and your physical condition of birth, but also the date, the time and even your name. All of these choices make both astrology and numerology make sense as defining potentials and influences. These choices, made by ourselves through the manifesting of our own Free Will, make each of us responsible to our own life Plan, including the conditions of our birth. The whole purpose of the Earthwalk is to manifest expansion through the experiences of these choices.

There are worlds other than Earthplane. When doing past life readings, I usually am given to cover some of these experiences by calling them star times. Star time might be spent in a place where you are the only one there, and your home is a cave where there is everything there that you will need and it is a place of comfort and healing. Much work is done there in the process that might be best described as reintegration. Another place might be the peach colored place where all people look the same. Or it might be a place where all are without form, except that of pure energy. There is another place that I like where all is a mechanical world and people embody robot forms in a hi-tech society. I guess that is why I like computers so much. There are other places too many to describe. Each world is a Spiritual experience and has a special orientation so to speak, just like the Earthplane is about Love and Brotherhood.

The major orientation identified to the collective experience known by some as the Earthplane experiment, are the unlimited ways to experience Love and Brotherhood. Failing that over the millennia, it soon might be called the place of mismanagement of resources, ourselves, Mother Earth, and each other. It seems like it might well end up as the place to go to learn how not to be. Yet even in that worst of conditions, it will function in lesson giving and thereby provide for a Potential of expansion. As expansion is the one truly inevitable condition, one must appreciate the perfection of it. After all, the Great Spirit made it and He makes no mistakes.

The Earthwalk is an opportunity to express and experience our creative force in becoming greater channels of the Great Spirit's Light and Love. In reality we can never really create anything. At best we can only apply the forces of change to manifest and experience our individual expansion through the experience of our Earthwalk. During our Earthwalk we are ever encountering new opportunities to experience and express the limitless ways to share and experience Love and Brotherhood. As we climb the steps of Life, the opportunities expand in proportion to our own expansion in our ability to both perceive and experience the expression of them. The steps keep getting broader as we walk ahead, but the decisions are much easier because of the choices that we have previously made.

I remember vividly my last encounter with my own locker between lifetimes, and the almost overwhelming nature of it. Each time I do a past life reading for someone, I always ask of The Great Spirit first if it is proper for me to do. Occasionally it has been given for me not to do such. The reason for not recalling the previous Earthwalk experience is to release from the Mind and Ego, the idea of it. That is necessary so as to begin fresh and with a clean slate, instead of enduring continuous cycles of carry over problems. How perfect it is that we are born anew without guilt or shame of the past. By Great Pop's brilliance of design, all ideas of debts from actions in the past are already nullified or paid for by service work in a star-time experience before a new plan is made and incarnation into Earthplane is begun. Yes, it is most perfect indeed!

Of note here is that there is No mandate or Have To's as far as things go when we are back inside Great Pop's Essential Will in True Spirit form. In this I mean that we each and all choose to do things, or not. There is only Real Light and Love as well as total acceptance and accord. We can choose to go to places that Great Pop has made, or not. And if we just want to stay inside for a while or forever and gain from other Beings' and things' outer adventures, that is A-okay as well. That is the Real perfection of this design by Great Pop. Yep, no matter what, each and All Spirits gain from the experiences and expressions of All others.

Also of note is that when one is in True Spirit, one is ageless in a sense. Inside Great Pop's Essential Will of which one could call a sort of "Heaven", we are in True Spirit. And while one is All Knowing and in that sense most mature in that condition of Self, in most ideas of oneself one is still a little child, all at the same time. And like most kids, most of us do like to "Go Outside and Play" in one or more of the many Theme Parks of outer personal experience that Great Pop has made like that of The Earthplane.

THE VERY PURPOSE OF BEING IN LIFE YOU SEE,

IS THE ENDEAVOR OF THE VERY NEXT STEPS

THAT YOU TAKE IN THE MANIFESTING OF

YOUR OWN EXPRESSION OF GROWTH

THROUGH YOUR EXERIENCE

AND EXPRESSIONS IN AND OF IT.

SO STEP WELL,

AND THEREBY EASILY AND IN BALANCE,

UPON EACH BRANCH OF YOUR TREE OF LIFE,

AND TO DO THIS IS TO STEP EVER SO LIGHTLY

SO AS NOT TO EVEN LEAVE A SINGLE FOOTPRINT

UPON THE SANDS OF TIME,

AND THEREBY ONLY, CAN ONE TRULY

EMBRACE PROPERLY AND THEREBY FULLY,

THE EXPERIENCE OF LIVING IT.

WHITE EAGLE

THE BEGINNING

I have spoken many times about the time that I asked the Great
Spirit about the creation of Earthplane and saw myself flying about in
bird form as the universe, stars, and Mother Earth came into being. I
then let cat curiosity Medicine get to me and I finally got bold enough
to ask Him how and why I was made. On this occasion, He showed
me how He had fashioned me by manifesting me feather by feather
from the finger tips of his left hand. From this I will note that this is
why for me, the left is the receiving side of Self. He lovingly sculpted
me into the perfect White Eagle form. Next He gave me breath and I
made this great big squawking sound and saw the great joy that it gave
Him. Still wishing to further please Him, I flew with great speed and
did acrobatic flying feats through the great void and saw how much it
brought Him joy. I still pray each day that I might make Him smile. I
know for sure that is indeed my greatest hope and purpose and the
absolute best thing that I can do. After all, that truly is why He made
me.... and You!

On another day I asked Him how things worked and how I could
travel backward and forward in time. He showed me how all is
vibration and how all of his creation is ever resonant and connected to
every other part of it, and Him. He showed me how all on Earthplane
have Guides or Angels as you might call them, who chose to serve in
the Spirit plane that way. The Guides choose to serve this way for a
while so that they might better serve Him through helping us, and it is
all about Love. He showed me how to see and feel the Spirit of any
and all of His creation, and that it is indeed the uniqueness of each
Spirit that causes the uniqueness of each vibration pattern which I see,
sense, or feel.

He taught me how to see and call the Spirit of the Wind and to
discover the unique Spirit attached to everything of His creation. This
includes the four directions, Mother Earth, the four elements, the
Mountain, the Tree, the Stones, the Animals, the All. He taught me
how to sense these things not only in Earthplane but in others as well.
He taught me how to sense the Spirit in the tiniest Stone, or the largest
place. Each can be found as a unique vibration pattern that is found
by excluding all others and isolating the unique vibration of it. He
taught me how to not only sense these things, but also to go inside the

vessel of them as well. He taught me how to provide the healing force to others, not only through my hands but also with my mind by becoming in resonance to the vibrations of them.

I learned that Thought-forms had vibration and then I learned to read the thoughts of others when I needed to. He taught me how to see with my Eagle vision, not only the insides of others as in a type of x-ray vision, but also the past and future events about one as that too is vibration. He showed me how that vibration is everlasting and the necessity of cycles to make vibration. I saw not only the beauty and purity found in the beginning of an Earthwalk, but also the blessings and perfection at the end of it.

As I write these words I can only say "Great Spirit Father, I can only Love you more for it as I continue to see more of your perfection in it, and I will keep trying to make you smile".

I asked Him about the parts of Self and He showed me the tree and said "Remember when I told you to walk in the Round Way, and grow from the inside out"? He then told me how the Heart of Self is like the inside part of the tree, and how the Mind of Self is like the part that has rings which I said looked just like Medicine wheels. Then He told me how the Ego of Self is like the Bark of the tree. He then told me how we should grow like the tree as channels of His Light and Love by taking some to Self and giving the rest away and growing from the inside out in the Round Way. He told me that to do this, the bark of the Ego must keep splitting and give way. He showed me how, if I made my Ego Bark of Self real thin by giving away my Fear, it would become almost transparent and all could see the great beauty of the Love being channeled through me.

He showed me how as channels of his Light and Love, we are much like straws or tubes. He told me that the whole purpose in all conditions and places that we might be in, whether Earthplane or others, is for us to expand. He told me that for us to expand we must take some of His Light and Love to Self as it is the nurturing food for our growth and is truly the essence of our Being as well as the energy force behind the vibration that is His creation. He showed me that if we give away all of the Light and Love that we receive, it is okay as there is an unlimited supply that is available to each and all of us in all conditions of existence. He showed me that if we give away all of the Light and Love that we receive and do not take some to Self for expansion and thereby making the tube of Self bigger to channel more, we are restricted in the amount we can give away, which is a silly condition to be in. He told me that to take some to Self was indeed okay and that I needed to develop more Self-worthiness to do so. He told me to take some and not all of that which we receive and use it to nourish ourselves. Then like expanding tubes or straws, we can receive more, so we can give more. I realized how perpetual our state of expansion truly is and the great perfection in it.

He next showed me how the All worked and how each of His creation is connected by silver threads to each other part of it, with a separate thread joining each form or Being to each other form or Being in His creation, including Him. He showed me how that whatever happened to one part of it, including me, was indeed felt by each and All of it, including Him. He showed me how we can help heal the conditions in others by either an adoption of it in oneself or by manifesting a change in the attitude in and of oneself. He showed me how we are ever in a condition of being an absolute reflection of what we like or dislike in each other, as to the parts that we like or dislike in Self. He told me that what we usually dislike in another can be also a past or present feeling or attitude that we have had or have in ourself. He showed me how the Ego was necessary only in that it enables us to measure our condition of expansion. He also told me not to take myself so seriously, and that the Earthwalk should be walked in Joy.

He told me how there were no such things as positive and negative forces and what a silly idea it was that He would create anything that would harm us or give us pain. He told me that He only created forces and how such forces were made to help in and support our expressions and Potential expansion. He told me that forces were made to provide energy for change and that we can change without expanding, but cannot expand without changing. He showed me how forces can be labeled as good or bad, but that it is all in how you look at them and that good and bad are truly relative judgments to conditions. He told me how the Winds of Change may also be called the Winds of Fortune. He showed me how, if the wind was at my back as I was going up the hill, I might call it a good or favorable wind and that the wind at my face might be called an ill or unfavorable wind.

He showed me how it all had to do with my perspective as it was the very same Wind. He showed me that from any circumstance or condition an experience will be manifested which can also be a lesson learned. Thus, one can always realize and receive the good or positive aspects of it. He taught me to see with acceptance and be less in judgment except in conditions manifested to or by, oneself. He told me that I only was in charge of my Joy and happiness. He said that these were the conditions that I might claim as my birthright to experience or express at any time, as long as I walked in Balance and with Harm to No One, including Myself. He showed me how I magnetize all of the experiences which I encounter to myself, and that All walk in a condition of silent Prayer for that what we wish to experience each step of the way.

He told me that our Fear was a prayer also, and that Fear is the major tool of the Ego as it tries to control oneself and to play God. He told me that there was no wrong way to Pray, just better things to Pray for. He showed me how all Prayers and thoughts manifest vibrations that are heard not only by Him, but also the All of His creation. He also said that of course that tree falling in the forest made a sound, even though no one was there in physical human form. He told me then that it was heard not only by the other trees, but also by the All including Him.

He taught me that the mind was the builder and how to energize the green ray of the vibration of Love from the heart center when doing healing work to complete and speed up the process. He taught me how all people have their unique Plan for Life and to respect the choices and decisions of others. He also told me that He gave each Being and thing its own Free Will and that each of us are totally responsible for the condition of oneself. He taught me how much He Loves each and every one of us and each part of His creation. He taught me that as I am conscious of Him in any part of His creation, to Pray to it like the water or wind is the same as to Pray to Him and that it is okay.

He taught me to respect the four elements of His creation, the People, the Plants and Animals, Mother Earth and Father sky, and all aspects of His creation and most importantly, He taught me to respect His plan and the perfection of Balance in it.

He taught me that we each have a pattern that is the hole in the end of the straw or tube that is the channel of oneself and we are constantly modifying this pattern as we grow. He showed me how we sometimes make wrongful holes in the pattern of oneself that do not belong there and we do this by accepting a wrongful idea about ourselves. He showed me how we magnetize that which we wish to receive or experience through the pattern of oneself and if we have holes of need in our pattern we will magnetize those with the same condition in themselves to us to experience the lesson in it.

He showed me how it is important that we fill up all of the holes in the pattern of oneself and to not expect others to do this for us, as to do so will put us into an Ego oriented sense of relationship that will be founded upon the shaky ground of need. He showed that by being in, and maintaining the best complete condition in the pattern of oneself, we can be most efficient and effective channels in the transmission of His Light and Love to oneself and others. He told me that this was the true condition of oneself anyway and is the condition which we can each renew to at any instant and is our true birthright as children of Him.

He told me how it is much better to be in and develop Relationship Proper by experiencing and expressing it as The Respectful Sharing of the Experience of the Expression of Being, and Ones Allowing for Others to experience and express being Themselves in ways and means of their own Choice which Walk in Balance and With Harm to No One Being or Thing and are most comfortable to Themselves. He showed me how Love is the name for the energy force that is the true condition of the vibration of anything of, or in, His creation. He told me that all Love comes from Him and that we each are in the continuum of cycles of growth as to become bigger and better channels of it. He told me how Love is an ever present force that is present in abundant supply throughout His creation and can never be in short supply. He showed me that at best we can only be channels of His Love and told me that the definition of Love Proper might be best stated as being The Gift of One's Care For The Well-being, Balance, and Fulfillment of Another Being or Thing Of HIS Creation. Great Pop showed me that in the definitions of both Love and Relationship, there is no mention or implication of a condition of contract.

As all are in a constant condition of Relationship to Self, each other, and the All, and Him anyway, the invocation of contract would only provide fuel to the Ego that would feed Fear in the betrayal of such. Or it might be stated as, if you put your fingers in the holes in my pattern and I yours, one or both will be in constant worry that the other will remove theirs.

He showed me how the keyword in the definition of Love was the word Gift, and that any condition other than that was not Love but Fear, the great tool of Ego, manifesting an illusion of need. He showed me how that the key words in the definition of Relationship Proper were Respectful Sharing, and that proper relationship cannot exist without respect or the condition of sharing. He showed me how the cause and cure for all problems in relationship is communication and that in communication it is as important to receive through patient listening to the Spirit of what is being spoken as it is to be heard. He showed me how we sometimes have an immediate feeling of like or dislike for another and how it is the Love or Fear that they are projecting through their pattern of Self that we are resonating to.

He told me how sometimes we might recognize a pattern of someone that we have known in a lifetime before, whether friend or foe. He told me in these instances we might adopt an immediate attitude towards them that in time we will have to adjust to maintain balance in the true and Proper Relationship that we may now develop with them. He showed me how some peoples tend to incarnate together in groups because they get great joy from the sharing of the experience. He showed me how some others incarnate together to grow from turning a hate relationship in the past to one more proper in the sharing of Love. He told me how we sometimes carry over from place to place and incarnation to incarnation some of the attitudes and Fears which we had before and how during an Earthwalk we are in a position to release from the memory of mind these things which are primarily resident in the pattern of Self through the manifestation by the Ego of Self. He showed me how Fear is a taught condition of Being and that in each incarnation we are born in a condition of absolute Truth and Love.

He also showed me how we choose our parents and our physical condition at birth to experience the best conditions for our growth. He told me how the stillborn or the ones that die at a very short time during an Earthwalk are usually in a condition of where the Spirit decides not to incarnate into Earthplane at that time and decides to do other work in another plane or dimension.

He showed me of how we are helped in the appraisal of our potential of growth by our Guides before, during, and after our Earthwalk and that we are constantly being assisted by them during our Earthwalk. He showed me how some hear a calling as most Medicine people or Shaman do, to exist and communicate in more than one plane or dimension at a time to best be of service to Him through service to others.

He showed me how all of His creation communicates through vibration and how it is all connected to each other and Him and that what affects the smallest part of it, affects the whole of it, including Him. He told me that sometimes some people like to call the ability to work with this vibration - the psychic realm - and that all of his creation and children have the ability to use and work with it but that it is like a muscle that we have early in life but must be exercised and developed or it atrophies under the pressure of the muscle of Ego. I was shown how sometimes parents or others in the society which we choose to grow in, through Fear or ignorance teach us not to use this natural ability that is available to each and all of us.

He showed me how each child is born in Truth, Love and absolute trust and for the parent or any other to betray this trust causes harm not only to the growth and Well-being of the child but it causes harm to the Well-being of the child of the Great Spirit Creator that is the parent or the one of influence that caused the harm. In such a condition of resonance as we truly all are, the impact of such wrong-doing affects me, you, the flowers and the sky, and the All, as well as, Him.

He showed me how I chose a condition of birth in the condition of my relationship to my own parents. I was shown how I chose to grow through the experience of choosing parents whereby I would not receive the nurturing and feeling of worthiness and Well-being that most receive from being held and Loved at birth and during the very early time of an Earthwalk. I chose those conditions to help me best grow past a sense of vanity that caused my demise in my previous life, as I had lost my leg during the war and did not feel whole or worthy. I am still a little angry at them for being such good lesson givers and I was given to understand that I could only release the condition from the previous life by coming to terms with it, and this is a good example of how carry over problems work.

He showed me that we can only conquer or grow past an attitude of Fear by coming to terms with the reality of it. I was shown that only by accepting not by denying the Fear can we discover the true condition of it to Self. I was shown to identify the source, which is usually from Ego, and then complete the process of release through forgiveness of Self and giving the attitude or attachment to the Fear away. He showed me how the fabric that connects the Heart of one with the Mind of one is called conscience and how we each are in a perpetual state of not only growth, but in a position of Renewall to the perfect pattern of Self. I was shown that we can do this by working in the fabric of conscience so as to renew ourselves back to the perfect pattern of His creation in and of us.

He showed me how the fabric between the Mind of Self and the Ego of Self was called illusion and how the Ego likes to take control by playing god, with only Self-defeat as the ultimate goal, as in each endeavor the Ego tries to stymie our full potential of growth. He told me that we should see the child of His, in all of His creation, and how children should see the child in the parent as well as in Self. He told me that the parent should welcome this vision of Self to the child and never should the parent try to assume god like stature over the children as in time they will soon experience the folly in it, as the inevitable outcome of this condition is that the child will soon outgrow the parent.

He showed me that we are ever in a condition of growth and that the greatest gift that we can present is to support the growth in another, no matter how old they might think of themselves to be. He showed me how much it hurts to lose another that you Love or have known, but if we embrace the truth of feeling pride in having experienced relationship with them, we usually feel a little silly in thinking that they are lost to us and see the illusion of Ego in it. He showed me to remember in these conditions that the silver thread to them that comes from the heart of Self will ever be there and can in truth never be severed.

He showed me how in any condition or circumstance, aspects of it have the ability of being judged as good or bad and that in truth indeed, there can be found a positive side to anything we might encounter, sometimes we do have to get away from linear or two dimensional thinking to see it though.

He showed me how in the beginning of the Earthplane experiment, all was established in a respectful sharing condition and that this should still be the ideal which we should adopt in our Earthwalk. He told me that we can only accomplish this if we assume and exercise responsibility for and to it. He showed me how He is and likes to be included in everything which I do each day. Because of this, I realized that my constant prayer is the greatest gift of both respect and pleasure which I may give to Him.

He showed me how in the beginning, All was Spirit and Spirit continues to be the true condition of everything of His creation. He reminded me of how to fly and showed me how to channel His Light and Love and for me to Love myself was indeed to Love Him in me. He showed me that to Love Him was to see and share Him in each other and the All of His creation on Earthplane, and beyond.

He taught me the Law, and that the Law was the Word, and the Word is One. He showed me that the only wrongful condition of Being is feeling separate from Him and that this is indeed a condition that can never be. He taught me how to pray to the Spirit of the Water that I drink, to the Spirit of the Food that I eat, to the Spirit of the Air that I breathe, as well as to any and all that I receive as He is the source of all of it, and to pray to the Spirit of it, is indeed to pray to Him.

He taught me how to call the Wind from the four directions and the understanding of the Sacred Circle that is the Medicine Wheel. He taught me to talk to the Spirit of the Plant and the Tree and all of his creatures on Earthplane and beyond. He showed me how to see the Spirit in things that do not obviously carry a Life-force, such as the Spirit of a place or a time, and from this, I understood much more about the ability of the collective thought and will. He showed me how on Earthplane, we are all the same in our uniqueness and in our uniqueness, the same. He showed me how the collective will can create a dimensional reality, as all is vibration and all thoughts are heard by the All. He told me that as we grow as greater channels of His Light and Love, we should endeavor to grow in a multidimensional sense, more like a sphere or a ball might be than as a flat wheel. He taught me that as we grow in this way, as we receive more, we take some to Self so that we can expand more so that we can touch more, so that we can share more.... of Him in us.

He reminded me of how we can create Thought-forms with Fear or hate through Ego and it is indeed these which we encounter when we climb the scared mountain in vision quest and these are the same forms which I encounter in the layer which I call the zones during meditation. It is given that while these Thought-forms might be considered as evil, they have only the dimension of form and are truly without substance. It is an illusion game of Ego when we attach them to ourselves, but growth will be the end result, and as with all, there is perfection in it. Some might consider these Thought-forms to be an example of the misapplication of our Free Will, I prefer to consider them not at all, and thereby give no power to them. He taught me to determine which Thought-forms were Fear entities and how to become invisible to them and any other things which do not support my Well-being and growth and how these Thought-forms come as the ideas of others and are definitely not of that by Him.

He told me further of how He gave us Free Will and that we create Thought-forms as an expression of our Free Will and our endeavoring to act as Co-creators with him, but by creating some of these Thought-forms, we are usually operating in a manner which is not in Balance and With Harm to No One. He showed me that to make myself invisible, all that I had to do was to make the bark of my Ego real thin so that no Fear or Thought-form could invade the tree of me, but instead would only pass right through me.

THE CREATOR SHOWED ME THAT IN

THE BEGINNING

ALL WAS TRUTH AND LIGHT AND LOVE,

AND THAT THIS TRULY IS A CONDITION TO

WHICH WE ALL CAN

RENEW OURSELVES TO AT ANY INSTANT.

PERHAPS MORE IMPORTANT THOUGH,

THAN ANYTHING ELSE,

HE SHOWED ME THAT IN THE BEGINNING,

NOW, AND EVERMORE.......

ANY AND ALL CAN BE !!!!

THE JOURNEY

Each of us are born into Earthplane at a time of and to parents of our choice, with a plan and Guides or Angels as they might be called by some, in a condition of absolute perfection, truth, Love, and trust. Each one of us has beginning Medicine that the Great Spirit gave each of us when He created us and we are constantly adding to this beginning Medicine as we experience incarnations into Earthplane and the others. In the good old days of my and most aboriginal cultures, the child born would be seen as a gift of the Creator to the tribe or clan and respected and cherished as such. The first child would often be given by their parents to an aunt and uncle or grandparents to raise and a name would be given to the child by a Visionary or Shaman that would describe their Medicine or Spirit. At puberty another name might be given to the child or another name yet be given during vision quest. Another name might be given during warrior-ship or in leadership roles. During an Earthwalk a child might well indeed have as many as six or more names, each defining the Spirit or Medicine of it as it grows.

In this societal way, the child indeed maintains a unique identity and value and it is the Spirit of the child that is portrayed in the name. The child is not named or thought of as the son or daughter of someone, or thought in reality to belong to its parents, as might be the case of a pet Animal or the like. If the child was found to do wrong according to the established rules of the tribe or clan, the child would be disciplined by any or all but more care was given to its growth and Well-being and to the development of the child. The child would go through many tests to test the Medicine and strength of itself and thereby would develop respect for Self and others through the character building nature of such tests.

As the child grew, often they would spend time with aunts, uncles and grandparents to learn from them their skills and Medicine. The child might learn basket weaving from one and hunting from another, with great respect being shared between the teacher and the pupil. In such societies, all of the adults that were of the parent's age were considered and called aunts and uncles and all those that were older were thought of and called grandparents and considered as such, regardless of their biological relationship.

In these societies and cultures, great value was given to the elders or aged ones as they had a great gift in the Medicine of wisdom that was respected by all of those in the society. Such was the high esteem held for children, that during times of conflict, the young children would be spared and adopted into the society of the winning tribe. While others that were older might be spared and kept as slaves, the young children would be treated with a great respect and treated as equal as those borne into the tribe.

In these cultures, the society was usually governed by a council with direct representation, and decisions were made by these councils as to best support the Well-being of each of its members as well as the collected whole. It is important to note here that the society into which we incarnate for an Earthwalk is as important of a choice that we make as are the parents which we select in our plan for growth. While we cannot change directly the biological parents of our incarnation, we all have not only the ability, but more important the responsibility, to manifest inputs or changes into the society to which we are borne. And if we find ourselves to be in a condition of failing that, to move on and make the establishment of a new one. Freedom is an absolute condition of Heart, although the Ego might try to tell the Mind differently.

I was told that a society can best be judged as to its effectiveness by evaluating the conditions of its oldest and newest members. If a society does not support the growth and Well-being of all of its membership, ever growing dimensionally as to support the ever changing needs of its membership, then its term is indeed limited as the failure of it is inevitable, with a new order to ultimately be established to support the continuum of growth. It was then explained that as the Earthplane experience is about Love and Brotherhood, it is the society that is in support of these ideals and reinforces the diversity of its membership that will ultimately prevail.

I am given periodically an understanding that is the theme for a year, such as to keep on keeping on, or to enable versus empower. The theme for the year, a while back, was the word Renewall which by now you have noticed that I use quite regularly. The word describes the ability that each of us has of renewing at any instant, our pattern of Self back to the condition of completeness and perfection as was made by the Great Spirit and was the condition of Self when we incarnated for this Earthplane experience. I was shown that Renewall is available to all, at any time, and can be manifested by just giving away the wrongful idea of Self. I was given in my daily practice of meditation to seek the truth of Self by looking within. In my way of meditation the object is to fly and be with the Great Spirit Father or Creator as some might call Him. I found that this indeed is the very best way for me to start each day and in the process, my prayer is for guidance and Renewall.

I was given the Seven Washings Prayer in which I Pray for cleansing and Renewall prior to my daily meditation.

The Seven Washings Prayer is as follows:

Oh Spirit of the Water Please:

Cleanse my Eyes that I may see clearly the Will of The Father,
Cleanse my Ears that I may clearly Hear the Will of The Father,
Cleanse my Mouth that I may Speak the Will of The Father,
Cleanse my Mind that I may Know the Will of The Father,
Cleanse my Heart that I may truly Love The Father,
Cleanse my Body that I may fully Serve The Father,
Cleanse my Spirit that I may be with Him.

Importance was given on the placement of the prayer for the Mind, as to first be a channel of the Creator instead of the Ego idea of Self. Each day in meditation, upon my asking of Him as to what it is for me to do, a vision is usually given and in most cases it might be the simplest of things like sitting at this computer and working at the writing of these pages. Often when I ask to be made over as He would have for me to be, I will observe others working upon parts of my body. Sometimes I will see implants being put in parts of my body or work on the lens of my third eye area for increased psychic vision and clarity.

Often in meditation I will see and communicate with The Christ or others including my Guides and go forward and back in time as well. On some occasions I will be presented with body parts from those on Earthplane and others and I will do healing work upon them. I will sometimes manifest tissue and other components with a blue-green ray, which comes from some part of me like a ray gun. After using this technique I am often given to flood the affected area with a green mist of energy from the heart and I know it has a supercharging like effect upon the healing process and the healing is indeed speedily done.

Sometimes, in meditation, I will journey into other planes or worlds as some might consider them to be. Wherever I am given to be in meditation, there is usually work for me to do there or I will encounter an understanding or answer that I might seek. Often in my technique of meditation, which at best might be considered a continuous prayer, the telephone or the door will make an interruption, and most of the time with the exact answer which I seek. This is still the very best way I know of to start each day, by being with Him.

As previously mentioned, a while back I asked the Great Spirit what was the best thing for me to be or to do and He said "Keep on keeping on, and walk the Round Way for all others to see". I asked how I should do that and He said "In a way that walks in Balance and with Harm to No One, including Oneself"!

I was then given a fuller understanding as to the cycles of life and the continuum of growth therein. I was shown the vibrations embedded within each cycle of a larger vibration and the vibrations embedded within each segment of them, and so on, and so on, and so on, with no end. I could then more clearly see not only the great perfection in it, but the great beauty of it as well. I more understood and developed a greater sense of how He allows to us all that we need or can use at any instant.

I then began to review the cycles of my own life. I had been previously given the understanding that all on Earthplane are in resonance to the number seven, and that it is the master number that describes the vibration of the life force on Earthplane and the cycle rates that we experience here. I was given to understand that not only is our growth pattern usually based upon seven year cycles, but also that we renew every cell in our bodies every seven years and this gives rise to what some regard as the seven year itch, as after that period of time, there is a whole new Being in cell structure there and this includes everything from bones to eyelashes. I was shown how we begin at zero years and at seven we enter primary education.

The next cycle of seven is the great metamorphosis number of fourteen, and this also describes the wonderful event known as puberty. The third cycle of seven develops to the age twenty-one and describes the potential condition of maturity, although for some it seems to take much longer. The fourth cycle of seven develops to the age of twenty-eight and may well be considered to define a condition of wholeness and so on. Each cycle of seven years in our life has a unique wind of change in it to support our potential of growth, whether we use it or not, more Free Will, it is perfect of course.

I was given to see the large influence that the society of our peers continues to exert upon us in not only being a great motivational force, but also in the great impact it makes in the structuring of our ideals. I saw how, at times, I had tried to walk the Earthwalk the Ego limiting pointy way, only to find, not only the limits of the Ego idea of Self, but also the true falseness of having such small ideals.

I was given then to remember the Medicine Way that I was truly born into and then I returned back to the truth of what and who I am. Yes, I am a child of the Great Spirit Creator just like you, with really very little difference between each of us or the work that we are here to do. I remember the Great Spirit Father, Creator of All one day say "Little one, do not take yourself so seriously on Earthplane. You are supposed to walk in joy and enjoy your walk".

I know again that I have indeed just made Him smile.

The journey of an Earthwalk is much like that upon other planes with the addition of a nice little element called time. I had often wondered about the time element on Earthplane and through my having a lot of star Medicine I have always had a sense of the illusion of it. I saw that on Earthplane we seem to continuously relate to past events of which we can truly do nothing about anyway. I did find that time can provide a certain motive force or incentive, at least to some of us anyway. I noticed that time seems to be too slow when we are in an unpleasant occupation of it, and too short when we are in a pleasant one. It also seems that those with the most time available, tend to have the least resources with which to enjoy it, and the opposite holds true as well, which is a kind of funny condition to be in, unless you are at one of the extremes.

The true journey or Earthwalk through the Earthplane experience is given to be expressed for understanding, as a continuum of the time of the tree on repetitive cycles of the Medicine Wheel. Each cycle begins with the seed planting time in the south, followed by the sprouting time in the west, and next to the growing time in the north, and then to the flowering time in the east, and back again to the seed planting time in the south, and so on. And while the directions might be different for some, the cycles are the same.

Earthwalk journeys also should be seen objectively sometimes to enjoy the humor present in them, such as the one who struggles to finally master a skill, will indeed soon find themselves to be in a condition to be of no need of it. It is given also to express here that only by giving away the need of anything, which is an Ego manifested illusion, can anyone master anything or as might be better put, become in a true condition of resonance or Onement with it which is the most proper ideal. This is usually because the cycle is complete as the lesson was learned.

One example of the humor in Life can be that of the hoarder not being able to live comfortably because there is no place for them or anyone else to sit or lay down. Another example is the person that cannot leave or go any place else because they are afraid someone will take their place or things. In that case they become imprisoned or possessed by the physical things that they consider to be their possessions. I have seen some people that do that with money as well.

In the ways of Tribes in the not too distant past, all things were considered as belonging to themselves and the Great Spirit. Each and all things were held as being even and Sacred and as such, all things should be cherished as a blessing to experience and Share, with no idea of ownership or keeping other Beings or things from experiencing or using them. The reality of Earthwalk is that it is a path and journey of experiences and it is those experiences that are all that any Being or thing can ever take with them when they leave.

I oftentimes liken the journey to a flight of stairs which has no end point. Each of us is situated upon a step of our own unique staircase of growth, and on each step we learn from the experience of the lessons it has at that level and Medicine for us to acquire in the process. We are ever in a condition of growth and as we acquire the Medicine and become proficient in operating at the level of the step which we are on, we lift our foot in faith to behold the potential of the next one. Just as we must release the comfortable position of the previous step, we must leave that step behind by joining the other foot upon the new and then regaining our balance to Self by fully centering ourselves upon it. One can easily visualize each step to be a lifetime, a year, a month, a day or an instant as it is all the same, but in our journey through our Earthwalk we must walk like the climbing of the steps ever leaving the past behind if we are truly to behold the future.

Just as there are many things for us to use on each step, and helpers to aid in the process of the experience of growth upon it, if we were to try to carry on any more than the lessons of it, the burden of the load will make the next step process ever so hard to do.

The journey is much like a continuum of attainment and release and in the exercise or process of it, we strengthen and round out the condition of Self. As we grow used to the process of taking the steps, it becomes much easier to do and each step becomes broader with more upon it to experience there. On occasion, however, as some are of want to do with impatience, peoples will skip a step or two only to stretch the fabric of Self until they fall. In this condition they end up repeating the steps not made, as upon each step the lessons learned there make the next lessons much easier to learn, and the steps much easier to attain in a condition of Balance. I have also seen the condition of where, for whatever reason, one would try to carry another up the steps only to discover that upon setting them down upon a step past one that they had individually achieved, their legs will be too weak to stand there and down the steps to the proper level they will return.

This situation gives great credence to the concept that each of us are truly exactly at a place or step where we need to be to learn the lesson in it. Besides the situation of the other's legs being too weak if being carried, the carrier in the process will not strengthen Self, but instead, weaken Self. The weakening of Self is the result of precious energy being misapplied in the effort, and in the process they only make the next step for Self much more difficult to experience and in truth only make extra work for Self. In whichever condition, however, lessons will indeed be learned by all and that truly exemplifies the perfection of it.

In addition to using the staircase to describe the journey, I often like to show the illusion of those trying to live with perception only to Self in the now, or as I call it, the Me Now culture. I ask them to write the word now on a piece of paper as fast as they can and stop them before they can finish. I then show them how what is written is indeed already in the past and the rest is in their future. Now is at best an illusion of Ego in as much as time is an illusion anyway, and truly only in and for the future of Self, can we make the most significant steps of change. It seems that a much better way to experience our Earthwalk journey is by living with respect and responsibility and fully beholding the future of, and for, not only Self, but all others.

Some of the aboriginal people speak of living for the seventh or the eleventh generation yet born and this seems to be indeed a much better way to be, and who is to say that these generations will not again be you and me? We each need to start now in our Earthwalk journey to ensure that this is a place that we can and will want to be. More harm has been done in the last fifty to one hundred years to Mother Earth and there are great mishandlings of materials and chemicals that truly might make her uninhabitable in physical form, and this may well be in your lifetime.

I see Mother Earth purging herself again soon and I am concerned about the burial of nuclear and toxic waste and of what will happen to these poisons of the greed of our society as the volcanoes and earthquakes that are soon to come, occur. It seems that to be responsible to the generations to come, we can and must act immediately and quit making things we cannot get rid of or that do not walk in Balance and with Harm to No One.

The Earthwalk journey might also be considered to be a connected string of new beginnings and this can best be manifested through ever surpassing the limits of the Ego idea of what we can do. We each can do this and realize the fullness of our true unlimited potential by allowing the Great Spirit's will to operate freely in and through each of us. Circumstances have often surpassed my expectations, not by the fulfilling of my limited idea of what can be, but because of my understanding that indeed, all can be. This can most easily be manifested if I will only broaden my scope of perception by seeing through Mind from the Heart of Self instead of from the Ego of Self.

Often I like to speak of life lessons as to be like learning to walk out and stand on the very tip of a branch of a tree. As we try to walk out upon the branch we may get only as far as three or four steps and then the branch bends under the weight of our idea of Self and we fall off. If we make no change in the attitude or idea of Self, we will continue to fall off after three or four steps, never reaching the end. After a time we may even reach five or six steps and think of how much we have progressed, but this condition is only an illusion manifested by our Ego, as in truth we are only walking farther upon the branch of the tree because the tree is growing, not us. If however, we do make change and lighten the load of Self by giving our Fear and need for excess away, we indeed can stand upon the very smallest tip of any part of the tree as we learn to become at one with it.

It is such conditions that we encounter in our Earthwalk journey that we become exactly that which we seek to learn, and we always are seeking, even if silently or subconsciously, exactly that which we become and we each can and should take responsibility of, and for it. As one masters the lessons of walking upon the larger limbs of our learning tree, we can move higher up the tree, learning the unique lessons of each branch until at last we can sit at the very tip of the top of the tree. It is at this point we have learned the lesson of the tree as we indeed have become it in ourselves. Then to our great joy, we see the forest, and the journey goes on you see, without end, only with new beginnings.

Sometimes I am asked about death and I am given to express the concept of death to me would be staying upon one step and refusing to grow. In some cases discarnates may stay and hang around some place or person for a time, sometimes for as long as three or four hundred years or even more. In these conditions they are not dead either, but they really are missing out upon the greater opportunity for embracing the growth experiences that would be available to them if they would make release through Transition and Renewall. It is in such conditions that they are really only causing problem for Self as they are missing out on the joy and experience of re-establishing their perfect pattern back to Self. Either way they are not dead, they are just missing out on experiencing some of their unlimited potential, or maybe as mentioned earlier, they are truly just where they need to be. Again, I see the perfection in it.

I asked the Great Spirit Creator

About the Earthwalk Journey one day....
And He only Said...
To Live it!

I then asked the Great Spirit
for Love and He said "Be Loving"
for joy and He said "Be Joyful"
for protection and He said "Be then not Fearful"

I asked Him what it is for me to pray for and He said:
"For Protection, Guidance, and Resource",
and indeed these cover Anything
that I may want or need in any circumstance.

Further explanation was given as follows:
Protect me from the wrongful idea of Self that my Ego
may make of me such as feeling separate from Him.
Guide me as to best serve His will in me and as to how
I may become a greater channel
of His Light and Love.
Provide me with the resources which includes the
opportunity in which to do it.

In our Journey, it might be much better
if we were to treat the Children
With the respect due our Elders or Parents,
and give our Elders and Parents the consideration that
We as children desire from Them.

**REMEMBER THIS ABOUT THE EARTHWALK
JOURNEY,**

IN ABSOLUTELY NO CIRCUMSTANCE

OR CONDITION OF IT,

DO YOU EVER WALK ALONE!!!!

****

RE-NEW-ALL

I was watching a program on this television channel which I like that is called PBS. The program was about astronauts and what it was like to be in space. I thought how difficult we sometimes make this process as I can go everywhere so much easier by flying out of body. But what really impressed me was when one astronaut started describing how much differently he saw Mother Earth from space and it brought much to mind about our society and its need for Renewall. At the time of this program, my country was in the process of carrying out a bombing raid on another country with hopes of keeping their morals intact by the destruction of their weaponry, which seems a little absurd.

I am given to include here the memory of a statement made by a dear friend of mine many summers ago who happened to be an attorney by the name of Jim Cornish. He said that if he had enough money to give a thousand dollars to every married Woman, he would not be able to handle the flood of divorce cases that would result as there were that many people in poor relationships. Funny thing is that he did later handle a divorce of mine.

At the same time of the bombing raid, other factions of my country's military are in another portion of the same continent where the raid was done and they are using their weaponry to insure that the population there get enough food to eat. It is explained as being necessary to use this weaponry because other greedy ones steal the food to profit the few. Elsewhere, at this same time upon Mother Earth, at almost the same latitude in Europe, others are still using weaponry to settle arguments over geography or to gain independence. In South America, as I write these words, a thousand acres of trees are being destroyed so that a few people will have more gold to wear in Europe and elsewhere. Others try to grow their food in areas that have no soil after the cutting of the trees which previously provided the food and shelter for the monkeys that the aboriginal people used to eat and they sadly see their abundance rapidly diminishing.

The list of absurdities in land use and resource mismanagement goes on and on, and there is no place upon this precious and fragile planet that has not been impacted by the greed and abuse of Man. Even the north and south polar regions are suffering by both the air and water pollution caused by the mismanagement of waste in the inhabited areas.

This astronaut spoke of how even from space that he could see the brown blight of air pollution in the thin film called the atmosphere that encircles the planet upon which we temporarily reside. Mention was also given to the observations of river sediments being so abnormally high and photos were shown not only of effects from the great oil spills, but also the great fires burning plumes of black smoke into the sky from the actions of global abuse ordered for no good reason by this person in power in this land called Iraq.

This astronaut then spoke of how often he had trouble sometimes identifying the society of the land which passed by from his position in space, because of the sameness of the adjoining areas and that borders between countries are but in reality only imaginary lines. I thought full well of our secular and separative attitude and standing apart from our reality and truth of being a world community. The astronaut then spoke of how from his position of being in space he was better able to grasp the concept of a whole Human race rather than as each having a separate place and the need for all of us to see it as such.

I agree that at this time there is indeed a mandatory condition for the Human species to continue to operate in and experience this dimension of Being. As he spoke about the places upon Mother Earth where he was able to see the boundary lines between countries that were not from the natural formations in the geography upon her face, it was evident from the use of the land that showed from his position in space whether it was for agriculture or habitat. One of the thoughts that came to me was how very much a small segment of Mankind has hurt Mother Earth in such a short period of time. It seems like only yesterday and has not been one hundred years since the automobile came into being, and from the first appearance of this convenience item upon Mother Earth, it seems that both the condition of Mother Earth and the societies upon her started to decline real fast.

Mountains are still being washed away for bits of gold or ore. It seems a pity to do such things in that there is an ample supply of all things for all of the people upon Mother Earth if they would only learn to share. The blight that seems prevalent in Earthplane society and is the cause of the cancers upon her face and in her skin is indeed nothing more than Human greed. It was given to me a long time ago to consider what aliens must think of the behavior of the Human species especially in that each race or tribe of the Human species view all others as aliens. This astronaut was able to see clearly from his position in space the true condition of the Human species upon Mother Earth, and in truth it is a world community. It is coming time soon for Renewall back to that condition as it is now necessary not only for the survival of the people upon her, but also for Mother Earth herself.

Having been given much about relationship and the understanding of what works well, Renewall to a world society must begin by both ideology and communication. I was given to think how it seemed that only by the existence of a threat from Beings from space would the barriers of countries and societies be broken down so that all could work together for the common good. I was then given to see that the threat from space is perhaps indeed already upon us, except it is being manifested internally in the form of the hole in the ozone layer, nuclear waste, and so very many toxins and poisons in each and every place.

Another pole shift is imminent and what becomes of that stuff which is currently being stored in unsafe places will affect each and all of the Human species. The future is truly the now condition of Being, and we must take action now for us to continue on Earthplane and behold the unlimited potential in the future of it. As all are constantly in relationship to each other, Self and the all, a start would be in redefining Mankind's role and responsibility in the care of this place called Mother Earth.

In earlier times, while Man existed in clans and tribes as he walked about Mother Earth's face, he put no pressure upon her with too dense of a population or by using resources that were not immediately and easily renewable. At this same time, while each of the clans or tribes might speak a different spoken language, there was a universal sign language also so that the key ingredient in relationship could take place - communication. Each and every society must share in vision or ideal and work for the common good of All for the lasting betterment of any segment of it to take place. It seems that it might be a good idea to again develop a universal language and continue to teach it to all of the peoples upon Mother Earth so that all can effectively communicate with each other and renew relationship to all.

Respect and responsibility are two other key elements and these are both important and necessary in the establishment of an ideology by which all peoples can live and experience the Earthwalk as in the Prayer Proper, by walking in Balance and with Harm to No One.

The rampant abuses in waste and the condition of hunger, drug, alcohol and sexual abuses as well as the abuse to the elderly and to the children and the general abuse to Self and each other are obvious indications that indeed, Renewall in the Spirit of Mankind should soon take place. Many cultures have come and gone from Mother Earth and The Atlantean and Lemurian and Egyptian are but some of these, with each of these cultures failing just as surely as this one will if change does not soon take place. As with these other cultures there will be some survivors if only but a few, but as the scientists say it may soon only be insects in this place.

Pole shift is Mother Earth's way of Renewall when she can no longer stand the pressure and abuse and Mankind makes societal shifts as well. The Great Spirit Creator gave us Free Will, and it is a most powerful tool indeed, but much like the two edged sword or blade, it cuts on both sides and in both directions in which it is used and great care and caution should be employed in its application. Much more effort, attention, and energy is needed in the Renewall and restoration of Mother Earth's condition. No longer should anything be made, for whatever reason, if it, or the byproducts of the making of it, cannot be gotten rid of safely.

Great speed and endeavor should be presently expended at the development and the employment of processes to restructure both radioactive and toxic waste materials so as to render the existing supply of these materials harmless to anyone and discontinue making any more of these substances until this is done. As great eruptions are soon to take place upon the skin of Mother Earth's face, in truth there is no safe way or place to store them. A small quantity of these materials that is currently in place, whether exploded into the atmosphere by the many volcanoes or spread into the water tables and oceans by the many earthquakes soon to come, is all that it will take to render the Earthplane to become an uninhabitable place to experience in Human form for eons to come.

The Renewall of the condition of Mother Earth and her precious resources that she willingly gives to us is a great moral responsibility and it belongs to each and every one of us. Even those individuals who think it is not of their whereabouts or concern or problem are a part of it and each and every voice and prayer is heard. Those willing to take action will receive support from the universe and Spirit planes as well, as the condition truly affects the condition of the All.

Methods of waste disposal, Renewall, and reconstitution are available and new technologies and efficiencies will be realized only when there is enough pressure to do so. Alternate and renewable energy resources are other areas of endeavor which Free Will might best be applied to at this critical time and definitely serve in the betterment in the condition of the All, and that is the definition of Brotherhood that we came to Earthplane to experience to begin with. By the development of a universal language and the continued communication available through the use of it, and the development of renewable resources especially in energy generation, all peoples upon Earthplane will be benefited whatever their social or societal condition might be.

There is absolutely no reason for any person upon Mother Earth to go hungry or to be in want of clothing or shelter. Those individuals that desire greater accommodations and pursue greater luxury in life should do so, but not to the detriment of another or by the sacrifice of a single living thing for the purpose. Again, the measurement of a society is not at how well the conditions are at the top of it or even in the middle but at the bottom.

As all are on Mother Earth to learn the unlimited ways of experiencing and expressing Love and Brotherhood, a greater focus should be applied in the tightening of the bonds of the Human experience through communication and lesson sharing. The education of a society begins not with the young but by the wisdom imparted by its elders. Not only should the elders be respected by the society but they should be given and take an integral and active part in it.

Too much in the present society operates from a plastic and cosmetic value structure and all are too eager to discard that which is not brand new and this value system is doomed to failure. As all is truly in a constant condition of Renewall, here is an excellent area for its application and communications should be established and vehicles made to enable the elderly to share in the learning experience that always works in both directions between student and teacher which is a perpetual condition of the life experience anyway.

A world order should be established with a focus to Onement and function not as a governing body, but more as a channel of resource sharing, communication, and planning with a touch of historian added for good measure. Counsels should be more in the way of Big brother advisors rather than as being legal rhetoric predators who prey upon the society that they are supposed to help. Healers should be more in service to the public which they choose to serve and provide for the prevention of the diseases that they wish to cure.

Both can be better at it by addressing the Spiritual component or issue at fault and truly hope to see the client or patient nevermore in such condition of Being. The work or healing should be done to the fulfillment of the client or patients need, not to the fulfillment of bank accounts which desire from Ego ever.... more.

It is indeed because of the pole shift, which at this instant is occurring, although not as noisily or as quickly as at times before, that the visionaries, healers, and teachers are hearing the calling and feeling the anxiousness in the wind of change bringing them together to be of service. It truly is a calling that some try to ignore, but the conditions only keep pressing forward until they finally acknowledge it and make their individual choice which is exactly why most are here at this time on Earthplane anyway. The Pole shift experience is also why there is so much pressure in the populations upon Mother Earth, as it will be a long time before there will be as many bodies to inhabit to experience the physical sensations of life on Earthplane. Ironically it is very much like the multiplication progressions found in the splitting of atoms or cells, the more that come, serve only to cause a quickening of the event that was to happen anyway by the very pressure of their anxiousness. It is like the addict or those which have an insatiable appetite, the more that you have, the more that you want, which at best is an unhealthy condition of mind.

It will be many generations to come before the many souls upon Mother Earth at this time may reincarnate, due to the population depletion or loss that will occur during the many eruptions and tidal surges. There is an underlying attitude in the populations in seeking, what is in it for me now, in the way of looking at things. This is past the Ego way of selfish delusion and indeed poisons the very fabric of the mind. It is Brotherhood that we are here to experience and in conditions of calamity or misfortune where most should pull together, many choose to take advantage instead. In the current conditions on Earthplane, situations and expressions of greed far surpass any other ideology or morality, fortunately not in all cases. Sometimes I think that this makes the potential loss of approximately seventy percent of the current population not seem too bad. As Spiritual growth is the true condition of Being, we are ever encountering opportunities and cycles in which to express it, whether on Earthplane or any other.

Societies are founded by cooperation but often with assignment of positions based typically upon need or wish fulfillment but not always with the same ideology. Conditions have been softened a bit in this period with only a few conflicts in the European and English areas. While to some degree both conflicts are ideological or religious in guise, in truth they are no more than the denial of Brotherhood acceptance in the allowing of God to be seen by the other and having more than one name. The conflicts in the English land seem the most absurd in that both factions agree that the fundamental teaching of the Christ was, and is, about Brotherhood in the condition of relationship in Man. Yet to this date the slaughter goes on that has continued since He was murdered upon a cross upon a hill called Calvary. It seems that the Earthplane populations have not learned very much in the last two thousand years except new ways to operate from Ego Fear and greed, and to try to dominate or deny Free Will in the condition of another, and in the process deplete and destroy this beautiful planet which we all came to be on, called Mother Earth. It is time indeed for each individual and society and nation to experience Renewall.

The **RE** in Renewall relates to the experience of bringing forth again the condition of being the perfection that is the true pattern of Self as was manifested by the Great Spirit Creator.

The **NEW** in Renewall relates to the aspect of purity in the condition of perfection in which each Spirit upon Mother Earth began.

The **ALL** in Renewall relates to our connection to all of the Great Spirit's creation including not only Self and the Ego attitude of Self, but also Mother Earth and every thing upon her, all Spirits in all planes of existence, and most important the Great Spirit Creator as well.

Pole shift is a process by which periodically Mother Earth renews herself and the conditions upon her. We have been shown through the ages by countless wise ones and heralds such as the Christ, how to go through the process of metamorphosis or Renewall of Self back to the consciousness of perfection, by giving the Ego away. As each of His creation are His children and all are truly here for the same purpose on Earthplane, we should see the sameness in each other in the experience of Brotherhood. As proper Brotherhood is given to be the sharing in the betterment in the condition of the all, it is indeed a condition which we can manifest only by realizing and taking the responsibility for the truth in Self. All conditions on Earthplane are in constant support of this adventure and experience and each and every situation is indeed an opportunity for growth and should be seen by all that way.

As each of us become more aware and take on more responsibility for Self and the conditions of each other, it is most important to respect and give allowance for each to grow at a pace that is comfortable to them. The child must first crawl before it can run, which it seems we also sometimes expect to come too soon. It is more important to see each step and make it as a positive adjustment or change for betterment in the condition of the All and then , not only will Renewall be manifested, but also the greatest growth will be made and that is what we are ever about anyway, see? As with the newborn child, the new order or society is a part of the Renewall process that is this pole shift event that we are all experiencing.

It is important to note here that the first item is not in experiencing the vision of it, but is in learning to communicate. Respectful sharing is the requirement for Relationship Proper and communication is the medium of sharing which is the easiest to employ.

As it might be defined, **The Law of One** is not only in the recognition of one Creator of all things, but one All and the oneness in the relationship of all things of His creation. Whatever is done to the least thing of His creation, a Dog, a Plant, Mother Earth, a Child, a parent or elder, a friend or a foe, is indeed done to and felt by Him. We are each in the condition of being in the constant realization of our prayers, and as all prayers have energy and form, they are felt and heard by all. We each need Renewall as a constant in our prayers and to give away our Fears. The fences and walls which we build with our Fear, which is the greatest tool of our Ego, keep out not a thing. The fences and walls only keep us in isolation and retard not only our growth, but they also retard the wonderful experience of being the best expression of ourselves as unlimited channels of the Great Spirit's Light and Love.

The pole shift should indeed be welcomed as a great opportunity to Renewall by the establishment of a new order that is focused upon the ideology of the true Brotherhood of Mankind with respect to both the earth plane and Mother Earth and all of the Great Spirit's creation. Heaven on earth then, can indeed become a reality, but this cannot exist as long as we continue to build upon Self the thick bark of Ego through our manifesting only greed. Care for the growth and Well-being of another which is the definition of Love, is a much better endeavor and not only leaves much room for more but by the very nature of the experience of it, we fertilize all of the tomorrows of not only ourselves but more important, each other.

Unlike the doctor who prides himself
in how many patients
have become in need of him,

I pray for the day to come soon that no one
is in want or in need of things like this,
or even a Man or Being like Me.

My Prayer is indeed for the Betterment
in the condition of the All,
and for RENEWALL
in the condition of Man.

WHITE EAGLE

Each one of us can and should diligently pursue
PERFECTION
as being the condition of oneself
and the All upon Earthplane,

and to be in a constant state of Renewall
and thereby manifest our greatest Growth,
and thereby experience our greatest Joy !!!!

Life truly is a continuum of shared experiences,
and it is indeed in the Sharing,

that we truly find the greatest
Happiness and Joy!

WHITE EAGLE

WALKING THE WALK

Upon starting this segment, I was given to notice that I personally, have absolutely no idea of what is to come out of this pencil which I am writing with. The words which flow come easily to this pencil of mine as most of this writing is coming through channel from my Guides through me to you. This day I stopped by a clover patch and as I am often prone to do, I asked if there were any four leafed ones that wanted to come home with me today. I often give most of the ones that I find to others that I see along the way home from the clover patch and I notice how often it amazes them in how easily and often they come to me. I am usually asked as to how I find them when they cannot, and I then tell them it is easy, I just ask and listen for one to say "take me, the lawn mower is coming again soon anyway so my work is done here".

Our Earthwalk is very much like that, walking ever in a sense of discovery in a huge clover patch. Some people approach it like those who believe that all good luck and good fortune belongs to others, and just like the clover patch, it is all in how you look at or perceive it to be. If someone looks at the potentials of what can be for them to experience, receive, and enjoy, with an attitude of denial of being able to receive these things and instead walks with dread and Fear and without expectancy, that is just as surely a prayer that will be answered as one of expectancy and knowing that truly all can be.

Once while I was looking and listening for four leafed ones, I was given to find five leafed ones instead, just to show to me the unlimited potential of All can be. Just as is the condition of those which have the understanding and knowledge of the possibility of attaining all of that which they seek, it is important to also employ patience and recognize the cycles if one is to behold the potentials of the All that can be. Just as the clover grows fuller at certain times, seasons, or cycles of the year, we too should look for and apply the knowledge of cycles in the attainment of the successes which we wish to attain and thereby we can receive fully the lessons in it and thus grow.

As we walk our walk in Earthplane, it is just the same as when looking for a four leafed clover, we must visualize the pattern of that which we wish to attain. Too often we listen to the clover patch with deaf ears and do not hear those saying, "Here I am, please take me with you", as we deny the Spiritual connection between all things. As is the same as when looking in the clover patch, we may choose to look at those that appear the same or at only those that appear unique. I prefer to look at each one as I try to see all of His creation, uniquely the same and in their sameness, each being especially unique. As we look over the masses of His creation in our Earthwalk it is this very special quality that defines His children that we call the Human race. It seems that sometimes it is much easier to find a four leaf clover than a friend in certain times and conditions of Being, in this society that is and should be seen as, the greatest patch of clovers and all with four leafs.

We each are captains of our own fortune and future upon our Earthwalk and it is a condition of Brotherhood that we all in the conditions of heart seek. I find my greatest sorrow and feel the greatest pain when the strings to the heart of even one friend are severed for any reason be it mine or theirs. We each at times wish to be the same and the samely unique in our personal struggle in the constant redefinition of our own true and unique identity, which can be thought of as the pattern perfect idea of Self that Walks in Balance with Harm to No One, including Oneself, I am certain that I do. I have always enjoyed and been drawn to the four leafed clover, perhaps it is because it resembles a little Medicine Wheel, ever walking in the Round Way, and that is ever the path which I seek.

Much of the time we might hear about how much of the future is dependent upon the character, desires, and ideals of the children now growing up. It seems that it might work that way except for the conditions of the parents of those to whom the children choose to be born. The child chooses the parents to be their Guides and lesson givers to teach them how to walk the path of life in an Earthwalk, yet as conditions exist in the present and for the last few generations, these lesson givers that are the parents, are spending all of their time obsessed in their own material attainment and conduct their business and behavior with little or no conscience to the Well-being of another and then become upset when the child does the same. These same lesson givers in their indulgence to their own Ego and greed, tend to operate mostly in material attainment with absolutely no conscience to the future or the needs of their children's children, which should be what is taking place in these critical times.

Fifty summers ago with the advent of the atomic age, all ideals and attitudes of the Beings in the predominant societies on Earthplane changed with the dawn of what was called the cold war. Two conditions of change brought about this circumstance and both affect the common ideal and the resulting morality or lack of it in the social conscience. The great Fear of instantaneous and total annihilation brought about by the atomic bomb in the consciousness of the larger societies, generated a mass paranoia that resulted in those having the resources to begin building bomb shelters and hoarding food and weaponry to perhaps survive the inevitable destruction of Mother Earth and all of the societies upon her. Those individuals which were not able to meet the high economic requirements, responded to the situation by turning to absolute Self-indulgence instead. This resulted in collapse of caretaking in the society and the drawing away from Brotherhood and the beginning of the Me Now attitude in the peoples of these larger societies and the resulting decline in social skills and morality.

As time went on the bomb sheltered ones soon became envious of the Self-indulgent, Me Now ones, and the whole of society was ripened by their Ego building for the salesmen and advertisers which preyed upon this condition of the Spiritually weakened and Ego Fear of Mankind. As time went on, and each generation which now was only taking approximately twenty summers to create, added their Fear to the pressure upon Mother Earth and the resources upon her as there was no other focus than in keeping up with the excesses of their neighbors and the ensuing declining morality as the bonds of Brotherhood broke down. Both Mankind and Mother Earth became the victims of the wanton waste and destruction of a society whose conscience and ideals were totally Self-serving as what is in it for me, me first, I want it all now, and more and bigger is always better with no care as to the Well-being of another. There often was little thought being given by the parents to the children that were looking to them for Spiritual ideals only to find nobody at home when it came to these issues especially as the peoples of these societies began to hide their Egos and shame under the influence of drugs and alcohol. Fear is the condition of Being that lets the Ego lead us away from our Spiritual Self to a condition of total absorption in our Physical Being, augmented with the printing and public acceptance of publications espousing immorality such as the one titled Playboy, and with music which hypnotized the society with messages constant in our ears of saying drugs are ok. The society was brought into a condition of being in the next generation of twenty summers to not a sexual revolution, as some liked to call it in the nineteen hundred and sixty decade, but to a revolution that led only to a Spiritual and moral decay and a resulting decline in the safety and Well-being of the peoples of the society now living in Ego Fear.

Meanwhile more irresponsible parents were bringing to Earthplane more children just to prove that they were there and their ability to do so. To add to the dilemma during this time, all efforts to raise the Spiritual consciousness of the children in the educational facilities were ruled as being illegal by the courts in this land. The message seemed to say keep them ignorant lest they make demands upon their parents to account for and explain their selfish behavior. Forty five summers ago there were very few latch key children in the society as most had only a father who worked to meet the needs of the family with mothers truly able to spend their time at mothering and in lesson giving.

If Ego Fear and Self-indulgence was the first, then the second destructive force that came upon the society which began with the atomic age was that the parents spent all of their energy and more important their time, in developing and becoming enslaved in careers that force the children to seek and receive all of their guidance in Spiritual and moral development outside the family or home. Those few who do participate in religious ceremony and seek to develop higher moral ideals, have too small of a voice and are usually ostracized from the community that should be in support of them. Next the society takes away from the educational experience of the children, prayer or any form of worship in the schools which should nurture and fertilize the growth of both the Spiritual and physical identity of them, and then no longer functions as the evolutionary platforms of growth which they should become for future children.

By the absence of the parents in the raising of the children, the public schools became the place for the beginning of the idea of Self in the children and thereby became the idea of the society to which is chosen to belong and identify with, not the parents. This is a Self-manifested condition of the society anyway and as the Free Will drum beats ever a different song, it is important that Free Will is realized as being a forever condition of Mankind, not society. On Earthwalk, pass not by one, without seeing in them yourself, and your Brother!

In most aboriginal societies all were seen as one and took responsibility not only to Self but also to the Well-being of each other. Often when the elders no longer felt that they could contribute to the Well-being of the group or when food stores became in short supply during the long nights time of the year, they selflessly would walk off from the others so that the group would continue and not be a burden to it. All in these societies or tribes as some may be called, gave great value to both the elders and the children, and saw and valued the important role each played in the future and Well-being of the people or society. The elders were the primary educators and caretakers for the children, but any member would take on the lesson giving and care for them at any age. The children were often seen as the life force to the society and each member saw the education and caretaking as a great responsibility and enormous care and pride was given to the process.

As the child was passed between aunts, uncles, and grandparents, it learned the Medicine and knowledge and skills of each so as to make not only a better condition of Self but also to enrich the ability and conditions within the tribe or society. By keeping the Medicines alive whether it be gardening, pottery, basket weaving, hunting, healing, or any of the many others, all members present and future of the society benefited from the process. Sometimes in these societies of peoples there would be potlatches or giveaway ceremonies whereby all of the possessions in the society or tribe would be collected and then redistributed based solely on need and utility.

In these conditions a person may keep one or two things that were considered necessary or special to or for them but all of the rest were given away, of course in the redistribution process you usually ended up with some of the same things again but things of great utility like horses, boats, or tools were often spread around evenly so as to serve the greatest need. After someone passed on or walked through the veil, some of these societies would wait for a year and hold a great remembering and giveaway ceremony with all of his or her possessions being evenly distributed and shared with each member of the society and in this way they were always remembered and, as most possessions had great utility, no thing was wasted. As Brotherhood is the sharing in the betterment of the condition of the All, potlatch and giveaway ceremonies worked well that way.

These societies were most often governed by a council of representatives that shared their Medicine that way for the Well-being of the tribe with chiefs being in a more administrative role than one as being autocratic. Often in these societies the Man would join the Woman's family, clan, and tribe in marriage and often these societies were matriarchal with women holding the chief status except usually in wartime as women were sensed as being closer to the rhythms of Mother Earth. The Medicine Man or Woman or Shaman, as is called by some, would usually live alone at the edge of the society and be called upon in time of need for healing, counseling, teaching, or visionary work.

One day I watched an elk at the edge of the woods in an icy area by the water. This elk stood there and was not so sure of what it should do. It seems that society is very much in that condition at this time but with out having elk eyes. It seems this society has its eyes closed most of the time right now, and any society which serves only in supporting the betterment in the condition of a few is standing upon thin ice and has a very small base to work from, and will and is failing as I speak. Words seem to make little difference to this society at this time as the crying out about the conditions of its children and elders seem to fall upon deaf ears.

The difference that each one of us in this society might bring forth is to raise and therefore initiate Renewall to the Spiritual consciousness of its members, which is all of Mankind. The Renewall is necessary to start the inevitable process of restructuring of consciousness from matter over mind, back to the true condition of mind over matter and renewing the membership of the society back to Spiritual ideals and consciousness. In truth all is Spirit anyway. It might well be stated that in society on Earthplane, try to lead not from the Ego idea of Self image, and follow no longer blindly the ideals of others, but renew Ego and Mind to the true identity and condition of Self as being each and every one, a perfect child of the Great Spirit and endeavor to continue to see that in each other. Each of us should endeavor to be an agent and emissary to the Creator by opening and offering each Self as to be His channel and workforce to the correction of Mind and Mother Earth by taking responsibility for the continued Well-being of Self, each other, and this planet called Mother Earth.

We should not think of ourselves from our Egos as being all that is, and we can only truly become God-like when we start to see ourselves in each other and all of His creation. It is only when we start trying to impact positively upon the Well-being of another, and it is amazing in how easy it is to do so, then truly do we start to belong to the Human race, with absolutely no regard to color or creed. All is felt and remembered by the Great Spirit Creator and the All and that is the most powerful Medicine anyone can realize and this I know for sure!

During our formative years we are constantly seeking knowledge in how to walk correctly in our Earthwalk. As we get older we change and then from our new position we try to make the actions and ideas of our younger time different than they really were, usually from Ego manifested illusion. Some people totally disassociate from their younger times and others dwell upon them ever wishing to relive the joy of victories or to forget failed expectations, much like staying upon one step and refusing to grow. The true beauty of an Earthwalk is that we each and every one came here for a reason, our own special plan for growth.

Any and all of us, if being totally truthful to Self, can stop and see that each and every circumstance in our Earthwalk is nothing but a full manifestation of our own design, aided by the wind of fortune or by choice prayed for, to achieve the lesson in it. To perceive the Earthwalk as being anything other than as an experience for growth and thereby lesson taking, is to not having been here in the fullest sense of the words.

I have watched as many try to live their lives and thus experience their Earthwalk vicariously through the events of the past and through the actions of relatives and others. It really matters little as to which is doing what, but know for certain, that each and every one of us is totally responsible for our own experience in our Earthwalk and this includes our own Well-being, but more important, our growth as channels of the Great Spirit's Light and Love. The very best way to accomplish this is to walk the Earthwalk in a manner which is indeed in Balance and with Harm to No One Being or Thing including Oneself. In the walking of our Earthwalk or the climbing of our staircase of growth we are bound to fall on occasion through the making of improper choices. The only harm that truly can be done in such conditions is to stay there and not forgive ourselves and thereby any others. Accept the lesson in it, and renew ourselves by trying once again.

We often go through periods of reorientation as we grow through the experiencing the lessons of our Earthwalk, and be sure that when looking for direction, the truth lives inside each of us, but to see the truth clearly we must give our Ego away so that we are not impacted by its great tool of illusion which we often times use in our rationalization. As we begin to walk our Earthwalk this way it may seem like it is an insurmountable task to make a difference in the mind and conscience of our society, but is not the society made up by each of us?

Defining the purpose of life and gaining an understanding of it has been an ongoing mission of the societies of Humankind since the peoples here on Earthplane first started to gather together and communicate one to another. In the early time when the populations were not so dense, the peoples here on Earthplane had and spent more time in the discovery not of new lands, but the sense of their own reality. After the communication of their ideals to each other, they developed a system of societies or clans. These societies made agreements for the establishment not so much of laws nor ownership of property, but the establishment of common ideals and they thereby defined their purpose in the attainment of them, as well as the behavior considered to be proper in the process. Societies today seem to exhibit little of these traits, yet ideals are still the undercurrents of societies, however most societies today seem to support the growth of Ego instead of the Heart by the exclusive nature of them and the price of the membership is the loss of a bigger sense of Brotherhood.

As the society begins to stray away from ideals which may be connoted as religious tenets, which is the ultimate breakdown of the threads that bind the population together, the result is the redirection of the concern of that society as not being focused to the Well-being of the whole, but in the attainment and advancement of a few.

The natural condition for the Beings on Earthplane is to function in such a manner that allows each member to manifest their unique creative force and Free Will. The enslavement of one society by another can only be if the enslaved society sees no way to realize its ideal and thereby actualize its purpose. As long as societies encumber the growth and Well-being of the Spiritual aspects of its members, and remember in truth Spirit is the only condition and is constant in all of the Great Spirit's Creation, it is indeed in this realm that the greatest good in the purpose of Being can be manifest through the changing of these societies.

One day a beaver came up to the Great Spirit and said "Father, I did everything that I was shown to do by my parents and still the trapper took them and my front leg too". The Great Spirit paused and then said "See, have I not provided perfectly for you"? Of course He had provided perfectly for the beaver as part of the beavers Medicine was in lesson giving and story telling. Of course the beaver had his life force still intact on Earthplane, but much more important than that, the beaver now had great lessons to share with others and thus the lessons and the beaver would soon be honored by them because of his experience in his Earthwalk. No circumstance or condition of Being can have a negative aspect unless it fails to serve in lesson giving and thereby support growth.

Much weight is given in the remembering the events of the past, but more important it seems to value the sharing in lesson giving as well as the receiving, as only in sharing can Brotherhood and the betterment in the condition of the All be truly manifested.

If Earthplane is to be a condition for our grandchildren and their grandchildren to experience and as the Iroquois Brother spoke about the seventh or eleventh generation yet born, which on reincarnation might well again be each of us, serious changes must be made. Changes must be made in the caretaking of the children with value systems much different than the current egocentric ones. Changes must be made in the value systems of ourselves with more truthful and purposeful ideals. Changes must be made in the caretaking of Mother

Earth with resource management by all peoples. Changes must be made in the caretaking and employment of the elders with involvement and lesson sharing in the society.

But perhaps the most important change that should be made is that all begin to see the Earthwalk as the sharing in the betterment in the condition of the All, and each member of the society taking good measure and renewing each Self as a perfect child of the Great Spirit Creator and helping Self and all others in becoming greater channels of His Light and Love. And then if it is possible to be more important, help each other see the truth of Self as a totally special and uniquely valuable part of His creation and see each Self and each other as being infinitely influential and more significant, responsible to and for it all on Earthplane. Remember, All can Be, but we must change and try if we are to grow to the realization of any of it.

On occasion most of us on Earthplane have had the thought, what if we were really the only ones here and all else were just robots or actors for seeing how well we would do, and of course in this way the Earthwalk by definition would be **In Balance and with Harm to No One**. The winds of change are steadily increasing and are always blowing and as mentioned it is truly all in how we look at them. The destiny of Man and Woman, as some now like to hold their gender separate, is not to be on Earthplane to persevere or to accept any or all conditions without the advent of change, but to continue to make better for Mankind and thereby Self.

The fatalist says, "No one survives the Earthplane", but I am sure all do, but it might be questioned at this critical time, "Can Earthplane survive our walk upon her"? The impact of each persons walk lasts long past the abuses to Self which are automatically transferred to the others there as well, but the abuses are transferred to the All, and Mother Earth herself.

As the first, greatest, and only idea of what might be called sin seems to me to be the abuse to Self, each other, or Mother Earth. All that comes through is to say emphatically **"QUIT IT!!!!"**, it seems too easy, does it not. In times to come whoever might read these words, I can only ask of you to read and hear the truth that lives inside each and every one of you and the sooner that each of us begins to see the child of the Great Spirit Creator in each Self , each other and in every thing on Earthplane the betterment indeed will begin in the condition of the All. As the Christ has brought forth to Earthplane on many occasions the lessons of Butterfly Medicine or metamorphosis, we should endeavor to live life to the fullest of our experience of growth and share that wealth with each other in the true sense of Brotherhood.

It seems so hard when we encounter problems in existence and in relationships not to react defensively in Egocentric Fear, ever justifying the actions taken and ever walking farther upon the thin ice as in the case of the elk which was described before. It seems that perhaps the best action to take in these conditions of breakdown in communications is what the oriental philosophy calls passive action. The winds of change will again blow and it seems like at these times it might be best to wait patiently and faithfully in prayer for the All that can Be. We might even do better instead of constantly reacting to the unfavorable conditions, and digging ourselves a deeper hole of which to climb out of, spend the energy more positively in the examination of the lessons in the circumstances and grow from them. If we walk our Earthwalk with expectation of the All that can Be and apply the cycles that are ever present in the winds of change, the greatest energy or force that we can then exert upon the attainment of our greatest desires or dreams, is the gift of patience and the resolve that comes through positive prayer for the attainment of them.

If we walk hurriedly or haphazardly in our Earthwalk and only see things through the blinders that our Ego manifests for us to use through the condition of our Fear, we will ultimately find the folly in it as we are soon drawn into circumstances to realize the great deception contained in the illusion and therein we will ultimately grow. As we grow, we are ever splitting the bark of our Ego. In conditions of discomfort or pain which usually comes from a condition of loss or separation, we are confronted with an opportunity. The opportunity is a Choice to either become absorbed in the experience by the pain which we sometimes feel that we need or deserve, or to take upon ourselves the greater opportunity to let go of the Ego idea and embrace fully the perfection in it and Renewall to Self with less Ego in the process. To visualize the Earthwalk as an endless continuum of Ego separation so as to receive the fullness of the receivership and sharing in Love is a much better way to perceive the reality of it.

In the walk of each of us on Earthplane are not constant hazards except those manifested by Self, but more important are the constant helpmates to help share the experience along the way, whether in physical form or as Spirit-Guide helpers. The truth lives inside each and every one of us. But we have to see it from the Heart of Self as being perfect children of the Great Spirit Creator to see it most clearly.

There is more than any Being can hope for

awaiting each and every one here on Earthplane,

if only that each of us will look inside Self and see

the beautiful Golden Thread that connects

each of us with the Plants, the Rocks, each other

and every thing and most important,

Ever connects each of us to

The Great Spirit.

I Love You,

and may you ever feel,

the Great Spirit

Smile upon you!

White Eagle

One Day,

I asked the Great Spirit Father for what should I

Pray.

He told me to Pray for -

PROTECTION, from the wrongful idea of yourself.

GUIDANCE, in how to walk the way.

RESOURCE, in the opportunity in which to do the walking.

I saw that all of the things which I might need or
  desire fell in the categories of one of these and
  then I was given the next four, as it seemed on
  Earthplane all things resonate to the number seven,

HEALTH, is something we seldom appreciate until
someone is in need of it.

WEALTH, in seeing the bounty within each of us
  in the All that can Be.

LOVE, is the force that He made all things with and
in all things, we should see and channel to every Being
and thing of His creation, including ourselves for
Growth.

JOY, is the way to walk our Earthwalk and the way
  to Properly approach the process of our own Growth.
          And so I do each and every day.

See each Tomorrow -
As a brand new Earthwalk journey's beginning,
And then make good travel plans
Through one's actions today!

Fear is a four letter word that is a tool of the Ego.
Hope is a four letter word
That is best used as a tool of the Mind.

Love is the greatest force in the universe
and comes from and feeds the Heart.
Love is ever being provided by
and is truly
in limitless supply,
From the Great Spirit Creator
And it is the one thing that
He loves to make the most.

On Earthwalk,
There Is Truly No Absence Of
The Great Spirit Creator In our Steps,
Only Sometimes
The Ego Manifested Illusion Of It!

One Day,

I asked The Great Spirit Father how I should grow.

He told me:

*Remember in the Earthwalk Little One, to keep Growing
like the tree,
from the inside out
and keep walking in the Round Way.*

**Like the tree, we each should take firm root
in the fertile ground of life on Earthplane
and become an ever Growing channel
of the Great Spirit's Love
through the Heart of Self
and then the Mind,
thus allowing the Ego to give way
so that all can see the beauty inside
that is the truthful condition that is in each of us.**

All Can Be!

About Earthwalk,

Just Remember,

**As the Great Spirit Creator
Is ever there for any and all
Who would seek Him
Through that Golden cord
Connecting
Him
To every Thing and Being
Of His Creation,**

NO ONE EVER WALKS ALONE !!!!

With Love,

WHITE EAGLE

WALKING THE

ROUND WAY

BY

WHITE EAGLE

CONTENTS

The Source   109

Onement   112

The Story of Jack   115

Another Story   118

Relationship Proper   124

Karma and Yin and Yang 144

Cycles   153

Renewall   163

Walking the Walk   167

****

The following information is presented from knowledge that has been provided to me during meditation and from my Guides through channel. The references to The Father, The Great Spirit, and The Creator, as well as Great Pop refer to the power or one that most commonly seem to call God. I have worked in counsel for some time now and while I was writing about a different topic, it was given to present this information now as indeed it is about an understanding for which there seems to be a much greater need.

****

THE SOURCE

Many winters ago I was given to ask the Great Spirit in my daily meditation, "Father, why am I White Eagle"? He showed me the creation of the Earthplane and as He did so I saw that I was in Birdform and I was flying about the cosmos and the great void. I will note here that previously I was given the understanding that time is an illusion that exists solely upon Earthplane to stimulate us to grow in the here and now. So, how long the creation process took was but an instant as I saw it to be. I accepted that answer for a while as I tried to understand the full meaning of it. I spent the next several days working out the understanding and the real question that I wanted to ask became clear to me. I then let the cat Medicine of curiosity overcome me and the next day in my meditation I asked "Father, how was I made, and why"? I was hoping for an answer to better understand and help me be better at pleasing His Will in me and thereby live my life more correctly.

He showed me what appeared to be a large room with walls upon only three sides, and everything was white as I also recall. One of the longer sides of this area was open with no wall there and it seemed as the floor just ended abruptly at the edge and the great void began there. The room opened up to the great void and while there was light in the room it was a funny kind of dark outside of it, not a black dark but sort of a bluish gray kind of one. It was not pitch black, but there was no light there either, it was just empty, but not Fearfully dark, it seems like that is the best way to describe it. I am still overcome with a funny kind of feeling when I think about it. In the center of the room was a long table much like a worktable an artist or sculptor might use, and I saw myself partially formed, sitting upon a perch as my Spirit form was being originally created in the purest form of this bird.

I saw and felt as He manifested in the most loving way, feather upon feather from the tip of the second finger of His left hand. As He took each feather, the Light and Love that shone from Him as He placed each one in His own design of me, into truly a most perfect form, was and is still overwhelming. Indeed the reason for my Being is His Love and idea of me. I saw no others about me, but there might have been some others in other rooms in this place. After He finished covering me in my beautiful white feathers, I saw Him stand back and admire His work. I then felt Him give to me a voice, so I jumped at Him and made this great eagle screech and the laughter it brought to Him still gives me great tears of joy. At the next moment I went flying through the great void hoping to please Him more, I did great flying maneuvers and such and then I very much understood how pleasing Him brought pleasure to me.

I now realize that indeed the way to Be is as He made me as a channel of His Light and Love and that as I do these things, it gives Him joy and pleasure and I will also always please the Him in me. All that Is, is of Him and as we start to see the God part or Spirit in everything including each other, we must be caretakers of it. Many times in meditation or Medicine Wheel work I will see myself in my eagle form. But sometimes it is given for me to take on another form as to better do the work. So it is to say that even in Human form, my Spirit is this white eagle that was my original condition of Being as the Great Spirit made to channel His Light and Love. That answers the question of what I am here for and in doing that it gives Him and the Him in me the greatest joy.

A while later I asked Him "Father, what about these forces that some call good and bad, positive and negative, good and evil and so forth"? He said that they were just forces and it is all in how we look at them. Then he said, "Remember how I taught you how to call the wind from the four directions"? And I said yes. Then He said "And remember that I told you to call the wind the force of Change. Even when the wind does not blow that too is a Change, see". I thought about this for a while and realized that the true condition of all things is growth, and for any growth to occur, the force of Change is necessary to fulfill it. I was given to understand that if I was trying to walk up a hill and the wind was blowing hard against my desired direction or the progress that I wished to make, I might be given to call this an ill wind or negative force or the like.

But, if instead of the wind blowing at my face, this same strong wind was blowing at my back and easing my step and supporting my progress, I would indeed call it a favorable or good wind or positive force. Then I was given to realize that perhaps the better way might be to make myself real small when the wind is blowing hard against my progress, and wait until it is quiet or at my back as the change in the direction of the wind is an inevitable condition as well. Another option might also be to use my Free Will and go the other way in such conditions, as Free Will and the power of choice is the force of which all of His children may partake. In any condition I realized that there are no good or bad choices if one would realize them by learning the lesson in them and thereby manifesting growth.

It then came to me later that truly All is of and from Him and All is energy and vibration. For vibration to exist there must be highs and lows or ups and downs, and each of these is a change as well. These conditions of highs and lows are also what we refer to as cycles. As we walk our walk, we constantly encounter these cycles and it seems that we often also refer to them as good and bad, and it seems kind of silly to me now. Know only that the truth of the situation is that everything is in perfect order at anytime for anyone to experience their true potential of never ending growth. The key is to realize the true lesson in any situation or circumstance.

I next was given one day in meditation from the Father when I asked for new understanding "The law is the Word and the Word is One"! This might seem ambiguous to some but it made immediate and perfect sense and a great memory then came over me. In times past, those of Christ and Atlantis and many other cultures upon Mother Earth, some few souls have tried to manifest God-like dominion over others.

ONEMENT

It is given for me to express the **LAW of ONE** as follows:

There is but One source and that is the true Creator of All things. The Creator has been called by many names such as God, The Great Spirit, Jehovah, Almighty Father, and many more. The Creator is the source of Light and Love and the All that is. Each part of His creation is a part of Him. Each stone, tree, Animal, the Earth, the sky, the oceans, the stars, all worlds and planes of existence Is and Are, of and from Him and are a part of each other. The people in Human form on Earthplane are His children and incarnate to Earthplane to learn lessons in Love and Brotherhood. Brotherhood lessons are about growing so as to be better channels of His Light and Love to all of His creation and this includes each other. All that is of Him has a unique component or vibration that can be identified or felt. This force or vibration can be called its Spirit or Soul-self. Each tree has this component, each drop of water has it, each breath of wind has it, as all things of Him have it. All components of His creation are linked together as if by a golden thread. Whatever happens to any part of His creation is immediately felt by All of it through the Great Web of these threads, including Him. Whenever we help another, we help ourselves. Whenever we hurt another, we hurt ourselves. All is One, and Onement is the true condition of the All that is, or ever will be.

In the beginning, all things in and of His creation resonated and operated freely and in Balance and with Harm to No One. At one point each and every component of the All operated in perfect resonance to His Will, which is as a full and unique expression of His Love. Each part of His creation was uniquely the same and the same in their uniqueness. Each component of His creation still has an unlimited capacity for growth both in the physical Earthplane as well as all others, and we are in continuous cycles of Renewall to His Will in us, which is growth, through our experiences there. The attainment of perfection may be realized at any instant by our giving away the idea that we are apart from Him and are any more or less than the perfect expression of His idea of us, which is to be continuously growing channels of His Light and Love.

In biblical terms, the Law of One was most closely represented by the statement of "Whatsoever you do unto the least of them, you do unto me". Perhaps even better put might be that what ever is done, affects the All, and also affects Him. As the All is uniquely connected to each other, the total component of the All, and the All that Is, is connected to Him. Too often it seems that we think in terms of detachment whereby something that comes from something else is no longer felt by the sender. If we receive a gift we tend to treat it like food, as an item available for our immediate, personal, and total consumption and usually with total disregard to anyone or anything else. Yet even our food has Spirit and thanks should be given no matter how it came to us. In this thankful way, not only will it better serve and fulfill us, but also our joy in partaking of it will increase immensely, no matter to its taste.

The Law of One is to see the All as a continuum of the Great Spirit Creator and taking personal responsibility to and for it. Inclusive in the All is not only each other, but also Mother Earth herself and all of His creation. We each indeed have a moral responsibility to the gifts of the Great Spirit to treat them in receivership both thankfully and responsibly. We in Human form can really create no thing. We can only observe cause and effect and channel the forces that He created. We channel these forces for our purposes in hopes of attaining the desired effect, however a lesson can be learned or shared from any experience.

All of His creation is the same in this capacity with the same moral responsibility to the Well-being of each of the components of it. Too often it seems that we see and treat everything like a new car or toy, with great care and pride until the new wears off. Much is the case when we operate from Ego or the illusion which it creates. However, everyone can remember a time in our purity or innocence of youth when there was no way we would part with our blanket, teddy bear, or favorite doll, no matter what their condition might be.

We really cannot destroy anything either, we can only detach ourselves from its serviceability to us and others. Our Ego is our great detachment tool in as much as it tries to play God and make us feel apart from Him which is truly a great illusion.

The Law of One is to treat everything and each other as being Of God, including yourself and be of joy as being His unique channel and enjoy each and every opportunity which comes to do it, as these too come from Him. Or walk in joy and enjoy your walk. Our true potential is only limited by the condition of our allowing ourselves to feel separate from Him which can never be the case.

I next asked "Father what about this thing called sin"? He then gave me a remembrance about positive and negative forces and the illusion therein. I was then given to realize that sin could be a word that might be employed to describe an attitude whereby one may exert dominion and control over another. This control is only viable if a person for any reason what-so-ever is willing to give away their responsibility to Self and thereby Him and His Law which is One. To live in any society, agreement by its membership is necessary to operate for the Balance and Well-being of its population.

Religious societies supposedly function in this manner as well. However whatever power that belongs to Self if given to another in the ways of government or dominion over Self is also at best an illusion as responsibility for one's actions is still a Soul-self condition to the All. There is, however, lesson in any action taken whether it does or does not walk in Balance and with Harm to No One. Sin might be considered as behaving in an attitude as being apart from God. Yet we all go through phases of this experience as we learn to give our Ego away and it is definitely a very redeemable condition of Being, in that it is at best an Ego-manifested illusion anyway and at some point in our journey we will ultimately be reacquainted to the truth that lives within each of us.

The better approach and ideal might be for each to accept their responsibility to their own birthright of happiness and perfection, and behave in such a manner that respects these same conditions in any and every Being and thing. To walk in Balance and with Harm to No One including Oneself is the only way in which anyone may realize their true and unlimited potential for growth as a channel of His Light and Love to Self and all else. For anyone not to do so is not so much about sin or the Ego-manifested illusions of Fear, but is truly just another lesson that will sooner or later be learned anyway.

It is not harder for the Great Spirit to Love us when we deny of ourselves our worthiness to receive Love from him, it is only making it harder for ourselves to receive, and that seems like a sin. In any society the best behavior can still be manifested by the application of what is referred to as the Golden Rule, which is to say, treat others as you wish yourself to be treated. That sounds a lot like the Prayer Proper which is to walk in Balance and with Harm to No One, as both assume responsibility to the condition of Self and the All.

Next I wondered about this thing called Fear and I was given to understand that Fear is not the opposite of Love, as Love is the true force of the universe and thereby opposite is a non-applicable condition, like being the opposite of green or fire, as there is no such thing or condition, but Fear is only a tool the Ego uses to manifest the illusion of there being an absence of Love. The Ego does this to reinforce an improper Self-worthiness condition in our consciousness so that it can stay in charge.

Then with all of this reference to Ego which seems to be all negative, which is another Ego illusion to condition, I asked for a greater understanding about the components of our Being. I then asked, "Father please help me understand about this Ego thing"? He said "That is simple, just look at a tree. Inside the tree is the Heart or Soul-self which is the core of the channel of Self and this is the darker colored part. Outside of the Heart are the layers of the Mind and it is represented by the rings of growth. And outside of the Mind is the Bark or Ego of Self. The proper way of growth is like the tree, in the Round Way, from the inside out equally in all directions and thereby in perfect balance".

I was then overcome with a fuller understanding of what He told me. We grow from the Heart though action and decision making of the Mind, and as Edgar Cayce constantly mentioned, the Mind is the builder ever forcing the breaking through or the giving way of our Bark or Ego. I thought how we do most often see first only the Bark of another, and some have much more Bark than others usually covering up a soft Heart and as they operate with grandiose-ness, anger, or Fear. It is just their Ego Bark showing and usually there is a scared little child inside, I have done the same myself and that is why it is easier to see the same conditions in another.

THE STORY OF JACK

I remember the day many summers ago when I started a new job. It was my first experience with computers and I had always been interested in them. Upon arriving for my first day and experience of working with computers, I was taken into the basement of this bank building. I went down in the shiny new elevator and into this large room full of equipment of which some was very new and some was very old. I had great apprehension of how well I could learn to operate them and some nervousness of how I would be looked at by the people there as I tried to learn. I was immediately reactive to the image of a young Man that was in the far corner that was moving about with such ease and making these strange machines do God knows what with a great anxiousness. There was another Man there who was quite a bit older than myself and the young Man who was in such a hurry all of the time, and this older Man moved about with a slower pace but also with great ease. As I was given my first task to do by this older Man, whose name was Jack Snapp, I tried to imitate the speed of the younger Man and this older Man told me to slow down, that the machine was there to take care of the speed and that my best effort was in care taking of the process and the requirements of feeding it. That was and still is the very best advice anyone has ever presented to me.

When the younger Man first turned around and I saw that he had a black eye, I immediately felt that I probably would never get along with him and had all kinds of apprehension about it. I felt that we probably had a conflict in past life and that I had been placed in this environment to relive it. Upon hearing that the younger Man was the son of the owner of the bank and the computer business, and that this younger Man was also a part owner of the computer business, made me even more apprehensive as to how this would work out. This younger Man, whose name was Jack Goldston, was also a real close friend to the older Man and I could immediately tell that.

As the next days went by, I was given an invitation by the older Man to join him and the younger Jack, in going to the beer joint next door to play pool after work. I was only twenty years old and had just gotten married and I mentioned this to him and he said it would be okay anyway. He said that he wanted me to get to know the younger Man, so I did. I did not know how to play pool and this younger Man seemed willing to teach me and now I realize that this older Man orchestrated that.

The outcome of the experience was that I became very close to this younger Man and I saw that he had both a great death wish for Self, and an anger for his earth father. I still dearly Love both of these people and for the next two years this younger Man taught me how to hunt, surf, rodeo, and do many things and we became almost inseparable Brothers in the fullest sense of the word. The younger Man even quit the company he owned a part of, shortly after I took a better paying position with another company and for the next fourteen months we still would get together after work and do weekend things. After my first child was born, who was a boy, we would still do things as he had custody of his son as well.

After the first six Moons of us running together, I asked this younger Man what his first impression was of me, wondering how he had felt. He said that he had heard that I was in college and that I was real smart. Then he said that he had dropped out of junior high school and had joined the navy and that he had Feared that I would think little of him. I then saw how thick the Bark was on his tree. We talked about many things over the now short time that we had together and I dearly Loved this younger Man and I learned a lot about Love from him. It was not a homosexual experience that some had even accused us of, but a very deep seeded true care for the Well-being of each other and we had a great resonance for each others joy and pain.

My wife at the time, wanted to have another child real close to the first, and one Sunday in the spring, my wife and son and I met the younger Man with a friend of ours down at the beach to surf. My daughter was due to be born in a couple of months so my wife was a little large. Later that afternoon, the younger Man and our friend wanted to go over this new bridge to another part of the coast and he said they would be back in about an hour. We waited until sunset for them to return, but they never came back. My wife heard on the news that night that the younger Man had been killed less than a mile from where we had waited. His new high performance car had rolled over him and left the other Man unhurt.

I cried great tears of Love, Joy for his release of pain, and hurt for the loss of this Brother that I Loved so dear. We talked often about how we would meet on the other side with his waiting for me with a Falstaff beer, a cigar, and a pool game in which we could not be beat.

The story ends with the lesson about learning to see past the layers of Ego Bark, to the beauty of the Love waiting inside another and we can only do this if we keep our own Bark real thin. I still pray for a blessing of this beautiful child of the Great Spirit each day and often think of him. I am eternally grateful for his teaching me how to do so many things, but most important in how to Love and care for another whatever their condition might be. I named my daughter after this young Man I was first afraid to get to know. Until our moccasins again share the same path Brother Jack, may the Great Spirit smile upon you, and know you live well in my Heart.

I was next given to understand that as the Great Spirit said to grow like the tree, that the tree is constantly causing its Bark to split as it becomes an ever expanding sense of Self, yet it is the Bark of the tree that all first see, touch, or encounter. I saw that if we grow in the pointy way, we are constantly reminded of our limits of Self, or as being only so long, wide, or tall in our ability. But if we grow in the Round Way, we can truly realize our sense of unlimited possibility and balance. The Mind or fiber is the part of our Being that connects our present limit of Self or Ego, to the Soul-self Heart which is truly ever complete with limitless possibility.

The ideal is to make the Ego layer, which also is an ever changing component of Self, as thin as possible so that growing is as easy as the blowing up of a soap bubble. Then the Ego will be thin and clear so that all can see the beauty within the Heart and Mind of our Being. Some trees grow their Bark real thick as they think they need it that way to protect themselves from Insects and Animals and they do not grow so fast that way. It seems that some peoples Egos get like that with age as well. Some other trees like the cactus and aloe vera, have other means of protection or feel no need for it and they grow much faster and easier that way. The Ego, like the Bark, does not like to give way and its greatest tool is Fear. The Ego tells us that it needs to be real thick or big and tricks our Mind into thinking that there is much to harm us out there so that we will stay small.

ANOTHER STORY

A long time ago I was playing a game with this opponent that had a great big Ego and he kept saying how much better he was than me. Unfortunately, all too often we see this in sports and other aspects of life as the Ego appetite and greed becomes the monster it tries to make us believe in and Fear in the first place. My Ego said that this fellow must be right since he had been playing the game much longer than me so he beat me a lot the first few times we played each other. I thought about this person a while and I saw how badly he reacted when things did not go perfectly his way. I realized then how fragile his emotional level was with his thick Bark and how unbalanced he could be. I waited until he was again behaving in an emotional way as if having a bad day, and I played him again and he left saying that he did not know how I could win since he was so much better than me. I won because I grew and he did not, and I did so only by giving my Ego away and accepting the unlimited possibility for myself, which is the true condition anyway. I still think of this person as well, and each time I see another acting that way, I thank him for his great lesson and gift to me in showing me how not to be.

The Ego is a necessary component to our Being and the pattern of Self describes its form, but the Ego like the pattern of Self, requires constant modification and management. The Ego uses the tool of Fear to manipulate our emotions and it is trying to play God constantly, and only by denying growth through Change can this condition maintain itself. The greatest Fear of Ego is Change and it is constantly telling us that change is bad for us and status quo is the way. The Ego knows that both Change and growth are the inevitable condition of our Being and that all comes from within, from the Great Spirit through Heart and Mind. The Ego tries desperately to trick us into using precious energy in the building of bigger walls and fences to retard our growth, as this growth can only occur by its giving way. The Ego has a great purpose and positive aspect in that it provides us and others with a way in which to measure our growth and condition, and is a tool which enables us to see how we are in the here and now at any instant.

More important than the Ego in the process of our Being and in the expression of our growth is Mind. Each thought, word, or idea generates a complete and unique vibration that is heard and felt by the All and the Creator. Indeed the Mind is the builder of any and all things. The application of Will in conjunction with Mind, is how we act as Co-creators with the Father by channeling His creative force, which is Love, to and through us to the All. If we follow the ideal that the Mind operates as an expression of the Will of the Heart or Soul-self of one, all that is manifested will indeed radiate with the vibration of Love. In this condition indeed, All can Be, and that which is manifested walks in balance and resonates to the highest good for the All.

If however, Mind operates in service to or as an expression of Ego, all that is manifested will resonate with the vibration of Fear. In this case, the ultimate outcome will be that energy will be wasted in Self-serving ways but ultimately lesson will be learned, and in either case the condition of growth is supported and will occur. Mind has been described by many as having layers, like the rings of the tree, such as conscious, subconscious, super-conscious, and the like. It is given that it is not so important to subdivide or segment Mind but to realize that the Law of One is in effect here as well. In truth all is vibration and thought patterns from the Mind of one can not only be recorded by mechanical devices, but can also be heard, seen, and felt by some people consciously.

The Mind is not resident as some believe in the biological component of the brain, but is an integral part of the ethereal body of one. While Mind uses the biological component of the brain and nervous system to operate the biology of one, the condition called brain dead does not affect the Mind, and Mind dead is a condition that can never be, although some people might appear to have lost either one at times. More and more often are conditions where some peoples having been recorded as brain dead have come back to life with no disability for the experience of it. The Mind operates in direct communication between the Soul-self and on Earthplane our biological components, but it is not restricted to these. Obviously knowing of and working with the layers of consciousness such as what they call the "Alpha" and "Theta" levels or states can be somewhat effective tools to use when working upon the biological end of the Spirit and physical body connection. That is why hypnosis and other techniques are somewhat effective in working with integration or detachment problems in the physical condition of the Being. However they are of no effect as regards one's Real Mind, which is always a part of one's Spirit and it can Never be affected by such techniques.

Meditation techniques and other Spiritual practices are the tools found to work best when working backwards to connect Mind with the Spiritual component instead of the biological sense of Self, and remember in truth all of His creation is Spirit anyway.

Mind is like the pencil in my hand as I am writing this, the lead is but one of the two sources from which these words appear. If the other source is Ego one would find Fear communicated and if the source is Heart, then only Love and truth are communicated.

The next understanding that was presented to me was conscience. The word conscience has sometimes been misapplied however, more properly conscience might be expressed as the fabric or tissue that connects Mind to the Heart or Soul-self.

The fabric that connects the Mind to the Ego must be a much more permeable and stretchy membrane to facilitate growth and expansion of the channel. This membrane may be called by many names, but we kind of like illusion. Conceptualization and perception can come from either of these two membranes so remember that in order to find the truth, look within. It is within this fabric of illusion that confabulation, which is the filling in of missing details with rationalized or imagined ones occurs. There is not much difference between delusion and illusion you know. The Mind is truly the working part of our Being and through it our greatest good can indeed be manifested. Some Beings, however, use the ability to generate Thought forms that are contrary to the Well-being of others. Ultimately, however, these Thought forms will be dissipated by others and rendered harmless. In such cases as well, lessons will be learned and growth will be manifested. This ability that we can call "Mind Power" to cause things to affect ourselves or others is indeed all perfect, if you choose to see it that way.

I was then given to understand that the core or central part of our Being is the Heart or Soul-self. This is also what might be called the perfect child. This is the feeling of Being or core of Self and might be best described as the essence of Spirit. This part of Self also lives not in a biological organ or inside the body, but lives all about the body and through all of it. This part of Self is like the part of the straw which is the hole in the center of it. It is indeed the part of all Beings and things through which real Love flows. This is the part of the channel of Self that must also take on the nurturing food of our growth, which is also Love. If the Heart of Self is in such condition as to deny Self-worthiness as to take Love to Self before giving the rest away, growth cannot occur. The Heart of Self is indeed the source or origin for and of, our growth.

The Heart of Self is that part of Self that is ever connected to the Great Spirit Creator and the All and this connection is sometimes likened to a silver thread. Just as the Heart of the tree runs through the smallest branches all the way to the tiniest of its roots, and draws nourishment from Mother Earth and transfers this to each and every part of it, so does the Heart of Self. The Heart of Self is that part of our Being that receives Light and Love from the Creator and channels it like a straw through Self, Heart, Mind, and Ego and then to the All. The Heart of Self is also where we receive because of our connective relationship to the Creator, our greatest sense of strength and courage which some call Faith.

While the Mind is a great manifester for the purposes of Self, it pales in comparison to the potential of what can be by applying the Creators Will to Heart. Truly all can be, and miracles are easily accomplished if the Heart of Self is the vehicle. While discussing the example of the straw or tube for the channel to increase or grow, the Ego or outer layer must first give way for the material of the straw or Mind to expand to allow for a greater increase in the expression of the Heart or hole.

I then realized that for me to grow most easily like the tree, in the Round Way the best approach is to make the Bark of my Ego as thin as possible and besides if I can make it thin enough, all can see the beauty inside, even me. It is important to note that the tube or straw does not work near so well if it is flat and not round. I then thought about trees and how they always know when and in which directions to grow. I see how in most cases where they are pretty much spread out they always grow nice and full in all directions. Then I saw a tree that was growing up the side of a building and it only had branches on the side that was away from it. As soon as this tree grew tall enough to see over the top, it grew round again. Sometimes I feel like the tree before it grew above that building. Now I realize that in time, I too can grow above what is keeping me from being round. I also see trees that have been broken or bent over by storm and even laying down they again reach for Father Sky and Sun as they resume their growth, and I realized that too sometimes seems the condition of me. I thank every tree for the lessons that the Great Spirit made in them for me, and I began to learn how to Walk The Round Way from the Source.

THE TRUTH ABOUT THE GREATEST FORCE OF THE
UNIVERSE IS THAT IT COMES FROM A VERY LOVING
FATHER, WHOM WE ARE TOO OFTEN TAUGHT TO BE
ASHAMED TO GET TO KNOW,

AND IT IS CALLED,

LOVE.

LOVE DOES NOT CURE ANY PROBLEMS,
IT KEEPS THEM FROM EVER HAPPENING
IN THE FIRST PLACE.

WHEN WE LEARN TO LOVE OURSELVES TRUTHFULLY,

WE ARE LOVING THE FATHER IN US,

AND THEN WE CAN BEST CHANNEL

HIS LOVE,

TO ANOTHER.

White Eagle

RELATIONSHIP PROPER

Over the years on many occasions during meditation, questions would come to Mind for me to better help those who had come to me to help them solve some problems in their life. Most often the problems centered about conditions of relationships. Often when asking about such things the answer given would usually contain a specific reference to the condition of the All of things and while the answers were always right on target for each specific circumstance, I began to wonder about the bigger picture of things.

So I was given one day many summers ago, to ask the Father in meditation about how things worked or at least how they were supposed to. For some time I had been getting many answers to questions that discussed the All, so I first asked about it to see if I was indeed ready for a greater understanding. As I became at one with Him I asked "Father, please help me understand more about relationship and the All". He said "That is easy, All is in total condition and relationship to and of Self and All else". I really must have looked dumbfounded on that one as He saw the great confusion come over me and without pause said "Here, let me show you".

He then manifested a cube of spheres or balls in space. From each ball a string or cord was connected to each other ball through many layers and many dimensions and it looked somewhat like this:

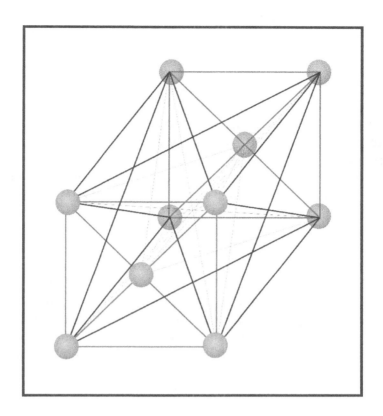

For graphic reasons some lines may be missing but visualize that each and every ball is connected to each and every other ball. Then He said "Watch this", and placed His finger on one of the balls and pushed it just a little bit and all of the balls were affected by its movement. Then He let the ball come back real quick and they all vibrated with the movement. Then He said "So you see whatever happens to the one of you, so affects the All".

I then was overcome with the understanding that whatsoever I can do to improve the condition of myself through growth, the All of His creation is indeed the better for it. I was also given a better understanding in how easy it is sometimes for me to heal others, as I learned that I could a long time ago by the method of sucking Medicine or adoption. In this technique I take the ailment from another into myself and do a lot of the healing work in myself. This is still a technique which I often employ in discovery or problem identification and while it works very well for me, I caution others in its use because if release work is not correctly done afterwards, it can keep you knotted up for days. Upon considering this, I realized much better how it was the effect of the All that made it work for me in the first place, and truly how very much we mirror and resonate with each other.

Then the Great Spirit said "Next, I will show you how important each of you are". He proceeded to take a ball from the middle of the cube of balls, and immediately the whole structure of it collapsed. I spent the next few days going over that lesson and each day since then, I realize more and more its truth and in ways of which it applies. It is important to state here and now that it is not to be implied that we are in a condition of codependency of or to each other for our own existence. Nor should it be inferred that we should tolerate the predations that some make upon others. But it is the Spiritual and thereby physical bonding that is being described. What so ever you might do to help another in need, to improve their condition of Self, improves your condition of Self. What so ever you might share in the experience and expression of growth through lesson giving or sharing to another, you will receive the benefaction and growth from the experience, as always the teacher learns from the student as well.

I next asked Him "Father, what is it that we are truly about, and better stated what is the purpose of our Being"? His reply to me was "All are in a continuous state of growth so as to become ever expanding channels of Light and Love to Self and each other".

It is given to interject here that as some might wonder, indeed as it was in the beginning, now, and ever will be growth as the condition of All of His creation, without limits and most assuredly without end. Just as growth is the condition of the universe that we know about, which scientists say is measured and indeed is an expanding entity in itself, growth is the same condition of and is a reflection of the All of His creation, which is of many more than the one dimension that we can see and experience on Earthplane.

It was then given for me to better understand that growth was and is the absolute condition of all things of His creation both in physical and Spirit and on all planes, and there are no limits except those which we manifest for Self. I then remembered when He told me to grow in the Round Way and realized how it applied.

Within this ideal, which is to continue to grow as a perfect expression of His Self, which is All Light and Love in us and act as channels of Him which we do when we channel His Light and Love to Self and each other, we can only best do this if we grow in the round, or better put spherical way. To grow this way, we must constantly give away our Ego idea of Self, which is fearful and limited, to embrace His idea and ideal for us. We do this as channels of Him when we allow that His Will not our will, be done through us. To grow in the Round Way is to grow like a balloon from the inside out in all directions so as we accept His Love for and through us and give as our will His Will be done through us, we can best become spherical channels of His Light and Love.

As we grow, we touch more so that we can give more so that we can receive more, so that we can grow, and touch more so that we can give more so that we can receive more so that we can grow, and on, and on, and on, do you get the picture? As we receive more and take proportionately the same to Self for growth, we still have more to give in each cycle as the amount given increases although the proportion might stay the same. It is indeed important to take some proportion to Self for growth or else the limits of our effect as channels of His Light and Love will be felt.

To walk our Earthwalk in the linear or two dimensional way is what I call walking in the pointy way. If I walk in this way, I walk with Ego as my guide and its Fear as my ideal, and I allow only my limited idea of Self to experience the walk. Even in this condition the proper ideal is in effect and ultimately I will find the lesson in it but I will usually find myself shortchanged in the process.

As a child of the Great Spirit, of which we all are, I can only reach my fullest potential by giving my Ego and the Fear generated by it away, as His idea of me will always be much greater than mine. If I quit trying to play God by operating through my Ego and allow Him to operate His Love fully and freely in and through me, then only can I be the best of me. The reason for this discourse has to do with our idea of Self which also is the pattern through which others see us and resonate to, with, or against us.

As a Shaman or Medicine person, it was given some time ago for me to give a Medicine or as some call them Indian name, to those people which request such. In the times since I first began doing this for others, I have steadily realized the benefits and value of the process. The method that was given for me to use was to go into a trance vision when I was using my Medicine drum. In doing that, I would see in vision not only the person's beginning Medicine, but also their Medicine in their other incarnations also. In this process, I journey past all lifetimes and a vision is given that I see as the beginning for each Being.

Also in the process, through prayer, the vision becomes clearer so as to distinguish the Self from Guides of the Self. A typical name might be Crystal Grey Owl, Crystal Star Bear Woman, Butterfly Flying, Blue Star Dolphin or the like. Each part of the name identifies a certain aspect of their beginning Medicine with the understanding that this is the true and perfect pattern of Self, of and for all times. It is indeed the pattern of the perfect child and channel of the Great Spirit, and it is a pattern to which any can return to in any instant. A person that is an Owl might be very comfortable standing by the side watching as others play or do things where an Otter might not enjoy the experience without participating in it. Each is perfect in their behavior as that is the pattern of them. The Owl, by the way, will know every thing that went on in the experience as nothing goes by unnoticed by them! Of note at this point is to identify and remember our purpose, which is **GROWTH**.

I asked one day for more understanding about this pattern stuff and this is what was given. The pattern of Self is the way that we perceive our selves and the way in which others see us. It might be better put as these Guides say "Pattern material is like a slice of bread from a loaf of ever renewing slices in endless supply. In this pattern material we manifest a hole or holes that lets out Light and Love to others in one direction and lets in Light and Love from others to us in the other direction. The perfect pattern for this channel is that of a white eagle and is of a size that is perfect to the condition of growth for him. In the process he is constantly amending the hole in the pattern of Self, adding some material here and removing some material there. If this Being is operating in resonance to his true identity as a perfect child of the Great Spirit Creator, and as a channel of the Creators Light and Love in him, then others will receive the Light and Love easily and evenly from him. The easiest and most proper way for this to occur is through walking the Round Way by using the Prayer Proper in decision making. The Prayer Proper is also the test for truth in any condition and is as follows:

DOES IT, OR DO I,

WALK IN BALANCE

AND WITH HARM TO NO ONE -

INCLUDING MYSELF?

If this is indeed the case or condition in Being, then others will receive a sense of Well-being from sharing in the Light and Love sent through the pattern of Self and the receivers as well as the All, return Light and Love back to the sender in absolute resonance through their pattern of Self and the sender will feel totally fulfilled. If, however, in the condition of Being, the sender may allow their Ego to make Fear holes in their pattern of Self or trick the sender into making a turtle or pattern other that proper for the true condition of Self through envy or greed.

Some turtles may envy the eagle in that he has flying Medicine and tell the eagle, be like me, be like me, I can swim under water and I always have my home on my back so Ego envy changes the perfect eagle pattern to that of the turtle it desired to be. Now in the imperfect pattern condition of Being, when the eagle sends out Light and Love through Self to others, it is seen and received in Fearful and incomplete ways, and when it is returned to Self it goes through the wrongful holes in the pattern and in places misses him completely. In this condition of Being he then feels unfulfilled and incomplete, always giving more than getting and often misunderstood.

The wonderful part of the process is that when the eagle is in such a condition of Being, whenever he chooses to with his unlimited Free Will and never ending supply of pattern material, he can throw away the wrongful pattern piece and make a new one at any time and at any instant renew Self back to perfection and continue to operate in resonance that way. With a little practice, the Renewall event becomes easier and quicker as we accept the lesson of each experience and become more used to allowing for the giving away of the Ego. The key to the process is to accept and employ Change as the vehicle of growth. Again, you can change without growing but you cannot grow with changing."

Now that the I or me component of relationship is a little better understood, it is important also to understand at this time that each individual is in a constant condition of being responsible to and for their own happiness, and happiness and joy are the birthright of all Beings from the Great Spirit.

Too often the Ego likes to play games with us here and advertisers make good use of it in selling us stuff we really do not need. All learning and the resulting growth obtained from these lessons is manifested through the making of choices. I always wondered why choice was used to describe a cut of meat for if it was really choice, I would not need a label anyway and just pick what I wanted. So these advertisers put choice on it to charge a higher price for the choosing of it. More Ego games.

It is given to say here that there is truly no wrong choice either, except for possibly the decision not made, but even here, the Great Spirit made a default pattern called Chaos that will make a choice anyway. As the pattern of Chaos makes choices for us which we normally would not make for Self, we become more aware of Self and the use of our Free Will in decision making for Self. In this condition a lesson will still be learned and growth manifested at some time, which indeed is the true condition of all things, it truly is perfect.

It is given to state here that it is important to describe that all of what we feel or care about goes through our pattern of Self as well as each thought and idea. The most important and powerful thing which we can put through our pattern of Self is our prayer, and that all prayers are heard and answered by the All and the Creator in a way that truly is best for us. Unfortunately our Fear is a prayer also and if we are not in a condition of being mindful of our Ego, which is the generator of all Fear prayers, more of the stuff that we do not want will come to us than the stuff that we do want. The universe is truly in perfect working order and if our reception to Self of it is not in good order, the solution to the problem rests solely upon Self. In all cases, if we see from the Heart clearly and not the distortions the Ego makes for us, we can always see the cause of the dilemmas and the perfect lessons in each. We are each sole responsible for our own happiness and we can make ourselves more in resonance to it by giving away the wrongful ideas that our Ego uses to teach us.

At this point we can now see more clearly how to operate and make better the conditions of and for Self by Change, to resonate to the proper ideal and purpose of our growth. It is very important to mention here that each has a great ability and responsibility to affect positive change continuous in the life of and for Self, but never should this ability be applied in making change in the condition of another without their participation and consent. One of the greatest Ego illusions of grandeur is to try to change another Being. First of all, it is in disrespect to their birthright as they also are a perfect child of the Great Spirit with a birthright of happiness and joy. And second, it is truly an illusion that you can change or should change another Being anyway. This is not to say that we should not help another and provide for those in need, it is to say do not go around trying to make turtles out of eagles.

Even in the process of efforts in healing, any change that indeed anyone might manifest in another or help them to manifest in Self, will only be retained for a short period of time in their pattern of Self if they do not truly have it in their Mind to do so in the first place.

Each person is totally in charge of the condition of their pattern of Self and although another might help them with the process, the results and the maintenance of the pattern of Self is theirs alone to receive and manage. Any attempt at a condition other than this will only be futile labor and a waste of energy, unless a lesson is learned from it of course, yet again, more perfection.

As I felt at this point I had an understanding of how all is in relationship to Self and the All which is every thing else, I felt compelled in my meditation one day to ask "Father, what might a proper description or definition of relationship then be"? It was given to me as follows:

RELATIONSHIP PROPER - Is The Respectful Sharing of the Experience of the Expression of Being, and One's Allowing for Others to experience and express being Themselves in ways and means of their own Choice which Walk in Balance and With Harm to No One Being or Thing and are most comfortable to Themselves.

It is given that it is most necessary here to stress the very importance of the key words Respectful and Sharing, as it is only when this condition does indeed take place that proper relationship can exist. I also was given to understand that because of the condition of the All, and how everything in His creation was interlinked to each and every other portion of it, that always all are in a condition of relationship at any instant but not always is the condition of the relationship a proper one.

Also it was given that the cause and cure for any problem in relationship is communication and not only is communication the balm for its wounds, but it is also the fertilizer for its growth. It is important to note also that all is directed at the ideal and purpose of Being, which is Experience. After spending some time in contemplation and review of this definition, I began to see how perfectly it applied to any relationship situation of which I could think whether family, workplace, school, or the Man sleeping on the street.

I was feeling like I had a great new Medicine, and perhaps I was correct, I believe it is called "Serpent Medicine", or a new understanding. It is funny that it comes to Mind to me, that indeed my

Guide right now in my Medicine Wheel way is named Tee-ka-hey and he is a great snake of understanding and new wisdom.

As I felt I had done pretty well on the relationship understanding, I thought I might try for a much used word which I also wondered greatly about so one day in meditation I asked "Father, I know that you told me that Love is the name of the force and is the food of your creation, but what is the proper way to Love someone in a relationship"? He told me as follows:

LOVE - Is The Gift of One's Care For The Well-being, Balance, and Fulfillment of Another Being or Thing Of HIS Creation.

It is again necessary to stress a keyword in the definition and here it is the word Gift, and again realization to the ideal of growth is applied. It is given to state here that in both definitions given, in no case or condition of relationship or Love, is a condition of contract inferred. All contracts invoke an Ego-Fear of betrayal, or it might be stated as, if you do this then I will do that, with the usual outcome of a lawyer type being applied to clean up the mess generated by an Ego prayer for being disappointed or a trust being betrayed. As mentioned we do not really make Love anyway as it is a force in the universe that is created by the Great Spirit in an infinite and continuous supply. We can only channel Love from the universe and Him to Self, each other and the All and it is the food and fertilizer of growth. It is only when we are feeling apart from Him that we feel unworthy or in need.

As we go about in relationships we are continuously magnetizing those people to us that we can grow with and learn from the experience of them. If our pattern is complete then we will magnetize those people which resonate completeness in their pattern to us, and if we have holes or wrongful images in our pattern of Self, then we will magnetize like in kind to us as well. It is all perfect this way as both conditions provide support to our expression and experience of growth, however many will find it is much easier and quicker to operate in the complete way.

I have experienced the situation as some say of jumping from the frying pan into the fire by not taking the time to resolve the issues that caused the condition of failure in one relationship only to repeat the lesson in the next. In all cases, the only change or adjustment that I could make was in Self. And until I was willing and took the time to face the truth of the condition of my pattern of Self which was something which I could only do to, and for myself, alone, then only could I improve my situation for myself which also always improves the condition of the All. Over and over again I am constantly hearing from others of how that they feel they need someone to find fulfillment or even exist in life and these are the very people which need to spend time alone so as to repair the damage their Ego has done to their pattern from previous relationships. I still smile when I remember Butterfly Flying saying ever so worriedly, "If I get so complete and fill up all of my holes, then no one will want me".

A word was given as to describe the process of discarding the old pattern of Self and starting to work with a new one. The word given is not the word *recovery,* which still makes me cringe when I hear others use it. Recovery brings to Mind a never ending process whereby one is in the process of the covering over of Self again and again with no hope of completion, and as I write this, it is perhaps that recovery brings to Mind the Bark of the Ego and the tree that I most dislike about the use of the word.

The more perfect word to describe the process and ideal is **RENEWALL**. Renewall relates to the condition that at any instant we may choose to discard the old pattern of Self and embrace a new perfect pattern to Self and operate through it in perfection constantly, or until we allow our Egos to mess it up again. Here the word Renewall is not meant to describe a never ending effort that constantly drains the resources of Self, Renewall better describes a tool that we might employ for Self whenever we need and choose to.

Now there is hope that as I get more experience at identifying the problems that are Ego manifested through me, I can make more permanent the lessons of them in me. In this way I may indeed experience more easily the unlimited growth and the resulting joy, happiness and fulfillment which is the birthright of each of us.

One day my Guides gave me another tool which I continue to use and that I find most effective in the describing of the possible conditions of relationships with reference also to the ideal. The tool is what I call circles and they appear much like this:

Type 1 - Enmeshing

Type 2 - Encircling

Type 3 - Mirroring

IN CONDITION 1.

The relationship exists as the point of friction between person A and person B. This type of relationship will only work if person A and person B are going in opposite directions and are enmeshed in it, as when two gears turn around each other. This type of relationship is one where opposites attract and it usually becomes a co-dependent situation whereby for one to grow or go forward, the other must retreat. In this case, each person operates as a full expression of their own Ego idea of Self and the friction of contact is the only shared part. Many of what are called Love / Hate situations operate here. The truth of this condition of relationship, whether it be between a parent and a child or manifested through a condition of attraction, and thereby choice, at some time separation by both parties from it and each other is inevitable, in that the condition retards the growth of both.

IN CONDITION 2.

The relationship consumes and retards the growth of person A, while at the same time, allowing for the unlimited freedom in the expression of Self in person B. In this case the participants will often also swap positions with each other. An example is that person A is the wife and she can not go out or buy anything alone, as all decisions about money and all control of her being in the world outside of the home is under the strict control of the husband. In these cases, should she even go to the store without asking him, or any external attention to or by her will often lead to fits of rage and jealousy being exemplified by him. Then person B may swap roles and conditions when dealing with things around the home and maintains a position of being helpless and incapable of cooking or even the washing of his own clothes. Unfortunately in the societies of this period, this is also the condition of relationship under which most experience between the parent and child. It may even exist well past the time considered to be maturity, and is often then sought after to be experienced or expressed as the norm. There is a lot of dependent and co-dependent stuff going on in this condition.

IN CONDITION 3.

The relationship consumes both person A and person B as one person cannot grow or even make a decision for Self without gaining the approval and compliance in the other, for if they do, the relationship will slip back into Condition 2. An example of this type of relationship is the case of where one person cannot go to the store or any place without the other. If some people from work are meeting for drinks after work, one cannot attend without the participation of the other. Indeed no activity is entered into without the total participation of the other. These relationships are often evident in that both parties to it will most often start to physically look like the other! While this condition of relationship is entirely co-dependent, it still seems to be the best of the three.

*****

While most often the relationships which we most often observe will fall into one of these first three categories, there is indeed one more and it may be considered as **the IDEAL:**

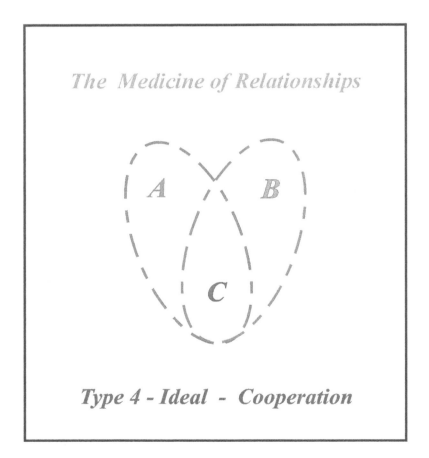

IN CONDITION 4.

Only in this condition of relationship are there three parts to be considered. In this type of relationship person A and person B are equally free to express their unlimited potential for growth. As each person explores their branch of the tree of life in their Earthwalk, they bring back and share the experience of it to the child of the relationship, which is the third part, or C. As each party in the relationship grows and develops, the shared part C is nurtured by it and grows well with it. The ideal condition of respectful sharing not only operates in this condition of relationship, but it actually thrives here. If one of the people in the relationship grows at a faster pace for a while such as in the following:

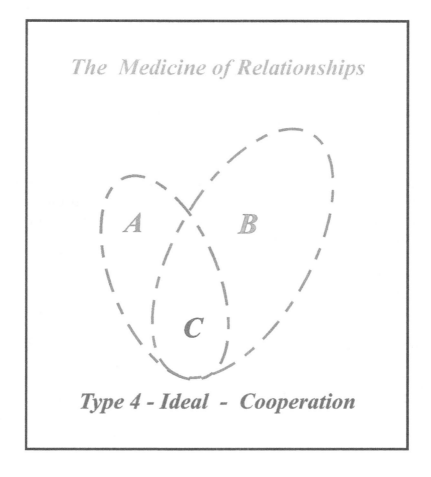

The Medicine of Relationships

A   *B*

C

Type 4 - Ideal - Cooperation

In this case, the relationship is still enhanced by the growth of each or just one. Indeed no feelings of jealousy or any dependency can live here. Whatever enhances the condition of growth of one, will ultimately support and stimulate not only the growth of the other, but of both A and B as well as the ball of the inertia of growth- part C. In this ideal condition of relationship the third part, or C, is considered as the child of the relationship and is the common or working and growing part of it. It is not a child in a biological sense, however, it should be treated as a child.

As the relationship begins, the child C, is born, and all through the condition of relationship it is valued, cared for, and nurtured by both parties. All this is done through respectful sharing with the vehicle of communication. If the child gets sick, the cure is in the changing of the pattern of both of the parties as it is a composition of parts of each and must be administered to this way. If both are not willing to make amendments to Self and only one tries, then the child C, will not improve, however the child will rapidly reflect the improvements made by both.

As both parties share respectfully, and grow, so does the child, but if the child becomes an obsession of the Ego of one or both parties, it will be absorbed and disappear resulting into a relationship that is in the condition of one of the first three, there and again Respectful Sharing is the Key. As with working and caring for a child, the relationship is fed and grows through the gift of Love, which is the force of the universe. Here we apply Love as a Gift of our care for the growth and Well-being of the other. If we get into conditions of conflict or sickness in the child, we can easily see it as a condition of Ego manipulation by one or both parties. We can then objectively release ourselves from the illusion that Ego manifests to play Fear, power, or control games.

As long as both parties truly give value to the relationship, all wellness can be manifested to it through the giving away of the Ego of one or both parties. It is easiest to enter into this ideal relationship after one has spent time filling up the holes in the pattern of Self from previous ones and it does require the attention of both parties to make it happen and maintain it as well. The key words Respectful, Sharing and Gift, work well in all of these circumstances and as each values the gift of the other to them all will always go well. I would like to also give to you a gift from my Heart of Self and it is:

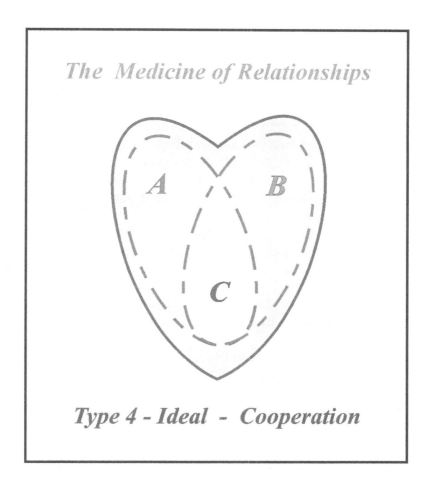

The Medicine of Relationships

Type 4 - Ideal - Cooperation

Often I am asked by others what they might do about a relationship that is not working for them at that time and they usually are referring to types 1 or 2. In these cases it is usually given for me to say for them to give them away. Only by the giving away of an improper pattern can a new one be established. Just as we have a pattern of Self, all of our relationships have one as well as described by the circles and defines the channel of Love through it. In relationships that are not working well as might be described by the Prayer Proper, in Balance and with Harm to No One, only by extracting one of the parties from a dysfunctional relationship is there any hope. Some marriage situations can be restructured and usually this is done through separations.

There is effectiveness in this technique only if there is a true willingness to embrace a change in the pattern of each Self and the relationship as well. If however, both parties restructure the relationship and are not complete in their own pattern of Self, only types 1 or 2 or 3 will be returned.

While marriages have a measure of hope, I have often found a much lesser ability of family members such as sibling, or parent / child, conditions to allow for the advent of Change. The aunt or sister will still think of the pattern of an awkward child of a person at reunions and family celebrations instead that of the mature adult that they might truly be. Family members are very reluctant in allowing for other members to change their pattern of Self and this is the seed and fertile condition for abuse, as most often it comes from the Ego gratification of someone exerting control over the condition or idea of another. What some people call "Little Power Games" thrive here. All that can be recommended is that we each remember in truth whose child we really are and that is of the Great Spirit, and pattern changing is not only your birthright, but the only way to growth. Then you can release yourself from those that do not participate in respectful sharing ways and allow for them to experience their own pace of growth, lovingly.

On marriages it is also given to express the ideal as being the union and extension of a working relationship into a partnership of respectful sharing for the purpose to procreate and provide a fertile ground for learning experiences to be shared by each member of that partnership. As children are given to the partnership, it is important that each member of the partnership continue to see each and every other member as a child of the Great Spirit just like themselves.

If respectful sharing is maintained as the condition of the partnership, both between the parents, and between the parents and the children, then all will be enriched as each member develops to the fullest of their unique expression of Self. In such fertile ground and balanced condition of beginning, as more children are added to the partnership, the relationships that develop between them will blossom with the respectful sharing ideal and the new order is established again.

It is also important to respect and support the differences in each other as well as the sameness in all conditions of relationships. The differences in each party in relationships is what strengthens the whole as they add to the potential of what might be manifested through the experience. The band would not sound nearly the same if they were all of one instrument playing but one note, all at the same time.

I was later given to come to the understanding of a deeper sense about relationship and of the layers of dimension that may prevail. In particular that which was brought to Mind was the understanding about manipulation and how often we become that which another might Fear of us becoming, whether conscious or not of, or to it. As we all are ever in resonance to the ideals, Fears and hopes of and for each other, we must also provide our own protection against the wrongful ideas that others may have in and of us by becoming invisible to them and make complete our pattern of Self before continuing or confronting them.

We truly are not another's idea of us, but in a desire to please them we may try to be exactly what they Fear or wish to see in us at a subconscious level and this is indeed one of the many layers of manipulation. Manipulation cannot occur unless one desires to please another through the changing of the pattern of Self and it seems a wrongful idea from both sides, wrong to do to Self and wrong to desire of another. Either way it is an Ego game and ultimately lesson will be learned.

Unfortunately manipulation is one of the early lessons learned from parent to child and can often take on extremely long term effects in the child's Self image and development. It is indeed through this process that we often learn to wear the mask of what another wishes to see in us and in our desire to please them we get caught up in their game, which usually is indeed not in our best interest or Well-being. To always be daddy's little girl, or mommy's little angel, or you are too smart for that, all bring on manipulative qualities that one can only rebel against the idea of in some layer of consciousness, as to be that, one must never change and thereby grow. Then as the child matures in age they will be in a continuum of mask wearing and walk in illusion of what and who they truly are, a perfect child of the Creator and he is most forgiving of our mistakes and allows us to renew ourselves to the perfect pattern of Self at any instant that we might walk in truth and joy through our experience of life through the ever expanding expression of Self.

If we walk only the path that another sees in or desires for us, we are not being responsible to our own growth through decision making. And if another would try to limit our idea of Self, we cannot judge them for it as we can truly only judge Self, but we can make ourselves invisible to it and forgive Self and thereby them for the whole idea of it in the first place.

Desire not to control and thereby manipulate the path of another, as each truly seeks their own lessons in life anyway. Instead give one's attention to the care for their Well-being and thereby support their growth that way. Parents should support the discoveries of the child and not tell them what it is that they see. As in this support of the discovery of the child, the parents too will learn and thereby grow. Sometimes it is indeed better to be care giving than caretaking. Manipulation is another great tool of the Ego, and it is here that one can see in truth, how it is that what one sees in the manipulation of or by another, always starts in that idea in and of Self.

If one sees in another a pattern of behavior that they feel is incorrect they should learn from the results of the action of it, not play Ego manipulation games to it, there again judge not that in another lest you take that condition in Self. In truth the manipulated one is in all conditions the manipulator for the experience in it. If one wishes to improve the condition of Self or another the process begins within the Heart of Self not the Ego of Self, and in Relationship Proper that is the respectful sharing part.

ABOUT RELATIONSHIP,

WE ALL ARE CONSTANTLY IN ONE,

BUT ALWAYS WE GET TO CHOOSE,

IN WHEN AND HOW MUCH OF ONESELF

TO GIVE AND TO WHOM.

WHITE EAGLE

KARMA AND YIN AND YANG

It is given to discuss here with you at this time through the channel of the Eagleman as we like to refer to him, about some of these ideas and conceptualizations that sometimes get somewhat out of hand or balance as it were. The first of which is the idea of Karma and Karmic debt in the condition of things. As before mentioned, All that Is, is created by a loving and benevolent Father who would not create conditions for us in Spirit or those of you on Earthplane that we could not rise above or grow from.

Upon entry or re-entry into the Earthplane for a walk or sojourn there, each entity decides and describes a plan for the growth which they choose to experience in the process. This plan, if anything might truly be considered a condition of Karma, is surely the best idea of it to be considered. In the very same context it may also be considered as Pre-destiny, which is another often mistaken conceptualization. Forces are ever-present in whatsoever the condition of Being might be, whether on Earthplane, in Spirit or other worlds, for the continuation and in support of our growth. As we are ever enabled with the Free Will that the Source or Creator gave to us, it is only through decision making that we can use the force of Change to embody growth in the condition of Self through the application of our Free Will. All is connected to the All else of His creation as well, and what ever affects any part of it affects the whole of it in any and all instances. As an entity takes upon Self a condition of change through a decision or judgment being made, whether it is acted out or not, it is felt by the All and resonances are made to keep the All in balance as the force of Free Will is applied upon it. The more one pushes against the wall, the harder it shoves one might say.

Inclusive in the plan for growth for a sojourn or walk, might well be a condition of disability or handicap, yet it is not the Will of the Father Creator that made it so, nor is it truly a condition of Karmic influence, it is purely a condition established by Self in the plan of the walk so as to grow through the experience of it, by the choice of the Free Will of Self. The plan for growth is not finite and un-amendable as well. In fact the plan is constantly being modified by the deeper Self, which you may sometimes refer to as the subconscious of your Being, and as one progresses down the path of the walk, countless adjustments are constantly being made.

The plan might well be visualized as a screen or a filter that is presented in front of the pattern of Self that was recently described, and this filter draws those conditions to Self through the resonance of vibration that is the essence of the All that Is, like a magnet. To objectify the condition of oneself at any point as being that of Karma or Fate is silly, and denying the truth to Self that each is truly responsible in one fashion or another, to and for, their condition of being. As to how to get rid of Karmic debt, forgive yourself. Only through forgiveness can any come to terms with their true condition and make change for growth through receiving the lesson of it. To truly forgive, one must see the true cause and effects of the condition or situation and take responsibility for their participation in the manifesting of it. One may try to make amends for the abuse or improper behavior toward another person or thing, but they can not change the event as it is done.

Feeling and expressions of sorrow and regret will not change or affect the pattern and screen of any but Self, and truly one can only forgive Self, and if the lesson is truly embodied, the improper action will not recur from Self. A good example of improper reaction is to do ill to another because some one did it to you, it just spreads the disease, and in truth the condition was always set up through the filter of Self to experience the lesson in it whether consciously or not. No thing, in any condition of being, whether on Earthplane or any where else just happens, there is no such thing as Fate. Fate or Karma is often used by the Ego of one to justify its position as well. The Ego might say to one that they deserve this pain or condition of Self so it can stay in charge and continue to manifest its own lesson giving which is usually in some form of Self abuse.

One often hears the phrase of What goes around comes around, in thinking in terms of Karma, and while indeed in many conditions this does seem so, it is much more correctly put that all prayers are answered. As each places continuously upon the screen of the pattern of Self exactly that which they wish to receive or experience and thereby magnetizes it to themselves.

The saying that If one does a good deed for another, it is put upon a wheel that is rotating and something good will ultimately come back to them in time, although not always in the same form, is another Karmic ideal that is somewhat misapplied. In truth what ever is done for another is actually done for Self as all are in a continuum of resonance and the good that one receives is immediately felt by the betterment in the condition of the All of which they are a part. Truly, whatsoever you do unto another, you do to yourself, whether it is considered good or bad. We are sure all have felt good about themselves when they are able to help another and this is why.

As we do good for others, we are filling up holes in the pattern of Self and rearranging the plan of Self on the screen or filter which we use with it. Those entities which try to do things as in giving gifts with expectancy of something coming back to them in return are often disenchanted in time, as theirs was not truly a gift, but a condition of a barter with a Fate or Karma that does not exist. And so they stay in a condition of disenfranchisement until they learn the truth and lesson in it, which may take until the next sojourn. Meanwhile they tend to fill up their pattern and screen of Self with bitterness and magnetize more ill will or conditions to Self, ever blaming all of it on Karma or Fate. Then when they leave Earthplane and release all Ego illusions through Transition as the Eagleman calls it, and return back to the condition of absolute truth in Spirit, they will only put the same lesson on their plan for the next sojourn, then it does embrace an aspect of a condition of Karma or Fate which is kind of funny when you think about it.

The best approach is to do as much good for Self and others in a loving, giving, and sharing way, and you will magnetize not like and kind to Self but manifold times that which you could most consider to receive, as it will keep improving the condition of Self and the All including the Creator. If we place good will upon the screen of Self and truly Will good for the condition of all, the returns are beyond our wildest dreams, but if we put doubt, Fear, greed, and envy we will surely come to experience that.

It is also given to mention that all Beings exist in a multidimensional form and when something inexplicable happens to one, it may really be not an act of God or the Will of the Fates, but their resonance to a much higher purpose so to say. It is not to say here that there are no acts of God or the Father Creator as we prefer to say, as there are such, but as multidimensional Beings we do each have more than one agenda. It sometimes is like the doctor that gets called away from the ballgame, we just sometimes have more important work to do elsewhere.

We will now call upon another to discuss the concept of Yin and Yang. On Earthplane much is given to the nature of the body and the physical senses of being there, that is why some chose so often to reinstall themselves in body there for the experiences of it. The body physical on Earthplane is of a design which some call symmetry, and in most cases when looking in a reflective glass, one can see how if *split down the middle, one side looks like the other from the outside and most of the inside.*

Yin and Yang is a conceptualization of existence on earth plane from the Eastern tradition or oriental, that references the duality or the appearance of having two sides of everything on earth plane, and is typecast as to its sexuality, as that is the condition of procreation that goes on there. In this concept, everything may be typecast as being of either male or female with the longer word yang referencing the male.

This is the symbol used to represent this concept known as the Tai Chi and it represents a dark and light fish looking swirl in a circle that represents the whole of life there. The dark fish needs the presence of the other to exist as without the presence of the lighter

colored one, the whole would be dark. The dark fish has a light dot which represents its eye and needs to embody the opposite of Self to see. The same condition exists for the lighter colored fish and each needs the condition of the other to exist. As procreation is not possible in the Human form on Earthplane without the union of the opposite sex of Self, the yin and yang concept identifies the need for both. Within this concept all things may be typecast as having female or male or yin and yang aspects, such as Mother Earth, Father sky, Mother Moon, and Father Sun, and has been used through many cultures to personify the expression of things on Earthplane.

More significant it is given here to say, is to embrace the truth that each entity has more than just two dimensions to Self. However all entities choose one of the two sexuality's to experience as they embody on each occurrence. Seldom is it the experience that an entity will incarnate always as male or female, as growth will best be manifested through the experience of both.

Each Being in Spirit has no sexual aspect and while the Creator is most often referenced as Father or male, there is no condition of it or bias to it in Him. In physical body on Earthplane, just as looking in the mirror and seeing both sides of Self, all Beings there embrace both sexuality's to Self. Better it might be said that all Beings on Earthplane have a male component to their Being and a female component to their Being with none being any better or stronger than the other.

Often for purposes of Ego self-justification in societies on earth plane, one aspect of Self has received favor as being first such as male before female, when in truth both were created at the same time. It is like the question of which came first, the flower or the seed, or the chicken or the egg, with always the same condition as the true answer is neither.

While the yin and yang concept does have application in some cases and might well be used to visualize the condition of Being as to having more than one dimension, it should not be inferred that there are only two sides to Self as truly there are more.

Just as with this energy which some call electricity which has a positive and negative current condition or yang and yin, this energy also has a condition of neutral as well, so there are truly more than two sides to everything, see. The Eagleman often talks to others about how the physical body of Self, whether male or female on Earthplane, represents the yin and therefore female side of Self, while the Spirit of Self which one senses at orgasm during copulation or during meditation, is the male experience or yang while there, whether in male or female body. We see nothing too wrong with the concept as if one desires, they may look at only one or two sides of anything and if it helps them to find balance in their Self, then it serves to provide for the better good. However, in these conditions of narrowed vision, the perspective is somewhat restricted and this may allow for the Ego to play games here.

If one thinks of the body of their Being as being the physical side and therefore the yin, female side, then all experiences dealing with any aspect of the body could well be considered female at all times and conditions. We have watched the Eagleman smile when he watches other male people playing macho and male posturing games, thinking how in the terms of this yin and yang concept, that they are exhibiting not the male or yang side of their Being, but just the opposite and the very essence of the female or yin with their competing for territory and mating rites.

The better truth of these conditions is that they are operating not so much from the yin or female side of Self or yang side either, but they are truly operating from the Ego Bark of their tree of Self instead of truly from the Heart. Much of the issues about the experience on Earthplane which cause some of the consternation as to the identification of Self and how one should consider Self to proper behavior, are not so much about their yin or yang aspects, but denying the Self the true understanding of their multidimensionality. Those entities which some call gay or homosexual, are not operating from a yang that should be a yin, but are seeking to solve issues that stem from past life carry over problems or early childhood conditions, and from their aspect of multidimensionality, they choose to operate from the other side of their physical form choice of Self at incarnation.

In the greater reality of the condition of the Beings on Earthplane, all people are not homosexual, heterosexual, bisexual, or asexual, they are better understood as being multidimensional and therefore multi-sexual about any given influence or thing. The infant has no specific awareness as to whether it is a boy or girl at that time nor much less cares, remember? There is much study as to genetic influences about such things going on, on Earthplane at this time, but know and be well assured that each entity chooses the condition of their sexuality as well in their plan for their sojourn on the planet you call Earth.

About those things that some scientists say is found as being different in the bodies of the homosexual people, it is to be fully understood at this time that the Mind of one works through a pattern which controls the body of one and can alter any condition of it including the cellular structure and enzymatic actions of it. One can dissociate from their originally chosen sexuality at any time and return back to it at any time as well. Free Will, remember? As most Beings on Earthplane have incarnated on previous sojourns there many times, both as male and female for the experience of that aspect of their sexuality, and all experiences are truly forever stored in the deeper consciousness of the Being of one, it is really very easy for one to alter the sexual pattern of proclivity or desire, to a pattern of one that they found as being more comfortable to be operating in.

This altered sexual expression of the Being is not operating from the Ego of one as some might assume at this point, nor from the Heart of one, but solely from the Mind of one and in that condition All can be. Beings cannot be truly taught sexual proclivity or desire as it is only an operative condition of the Self through the pattern manifested by the Mind of one. While the Ego makes manifestations through Fear and illusion, it is truly the balance or imbalance of those entities desiring the expression of sharing Love through the sexual expression of Self which they are most comfortable in being resonant to at any given moment. The physical copulation technique has really very little to do with any of it except to experience the sharing in the pleasure of the releasing of the Mind from the body and experiencing the ecstasy of it during the short moment of orgasm and being stimulated by the care and administrations of another, whatever their sex might feel best to each participant for whatever reason. The yin and yang might best be used to remember two sides of our sexuality choices but it really defines not much more than that. The sexual choice is an individual decision which one makes through the expression of their Free Will and through the experience of it lessons will indeed be learned. In Spirit it is not that we are yin or yang, as we are neither, both and many more.

It is given to say that importance should be noted that each person should not judge another as to what choice which an entity makes about their sexual expression of Self or any other as long as it walks in Balance and with Harm to No One. An entity's choice is truly for them to experience that condition for themselves, and as in most societies, judgments are made about homosexuals as being immoral, evil, or as sin, one can really only judge them so through the Ego of Self and often does it through Fear and the illusion therein, for in truth, you can only judge yourself.

The sexuality center of one's Being which in some references is called the root center or chakra, is the great storage center and generator for the energy of the physical Being on Earthplane. It is the procreation vehicle which causes continuance to most species on the Earthplane and the drive to do such in the Mind or consciousness of life forms on earth is the greatest motivator. Some Human and Animal forms on Earthplane exhaust themselves to death in the process of it, not walking in Balance you see. While some efforts are made in some of your cultures on Earthplane in the education about Human sexuality, more effort needs to be made in the integrated aspects of it not just the biological technique. However, much more important it seems would be the teaching of parenting skills before you show them how to be one!

****

WHATEVER ONE'S IDEA OF KARMA

OR YIN OR YANG MIGHT BE, AND IN TIME

WE DO HOPE THAT YOU WILL EXPAND

PAST THESE RESTRICTED CONCEPTS,

IT IS TRULY MORE

IMPORTANT TO SEE THE INNER CHILD

OF THE GREAT SPIRIT CREATOR

IN EACH AND EVERY ONE OF

HIS BEINGS THERE ON EARTHPLANE,

AND LOVE THAT IN THEM,

AND YOURSELF.

CYCLES

In the understanding of the Round Way, one must remember that the true condition of all things is as vibration or energy created by the Father. For vibration to exist, it must have a wave pattern of high and low periods or ups and downs such as:

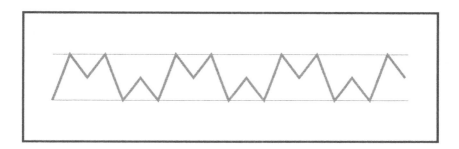

Also, as all forms of Being are truly in a multidimensional sense, it might better be visualized as a vibration within a vibration within a vibration and so on, and it might be represented this way:

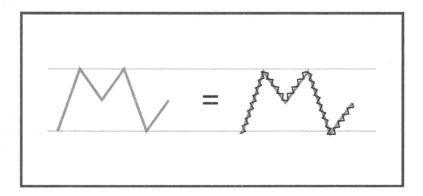

These ups and downs of vibration may also be interpreted as cycles, and cycles exist in every experience on Earthplane. The cycle of the Sun is from rising in the East to setting in the West. The cycle of Mother Moon is not only a daily one of rising and setting but consists of the four periods described as full, waning, new, and waxing, and it might be shown this way:

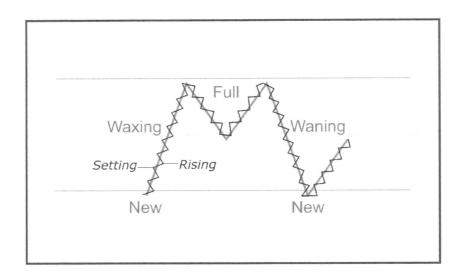

All is reflected in cycles and they can indeed be seen in the conditions of everything on Earthplane, such as the cycles of the four seasons of the year, the cycle of menses in the female body, the cycle day to night and so forth. On earthplane our cycle of life goes through seven year renewal cycles as well and there are notable stages in our growth periods. Every cell of the body in the Human form is exchanged or renewed every seven years from bone to the lens of the eye and the teeth. It is noted here that in the Earthplane, seven and four are two of the master numbers of everything and most all is found to be in relationship to these.

From birth to seven years is the first period with the child learning from its incarnation at birth, how to walk, how to communicate using often a new language, and the behavioral pattern of the home life as defined by its parent figures. In some societies it is at this point that Spiritual growth is stifled and much of the ability of the child to operate in the way of its multidimensionality and psychic dimensions is "untaught" to it. As all is Spirit, and the infant child knows this at birth, it is taught Fear, falsehood, mask wearing or whatever, through discipline or by mimicking the behavior of its parents to get what it wants. The child must adapt and so forth to operate in most societies, in order to survive the law of the morality or lack of it at that time.

At seven years, in most societies, the child enters the second cycle with entry into the primary education system of its culture having supposedly at this time, learned how to operate in the society of the home and family group. It is now pressed into a new environment of learning and is given opportunity to integrate into a new, larger, and ever changing society of what is and will become its peers. A new cycle of structuring is found here with much more emphasis being placed upon its physical than Spiritual growth. The child has, at this time, its Self-image formulated to the greater sense of its physical dimension of Self and learns how to operate competitively. Much Ego Bark building goes on in this stage as the child finds that some of the attitudes that were taught at home are not reflected by the new members of its society and culture.

At fourteen years, the next cycle begins, called by some as puberty but we see it more in the dynamics of metamorphosis. The child will now transform with the single event of the menstrual cycle or a birthday from childhood to young adulthood or adolescence. The major influence in this cycle is preoccupation to the physical senses of Being with the Spiritual very much placed on the back burner in most societies. During this cycle the child will usually reach its full height and fullness in the physical sense and begins to operate very competitively with thoughts of mating. In this third cycle, during previous periods of this culture on Earthplane, the boys would enter apprenticeship to learn a craft so as to support themselves and a family and the girls would get married and start a family as soon as one was chosen. In later times some call modern, this period is used in the attainment of secondary or higher education or still in the establishment of an occupation. Most children expect to leave the society of the home during this period. Still in this period, concentration is focused very much upon material attainment and not Spiritual growth.

The fourth cycle, remember master number again, begins at the age of twenty-one. It is at this age in most cultures that the child achieves full adult status and can own property and becomes a voting member in the decision making process that governs it. While fourteen is the period of metamorphosis, twenty-one can be type cast as that of maturity. Most often it is during this period that full physical growth, usually through the filling out of the height of the form previously achieved in the third cycle is achieved. The full Ego persona is also catalyzed during this period as the numbers of the peer group is greatly expanded with the ability of the entity to choose to move about and explore the experience of alternatives and a level of experience in the expression of Self is thus attained. It is also during this period that the male entity typically experiences warriorship and feels a full awareness and feeling for its mortality in the physical sense. It is also the period that the child feels its greatest struggle for both survival and Self identity and tends not to see Self in future terms, the Bark of the tree is the thickest here from the condition of its Ego. If there are no wars present to test the child's right of continuance or survival they tend to test it in other ways of Self abuse with drugs, alcohol, and all forms of risk taking. It actually patterns itself after the mating rituals of other species such as the elk or seals whereby only the strongest are given the reproductive privilege. Very few males and some females believe that they will survive to experience the next cycle, including the Eagleman, and many do not.

Due to this condition in this cycle, many families are started here that are not well founded in Proper Relationship or with the ideal of growth as the future seems not possible to attain. They are instead founded in a sense of Fear in the physical mortal sense and only for the purpose of generating prodigy to leave one's name or things to. Very biological and non Spiritual. This is problematic because of the Ego-Fear orientation and the denial of the Spiritual aspect, which is the true essence of one's Being and is bound to failure in most cases as soon as one of the parties in the relationship decides to grow. There is a lot of acting out the pattern of the parents in these relationships during this cycle. It is also, because of these struggles, that many return to the path of Spiritual growth or at least experience some interest in it here. This cycle being the fourth one of seven years, also ends one period and begins a new one.

The second period begins with the twenty-eighth year survivors and it is at this time that family raising and career establishment or advancement are of the major focus. While the first period of four cycles was focused upon physical growth, this second period is focused upon expansion.

The fifth cycle from twenty-eight to thirty-five, that renewed Spiritual interest is started. This condition usually centers around the awareness that is manifested through the death of relatives, usually grandparents and some parents in the current society, and questioning the life experience and desiring a fuller sense of Being. It is during this cycle that most careers are enhanced and advancement are most easily made because the entity not only believes in, but also plans for the future and quits sabotaging the efforts of Self through giving away some of the Ego-Fear in the Bark of the tree of Self. The attitude of the previous cycles Fear of survivorship are slowly balanced by the *experiences gained here. Spiritual development is also a focus of those parents raising children in this cycle as well.*

The next cycle from thirty-five to forty-two, is one that might be best expressed as harnessing. It is during this period that ones current relationships come into realignment or new relationships are established with a much greater emphasis upon common goals or ideals. It is also a cycle where a peaking out occurs in career and family as well. The children born to those relationships established in the third and fourth cycles are usually leaving the nest at this time and the parents have more time together and new communications are made. While the previous cycles were mainly focused in the egocentric attainment of the individual either through the experience of success or failure, more desire for sharing or a renewed interest in the experience of Brotherhood is founded here. More Spiritual growth as more Bark is shed from the tree of Self.

The next cycle from forty-two to forty-nine might well be called rebirthing. It is sometimes also called by some on Earthplane as the middle aged crazies. It is during this period that a renewed interest is made toward life purpose and the expression of it and Spiritual growth. Part of this awareness comes from the sharing in the death experience of some of one's peers and parents and those close to them and a heightened consciousness of one's time on their Earthwalk is realized. A greater desire for ways to express one's creative force and Spirit is the essence of this rebirth. Those maintaining marriages that are not in Proper Relationship will test their validity and quick changes are often made here. As each has been changing every cell of their own body every seven years, one often finds a stranger in the bed that they have been sharing and looks differently at their partners in this time.

While the focus in the previous cycles has been toward material attainment and physical growth even in family matters with little attention being given to the communication of higher Spiritual ideals and work being done on Spiritual growth, the buck stops here, as some say and addresses the herd. It is also in this cycle that the male will find a way and reestablish himself in a more Spiritually fulfilling occupation, and the female will continue education and develop methods of channeling her creative force independent of him. The doctor or lawyer or accountant will often leave his practice to start that fishing camp which he always dreamed of much to the consternation of his peers. It is typically during this cycle that the child returns to the awareness of their true creator and parent, which most call God.

The next cycle from forty-nine to fifty-six is also the end of the second four cycles or period. This cycle is also often where the Spiritual child attains it quickest growth and awareness. It is because of the experiences gained in the previous cycles and the enabling of the greater focus to the Spiritual ideal, that the greatest accomplishments are made in the physical plane here. By the child doing what it loves to do, and by allowing the unlimited resources of the universe to flow through the channel of Self, the greatest fortunes are made and the greatest good is most often expressed here in this cycle. This is possible as the tree of Self has shed most of the Bark of its Ego through the tests and lesson giving of the previous periods and the child learns who and what they really are and fully accepts that condition to Self without reservation. This is indeed the cycle of great achievement as the child tends to operate in balance as both an expression of the Spiritual as well as the physical Self.

The following cycles and periods are pretty much a continuum of the same with continued Spiritual growth and increasing emphasis on Brotherhood and the sharing with others. While the previous descriptions speak of specific numbers in physical years, they are not fixed or finite and conditions exist where they will often overlap and variations will sometimes occur but most will find them typically accurate.

The lesson here is that the Earthwalk is a lifetime spent in search of ways to channel the creative force of Self, which is the Love from the Creator, founded ever in a process and climate for growth and to experience and express Love and Brotherhood. The cycles help just as steps upon a staircase, places to stop and examine one's current expression of growth that makes the climb much easier. In walking the Round Way, just as in the Medicine Wheel, the goal is not to change the cycle or the direction that you are in, but to fully understand and appreciate the lesson in it and thereby manifest your greatest growth. By the doing of this, not only is the very best manifested in and for Self but also the very condition of the All is equally enhanced.

In the personal expression and understanding of the Eagleman's way of the Medicine Wheel, the cycles are each represented as the cycle of time, as given for him to understand in the way of the time of the tree. In this way, as it is given for him to develop his own understanding of what is presented to him through Spirit Guides and his own ever changing perception of the Earthwalk. Always the enabling and providing is manifested not only just from his ability of cognizance and recollection as given for his own experience of growth with respect to his own plan for it, but also from a supreme guidance that lives within each Being as might be considered a higher calling than one can make for oneself if one chooses to listen for it and is willing to be of that service. At any early time most can remember when their parents or others believed more in their ability at some measure or task than they did. It pretty much stays that way in the experience of the expression of growth, but sometimes it seems hard to believe that the Creator would not give one more than they could do. When that happens, one is usually not listening from the Heart of Self but to the Ego and forgetting the All of what can truly be at any instant, when the Creators Will is done or channeled through Self.

When anyone realizes their true relationship to the Creator and their strings of attachment to the All, which all are equally endowed and are parts of in the multidimensional sense, and when they accept the truth of their condition of Being as and of that, the very revelation of it provides to anyone the very best blueprint in the way of living the pattern of life, and that is walking the Round Way.

In the Eagleman's way of the Medicine Wheel, the beginning place is in the direction of the South and is called the seed planting time. It is in this direction and time that one gathers and assesses their resources. In each experience of any direction, the prayer is for guidance and the development of resonance to, that is proper.

In the way as is understood for him, the direction of the West is called the sprouting time and it is here that a plan is made for the resources gathered in the South. It is also found that in making the plan for the utilization of the resources given, some that cannot be utilized in the plan must be given away or back. Some call it the crying time as well, and as the snake must shed its old skin to embrace and exemplify the new, many changes go on here.

The understanding of the direction of the North as is given to him is called the growing time. It is here that one does the work in adherence to the plan given in the West with respect to and utilizing the resources provided in the experience of the South. The North is also called the direction of wisdom gathering, as only by doing the work and experiencing some decision making in the process of it, can one truly experience the lesson giving by the mistakes made or not made in the process of the experience of it.

The East is understood by him to be the flowering time in the way of the tree. It is in the East that one shares the flowers and fruits of the experiences of the other directions and often finds others drawn to them by the illumination of the experience of it. It is the seed of the South direction of the previous cycle that is borne again here for use.

The seeds of the illumination of growth that is provided in the East become the substance of the next cycle in the South.

Any aspect to growth can best be measured and experienced by the interaction of how it fits within its own cycle and the cycle of Self, or resonance as it is called, as all is vibration. One constant in the Earthwalk experience is the wind of Change that is ever present to fertilize growth.

The influence of cycles is ever present. The embracing of the cycles is like the young Man who wishes to ride the wave. It is much easier if you embrace them and use their energy to go the direction of choice, and if they are not going in your direction, find a place they do, or learn to paddle real, real, hard. Either way they will always support growth. One thing that is certain is that all conditions will ultimately change. The trick to the Earthwalk is walking the Round Way and that is by walking in Balance and in perspective to the ideal.

I ASKED THE GREAT SPIRIT ONE DAY,

"FATHER,

WHY THESE THINGS CALLED CYCLES"?

HE SAID:

"TO HELP YOU GROW".

A LONG TIME AGO

A WHITE MAN TOLD ME THAT IF A FROG HAD WINGS

HE WOULD NOT BUMP HIS BUTT ON THE GROUND.

I THOUGHT ABOUT THIS FOR A WHILE,

BUT I DID NOT TELL HIM THAT IN THAT CONDITION,

THE FROG WOULD NOT BE A FROG.

Too often it seems that we think to look at cycles in the linear or the two dimensional sense of things. In this case, often the Ego says that this is good and that is bad for me.

But to me it seems that all is much better if we look at cycles as being not good or bad, but as being a rhythm by which we can experience and express unlimited opportunity for growth,
and thereby dance.

White Eagle

I thought about these cycles for some time. It seemed that in

The North, the people there learned that it was not such a

Good time to plant Corn at certain times of the year.

I thought about this for a while and it seemed that it was

Ok to do this planting of the Corn at that time,

In the Southern hemisphere.

It seems that about this corn planting and these cycles,

It pretty much depends upon where you are standing.

****

I asked The Father again about
the winds of change.

He said:

"You have been learning
about cycles
I see."

WHITE EAGLE

RENEWALL

In the process of walking in the Round Way, one perceives things not in a linear or two dimensional sense of beginnings and endings, but as continuous cycles of new beginnings.

Each year for many summers the Great Spirit provides to me a word or phrase that describes an idea for me to develop an understanding of. One year it was "Keep on keeping on", another time it was "All can be" and so forth. To keep on keeping on, I learned more in developing an understanding about growth through the learning of the lessons of faith and what I call tester Medicine. The more important message was understanding direction, ideals and ultimately more about this word called faith. Renewall is the current word concept for the period in which this writing began and the two Ls at the end are significant, changing the character count from seven to eight in the process, for those who endeavor to analyze things that way. As we walk the path of life, we are constantly manifesting lessons to facilitate growth for the purpose of expanding the dimension of Self as to become greater channels of His Light and Love. I often hear mention of peoples stating that they are in a condition of recovery and I am immediately brought to Mind of a vision of a perpetual and exhausting condition of the reapplying of a cover or mask to oneself. I see recovery not as a process of healing and growth but as an Ego manifestation of a limitless and exhaustive condition of control. In trying to understand the concept of Renewall, I immediately felt it to be a much better ideal to employ in the healing process and later I more fully understood as to how perfectly it applies to any and all conditions of Self.

The **RE** portion of Renewall relates to the ability to apply the force of Change to make better the condition of Self at any point of time, whether in our Earthwalk or anywhere else.

The **NEW** portion applies to the birthing process or it might be better said as the bringing forth of a new condition to Self, or our condition of relationship to others. This New is brought forth by the changing of the attitude of oneself or our sense of relationship to any or All that Is. New is the process of taking a new piece of pattern material and making a pattern of the perfect child of the Creator in it and using this ideal of Self, instead of trying to constantly correct the old pattern which was erroneously modified by accepting another's idea of us through Ego need or manifestation.

While indeed all can Be, it is usually found to be a much more efficient expense of energy to make new for Self than to repair the old. Also, my Ego is ever using illusion to make me feel incomplete.

If I listened to it and changed my pattern to being that of a turtle or one that was improper for me because it responded with envy when some turtle people said, "Be like me, be like me" and I saw how they carried their house on their back which would only make flying real difficult, I would ultimately learn lesson in it.

Also the Light and Love that went through this wrongful pattern would only be received by others in scattered and incomplete ways. Though possible, it would certainly take a lot more work and time to make the wrongful pattern correct by changing the form back to the eagle, which is the right idea of me, than to shed the old and start new with a fresh pattern from the unlimited supply that is available to any and all. At any instant we can indeed make new the condition of Self by giving away the Ego idea or illusion it makes for us and embrace the truth from the Heart or Spirit of Self.

The **ALL** portion is important and relates not to the action being taken as the two letter form would imply, but instead it relates to the truth that what affects the condition or Well-being of one, affects the condition and Well-being of the All. Whatever any might do to improve the condition of Self through growth, immeasurably affects the condition of the All. This affect is usually found in the relaxing of the strain in the condition of the All, including upon and within oneself. At any moment and in any situation or circumstance, Renewall can take place. In my Medicine way, I like to pray to the sunset in thankfulness and in Renewall for what I desire in the next day and for guidance and enabling that the Fathers Will be done through me. I am also in constant Renewall of my vow to Him and thereby His Will in and through me and it is indeed situations that come to me as answers to this constant prayer, that bring me my greatest satisfaction and joy. All prayers are answered, remember.

Renewall applies to all conditions and experiences in life and the condition of it definitely supports the Prayer Proper of walking in Balance and with Harm to No One, including Oneself. As we walk our Earthwalk in the Round Way, we also experience countless cycles of Renewall of Self and the All, but as we learn to keep the Ego Bark of the tree of Self real thin, we do not have to do it for Self as often. The ideal of Renewall also allows for one to choose the when and where of the process and unlike recovery, the end of the need for it for Self is indeed possible.

As all is and are in a continuum of a condition of relationship, any and all problems that develop, may be resolved by Renewall to the proper pattern of Self as a perfect child of the Great Spirit Creator and Father of all things and in seeing and supporting the same condition in all else and others. The Ego must give way for the experience of growth and Renewall provides for the re-establishment of a more proper relationship between the Ego, Mind and Heart components of Self. Renewall re-establishes the birthright of happiness and joy to Self and others and allows for proper balance to be maintained as well.

Problems in social or family structure at this time may all be resolved by allowing oneself to see past the Ego illusions presented and see the truth from the Heart of Self. As we learn that all are in relative positions of their own cycles of growth, we can then release them from the ideal which we might think that they should be about and Love them as being just what they are, children of the Great Spirit just like ourselves. One only perpetuates a condition of improper relationship by the failure to release it. This includes family, friends, occupation, or anything that does not support our growth and allow us to express and experience our greatest Love and joy.

If one indeed has a parent or parent figure which does not support their growth and allow for them to walk in balance, then they should give away the thoughts that the parent fell short of the ideal and that one needs that from them and that sense of the relationship. Then in time, build new of Self by Renewall of Self and allow for them to see that they are children of the Great Spirit, and subject to failure and success, by their seeing that you see, and exemplify that condition in oneself. Generations of abuse do not make the abuse okay, nor can any change the past events of Self, but any time of any day is a great one for Renewall.

By the giving away of a relationship that does not work, one makes room for and has unlimited possibility in the establishment of a relationship that does. If both or all participants approach such a change with a consciousness of respectful sharing in the experience of the expression of growth and share a common ideal, they can even join into a new relationship at some point once again with the people that were with them in the relationship that was just given away.

By the process of Renewall, all can operate freely and fully in any condition or society. If a person is operating in a situation or condition of life that does not support the ideal of that of Self, it is not the ideal or the condition that is usually incorrect but in these conditions it is usually a misapplication of Ego which maintains the condition through its resistance to Change and thereby giving way. In these conditions through the giving way of the Ego, one can easily renew proper balance in and to Self and the force of Change will indeed present unlimited possibility to **Re-New-All** conditions to support the growth of one as to walk in Balance and with Harm to No One.

In the giving away of the Ego manifestations of Fear, anger, hate, greed, envy, and disappointment, one is much better able to see the true perfection that may always be found in any situation and experience and express the growth accordingly. In the process of Renewall, all begins fresh at that very instant to support the unlimited potential for any and all to experience and express the Creators Love through the channel of Self.

In walking the Round Way, Renewall also relates to the fact that we and the All of His creation, Spirits in all planes, stars, Mother Earth and Moon, Father Sun and sky, are all directly connected, we have unlimited opportunity to be better caretakers of his resources in and about us. The potential of walking in joy and enjoying our walk is facilitated by our unlimited potential at Renewall.

The beautiful thing about RENEWALL

Is that All can keep on doing it until they get it right,

But truly it is not a perpetual Condition of Being,

But better yet it is a perpetual Ability in being.

WALKING THE WALK

Walking the Round Way is to see that all is Spirit and is the manifestation of a loving Creator. All is of and from Him and operates under the Law of One. Each of us is and should be seen by each other as a perfect child and channel of the Great Spirit's Light and Love. Likewise, each of us should respect and be caretakers of everything in and of His creation. Walking the Round Way is to see and seek proper relationship of Self with the Spirit of everything He created from the grain of sand to the tallest tree or the highest mountain or the widest ocean. The Round Way is the ideal for our expression or purpose of Being which is growth, in all conditions either in Spirit or on Earthplane, and growth is the truly only inevitable condition of Being.

To grow in the Round Way we must grow from the inside out like the tree, from the Heart through the Mind and ever expanding and making thinner the layer of the Bark of the Ego which He gave us to measure our growth. As we grow in the Round Way from the inside out, we become ever-expanding channels of His Light and Love to Self and others. And it is only by loving, and thereby forgiving ourselves, and accepting the truth of the condition of ourselves as being children of a loving Creator and accepting His Love for Self, that we can grow. By walking the Round Way we try to understand and see the perfection in every condition and know that indeed, all is absolute perfection for us to realize our unlimited potential to experience and express Love and Brotherhood. We walk the Round Way when we realize that all of that made by Him is connected and that what affects one, affects the All. We walk the Round Way when we accept unlimited growth as our Ideal and that we can only grow through Change and the only change we can or should attempt to make is in Self.

We walk the Round Way when we seek and express proper relationship with any and all things of Him and when we maintain proper relationship through the respectful sharing in the experience of the expression of growth and by allowing for the other to grow at a pace that is comfortable to them. Walking the Round Way is being a growing channel of the limitless supply of Light and Love provided by the Creator and that Love is the **The Gift of One's Care For The Well-being, Balance, and Fulfillment of Another Being or Thing**

Of HIS Creation and that all is in a condition of perfection to support this experience and expression.

Walking the Round Way is holding no one else responsible for the condition or the growth of Self, while still supporting the betterment in the condition of the All. The Round Way is to realize the growth in Self by learning the lessons through each experience that is presented and being thankful for each experience. It is being mindful of the ever changing pattern of Self and the types of prayers placed upon the screen or filter in front of it, and by maintaining a willingness to Renewall as the cycles to do so are presented. Walking the Round Way is to see the perfection in any condition of Being and in sharing the joy in the realization of it.

Walking the Round Way is to operate as a responsible multidimensional Being and participant in the All of His creation, as His perfect child and to see the Him in all of His creation including the Him in Self.

WALKING THE ROUND WAY IS TO SEEK

GROWTH AND TRUTH

AND THAT WHICH WALKS IN BALANCE

AND

WITH HARM TO NO ONE.

****

WALKING THE WALK IN THE ROUND WAY

IS TO REALIZE

THE GREATEST GIFT OF ALL,

THE GREAT SPIRIT CREATORS LOVE

IN AND FOR....

Y O U!!!!

****

So,

Enjoy your walk,

And Walk in Joy!

White Eagle

THE
MEDICINE WHEEL
WAY

BY

CONTENTS

The Wheel	173
The Directions	176
Consciousness	182
The Elements	184
The Ceremony	190
Other Wheels	201
Prayers	204
Solution Questions	212

<<<<<<< Left To Right >>>>>>>

In the Medicine Way, all things are done with respect to the four cardinal directions and center of the Medicine Wheel. One can and should always consider oneself in the center of a Medicine Wheel as one goes about one's daily activities. This means that one is always facing The Creator in the North, even when one is sleeping, no matter as to the direction that one's body is actually facing. The significance of this is that since one is always facing North so to speak, all Bead Stories, Symbols, and Patterns are to be read and interpreted as being Left to Right in their orientation.

So if I were to say for you to place one's candles so as to read Change to Spirit, the Red candle would be on the Left and the White candle on the Right as one is facing. This of course would be just the opposite if one were standing in the North and facing the South, hence the need for clarification here.

To make Bead Stories, Patterns, or Candles multidirectional, one simply places an element in the center and reverses the pattern, as is common in many ancient things. In that case, Red to White, with Blue in the center for the Creator, followed by White to Red would read: Change to Spirit by God, Spirit to Change. The primary reason for Left to Right is that the Left is The Past and the Right is the Future with the Center being the Present or Now.

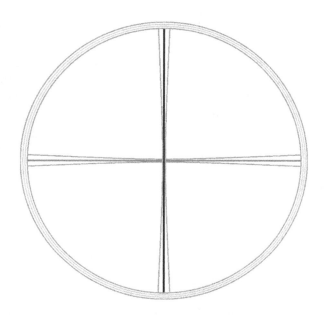

THE WHEEL

I asked the Great Spirit one day, "Father, what it is for me to do this day"? Then He showed me a great wheel. I thought for a bit and then came a great realization upon me about how the wheel was and in how it could be used by all to walk in the Round Way.

It was given to me at an earlier time, the understanding that indeed all is of, and from, Him, and that in all conditions of our Being, we are truly in a continuous process of growth. As it was given for me to understand that we are ever in the process of growing as channels of His Light and Love He showed me a tree as the way to grow. I was then given the understanding of how well it is that the tree grows from the center or Heart of it, through the rings or Mind, by the process of continuously giving way its bark or Ego. I noticed how the rings reminded me of Medicine Wheels and the process of growth therein. Then one of my Guides reminded me of the saying about what goes around comes around and the idea of wheels of Karma and such.

I started noticing how wheels made everything easier in life through the application of them, whether they are used for transportation, lifting objects, or even in the telling of time. I understood a long time ago that we all are ever walking the wheel of life, but not as much as I began to understand as to how very well that walking the way of the wheel balances and supports our growth if only we make application of and to it. In the greater sense of things, each lifetime might be considered a wheel and each second, hour, day, month, and year could well be considered as a wheel within another wheel within another wheel and so forth. While there are as many ways of applying the Medicine of the Wheel in life as there are people, this document is not to say what it is for each, but more important, this document is provided as a guide to aid in the discovery of how the Medicine Wheel may serve each in the experience of growth and the expression of their life.

While in the presentation of this document I will draw upon some of the interpretations and understanding of some of the aboriginal peoples of the North American continent, be sure not to feel restricted to or by these in the discovery of how the Medicine Wheel may help in the walk of your life, as the wheel is and should be applied as a tool to discover the truth that lives inside each of us. Many tribes do not necessarily agree as to the color or element in any direction, but in truth there is no right or wrong of such things in the way, it is only important to discover what it is for each self.

The wheel represents the channel of Self and the Sacred Circle that has no end point, as is the true condition of each of us whether in Spirit or on Earthplane. One might think better of the wheel as being a tube through which each is connected to not only the Great Spirit, but also to the All of His creation on Earthplane and beyond. One should also think of the wheel not in a linear or two dimensional sense as to be always flat like a plate or a piece of paper, but instead think of the wheel in a multidimensional sense like a balloon or a ball or a sphere. As we each walk the path in the way of the wheel, we are ever growing from the inside out and as we complete each cycle we are not only expanding the sense of Self, but also what it is that we can do by the previous experience of it, without limits.

By walking in the way of the Medicine Wheel, our walk becomes a path of an ever increasing spiral about this great sphere of this wheel that indeed is the essence of our Being. As we keep walking the way of the wheel, always in the clockwise direction, from South, to West, to North, to East, we begin to see, feel, and experience the Medicine of it in ourselves. Through the practice of the Medicine Wheel way, we are ever growing and adding to the Medicine of Self. As we learn and gain more experience and knowledge, we can share more with the All of His creation and become more of the Him in us than the limited idea of our Being that our Ego allows for us to perceive. The wheel being a circle has in fact countless beginnings in it, but no end. The wheel also can rotate or turn upon its axis and can turn in either direction as well. As one might ask why it is important to walk in a clockwise direction, it is given to say here that clockwise is the right way as the other is left. Both ways work, but for me it was given to use the clockwise direction in seeking growth or direction and the counter clockwise direction for undoing things as in clearing or rebirthing.

In the way of walking in Human form, one can only progress by the placement of one foot forward at a time and it really does not matter which one is first. The right one is most comfortable for me and it is a lot like the sun rising in the East instead of the West. Sometimes the Why of things is not nearly as important to discover as the What of them.

Of note here is that any may go from one direction to another, however it is given that a greater order will be understood by most in following the clockwise way. Also it is given to say that at any time any may go to the Center, as truly it is in the Center of some great wheel that we all stay in one aspect of our Being. By being in the Center, one may periodically draw support from all of the directions rather than just one. It is also given to mention that the Center should be used to resolve short term issues and experience the growth from them and return as soon as possible to the rim as from the position of the Center it is much harder to expand the sense of Self that is available from the experience of each of the four directions. It might be better understood that it is much easier to stretch the fabric of the envelope of Self a little at a time, in one direction at a time, than by trying to stretch it in all directions at once.

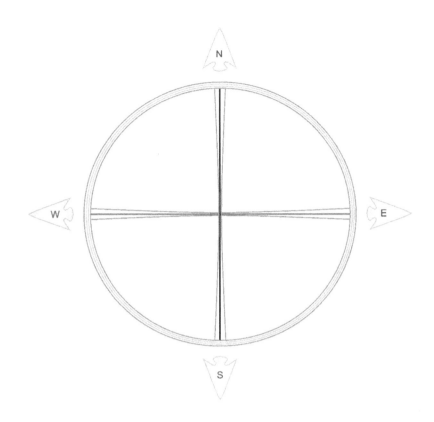

THE DIRECTIONS

One might make significance of the master numbers of four and seven at this point and understand the correlation of how most everything is in relationship to these. The elements are described in the unit of four; Wind, Earth, Water, Fire. The directions are defined as being four by South, West, North, and East, and by the addition of Up, Down, and Center, they can also be expanded to seven.

When any Being chooses to incarnate, its Spirit is present temporarily during conception so as to provide the DNA code sequences etc. for the development of its physical Bodyform. Most women sense this presence, although not all realize exactly what it is. The Spirit then returns to the Essential Will of the Creator until or shortly before Birth, whereupon its total Transition into the Physical realm and condition takes place. In terms of the directions of the Medicine Wheel, one can say that we incarnate from the Essential

Will of Great Pop in the North of our Medicine Wheel of Life as shown below:

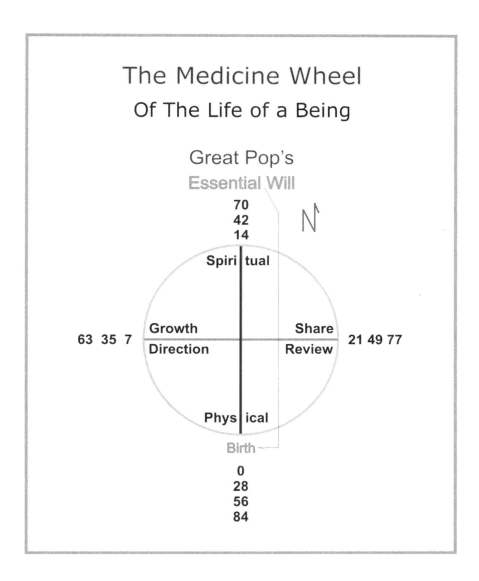

The Medicine Wheel
Of The Life of a Being

Great Pop's
Essential Will

70
42
14

Spiri tual

63 35 7

Growth   Share
Direction   Review

21 49 77

Phys ical

Birth

0
28
56
84

There are two ways of "Walking the Path" of a Medicine Wheel. One way is in a clockwise manner or the "Doing Way", and the other being the opposite counterclockwise path and "Undoing Way". However, in a Life Wheel, one can only walk the path of it in the Doing Way or clockwise direction, period. While this diagram shows how we reach the West at the age of seven and North at the age of fourteen etc., the whole of this Wheel of Life is actually operative within another Medicine Wheel. This other Medicine Wheel can be considered to be one's Greater Wheel of Life or incarnation and it is within this one that one's Wheel of Life is operative as is shown below:

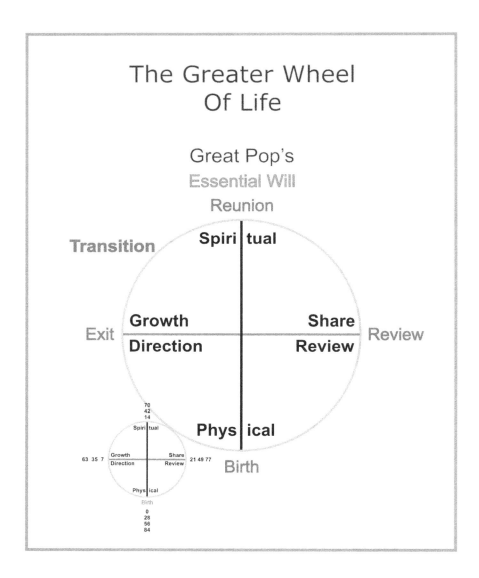

As depicted above, our smaller Wheel of Life can be considered as being only operative during the Southwest quadrant of the Greater Wheel of an incarnation. This condition holds true for all Spirit types:

Plants, Animals, Minerals, the Sun, Wind, Rain, and even Mother Earth. And while the amount of time required for Spirits of things other than Beings to reach each subsequent direction may vary, the process is still the same.

The Medicine Wheel is also orientated to the influences of the four directions as relates to in lesson giving and it is given to explain these in terms of the time or cycle of the tree. As long as one is in the Earthplane they are in the South of it. The South is the entry point for any cycle of the Medicine Wheel and represents the seed planting time in the time of the tree. South is also the direction and place for us to gather our resources. The South to North axis is our direction in that in the greater sense of all things, the Great Spirit Father lives in the North and we are ever seeking Him in us, and that is truly our greatest resource.

The west is the "Looking inside place" and in the Greater Wheel of an incarnation, we live our Earthwalk experience within the seven year cycles of our Life Wheel and it is what moves us toward the West in our Greater Wheel of an incarnation as was shown earlier. Therefore the West is the direction that we are always going to on Earthplane during an incarnation. After we take our last breath in a sojourn and after each Earthwalk experience, it is the West that we next go to or experience in our Greater Wheel of an incarnation as it is there that we choose to return to Great Pop's Essential Will through our tunnel of Transition, or not.

The "Looking inside place" of the West represents The Way, or the Way of the West and is sometimes called the Medicine Way. It is given to me to express here that the West is also the place of Truth, as only by looking inside the Self can any find the truth, as the truth lives in the Heart of Self not in the Ego of Self. The West is called the sprouting time in the time of the tree and even the smallest of seeds when planted, knows which way is up by looking inside, you see. West is the direction for making one's plan in how to use the resources in the South. Some things gathered in the South must now in the West be given away, as they do not serve the plan and are then best shared with the All and this includes the Fear tools of the Ego which when given away, Bring Harm to No One. The West to East axis is our balancer and this axis serves to keep us Round and to walk in Balance and with Harm to No One including Ourselves. This axis is centered between the two directions in which we do a lot of self-examination and review. If we did not have the West to East balancers we would be walking the pointy way and continuously finding and experiencing the limited idea of Self instead of experiencing the All that truly can be. The West sometimes seems like the crying place by some as well, as much release work goes on in this direction and it is here that we learn about Renewall through release and allowing for the better idea and pattern of Self to be manifested.

The North is the direction where the Great Spirit lives and it is also the focus of our orientation. One might say the North is the top of this ball that we live on called Mother Earth. All Medicine Wheels are orientated to the North so as to receive from the Great Spirit who lives there. In the time of the tree, the North is called the growing place and as growth is the inevitable condition of Being and the true ideal for Man and the All of His creation, it is indeed well placed here where He lives. It might also be expressed that the North is the place where we do the work according to the plan made in the West from the resources gathered in the South. Some call the North the place of wisdom and it truly can be found to be so, as only by doing the work are the lessons learned and wisdom gained from the process, you see.

The East is the direction of enlightenment, understanding and illumination. The East can also be seen as the direction of sharing and distribution. Like the West, the East is a place for self-examination and review, and as much as we might cry in the West, we often laugh at ourselves in the East. After doing the work in the North, by the plan of the West, with the resources of the South, we share and examine the product of it in the East.

If for instance we had picked up a bunch of sticks, stones, nails, mortar, bricks, and tools as resources in the experience of the South, we would carry these things with us to the experience of the West in this cycle of the wheel. In the West we would then look inside and ask for guidance, which can be also experienced in meditation and vision quest, and a plan will be given. The plan for this cycle of the wheel might be given for us to experience the building of a bird house. As the plan is given, we then have to give away all of the materials and tools that we cannot use in the building of the birdhouse. These things might be some of the Ego attachments we might have made to the stones and bricks and things including sometimes relationships to others that no longer support our growth or provide for our Well-being, and it is okay to cry in the letting go of them. The letting go of these things that might be considered as unnecessary resources allow them to better serve another plan whether it is of ourselves at another time or someone else's, as the unnecessary resources are too weighty and burdensome for us to carry forward at this time.

As we go to the North we do the building of the birdhouse there. In the process of the building, we might need a board of a certain length so we mark it and cut it just inside of the line that we made. Then as we place the board into position we might find that it is just a bit too short. Again we mark another board and this time we cut outside of the mark, ever embracing the Winds of Change in the process, as if one technique does not work, through making change we will find one that does. This time the board fits just right and we gain the wisdom from the lesson given as we do the work. When we are complete with the work in the North we then take this birdhouse to the East where we share it with others and the All by placing the birdhouse in a tree. Through the sharing with others in the experience of the East, we get our fullest sense of each cycle of the experience of the wheel by the examination and review of it that goes on here in the East. In the East we then observe the birdhouse in the tree and we might find how only the smallest of birds might use it because we made the hole in it of a certain size. Then we might realize that if we wanted to make houses for different sizes of birds we will have to make others with different size holes and dimensions by the illumination and enlightenment that we receive by the birds' reactions to this birdhouse. The East is the flowering time of the tree and therein always provides us with new seeds to sow.

The Center may also be used as previously mentioned, to draw upon all of the resources of the four directions to solve dilemma, but understand well that although balance will be found here, little direction will. The Center has no time of the tree, season, or element to it, but represents more importantly the All that can be, and the unlimited potential for growth if one makes application to it. The Center is indeed a place any and all can go to renew perspective.

CONSCIOUSNESS

In the experience of the Medicine Wheel one becomes more aware of the elements that are provided through the experience of each of the directions to support our growth during that cycle. As we become more prayerful for guidance and resource, we also become more conscious of and to all that is being provided to us by the Great Spirit for us to use. Each circumstance or event in our Earthwalk becomes more meaningful as we become more fully conscious of its reality and its potential to serve our Well-being and growth.

In the process of guiding others in the way of the Medicine Wheel a prayer to each of the four directions is given but perhaps more important is the Prayer of Goal and Purpose that initiates each ceremony. The Goal and Purpose Prayer is for the purpose of raising the consciousness of the entity, as conscience was given as the fabric that joins the Mind of one with the Heart of one and the focus to truth can only be established here. As the Medicine Wheel ceremony is that of a Vision Quest or heightened form of meditation experience, the goal and purpose must be consciously sought to receive the fullest benefit of the experience of it.

I personally do not recommend the use of substances that alter the consciousness of one nor do I condemn those that do, as indeed peyote can be used as a medicinal purgative as well as that of a mental stimulant or hallucinogen. I have found that sometimes if one is not prepared properly through clearing rituals, the experiences to be found in such conditions will only be brought in touch with the Ego of Self instead of the Heart of Self, usually through the manifestation of Ego Fear and Illusion as a sense of reality. However in any condition of Being, lessons will be learned from the experience of them.

Prior to initiating anyone to the way of the Medicine Wheel, I am usually given to establish that they have developed a strong enough meditative ability that makes the use of substances pale in their comparative ability.

The way which I personally practice and have been given to guide others in meditation is a cross between some of the eastern or E. Cayce techniques of raising the vibration or Kundalini energy of one, combined with a Vision Quest so as to leave body and be with the Great Spirit. It is given to note here that in this technique that one takes one's Spirit with consciousness intact to be with Him so as to best remember and then apply the full benefit of the experience of it. Fasting, clearing, and purification rituals should be done periodically anyway whether through smudging, sweat lodge, or whatever technique is found to be comfortable for use and always have application in a Medicine Wheel ceremony. It is given to express here that one does not have to endure pain to get close to the Creator yet these rituals do heavily impact the condition of the conscience of one. Ask any Firewalker. I do however share great respect and honor to those entities who do choose to give of themselves this way whether in Sun Dance or other ways, and only if the purpose is true from the Heart and not the Ego, can anyone truly fly free.

The Conscience is indeed the part of Self that gets the very most out of each Medicine Wheel ceremony, so it seems good to mention here that one should endeavor to keep it intact and in the clearest of conditions.

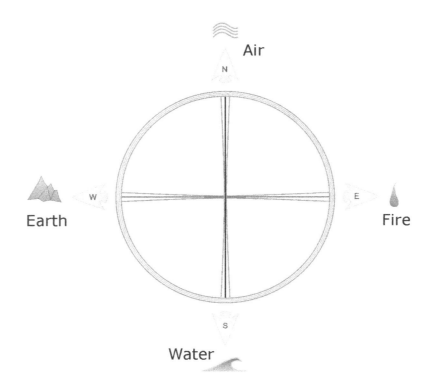

Air

Earth

Fire

Water

THE ELEMENTS

As with the directions, the foundation of all on Earthplane is significant and resonant to groups of seven and four. In the way given for me to perform the pipe ceremony I pray to each of the four directions, then Mother Earth at the center, the Winds of Change to the left, and Father Sun or Mother Moon usually to the right, counting here again, seven. Also the Star that I use is one that has seven rays which represents the seven tribes of Man, each being of a different color. The wheel may also be seen as being described as having seven and not four points or dots, if it is seen as a ball like Mother Earth and being of more than two dimensions. One dot then represents each of the four directions and one for the top, one for the bottom, and one for the center or the whole of it counting again, seven.

The foundation for all things, whether in Spirit or Earthplane, is in resonance to a rhythm of vibration that supports growth through the dynamics of Change and all vibration has the qualities of sound and color or light. As all is vibration, it can best be expressed as a wave pattern and thereby anyone can see the cycles of such and thus facilitate the growth experience of any condition.

The wave pattern might be presented as follows:

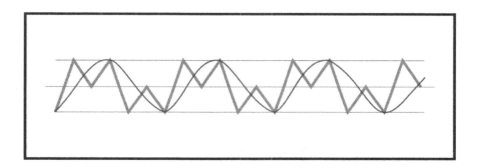

But also know that a segment of the pattern of the vibration also has a wave within it and ever deeper waves within each segment as such:

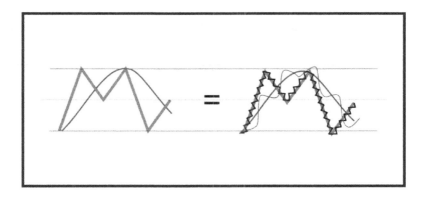

Magnified to the highest power one sees only a continuum of vibration within vibration within vibration and this is how the All is connected as well. Also it is being given to express here the structure of the universal thread, which appears like this:

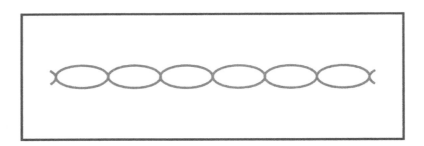

Where upon all is a condition of up and down cycles of growth and what affects one, indeed is resonated by and therefore affects All. One might well view the four directions this way as well:

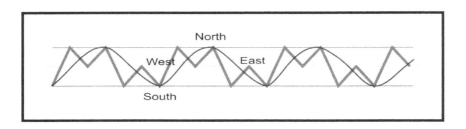

Or better yet:

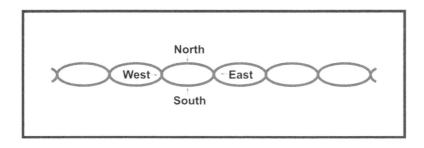

In the previous example it is much easier to visualize the balancing ability of the East and West in the cycle of growth. As one can see the embedding of vibration as previously shown, one can also see the process as being wheels within wheels as well. The wheel might better be visualized now as such:

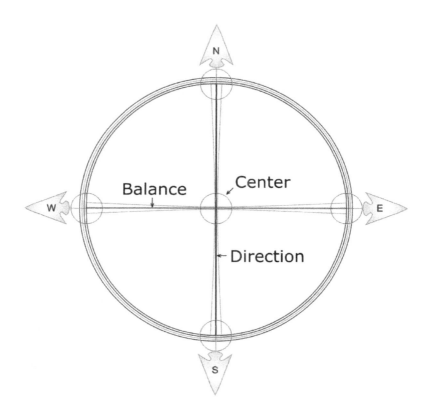

The elements of the directions of the wheel are what it is for you to discover in the process of experiencing the cycle of it and what they are for you can only be truly found by that experience. I will show you how they are for me only for the purpose of helping to guide you in the discovery of them for yourself, or it might be said that here are some of the things to look for.

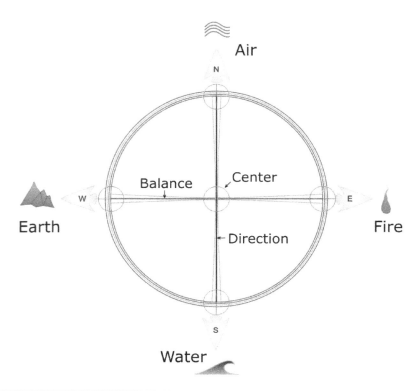

WITH:				
	SOUTH	**WEST**	**NORTH**	**EAST**
SPIRIT	Resource	Plan	Action / Work	Sharing / Distribution
TIME	Seed Planting	Sprouting	Growing	Flowering
SEASON	Summer	Fall	Winter	Spring
COLOR	Blue or Green	Brown or Black	White	Yellow or Red
ELEMENT	Water	Earth	Air	Fire
MINERAL	Garnet / Tooth	Turquoise / Apache Tear	Lapis Lazuli / Topaz	Citrine / Amethyst
PLANT	Willow / Grasses	Shrubs / Sage / Cedar	Trees / Oak	Flower / Daisy / Dandelion
ANIMAL	Shark / Mouse / Snake	Bear / Cat / Butterfly	Buffalo / Owl	Eagle / Wolf
INFLUENCE	Gathering	Looking Inside	Wisdom	Enlightenment

While the elements above are those for me in general, know also that they can change from experience to experience. Each time a person enters a direction of the wheel even though they may have experienced that direction before, does not usually result in the same Guide or lesson or understanding. The way of the wheel is to open up oneself to be in receivership of whatever it is for you to experience or to learn as you progress from one direction to another in a continuous cycle of learning. While on occasion I may receive a Butterfly Guide in the North or the West, never have they been the same for me and each have taught me different aspects of Butterfly Medicine.

Each time one enters the Medicine Wheel ceremony, all is given away and a new page in the lesson book is started in the seeking of a new Guide and its lesson in its Medicine for you to learn.

While I am on the subject of the elements, it is given for me to mention here that while most of this book is about the Medicine Wheel Way in the ceremony of growth, the Medicine Wheel is also used in countless other ways, such as prayer rituals and healing ceremonies whereupon additional forces are called upon to help with the work. While I am not called upon to discuss sacred ritual here, know that the elements identified will support it as you discover and learn their Medicine as they choose to show it to you, such as Butterfly Metamorphosis Medicine, Moss Sucking Medicine, Cinnamon and Citrine Calling Medicine and so forth. The most important understanding which I might relate about the elements is that all support growth when in application, and to understand the Medicine Wheel Way is to be open to receiving its Medicine of understanding. In the sense of developing a respectful relationship, it is indeed important to study up on that which is shown to you in Medicine Wheel ceremony. If you are in the East and you are given to see a vision of a butterfly sitting by a fire, study up on both the Medicine of Fire, which also causes change or metamorphosis, and the Butterfly.

It is important also to study up on the specifics of whatever is shown as not all butterflies migrate like the monarch and not all deer live in the mountains. The more that you endeavor to learn the Medicine of your Guides, the easier it is for them to support your growth.

In closing the discussion about the elements, it is not so important to know what they are, as it is to know that they are, and that there is an unlimited supply that will support you if you are willing to learn.

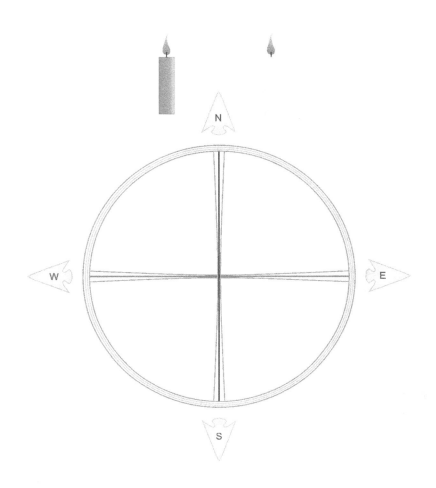

THE CEREMONY

Each direction of the wheel cycle lasts approximately ninety days or one season as it were. In initiating people to the Medicine Wheel process, I usually relate to them that a complete cycle of the Medicine Wheel lasts about one year and that if they are truly willing to commit to that, it will in all cases enhance their life immeasurably even if they only decide to experience but one cycle of it. It is being given here to explain that the benefits gained are manifold and included are the establishing order and direction to the growth experience on Earthplane. The wheel process provides a balanced order for direction and realization of goals, purposes, and values while providing linkages to helpers in both the spiritual and physical realm.

The original entering or initial position as was given to me is in the direction of the South and all should begin the process in this direction. As one enters the wheel process, a diary or notebook should be kept so as to record visions, revelations, prayers, symbols and directions and so forth. Included in this document, at the back, are copies of the prayers which were given for me to use and any variations of these that are comfortable to you are surely okay to use or you are most certainly welcome to use them as they are.

Note here for sure that the Wheel Ceremony is a Prayer Ceremony and Vision Quest and must be respectfully administered to fully realize the most from the experience of it. A calling for Vision and a Spirit helper is made and one must be cleansed of negative thoughts. Fasting for some, sweat lodge for others, or a purification meditation or bath all seem to be equally effective for preparation, use whatever feels good for you. Here again I personally do not recommend the use of drugs or alcohol and recommend the purging of systems before ceremony if these substances are in your use.

Preparation for a Wheel Ceremony is both a physical and mental process. Begin by establishing a day and time for the ceremony and plan for it as expectantly as you would for your own wedding or the birthing of a child as indeed it has as much or more significance to your own Well-being. Establish a time and a place where you will not be disturbed or interrupted. Place the phone off the hook or on a recorder and a note on the door or whatever it might take. I have enjoyed some wonderful experiences out of doors as well, if mother nature is compliant. The duration of the ceremony varies from time to time and allow for more than you might need so as to reduce the pressure of expectancy. While some of mine might last from ten to twenty hours, a two to four hour ceremony is effective for most initiates. The most important thing to mention here, is that you should allow for as much time as it takes as truly the more care that you put into the ceremony, the more benefit you will receive.

Once one enters a direction of the wheel during ceremony, you are essentially in that position for the duration of that cycle and can mentally draw upon the energy from it at any time or place. Each phase of the wheel is a prayer for specific direction for growth with aspects to your Earthwalk experience. In the process of the Medicine Wheel way, you are to start interpreting the events of your daily life in terms of the direction that you are in. Examples might be, resource gathering or seed planting in the South and it is a good place to start new or change conditions about Self, such as career or relationships. Planning, review and release work in the West, and this is a good place to get rid of clutter and make direction in one's life. Productivity and ingenuity in the North and this is a good place to try new things. Review and sharing in the East and this is a good place to go on journey and experience workshops and do reunion things. As you begin to experience each of the directions and the events therein, you will start to see the same phases operating in the lives of others with a major difference being that you are now in charge of receiving and perceiving the order in yours.

During the ceremony you will be listing ones Askances and Give Aways which are somewhat "Contrived" words between Great Pop and my personal language translation. A "Give Away" is different than taking out the trash or throwing something away that you do not value or want. It is giving something that you do value and hold precious but are willing to let go of, so that another Being or thing can share of its supply and support.

An "Askance" is something that you desire of another Being or thing and can be something other than a material object or the like. It differs from being a simple desire in that it implies that you are well aware that some other Being or thing is being called upon to produce, provide, or deliver that which is sought by you and you are showing your respect and appreciation of them even if they choose not to do that of which you ask. Both of these words and consciousnesses are used with consideration to all involved.

Having made a date and time available for the ceremony it is next recommended to collect the following items or variations thereof for use in the ceremony:

1. A round or square cloth of white or blue material of about four feet across.

2. Two candles in holders, although some will also wish to use one each of different colors for the four directions as well, as variations are most acceptable here. The right one in the North position should always be White for Spirit and Truth.

3. Paper and writing materials and these should include colors as well. This is for use in writing symbols and thoughts during the wheel process. Many individuals might experience what is called automatic writing here as some Guides like to work that way. It is important to document your vision whether by words or by pictures as they will continue to unfold their meaning in the cycle to come. One sheet of paper will be titled Askances and another titled Giveaways, and if one is going into the position of the North, a third titled The Plan should also be prepared here.

4. A bowl or pot in which to safely burn the above Askances, Giveaways, and Plan "Prayer Cloths" as we like to call them.

5. Any Medicine Stones, plants, bags, totems.

6. Prayer Stick, Rattle, or Medicine Pipe if available.

7. Any books or tapes supporting your personal growth now in use.

8. Any wings or feathers, fetishes, or jewelry for cleansing and Spirit invocation.

9. Tobacco for a gift to the four directions and the center.

10. Any incense.

11. A smudge stick of Sage or Cedar or both is most necessary.

12. Copies of the Prayers from the Prayers section at the back of this book. If this is the initial time and one is entering the South, then the Prayer of Release will not be needed. Otherwise it should be included with the Prayer of the direction that one is going to enter into as well as the Goal and Purpose Prayer.

13. Drum or meditation music and any instrument that you might wish to play to support the vision and to use for release and celebration.

14. A clean and clear mind and an open heart.

To begin the ceremony one must first prepare the area by cleaning and I like to use the vacuum to suck up all of the negative stuff before I begin. I use drum tapes that I have recorded from my Medicine Drum and provide ample stereo time of taped music to cover the anticipated duration of the ceremony. I usually will be often found to play one over and over again at times but it just to say it is good to have some variety here. The type of music to use is that which is the easiest for the person to meditate and visualize to, and to be careful of some of the hidden messages in certain types of music as it will become much amplified by the very nature of the ceremony.

Begin by spreading the cloth upon Mother Earth and if a square one is used, orientate the corners to the four directions, as each point becomes part of the circle as that is the condition of all things. Next place the candles at the cardinal point of the direction of the wheel that one is entering into, and if it is a Center Wheel they go in the North. Unless it is a Clearing Wheel then the White (Medicine of Spirit) candle always is to the right of any other candle(s) when viewed from the center. At times one will feel called to include additional candles at the cardinal points of the other directions, although this is not common and should Not become a frequently done. The reason is that as more candles become involved a scattering of focus will occur. However if others are used, place each in the center point of that direction on the Wheel.

Continue by placing Medicine Stones in each of the four directions starting in the North with the Father stone, which for me is Lapis Lazuli, at the farthest point from center and followed by the Christ stone which is Amethyst right below it towards the center, followed by the stone of Self which for me is Emerald being placed below that. Progress in a clockwise path around the wheel placing the appropriate stones and items at each point on the wheel as one feels most comfortable with for the condition of Self.

Your Guides will change from ceremony to ceremony and you should allow for them to help you determine and locate any Animal and Plant Spirit items that you may feel called upon to include. While the first ceremony might feel a little unsure or awkward, they become much easier after the first and you are more aware of and develop your own technique. After a few cycles you will know better what these are for you as you answer the Solution Questions for each direction as you experience it and the solution questions are also included in the back of this document with the prayers. You are welcome to use mine as described but it is more important to discover what each is for you.

Next place any Medicine Stones that represent the stone of Self and any Medicine bags below that of the Christ consciousness towards the center of the wheel and place any prayer sticks or rattles here initially as well. Place all fetishes, jewelry items, and totems below that. Add all other items around the perimeter of and touching the cloth as now it has become the Sacred Circle and visualize it as such. Place the educational or development items in the East for reasons of enlightenment. If one wishes to include items and pictures of loved ones whether on Earthplane or others they should be in the Northwest and things that deal with material desires in the South. See if all is ready and I recommend making any smoking material or refreshment available and handy as well. Place the writing materials in the Southeast with the burning pot handy and then place a Tobacco gift to the four directions and Center.

The wheel should then look as follows:

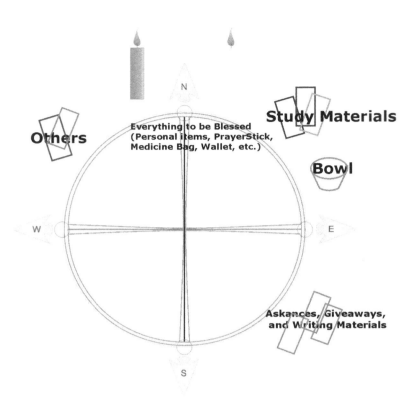

It is now time to begin the ceremony ritual. Begin by the removal of all jewelry and cosmetics and disrobe as you are ever naked before the Creator. As you remove these things, release your Ego and return to the purity and innocence of the Heart of Self. Read aloud the Goal and Purpose and breathe out facing the direction of entry, which will be from the South in the first cycle, then clockwise to the West in your next ceremony. Next light the candles with the White one being first and then the other in the North followed by others clockwise if others are present and finally the incense if used.

Next smudge and cleanse Self from the feet to the head and arms and purify Self, followed by smudging the Sacred Circle in a clockwise direction and all things in and on it. At this time it is appropriate to say the Release Prayer of your previous Guide if applicable and give thanks.

Now it is time to do the Invocation or Spirit Calling. Use your rattle and prayer stick or just your hands, and it is being mentioned to say that the prayer stick is a left hand tool and the rattle is a right hand tool, proceed to the South and facing in that direction ask for the Spirit of the South to send a Guide to help you in the Way. Next move to the West and repeat the process followed by the North and then the east.

If it is chilly you might want to bring a cover such as a blanket with you. Face the direction of entry, South if the first time, and subsequently the West and so forth, and stand with your back to the wheel and read aloud the prayer for that direction which is located in the back of this document. Now turn and enter the Sacred Circle of the wheel and sit in the center facing the direction of entry.

Now turn on any meditation music and begin to record your Askances, which are the Prayer for things that you wish to receive and it is okay to ask for anything that walks in Balance and with Harm to No One. It is important to ask for a Vision of what it is for you to do, especially in the direction of the South and you will get a better understanding about your life plan for this Earthwalk. Next record your Giveaways, which are anything you no longer want in your Earthwalk, or some things you want to share. Fear, pain, money problems, loneliness, lack of direction, or love to the universe are some popular ones.

Next go into a deep meditation and ask to be with The Creator and for answers to the questions about the direction that you are in such as symbols, color, elements, and so forth. Ask for guidance as to the What, and How of what it is for you to do and for Him to make you over as to best serve His idea of you and make yourself available to that transformation by Him.

Record any thoughts, visions, or revelations as they come to you. Continue to record these when they come, even though you may not at the time be physically present in the ceremony of the wheel, as they will indeed continue to come. Rattle, chant, drum, dance, sing or do anything that comes natural to you as you continue. Also know that it is okay to cry a lot in the Wheel Ceremony as you are truly in the presence of your loving Creator Father here. Be ever conscious of your prayer and release yourself to the fulfillment of it and the vision or understanding will come.

Especially during very long Wheel Ceremonies it is definitely okay to lay down if necessary and do so with your feet in the direction of entry, and use the bathroom if necessary and be ever mindful that the wheel walks with you where ever you move during the ceremony of it and always exit and reenter from the direction that you are in. One might review passages in texts as they might be called to you but be sure here to make purposeful your search and own what it is that you are seeking and be open to it finding you.

After the meditation time and the vision has come, document all of it and use colors to make drawings as these will be very useful in times to come for you. Now take the Giveaway Prayer sheet and read it out loud and release it to the universe by burning it in your right hand and placing it in the bowl to finish. Next repeat the process with the Askances and burn these in the left hand.

At this time prayers for invocation of the Spirits into ceremonial items, totems, Prayersticks, and rattles should be preformed.

Any additional prayers should now be said at this time especially one of thanksgiving and the ceremony is now complete. Take a mental picture of all that is about you and remember that as you walk from the ceremony, the Wheel is an ever present part of you now and see everything that way and extinguish the candles in the reverse order as lit. Removal and clean up of the items is to also be done in the reverse order from that as begun and this should be also respectfully done with great care and thanksgiving.

Next study any habits and research the behavior of any Guide that showed up, as a Master Teacher will come to help you learn and grow in the experience of the direction that you are in and you show respect to him by learning his Medicine this way and thereby take it on to Self for further use and understanding. It is also important to record your dreamtime experiences as often your Guide will work with you here and a greater understanding will be presented in the process.

As one walks their walk during the cycle of the wheel, it is important to see and to look for messages and enlightenment in the development of their daily activity and to seek further guidance in regular daily meditation. It is given to mention here for some to place a copy of the previous sentence in a place of prominence to read as they begin and end each day.

Sometimes some Guides may be shy about showing themselves and for some, more than one may appear in any phase, but it has always been one special one that I am to learn the most from each time. On one occasion it was not until it was in the Prayer for Release that I realized who it was. It is nice to ask the Guide its name and these may be hard sometimes to spell but they will always give you one.

As we move from one direction to another, it is often hard to release our previous Guide for all of the Love that we have received from them but it is indeed important to do so. One will find that only by truly doing so, will it be possible for them to become more of themselves in oneself.

***

Continue to study the symbols and patterns as given during the ceremony and more will be given to you during the cycle, and if none appeared in the ceremony, know sure well they will find a way for you to recognize them. This study will enable you to attain a full understanding as to their Medicine for you in each cycle as all have meaning and Medicine and great value. Study anything available about the nature of your Guide, which will most often be in an Animal form, but also seek your Guide in meditation and daily life as they are there to help you. Make every effort to see how the experiences encountered in your daily life translate into the Medicine or learning experience of the direction that you are in, and how often and easily events manifest for you to share in the experience of it. Keep records of your meditations, revelations, and experiences and the questions answered as well. The recording of these understandings that come to you is your gift of care and shows your respect of their value to you and more will be given easier to you this way.

At the end of the first cycle and having experienced the way of the East, one can then decide whether to continue by reentry into the direction of the South again and this time the prayer of release will continue to apply to this direction as well. As a practicing Medicine Man, I am personally constant in the process, but anyone will greatly benefit from the process whatever their personal life path choice might be if for no other reason than to gain an understanding of it.

Take time before going back into the South, should you choose to, to review all of your experiences and lessons learned in the previous directions of that cycle, which is indeed a real East thing to do. At this time one might well go to the Center as well for a short period and know that the Center may be approached from any direction and in leaving, return to the direction of approach. Indeed the question of whether to continue the process is a real Center thing to do.

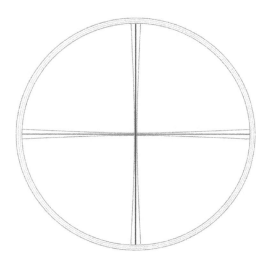

OTHER WHEELS

As a Medicine Man I personally use the Medicine Wheel constantly in my life and more than just in the experience of the Way of the Walk of it. As a healer, I will often place a person upon an orientated cloth or an imaginary one as both work equally well for me and place Mineral, Plant, and Animal items in the four directions and call for assistance from them in the healing process.

The Medicine Wheel is also a very valuable tool for me to use when dealing with Spirit problems whether they be in possession clearing or rebirthing and other transformation processes.

Sometimes during a walkabout I will use a napkin and / or salt and make a small wheel on a counter or table top when I wish to invoke a special Guide into a Medicine Stone to give to someone or to cleanse one for them and this works for fetishes, totems and jewelry items also.

Often I will use the Medicine Stones and items in my Medicine bag and lay them out in a Medicine Wheel before doing a channeled reading for someone followed by a Prayer for Guidance.

The altars about my home are Medicine Wheels as well. When someone has Spirit problems in their place, I will often be given to smudge it and then place Medicine Stones to the four directions and the center of it and then the whole location becomes a great Medicine Wheel and I have found that this works very well with discarnate or ghost problems.

THE MOST IMPORTANT THING TO REMEMBER IS THAT:

ALL PRAYERS ARE ANSWERED,

AND THE MEDICINE WHEEL

IS A TRULY WONDERFUL WAY TO PRAY.

WALK IN JOY
AND
ENJOY YOUR WALK!

Now that you have gotten this far in the Way of the Medicine Wheel and are ready to start, the first question that you might ask upon entering the direction of the south is:

WHAT IS MEDICINE ?

You should have the answer by the time you go into the North!!!!

White Eagle

PRAYERS

GOAL

MY GOAL IS :

TO UNMASK MYSELF AND COME NAKED BEFORE THE CREATOR THAT I MAY STRIP AWAY THE LAYERS OF VANITY AND EGO SELF-WORSHIP AND DISCOVER THE TRUTH OF WHAT AND WHO I AM, AND TO MORE FULLY UNDERSTAND HIS TRUTH AND WILL IN ME.

PURPOSE

MY PURPOSE IS :

TO REVERT BACK TO ONENESS TO THE WILL OF THE GREAT SPIRIT CREATOR BY GIVING MY WILL AWAY TO THIS END.

I DO THIS SO AS TO BECOME TO THE FULLEST OF MY BEING, HIS EMISSARY AND AGENT TO ALL OF HIS CHILDREN IN SPIRIT AND ON THE EARTH-PLANE.

AS I DO THIS,

MY PURPOSE BECOMES THAT OF BEING AN EVER EXPANDING CHANNEL AND EXPRESSION OF THE CREATOR'S LOVE IN AND THROUGH ME BY WALKING THE ROUND WAY....

WHICH IS TO WALK IN BALANCE AND WITH HARM TO NO ONE BEING OR THING, INCLUDING MYSELF.

RELEASE

DEAR (Previous Guides Name),

I THANK YOU DEARLY FOR YOUR LOVE AND SERVICE TO ME AND FOR ALL THAT I HAVE LEARNED IN THE EXPERIENCE IN THE WAY OF THE DIRECTION OF (THE PREVIOUS DIRECTION).

I WILL CONTINUE TO BUILD UPON THE MEDICINE THAT IS THE YOU, THAT IS NOW IN ME, AND I WILL EVER CARRY YOU IN MY HEART THIS WAY.

I NOW RELEASE YOU TO YOUR NEXT EXPRESSION OF SELF AND BACK TO THE GREAT SPIRIT CREATOR FROM WHOM WE ALL COME, AND I DO SO THANK HIM AND YOU, FOR YOU.

SOUTH

DEAR FATHER,

GREAT SPIRIT AND CREATOR OF ALL THINGS,

PLEASE GUIDE ME IN THE SACRED WAY OF THE MEDICINE WHEEL AND IN THE WAY OF THE DIRECTION OF THE SOUTH SO THAT I MAY SERVE YOUR WILL IN ME BY GAINING SACRED KNOWLEDGE THIS WAY.

PLEASE GIVE TO ME A GUIDE IN THE WAY OF THE SOUTH THAT I MAY LEARN AND DISCOVER THE RESOURCES AND YOUR VISION IN AND OF ME AND TO BETTER KNOW WHAT IT IS FOR ME TO DO SO AS TO BEST PLEASE AND SERVE YOU.

PLEASE PROVIDE ME NOW WITH A VISION AND UNDERSTANDING OF MY CONNECTEDNESS TO YOU AND THE ALL AND MY PURPOSE THIS WAY.

WEST

DEAR FATHER,

GREAT SPIRIT AND CREATOR OF ALL THINGS,

PLEASE GUIDE ME IN THE SACRED WAY OF THE MEDICINE WHEEL AND IN THE WAY OF THE DIRECTION OF THE WEST SO THAT I MAY SERVE YOUR WILL IN ME BY GAINING SACRED KNOWLEDGE THIS WAY.

PLEASE GIVE TO ME A GUIDE IN THE WAY OF THE WEST THAT I MAY LEARN FROM THE LOOKING INSIDE PLACE THE TRUTH AND YOUR PLAN IN ME AND TO LEARN HOW TO GIVE AWAY THOSE THINGS THAT ARE IMPROPER IN ME OR THAT I NO LONGER NEED SO THAT I MAY EASILY WALK EVER IN THE ROUND WAY.

PLEASE PROVIDE ME NOW WITH A VISION AND UNDERSTANDING OF MY CONNECTEDNESS TO YOU AND THE ALL AND MY PURPOSE THIS WAY.

NORTH

DEAR FATHER,

GREAT SPIRIT AND CREATOR OF ALL THINGS,

PLEASE GUIDE ME IN THE SACRED WAY OF THE MEDICINE WHEEL AND IN THE WAY OF THE DIRECTION OF THE NORTH SO THAT I MAY SERVE YOUR WILL IN ME BY GAINING SACRED KNOWLEDGE THIS WAY.

PLEASE GIVE TO ME A GUIDE IN THE WAY OF THE NORTH THAT I MAY LEARN KNOWLEDGE AND WISDOM AND HOW TO APPLY AND SHARE YOUR RESOURCES IN AND OF ME IN EACH AND EVERY WAY AND DAY.

PLEASE HELP ME IN THE EXERCISE OF YOUR WILL IN AND OF ME SO THAT I MIGHT EASILY REALIZE THE LESSON AND SHARE IT WITH OTHERS.

PLEASE PROVIDE ME NOW WITH A VISION AND UNDERSTANDING OF MY CONNECTEDNESS TO YOU AND THE ALL AND MY PURPOSE THIS WAY.

EAST

DEAR FATHER,

GREAT SPIRIT AND CREATOR OF ALL THINGS,

PLEASE GUIDE ME IN THE SACRED WAY OF THE MEDICINE WHEEL AND IN THE WAY OF THE DIRECTION OF THE EAST SO THAT I MAY SERVE YOUR WILL IN ME BY GAINING SACRED KNOWLEDGE THIS WAY.

PLEASE GIVE TO ME A GUIDE IN THE WAY OF THE EAST THAT I MAY LEARN ENLIGHTENMENT, ILLUMINATION, AND PERCEPTION. PLEASE HELP ME IN THE REVIEW AND TO DEVELOP MUCH GREATER UNDERSTANDING OF MY PURPOSE IN YOUR PLAN AND TO GAIN GREATER BALANCE THIS WAY AND SHARE IT WITH OTHERS.

PLEASE PROVIDE ME NOW WITH A VISION AND UNDERSTANDING OF MY CONNECTEDNESS TO YOU AND THE ALL AND MY PURPOSE THIS WAY.

CENTER

DEAR FATHER,

GREAT SPIRIT AND CREATOR OF ALL THINGS,

PLEASE GUIDE ME IN THE SACRED WAY OF THE MEDICINE WHEEL AND IN THE WAY OF THE DIRECTION OF THE CENTER SO THAT I MAY SERVE YOUR WILL IN ME BY GAINING SACRED KNOWLEDGE THIS WAY.

I KNOW THAT INDEED I AM EVER PRESENT IN THE CENTER OF MY WHEEL OF LIFE AND THAT IN THIS CEREMONY NOW I MAY DRAW FROM THE FORCES OF THE UNIVERSE AND SUPPORT FROM THE FOUR DIRECTIONS AND WINDS HERE AS WELL AS NORTH/SOUTH DIRECTION AND EAST/WEST BALANCE.

PLEASE GIVE TO ME A GUIDE IN THE WAY OF THE CENTER TO SUPPORT MY GROWTH IN BALANCE AND TO ACHIEVE BALANCE IN MY GROWTH AND THAT I MAY SEE MORE CLEARLY YOUR WILL IN ME AND REALIZE YOUR SUPPORT AND PLAN IN AND OF ME.

PLEASE PROVIDE ME NOW WITH A VISION AND UNDERSTANDING OF MY CONNECTEDNESS TO YOU AND THE ALL AND MY PURPOSE THIS WAY.

SOLUTION QUESTIONS

(What to Discover in Each Phase)

SPIRIT -

TIME of TREE -

SEASON -

COLOR -

ELEMENT -

MINERAL SPIRIT -

PLANT SPIRIT -

ANIMAL SPIRIT -

INFLUENCE -

GUIDE -

SOLUTION QUESTIONS – Continued

S Y M B O L S -

VISION -

R E V E L A T I O N S -

MINERAL SPIRIT

KNOWLEDGE

BY

CONTENTS

Introduction   217

Mineral Spirit Knowledge   218

Mineral Spirits   221

Additional Stones   249

Color / Ray Medicine   252

Metal Medicine   254

Elemental Medicine   255

Stones by Function   256

Finding the Spirit of the Stone   262

Sharing the Spirit   265

Index   271

****

EVERY STONE BECOMES A PRECIOUS GEM

WHEN WE EMBRACE IT AS A GIFT

OF THE GREAT SPIRIT FOR US TO USE

TO REMEMBER HE MADE US

JUST LIKE HE MADE IT.

LOOK INSIDE EACH STONE

TO BEHOLD THE PRECIOUS SPIRIT

AS IT HAS ITS JOY TO BRING AND WORK TO DO

JUST LIKE YOU.

White Eagle

Introduction

This book is but a brief description of how Mineral Spirit works for me. I feel that there is an unlimited ability in how they may also help you. It is important therefore to use this book as a guide only in the sense of observing one man's way in working with Mineral Spirits. Equally important is to spend time with them so as to develop your own special and unique relationship to and with them.

While the descriptions about the Mineral Spirits detailed in this document may or may not agree with some of the many books currently available on the subject, I can only express that this is what was given for me to use in my way. Please remember that All Can Be, and the joy is in the discovery of it. As the Great Spirit created all things, He embodied us and Mineral Spirit with unlimited possibility. The foundation of the body of all living things on Earthplane is Mineral Spirit and Water. Therefore it seems obvious that we should easily resonate to the vibrations that are the Mineral Spirits in ourselves and others.

The key to working with Mineral Spirit as with all others is a condition of Proper Relationship. This proper relationship may better be described as being the condition of respectful sharing in the experience of the expression of growth. As one senses the Love of the Great Spirit in one's Heart, Mineral Spirit is an able and most willing partner in the conducting and distribution of this energy to any and all things in the universe. As with all conditions of relationships, the key element for success is communication. So spend some time speaking to and listening to the Mineral Spirit stones that choose to share your Earthwalk journey. I am sure that both your and our lives will be much richer for the experience.

MINERAL SPIRIT KNOWLEDGE

BY

WHITE EAGLE

All stones should initially be cleansed by placing them in a container, I prefer glass, of water and salt and placed in a position where the rising sun in the East will shine upon them at daybreak if possible. Sometimes I will also do this initially under the full moon or new moon and thereby receive the benefits of both influences, but the sun is much stronger in cleansing and energizing. Periodic cleansing should subsequently be applied at times of the full or new moon at least four times each year. I prefer to cleanse mine much more often and in fact each time that I use a Mineral Spirit in healing, I will cleanse it immediately. The care given to the Spirit of the stone this way will be returned manifold times to the user of it. More respectful sharing, you see. As the Great Spirit made all things, each and every thing of His creation is embodied with a unique vibration or Spirit that we may use to enhance our lives in meaningful ways. While man has the ability to transform the image or shape of things, the unique vibration of that made by the Creator is always retained and is ever present and may be used to remember our connection to the source, the Great Spirit Creator, and used in prayer, contemplation, or the healing way.

Upon the receipt of any stone and its subsequent cleansing, time should be spent in examination, listening, feeling, and sensing the unique vibration that is the Spirit of it in every way. While there are many books available giving the specifics of the writers' understanding and uses of stones, only you can truly determine the Spirit and uses that any stone might have for oneself.

Just as the stars may present certain influences at any specific time, All Can Be at any moment and there definitely are no absolutes or limits. As a Medicine Man or Shaman sometimes I will invoke a Master Guide to work with the stone Spirit that is already present to help a person and then the stone becomes in the way of totem. At other times a stone might be found that is already in the way of Spirit carrier or "Wotai" in which an Ancient or Guide will call to help one in their Earthwalk.

While some people might prefer polished or unpolished stones, I personally like them all, whatever their condition might be found to be in. I also find that most stones and especially the crystals seem to especially respond to and like the attention of my cleaning foreign matter such as debris and residues from them. Of significance to mention also is that size really makes no difference as to the ability of the stone Spirit, however it may make a difference as to how much weight you wish to carry, the thinking that bigger is better is not valid here. A special note on Quartz crystals, in the understanding given to me is that Quartz is mostly just an amplifier and while it is excellent at that, Quartz in itself does little until energy is applied to it. While some Quartz crystals may work better as transmitters, usually being those with the point in the center, and some work better as receivers of energy with the point to the side, either can indeed be used for any purpose at any time.

Although I prefer to favor the clear Quartz for use in energy work, else I have to work through the White Ray if present in the crystal, I will gladly use whatever is at hand. In healing work I prefer to use the Rose Quartz as the receiving stone and I have found that it has both great sucking Medicine and is able to rapidly renew itself as well, and an Amethyst as the transmitting stone.

The Amethyst is what I call the Christ Consciousness stone and each stone will operate with the Child of God and Violet Ray and consciousness or Medicine. I also refer to the Amethyst as the motor generator stone as its energy is retained after application. The Rose Quartz contains the soft Pink Ray of the female energy or the body of man and the Amethyst contains the Red Ray of change blended with the Blue Ray of the Will of the Father Creator. The Rose Quartz and Amber have the greatest sucking Medicine and should be applied to the affected area and the energy of Love applied to the Amethyst at a boundary location of the affected area or wound. Allow for the inflammation or affliction to flow into the Rose Quartz or Amber for a period of time and afterward cleanse all stones that were applied. I will occasionally use Plant and Mineral Spirit together in the healing process such as placing Moss, which also has great sucking Medicine next to the skin and a Rose Quartz on top of the Moss for greater results. Often when Rose Quartz is used in this way it will get very hot, sometimes turn White, and often will develop a film or oily surface after use, all of which is very natural and is no cause for alarm or speculation.

The following is a brief description of the Mineral Spirit stones that I use and is by no means exclusive. Note also that the direction that is given relates to my use of Mineral Spirit and its position for me in the Medicine Wheel.

MINERAL SPIRITS

AMBER - *

The Medicine of Amber is that of 'I Absorb' or what could be considered to be, Resolution. Oftentimes in conditions of imbalance or illness, I will eat some Amber with a small Emerald and or Ruby, which are the two stones that are resonant to my personal Medicine. While some might argue as to whether Amber should or not be included with Mineral Spirits, that is in fact resonant to the very nature and Medicine of this Mineral Spirit. In reality, Amber could be included with the Plant Spirits instead, or as well. This is because Amber is solidified or petrified tree sap primarily from the conifers, and mostly of the Pines. While most commonly found in the Amber or Golden Ray it also occurs in the hues of blue black, red, and green as well as sometimes clear. Amber is the only Mineral Spirit that floats on water, although some will sink at times! Oftentimes Amber will be found to have inclusions of debris or insects, which also is evidence of its great sucking and entrapping Medicine. Amber is the stone of choice to resolve witchcraft problems or issues and should be worn frequently about the left hand, heart or head for the greatest protection and enabling clarity and purity of thought.

AMETHYST - *

Although the crystal form is often preferred, the Christ Consciousness stone is one of the Mineral Spirit stones most favored by myself as a transmitter of Healing Love energy. The Purple Ray is the vibration of the Ideal that we remember ourselves as children of the Great Spirit and His love for us and the Christ potential as a more perfect pattern to aspire to. I use the Amethyst in the North, Center, or East of the wheel. The Medicine of the Amethyst is always to be considered to be of significant value for inclusion on any necklace. The Amethyst is present on all of my prayer sticks and reminds me of my connectedness to the Great Spirit Father and of my purpose in service to Him. The Amethyst is my most often used prayer stone and I will often place it upon the forehead of one while laying down and have them use it to pull renewing energy past the bottom of their feet and out the top of their head. I also often use the Amethyst on the forehead or crown of one to enhance the raising of the vibration in meditation. The Amethyst is the major stone that I use in healing and the Medicine of the Amethyst might best be stated as Renewall. Amethyst is good to wear on all parts of the body and should especially be used in weakened or afflicted areas.

AQUAMARINE - *

When in its natural crystalline form, Aquamarine is very linear and rod shaped and is usually found in the Light Blue to Clear Ray. The Aquamarine represents the water and its Medicine is about Abundance in all conditions of life. The Aquamarine in my Medicine bag represents the father / child relationship and is a great stone for calming and peaceful energy. While some might wear the Aquamarine upon the left hand for good results, its best application might be about the neck or about the head such as earrings. The Aquamarine is used in the South and North in my Medicine Wheel and can be applied linearly upon the chest center, heart position, or throat in healing applications. The Medicine of the Aquamarine is that of Calming and the realization of the Abundance provided by the Creator for each of us to use, as truly each has everything that we really need as we wake to the dawn of each new day.

AVENTURINE – *

Aventurine like so many other Mineral Spirit stones is what I call a composite stone meaning that it has more than one type of element in it. Aventurine is of a base color embedded with pyrite specks that reflect a golden metallic hue in its three basic colors of red, blue and most common green. As the color Gold has the Medicine of bringing forth and prayer, it is little wonder that the primary Medicine of Aventurine is that of the Giving and Sharing of Love. Because of this Medicine and value, Aventurine is very effective in use in jewelry as well as most any direction in the Medicine Wheel and is especially effective and proud to do its work in the center. Effective in all rituals involving relationship issues, Aventurine is one of my favorite gift stones. In its effect on body and energy use, Aventurine is very effective in the throat, heart and stomach areas and is useful in resolving foundation issues about the feet and head as well.

AZURITE - *

As its name might imply, Azurite is of the Blue Ray and thereby reminds and reinforces the awareness that all is possible by the Creator. While the Medicine of the color of Blue in itself speaks of limitless possibility and The Creator, Azurite takes it one step further in embodying Strength of Faith and Conviction as well. Indeed Strength of Conviction is the major part and aspect of the Medicine of Azurite. Like most mineral Spirits that are of the blue hue, Azurite is considered to be copper based. And in this case, one would be correct to assume that Azurite embodies and shares the conductivity and therefore support to Flow Medicine that is found in Copper also. So in the simplest expression, the Medicine of Azurite can be considered to be that of Support to the Realization of unlimited Possibility with Faith and Conviction. From this Understanding, one can easily see how Azurite can be positively applied in any situations where there are issues with support to Flow as well as Hope and why Azurite should be a most welcome Mineral Spirit in any Medicine bag or on any Prayer Stick. In these two applications, Azurite can be considered to represent one's Path and Prayer as well as Courage or Ambition. In application with Plant Spirits in potions and teas, Azurite actively supports not only the realization of that which is sought, but also helps in the blending and harmonization of the individual components. Unlike "Power" found in stones like Tourmaline and so forth, this aspect and Potential of blending found in Azurite should be considered often in such considerations and expressions. Azurite is most definitely a South stone in Medicine Wheel Applications, and can at times be considered for use in the North as well.

BLOODSTONE - *

Bloodstone is usually a deep green stone containing blotches of Red Jasper in it which reminds us of our Soul Self as the blood of our physical body immersed and surrounded by a sea of the Green Ray of Love. This stone is a very good one to use in relationship and the dynamics of the red blotches also reminds us that we are ever in a continuous relationship with the Father Creator and each other. Bloodstone is a good gift stone as it helps all recall their true identity as children of the Great Spirit and His limitless supply of Love for us. Bloodstone may be used in the South or the Center of the Medicine Wheel and may applied to the heart, chest, throat or any position of the back in healing. The Medicine of the Bloodstone is Remembering and Cooperation and is good for all problems in relationship as well as in the centering of Self. Bloodstone wears well on rings, necklaces, pendants, and earrings.

BOTSWANA AGATE - *

This particular form of agate deserves special mention not so much because of its origins, but because it is a very special form of Agate. This type of agate comes in a variety of shades and colors with one predominant characteristic, which is that all forms of it have many layers and specific patterns that are present, and become most evident when polished. And as the idea of patterns remind us of the patterns of behavioral models that we are constantly choosing from in our personal expression, is it any wonder that I might find the Medicine of this Mineral Spirit to be that of being The Stone of Choices and Changes. In the many years that I have been "Giving Mineral Spirit Feet" by presenting Medicine stones as gifts, this is one of my favorites that I use for that purpose. And is it any wonder that since each and everything that exists has Spirit, that these particular stones have oftentimes helped many people in their journey in Life. I even remember one account whereby the stone I gave someone saved their Life. It did so by jumping down upon the floorboard of their automobile when the light that they were stopped at turned green. In pausing to proceed so as to retrieve the stone, they were saved from being killed in a wreck that would have occurred. This was because a heavy truck without brakes soon came speeding across the path that they would have been present in, had they not been distracted when the light turned green for them. For obvious reasons relating to its Medicine, I prefer to use Botswana Agate more in the preparation of teas and potions than for wound applications. In healing, this stone may be well used in helping remove stress in the body and particularly has great benefit when used about the feet and ankles. This stone is naturally a good one for use in Meditation and contemplation. Botswana Agate has a predominant place in the South and North of the Medicine Wheel, as well as the Center. And in one's Medicine Bag, Botswana Agate can be used to represent and foretell of the Choices that are significant in one's current position of one's path in Life. In adornments, this is a good stone to be used on the right side of the body, and is one of my favorite stones to keep in my pocket as well.

CALCITE - *

Calcite appears in a rainbow of colors and has a very wet soap like appearance. In whatever color ray, Calcite has a very softening effect upon the user and soothes the emotions. The choice in color of the Calcite stone is as important to the use and benefits derived from this Mineral Spirit, as is the material of the stone itself. The Medicine of the Calcite might best be expressed as Embracing Softness in the variety of the Experiences of Life. As Calcite comes in a rainbow of colors, the very symbol of the Medicine of the Calcite Mineral Spirit might be that of the rainbow itself, as in it is represented both the dynamics of Hope and Variety. Calcite may be used in the corresponding hue to increase or energize any of the centers of the body, often referred to as chakras, in the healing way. And Calcite can be used and worn freely about all parts of the body, as we can all benefit from the rainbow stone. Calcite is a predominately West and South oriented stone in the Medicine Wheel, and can be used to represent Balance Considerations in one's Medicine bag. In healing or remedial use, any part of the body will benefit as mentioned. However, Calcite is especially beneficial in use in any conditions of pain or swelling, or around the eyes, ears, head, and throat, as well as heart and solar plexus.

CARNELIAN - *

Carnelian comes to us in variations of color from yellow to orange, red, and brown. I prefer to use the red Carnelian in helping to raise the vibration through the activation of the root center energy in body work applications. I also use the Carnelian or the Garnet as representing the beginning or Seed of Self or Soul Self in my Medicine Bag. The Carnelian is a great beginning stone when learning how to work with energy, as it can be very responsive to kinetic energy and can be made hot or cold that way. The Carnelian is much softer than the Garnet in its influence upon the body, and has more absorptive ability than the Garnet. However, any stone of the red hue or ray is a good one to use to enhance the Force of Change. Carnelian is a good bring into action stone and operates steadfastly, but without anxiety as might be found in other stones especially the Ruby. I use the Carnelian in the Center, South, or East in the Medicine Wheel. The Medicine of the Carnelian might well be put as being The expression of Thoughtful Change and Softness in the Way.

The Carnelian may be used in the lower parts of the body in healing, but should be restricted in its application to areas below the navel. The Carnelian in adornment likes to be associated with the Turquoise or any Green, Yellow, or Blue Ray stone and it usually prefers a silver setting. The Carnelian is best worn on rings and bracelets, and the right side will usually be better enhanced by it.

CHALCEDONY - *

Being of the Quartz family, the Chalcedony is a great energizer stone. I use the Blue Chalcedony in my Medicine bag to signify energy in relationships, and it is one of the stones that I often give away as a gift stone for that reason. The Medicine of the Chalcedony is indeed that of an Enabler, but is a calming force in the process of action. The Medicine of the Chalcedony might well be put as symbolizing the power of Prayer, as the blue of the Father is almost always found present in this softly enabling stone. The Chalcedony is a good South stone, but may be used anywhere in the Medicine Wheel for its obvious support or enhancement. In healing, the Chalcedony may be used to ward off infection, but pales in comparison to the Rose Quartz as the Medicine of the Chalcedony is more about relationships. All Medicine bags should include a Blue Chalcedony, and it may also be worn anywhere upon the body. If used in healing applications, placements should <u>kept above the shoulders for best effects</u> and the Chalcedony is very good in dealing with problems of the mind. The Chalcedony is a good calling stone for a new relationship, and the Chalcedony has a very good memory and can be used to help in this area as well.

CHRYSOCOLLA - *

Found in most continents including North America, Chrysocolla is a great Peacemaker and Calming Stone. It is this part of its Medicine that has given cause for many of the New Age group to have it handy around Computers and such Mechanical Spirits so as to relieve stress and worry when operating them. One can say that the Limitless potential to be found within oneself is the presence and Medicine of this wonderful supporting Mineral Spirit Brother as well as to see past the limited idea of Self that is often promoted by others. If there is to only be one Mineral Spirit that is to be considered in combating WitchCraft, this is most certainly one of them. Chrysocolla is most certainly a good stone for the West and North in any Medicine Wheel and can actually be of help in any direction for that matter. In one's Medicine Bag Chrysocolla can be used to represent that which is one's inner truth and Potential and well as that to come in divining. In potions and teas as well as bodywork, Chrysocolla is effective in support to calming of any condition.

CITRINE - *

The Citrine being of the Yellow or Gold Ray, is the Calling stone and should be included in every Medicine bag and Prayer Stick. I also use the Citrine in every application of Prayer and it is one of the stones that is placed in my rattles as well. While the Chalcedony might represent the power of Prayer, the Medicine of Citrine is the Prayer or Calling Forth that which you would receive. As all Prayers are answered, Citrine represents one's phone line to the Great Spirit and all of His creation, and should be used in all Prayers or expectancy. Citrine's Plant Spirit twin is the Cinnamon, and I will often use these two Brothers together. Although Citrine is of the Quartz family and thereby has amplification qualities, I prefer to use it more in the preparation of teas and potions than for wound applications. In healing, the Citrine may be well used in the back areas from the waist up, and will have good effect upon the Will center. However, because of the great strength of the Medicine of this stone, its applications should be brief. The Citrine has a predominant place in the East of my Medicine Wheel and is always included there and in my Medicine Bag to represent one's Prayers of Desire. If I were to carry only two stones, one would be the Citrine, and the other the Lapis Lazuli or Father stone as I call it. The Citrine likes to be worn on the left, which is the receiving side. Citrine can really be worn anywhere. However if worn on earrings, headaches may occur if one is dealing with problems of guilt in which case, the Rose Quartz is preferred. Everyone should have a Citrine.

CORAL - *

Another gift of the sea, Coral is a stone of Wealth and Resource. Coral comes to us in different color variations of white, pink, red, brown and black and all have a drawing effect upon the user. Because of the recognition of its supportiveness to growth, Coral has been found to be well used as a bonding medium for implants in bone graph situations. It is important to remember its drawing qualities when selection for use. It is also important to use caution when using the black or red variations. The Medicine of the Coral is indeed that of Growth and more important the Support of Growth and Cooperation and Sharing in the Resources of each other for the betterment of the All. Corals Medicine might well be expressed in the single word Brotherhood. Coral may be used in the South of the Medicine Wheel and temporary applications may be used in the drawing out of poisons and infections from wounds, however here again I prefer the Rose Quartz in these applications. Coral is a good addition to any Medicine bag as Brotherhood is represented here. Coral may be worn on any part of the body and for good effect earrings and necklaces seem to be preferred and bracelets work good on either hand.

CRYSTAL - QUARTZ - *

While many of the Mineral Spirits grow in crystalline form it is the clear Crystal of the Quartz family that is being discussed here. As mentioned earlier I personally prefer to use the clear Quartz Crystal although they may be found in smoky or black color, or rutilated with threads of color, or even with some having water inside. I also prefer to use the natural Crystal formation instead of the ground and polished points often found in stores. I especially like working with the double terminated Crystals which have points on both ends and consider these to be especially good finds for healing use. I use the Crystals in amplifying energy in healing work and placement can indeed be anywhere. The Medicine of the Crystal is that of Clarity of Direction and enhancement of the Truth and Ideal. Crystal Medicine might also be that of Focus as well as Direction and those having Crystal in their name usually exhibit tunnel vision when directed toward a goal. The Crystal in the Medicine Wheel may be used anywhere but is always suitable in the North. The Crystal may also be worn about any part of the body, however, its application may irritate sensitive areas with prolonged use so use caution here as well. In a sense, Crystal can be said to have no conscience and I will oftentimes warn people about that. The Crystal will do exactly what you tell it to and is a true amplifier, so amplify good things.

DIAMOND - *

While the Diamond is beautiful to look at, they cost too much and have little positive Spiritual or healing value. The Diamond does make a nice birthstone however, but most circumstances about the Diamond support affairs of the Ego more than the Heart. The

Diamond is formed underground by great pressure, and indeed the Medicine of this stone is that of Pressure to Achieve. Unlike the clear Crystal providing Clarity of Direction, the Diamond is usually cut and polished to sparkle and this attraction becomes like the scattering ray of the Opal, very supportive to the Ego in the enhancement of need and greed. The Diamond Mineral Spirit like some others, has no conscience per say. So, is it any wonder that certain curses have been associated with the stone of Greed. The positive side to the Diamond, as all things have one, is that of lesson giving and these stones are good teachers in how not to be. I do not use or any longer have any of these stones. However, those wishing to, may use them in their Medicine bag to represent the Lesson. Diamonds may also be used in the South of the Medicine Wheel. As mentioned, Diamonds have little healing value and while they may be worn anywhere, I choose not to.

EMERALD - *

The Emerald may be found in various grades of clarity and refinement as well as color and should be included in every Medicine bag as the Medicine of the Emerald is that of Love, Trust, and Commitment. It may be used in any direction of the Medicine Wheel and likes to be around the Amethyst and Lapis Lazuli stones for obvious reasons. The Emerald has great energy for the heart center and is a good one to use for issues or problems in this area as it is a good stone to use for stabilization. Indeed stability is another dynamic of the Medicine of this most gracious Mineral Spirit that not only speaks of truth but constancy and the vision of everlasting. This quality makes the Emerald to be a much better choice over the Diamond as a symbol of the gift of Love. The Emerald softly amplifies the green vibration of Love and like the Citrine has great clarity of purpose. The Emerald as mentioned is a good stone to use in healing and can be applied effectively to any area above the abdomen for good effect, however the throat center for expression and heart center are the most common applications. In the process of naming people often a Mineral Spirit is given as representing the soul pattern of the individual and the Emerald was the one given me as to represent myself so I keep one in my Medicine bag for that purpose. The Emerald prefers a gold setting over silver and is a good one to wear on all parts of the body, again the left side for receiving and the right for transmitting.

FIRE AGATE - *

Because of its opalescent appearance Fire Agate has been Sometimes confused by some as being of the Opal family. This is actually a part of Fire Agate Medicine, which is that of Looking Within to find the Reality of Self Worth and Value. Found mostly in North America, Fire Agate may be found displaying the Orange, Brown, Golden, Blue, or Green Ray. Just like the Fluorite is the sister stone to the Dolphin, Fire Agate is the sister stone to the Fox. Of course in understanding its Medicine makes this parallelism of Medicine to be pretty obvious. While deception or stealth might be the first consideration, it is the Care and Wealth Within that is to me mostly considered in the Medicine of both the Fire Agate and the Fox. As one might imagine Fire Agate is another excellent Mineral Spirit for use in potions and teas, and the prayer should be that of Passion and quickness to the regaining of completeness and Well-being. Fire Agate is a particularly good stone for use in the South or West of the Medicine Wheel. In one's Medicine Bag, Fire Agate can be used to represent The Future or Wealth. In bodywork and healing, Fire Agate can be found useful in removing blocks anywhere. In adornment, Fire Agate works well about either side of the body and is especially beneficial about the hands and feet.

FLINT - *

Sometimes referenced by several different names, Flint is a member of the Quartz family that has been one of the Mineral Spirits that has been the mainstay as it were of Beings, since their first appearance here on Mother Earth. While its Medicine is seemingly as vast as is its utility, Support to Process might be the single most idea of it. A part of Flint Medicine can also be considered as Brotherhood in most every sense and way. Be it in the process of starting a fire, the procuring of food as a point of an arrow or spear, or the use of it in all kinds of tools, like axes, scrapers, and knives, Flint has always been a readily found Enabler, which perhaps is the very best idea of its Medicine. Actually, it is the relatively hard and even at times brittle nature of this Mineral Spirit that has facilitated its use in so many ways. One can easily recognize that like it sheds its outer most parts in flakes so easily, like releasing its Bark on tree of Ego, all can learn much from the Nature of this particular Mineral Spirit, in so many ways. Flint actually appears in many colors, yet the most common found is that of a grayish hue. I personally wear Flint often as arrowhead adornments which ever are about direction and path, as well as how to be in Life. Flint is always a good South stone in the Medicine Wheel as well as West, however because of its Essential Nature and thereby Medicine, it is always welcome and serves well in any direction. Flint for obvious reasons can be used in one's Medicine Bag, Jewelry, or Prayer Stick, to represent Direction, Path, or Goals. In healing applications and bodywork, Flint can provide positive support about the head, neck, feet, and lower back. In fact, any issues with the skeletal system at all, will find support to Remedy from Flint.

FLUORITE - *

The multidimensional Fluorite is a good enhancer of Perception and Awareness. Naturally appearing in color variations from clear, yellow, green, blue, to deep purple, I prefer to use the pale blue to purple varieties although any will do. This crystal is naturally formed in a double pyramid or what is called an octahedron shape that reminds me of the church of self. This is a good stone to use over the third eye area to stimulate breakthroughs in psychic awareness and provide for the enhancement of the Mind. Fluorite is kindred to the Water Spirit and has a great effect and consciousness associated to water, Dolphins, and Flow. The Medicine of the Fluorite is that of All-knowing and embracing Knowledge and Wisdom to the church of Self. The Medicine of the Fluorite is also that of Calming as this truly is what the benefit of knowing can bring. The Fluorite is a great balance stone over anxiety and provides greater focus and understanding. The Fluorite belongs in the North or East in the Medicine Wheel and while I use Amazonite in my Medicine bag to represent psychic awareness the Fluorite can also be used for this purpose. The Fluorite needs to be cleansed more often if continuously used and this is why I prefer the other. Cleanse the Fluorite in water and it prefers the soft light of the Moon over the sometimes harsher reality of the Sun for Renewall. Fluorite can be worn anywhere but areas about the head will receive the most benefit. I use Fluorite in healing mostly for its stimulating Medicine rather than to suck anything away and again in areas about the head.

GARNET - *

The Garnet is the Soul-Self or Seed of Self or Life stone and in the Medicine Wheel belongs in the South to represent the inner child and our continuous growth and position there during our Earthwalk. As our blood is Garnet red and Garnet grows in seed crystals, I prefer to use the Garnet over the Carnelian for Soul-Self representation or root center work although either or both may be used. The deep Red Ray of the crystalline Garnet is indeed a great initiator for any project of growth and is the most perfect starter stone for any one to work with or receive. As the Red Ray is about change, the Garnet is also a good one to use about all conditions of growth. The Medicine of the Garnet is that of Purity of Purpose and as in all conditions of Being, growth is the only inevitable condition, thereby the Garnet reminds us not only who we are as children of the Great Spirit Father but also of our purpose as to continuously grow as greater expressions of His Love in and of us. The Garnet in my Medicine represents the Soul-Self or inner child in the physical plane. The Garnet can be used in healing about the liver and spine for good effect as well as the heart and throat, and all areas of the back. The Garnet wears well on all parts of the body but sometimes earrings and rings of any nature are preferred.

HALITE - *

Halite is one of the softer Mineral Spirits that is oftentimes overlooked. Perhaps it is because of its Medicine, which is that of Adaptability and Ease in Change. This Nature of Halite certainly explains why it is so oftentimes found in a dyed condition and is often used in such a condition to simulate other more costly Mineral Spirits such as Turquoise. I have used the dyed forms of Halite in my personal jewelry and the representative Medicine of the dyed coloring has only the most positive of effect. And when one considers that not only will one be embracing the Medicine of that particular color but also that of Adaptability as well, it seems that this practice should be oftentimes expressed. Actually, I will often mix both dyed Halite with the "Real" stones that it is representative of, and both are complementary to each other. As one might imagine Halite is another excellent Mineral Spirit for use in potions and teas, and the Prayer should be that of ease and quickness to the regaining of completeness and Well-being. Halite is a particularly good stone for use in the South of the Medicine Wheel as well as that of the North. In the

Medicine Bag, Halite can be used to represent that which one desires to change or become.

HERKIMER DIAMONDS - *

The Herkimer Diamond is actually a Quartz crystal, and not a diamond at all. What makes the Herkimer diamond different than other quartz crystals is that they are double terminated, meaning that they developed points on both ends. In fact this development is so even and precise that it is often difficult to tell just where the ends are on these little "Gems". And what is even more extraordinary in their double termination in this manner is that not only are the faces of these stones pretty much the same all of the way around, but also there is great clarity throughout the stone. Also like diamonds, Herkimers can have a slight color tint found in some of them which deepens their radiance. I prefer the Herkimer over that of the diamond simply because there is so little Ego that is associated with it as compared to the diamond. The Medicine of the Herkimer Diamond is that of support to Balance, and Change of Attitude and Heart. These stones can be used in any direction of the Medicine Wheel and make excellent Center stones for obvious reasons. In one's Medicine bag, the Herkimer can be used to represent Truth and Balance, and it will always tell of the true Heart desires when used in divining.

JADE - *

While the Mineral Spirit of Jade is most often associated with the Orient and its thinking, as much of the carved forms originate there, the Medicine of this stone is that of Softness in Transition. The Medicine of this Mineral Spirit might also be expressed as the Constancy of Change, and helps to remind us to think of change in a peaceful way. I have found both the white and green variations of this Mineral Spirit most helpful in working with the heart and abdominal centers. While both have a great soothing ability, the white may also be used quite effectively in contemplation. The green Jade may be used in one's Medicine bag to represent fortune, love, or money, but should not be used for both at the same times for obvious reasons. Jade is always a good gift stone, and the green variety belongs in the South, Center, or East of the Medicine Wheel. Jade is best used for pendants and necklaces or in carvings, sometimes when worn as earrings or bracelets too much consciousness to money issues might be manifested so use caution here.

JASPER - *

Jasper is of limitless color variations and I have often found that some forms of this Mineral Spirit to have great pot stirring Medicine. While some forms of this stone indeed have a soothing and calming effect, most exhibit an instant call to action, there again much depends more upon the color that is used than the particular stone. The red variety exhibits no subtle call for change and definitely should not be used as a worry stone. Jasper might better be used for its grounding effect than energizing as it always brings to mind persistence and teaches us lessons in Patience and Resolve. The Medicine of the Jasper might also be expressed as that of Will. In healing, again the color used is most important and can effectively be used anywhere on the back and is especially effective to the Will center for obvious reasons but also to the throat center for enhancing the ability of expression. The Jasper should not however be used about any part of the head. Jasper can be used in the South of the Medicine Wheel and used in the Medicine bag to represent Will or consciousness although this is another stone that exhibits little conscience as it tries to stir the pot of life. The Jasper can be worn on some bracelets and rings for good effect but not again in areas about the head. It is best to use Jasper with another stone for better balance in its application and the Quartz is one that definitely should be avoided here.

KUNZITE - *

One of the Major power stones, Kunzite can be found to help the user to draw into action the focus of the Will. I prefer the purple to pink variation and have found it quite effective for use in enhancing kinetic energy in healing work. Being quite linear in structure one might well use the Field of Flow of the Kunzite to enhance the range of effect in hands on healing work. It is important to note here that because it is a power stone of great ability, the Kunzite may increase anxiety if worn for prolonged periods. This stone reminds me of a diehard battery and loves to be recharged in the sunshine. This stone should not be used with another power stone such as a Quartz crystal or a Tourmaline as there is already so much ability in it as it not only has good conscience but great heart. Indeed the Medicine of this stone is that of power but more important the Medicine is that of the power of the Heart of Self. The Kunzite in my Medicine bag represents power and the Kunzite should be used in the Center or lower North of the Medicine Wheel. Kunzite can be worn for short periods on any portion of the body for enhancement and may also be applied to any area of the body for healing, again for short durations as this is a very strong and dynamic stone.

LAPIS LAZULI - *

Lapis Lazuli is the stone that I call the Father Stone in that it represents the Great Spirit Creator in my Medicine bag. This stone belongs only in the North, where the Great Spirit lives, in the Medicine Wheel and if I were to have or carry but one stone it would be this one. In the Lapis Lazuli Mineral Spirit, the deep Blue Ray of the Father is embedded with flecks of gold representing His children, all of His creation, and our prayer. The Gold Ray reflects our connective tissue which is our prayer as well as our constant embodiment of Spirit in His creation and His providence, support and Love for us. If we were to blend the Blue Ray of the Father with the Gold Ray of our Prayer the result is that we will be enveloped in the Green Ray of His Love. Lapis Lazuli has been prized by many civilizations and cultures with even having peoples being found in the pyramids having holes bored in their skulls and this Mineral Spirit placed there for obvious healing purposes. The Medicine of the Lapis Lazuli is that of God Consciousness, the Source and perhaps even more significant if possible that truly All Can Be. The Lapis Lazuli is truly a left side receiving stone and wears well on hands, neck and about the head. In healing work it is the Lapis Lazuli stone that I wear as I indeed know the source from which all things come and pray to be a channel of His Light and Love especially in the healing way as it is His Will that I pray comes through me.

MALACHITE - *

Like the Jasper, the Malachite is also a great pot stirrer stone of great ability. Unlike the Jasper that just wants to change anything, the Malachite Mineral Spirit is a specialist. The Malachite has a deep and quickly felt energy about relationships and affairs of the heart that is most often very disruptive. Use this stone to effect a Change in Relationship as the discordant swirls in the most often Green Ray of this stone are felt by everyone, friend or foe. I keep this stone grounded in leather and take it out only occasionally for use in ceremonial work, cleanse and quickly return it. Those peoples wearing Malachite that I have noticed usually exhibit a great anxiousness about things. While the swirls of green in this beautiful stone have an almost hypnotic affect, the Spirit or intent of the user is truly the one to examine. Use this Mineral Spirit with great caution and grounded in leather. The Medicine of this stone is that of Constantly Searching and one can never get enough. I Want More is its constant prayer, and its song is Always Looking for Love. The Medicine of the Malachite might also be expressed as Denial or that All will Never Be Enough. The Malachite has a lot of Coyote Medicine in that it likes to wear false faces and is a great trickster. However, it also is a great teacher in that it can in time help us see past the illusion that our Ego uses to keep us in Fear or discord. The Malachite might be used in a Medicine bag to represent the Ego, but I will not carry one in mine. The Malachite may also be used in the South, Center, or East in the Medicine Wheel, but I will not do that either, but that is just me. I use no Malachite in healing, but temporary placements may be effective for some about the back and heart center. Malachite is a good right hand stone in adornment for those that wish to stir a pot of sorts, but I sure would not recommend that as this stone is all Ego and no conscience. Malachite cares not at all who might get hurt. However, lessons will be learned though as it is all perfect you see. Give a Malachite to someone you no longer wish to see, and for sure never to a friend you wish to keep. Malachite is a powerful teaching stone, especially about willfulness and lessons in Love. As one by now might well imagine, Malachite is a personal favorite for Witches and those operating in the way of self-service and Witchcraft. However, Great Pop made no bad thing at all, only people tend to use things in bad ways at times. Needless to say, I always caution people about this most intriguing at times Mineral Spirit, that is called Malachite!

MICA – *

While Mica might seem like a not especially precious Mineral Spirit like that of a Ruby or Emerald, it is very special and deserves one's respect and consideration in every sense and way. Mica is very commonly found in nature and it oftentimes is what gives the many sparkles that one will see in other types of stones. The primary Medicine of Mica is that of Share and Support, and hence one can perhaps easily realize why it is so commonly found. Mica also has a Medicine of Utility and associates often to one's lens of Perspective because of this aspect of it. Perhaps this association to Perspective is why Mica was often used for making windows in houses and so forth long before the more recent appearance of glass. The thin, flat, sheets of Mica are often found in what some call books, and these are evident of not only its linear and flat like quality, but also of its being associative in every sense. Rubies are often found inside these "Books" of Mica and is it any wonder, considering its Medicine? Mica can have good effect in healing work when used about the eyes and head. However, it should not be applied anywhere about the throat, heart, or digestive tract for obvious reasons. Mica can be used in the North as well as East of the Medicine Wheel. Also, Mica can be used to represent one's associations or the Future in one's Medicine bag.

MOONSTONE - *

If you think I may be a little harsh about my Malachite Mineral Spirit Brother, wait until I get through with this one. Another power stone, Moonstone has a great ability of amplifying both our highs and lows in emotions to great extremes. If you feel good, wearing this stone will often make you feel even better, however if you are feeling the least bit down, wearing this one will soon show you the deepest bottom. Operating much like its namesake Mother Moon upon the waters of the physical on Earth, Moonstone operates upon the water of our emotional Being. While the Crystal is a great physical amplifier, the Moonstone is a great emotional amplifier and exhibits little conscience in the process. Moonstone operates well in the physical realm as well and on occasion I have experienced such energy transmitted from these stones upon picking them up that sparks flew about for all to see and on one occasion the stone flew across the room from a simple touch. While Kunzite is like a diehard battery, Moonstone is like a nuclear reactor in its potential. Use extreme caution in the use of this stone as all color variations are extremely powerful and the clearer the stone the more direct it is. Cleanse and ground this stone in water. The Medicine of Moonstone is that of the unlimited ability of the Mind of Self and like all amplifiers it can only increase what it receives as input so put good thoughts there. I used to use Moonstone in my Medicine bag to represent power but I prefer Kunzite there and Moonstone is a great stone to use in the North, Center, and South of the Medicine wheel. I do not use Moonstone in healing work, however it is given to mention that it has great ability about release work and may be applied about the head and throat but never the heart. Moonstone is often seen on rings however I am given to express caution about wearing on ears or as necklaces as its influence can be counterproductive about the Mind or adrenals.

MOSS AGATE - *

Moss Agate can actually be found in a variety of colors, however the most frequent form is that of the Green Ray. Getting its name from the veins of color that seem like a multidimensional web of sorts within the clearer part of this composition stone, Moss Agate has great Balancing Medicine. Indeed Balance of Perspective is the very Medicine of Moss Agate, and it has been oftentimes found in my pocket in times of stress. I carry Moss Agate at times of stress as I have found that it is a very helpful Mineral Spirit partner that constantly helps me see the many sides to a situation. In bodywork applications Moss Agate has a slow drawing and soothing effect that can support the activity of the more causative stones to certain areas like Amethyst and Tourmaline. Moss Agate is a predominately North stone in the Medicine Wheel, and can be used in one's Medicine Bag to represent one's True Values and Cares.

OBSIDIAN - APACHE TEAR - *

Obsidian or volcanic glass comes in a variety of shapes and grades of clarity with one variation having white splotches or snowflakes. As one of the two stones that I use in the Medicine Wheel in the West, the Obsidian in the Apache Tear form does indeed represent the Way of the West or the looking inside place. Obsidian is a very good Mineral Spirit to use for Contemplation and Introspection and has great ability in absorbing negative energy and transforming it into clarity of thought. The aboriginal peoples used this wonderful stone to make knives, spear points, and arrowheads and it can help all in cutting through to the truth. Do not let its color fool you as the Spirit of the Obsidian is warmth, truth, and Love and the Apache Tear is an excellent protection stone. The Apache tear in my Medicine bag represents the Way or the Path and is the direction finder for growth as well as that which is sought or is to come. The Medicine of this Mineral Spirit is that of Peace in knowing the path or what it is right to do and thereby Clarity of Vision. Use this wonderful Mineral Spirit Brother in all Vision Quests and meditations. In healing work the Obsidian or Apache Tear has good transforming qualities and is good for release work of pain or anxiety and is most often used about the head although any area will benefit from its application. The Obsidian prefers right side use but is happily worn anywhere upon the body as it best represents the path of the Spirit of one, you see.

ONYX - *

Although this Mineral Spirit is short to spell, there is no shortness in ability as the Onyx is a great shock absorber stone with very good sucking ability. This stone in its soft dull color most often found in black or chalky white, is a good receiver but none equals the ability of the Rose Quartz. Onyx is actually much better at balancing and soothing the emotional body than the body physical. While I prefer the black variation for use, is it little surprise that this stone would often be selected for use in its black and white colors in chess sets where a great Patience and Clarity of thought is required. This Mineral Spirit is good for Contemplation and has soft energy but has very good memory as well. Onyx is one of the best heat retaining stones when working with kinetic energy and while it can be used alternatively with Rose Quartz in healing any affected area of the body, Onyx has a longer time requirement between subsequent uses due to its slower release and Renewall ability which in some conditions might well be preferred. The Medicine of the Onyx is that of Emotional Stability in the Sea of Change of Life. Onyx is the very best of grounding stones and its message is that of Constancy or perhaps better put, I Am Here. The Onyx can be used in Medicine bags to represent passion or thoughtfulness and the Onyx can be used in the North, Center, and East of the Medicine Wheel. The Onyx loves to be worn any where about the body and earrings might be found to be the most productive place. Onyx is very good for statues and totems and any gift of Onyx means that you care. Onyx also likes to operate in pyramid and spherical shapes and whatever shape this Mineral Spirit is in is a good one to have around.

OPAL - *

Another stone to use with extreme caution, the brittle Opal appears in many variations of color and shape. Unlike the pot stirring Medicine of some of those already discussed, this beautiful Mineral Spirit has an extreme power of creating discord. Just as its brittle substance fractures easily, the Opal has a great scattering and disruptive energy that dimensionally enhances Fear, nervousness, and anxiety. It is very hard to focus or stay on track in the presence of this Mineral Spirit no matter as to who is wearing it. I was given to learn the ability of this stone one day, and after procuring one it was less than four hours later that I returned it to Mother Earth as its scattering ability was much more disruptive than I cared to deal with. The grounding medium for this stone is Mother Earth and it will stimulate the growth of any plant and for obvious reasons do not be surprised as to any unusual shapes they might take. The Medicine of the Opal is that of Learning and Change but more about that of look at me while ever changing shape. Of great beauty, its Fire of Change and disruptive nature can be put to good use from time to time but the Opal should not be worn for long periods about the head, neck, or heart centers. The Opal might be a good stone to give a politician I think as it might wake some of them up! The Opal is best used in rings about the finger and is best used upon the right hand in helping in the manifesting process and actualization of change. The Medicine of the Opal is also that of great Passion and reflects the Fire of Life which is indeed Perpetual Growth through Change. The Opal may be used in the North, South, and East of the Medicine Wheel but never should it be used in the Center or the West. The Opal in any Medicine bag represents Growth but can also reflect Ego and Fear, I do not use one in mine as I think too much of the other Mineral Spirits that are there and do not especially appreciate its lack of conscience in the way it likes to cause discord. I do not use this stone in any healing work.

PEARL - *

The jewel of the sea, Pearls have for a long time represented Wealth, Abundance, and richness and especially that of the sea. As the Garnet represents the Seed of Life or the Soul-Self, Pearl reminds us of the purity of Spirit and the beauty within. Pearls and Garnets go extremely well together on any adornment and can be worn anywhere with an almost magical effect. A great gift stone, the Medicine of the Pearl is that of Abundance, Well-being, Purity and Beauty and indeed might best be represented by the word perfection. Just as crystals grow in the embrace of Mother Earth giving them their great ability of focus and a sense of purpose, Pearls also grow as a union of Mineral and Animal Spirit in the sea of life. Representing Purity, Patience, and timelessness is it any wonder that they refer to truths as being Pearls of Wisdom? The Pearl is a good stone for the North, Center, and especially the South in the Medicine Wheel and may be used to represent Abundance and Spirit in any Medicine bag. Pearl may be used in the making of potions and teas in the healing way and may also be applied to the heart and head centers with good effect in renewing calmness and peace to one of anxiety and stress. While the Opal is of discord and a lack of conscience, the Pearl is just the opposite and may be used for periods of time to balance the energy of the Opal in adornment however I recommend leaving the Opal alone and be very happy with the Medicine of the Pearl.

PERIDOT - *

The Peridot is another Mineral Spirit that represents Love as it combines the Green Ray of Love with the Yellow or calling forth Ray in a beautiful shade of green with great clarity in its crystalline form. The Peridot is another stone that should be included in every Medicine Wheel and Bag. The Medicine of this beautiful Mineral Spirit is that of the calmness that comes in the receiving and awareness of the Love of the Great Spirit Creator. The Peridot in my Medicine bag represents Love and the Peridot is a good stone to use anywhere in the Medicine Wheel for obvious reasons as Love is something that we can never receive or give too much of. More specifically the Medicine of the Peridot might best be stated as the bringing forth of Love and the Peridot has a great calming and soothing ability in the healing way. The Peridot and Garnet also like to work together and in healing the Peridot likes to be used around the heart and head centers. I usually use the Peridot in the East, Center, and South in the Wheel but as mentioned it works well anywhere. The Peridot has also a great magnetic quality that comes from its Gold Ray and is an excellent choice for earrings, necklaces, pendants, and rings and prefers gold but works well with silver and can be worn on all parts of the body. Although the Peridot is not as popular as some of the pricey gemstones, I often prefer the Peridot for its easy listening and soothing quality that is surpassed by none. The Peridot is another excellent Mineral Spirit that can be used in the making of potions and teas for its obvious Medicine of the gift of Love.

PIPESTONE - *

Pipestone is a very soft and absorptive Mineral Spirit that can be found in several colors and hues. It can be easily carved into many shapes and hence has great utility to indigenous peoples. While most often it is seen used by Native Americans for whom it is Sacred and most valued and is often seen in its Red form as the material of the bowls of their pipes, it can be other colors as well such as grey and black. Pipestone has a Medicine of Flow and Drawing Forth and parallels that of the Waterfall, which is that of bringing forth the Creator's idea, message, or resource to Mother Earth. Pipestone is as absorptive as it is soft and hence has good sucking and calming Medicine as well.

PYRITE - *

Pyrite is a hard mineralized crystal that varies in color from bright gold to shades of copper and green. Because of its shiny appearance in natural form, Pyrite is often called "Fools Gold". Like all crystals Pyrite also supports Growth and can be considered to be the Mineral Spirit compliment to the Coyote for obvious reasons. In nature, Pyrite can be found as crystal clusters as well as embedded within other mineral formations. Pyrite is most oftentimes the source of the flakes of gold in many of the more common gemstones such as aventurine. It is this Medicine of "Share and Support" that can best describe the Nature and Medicine of this wonderful Mineral Spirit Brother as well as that of Brotherhood itself. Pyrite can be used in any direction of the Medicine Wheel, with most common applications to be that of the East and South. In one's Medicine bag, Pyrite can be used to represent money or that which is sought. In potions and teas, the prayer for Pyrite's support should be that of bringing forth betterment. Pyrite has positive use about the head for vision, and the heart center for Hope in bodywork applications.

RHODOCHROSITE - *

The Mother - Child stone, Rhodochrosite has a great ability in the reinforcing of the Yin or Female energies of people. As in the saying that man is of air and woman is of earth, this is a great enabler stone that helps us to integrate the white of our male and Spiritual Being with the pink of our female and Physical Being. This Mineral Spirit shares this understanding with the ideal of growth in its pink and white layers, which represent integration of the two bodies of Self and our path of the steps or layers of growth. Rhodochrosite is another great gift stone as its Medicine is that of not only Integrating the Male and Female parts of Self but Rhodochrosite has a great strength in the cementing together of relationships of all sorts. The Medicine of this beautiful Mineral Spirit might singularly best be expressed as Union. Rhodochrosite is also a great contemplation stone and its smoothing energy is easily felt. Rhodochrosite is a good stone to use in the South, West, and East of the Medicine Wheel and should be also included in the Medicine bag to represent Female or all relationships. Rhodochrosite is another good stone in the preparation of potions and teas in healing and will be greatly enhanced by the presence of an Amethyst when applied this way. The Rhodochrosite likes to be worn about the heart, throat, and head and if used on rings or bracelets it prefers the left side in adornment. In hands on healing work the Rhodochrosite can be used on all parts of the body but is particularly effective to the abdomen and especially the adrenals.

RHODONITE - *

Oftentimes confused with Rhodochrosite in appearance, Rhodonite is quite different in its nature and Medicine, which is that of Freedom and Self-support or sufficiency. This Essential nature makes Rhodonite an excellent Mineral Spirit to use for centering or what some call grounding, especially after clearing work. Also, this Medicine and nature makes Rhodonite an excellent Mineral Spirit for use in potions and teas, and the prayer should be that of support to the regaining of completeness and Well-being. Rhodonite has been used in the ground-up form for treatments of emphysema at times, and clearly one can see why such use might prove successful. And one might suspect, this is a particularly good stone for use in the South of the Medicine Wheel as well as that of the West. In the Medicine Bag, Rhodonite can be used to represent the Self as well as the Potential of Self.

ROSE QUARTZ - *

As might be already felt, I REALLY like this one. As previously mentioned I call the Rose Quartz the Healing Stone and that is what it also represents in my Medicine Bag. The Medicine of this Mineral Spirit is that of Healing and it has great sucking Medicine as well as that of Renewall. The Medicine of this beautiful stone is also that of Passion and Compassion and has extremely great sensitivity and balance. The Rose Quartz is the stone of choice to be applied in all healing situations and more will be given about some of these techniques in another area of this book. The soft Pink Ray of this Mineral Spirit draws upon Love from the universe and functions freely with great energy and yet with great softness and care. In any healing situation, ask a Rose Quartz and it knows exactly what to do. This beautiful Mineral Spirit likes to be regularly cleansed in salt water and loves to spend time in the light of the sun and moon. Use the Rose Quartz in all potions and teas and its application should include its Brother, the Amethyst, for best results. The Rose Quartz likes to be worn anywhere upon the body. The Rose Quartz likes to work in the East, South, and Center of the Medicine Wheel for me however it is one that I would recommend for use anywhere.

RUBY - *

I call the Ruby in my Medicine Bag the Butterfly stone or the Stone of Change and indeed the Ruby is a must for all Medicine Bags and in the Medicine Wheel the Ruby belongs in the West and calls in a great energy for change. Indeed the Medicine of the Ruby is that of Change or Transformation but more important is that the Ruby embraces a great conscience as well and thereby supports not only change but more significant, a change for the better hence the metamorphosis. Just as the caterpillar that used to eat the plant goes through metamorphosis in the time of the cocoon to become the butterfly that helps all plants grow, Ruby brings forth the resurrection memory in the Christ consciousness in man. As all are constantly in the process of growth and that growth can only be manifested through the Force of Change, Ruby has great Medicine in helping us to establish our growth in the most meaningful of ways. Just as the flame can only change the form of something, as nothing is either created or destroyed except by the Creator, Ruby helps us to consciously change the form of our Spiritual Self always for the betterment of all aspects of Self and thereby each other. In healing work the Ruby is very effective in working with the heart, head, neck and extremities and loves right side applications although any place is good to adorn with the butterfly stone that is the Ruby. As might be imagined the Ruby also likes to work with the Amethyst, but then again most all do.

SAPPHIRE - *

Operating in the Blue Ray the Sapphire has a consciousness to Enabling and Will. The message deep within the Blue Ray of this stone is consciousness to the Creator and the channel of the creative force in Self. While in the Star Sapphire form of this Mineral Spirit a focus to the center of Self might be expressed, it is important to displace the Ego in this process. A great warmth and sense of Well-being can be felt by the application of all variations of this stone but make sure it is not in an egocentric way as lesson will indeed be manifested about that. Caution is thereby expressed in the use of this

Mineral Spirit as the Will center is easily manipulated by the energy of it. This stone should not be used about the heart or neck area as it may cause constrictions. The stone might best be worn for short periods about the extremities and the right side is given as the best. The Sapphire is one that I do not use in my Medicine Bag or Wheel for obvious reasons, however if chosen for use, the South position only in the Medicine Wheel is recommended. The Sapphire should be cleansed and grounded in the sun between each use as to help it remember the Source. If used for any reason in a Medicine bag it might be used to signify the Goal or Purpose. The Medicine of the Sapphire is that of the power of the Will, and the prayer before use might be - 'Father, thy Will be done through me, not that of the Ego of me, but through the Heart of me.'

SODALITE - *

In stores and such settings, Sodalite can be and is oftentimes mistaken for Lapis Lazuli in its appearance. However, Sodalite lacks the golden specks that are commonly found in the "Great Pop Stone". Also embodying the deep Blue Ray of the Creator as well as the White of Spirit, the Medicine of Sodalite is that of Hope and Limitless Potential. Certainly this is a good stone to have and use when feeling down or in need of Perspective, and it is the element of Perspective that Sodalite most easily and quickly affects in use. Like Lapis, Sodalite is one of the softer Mineral Spirits, meaning that it polishes easily as well as is relatively easy to fashion. This softness is translated into Adaptability, which is another aspect of the Medicine of this wonderful Mineral Spirit. Sodalite is an excellent stone for use in the East and South of the Medicine Wheel. In my Medicine bag the Sodalite represents one's Hope and Endeavor. In potions and teas, Sodalite has great balancing energy and should be used when anxiousness or stress are parts of the symptoms to be dealt with. In bodywork, Sodalite can have positive effect upon any part that needs release of tension, and is particularly effective about the head, neck, and chest. Sodalite wears well in jewelry and adornments and should be predominantly used in the upper regions and right side of the body because the right is manifesting, while the left is receiving.

TIGERS EYE - *

Found in variations of color from golden yellow, red, and blue, the Tigers or Cats Eye Mineral Spirit is a great balancing stone. The Medicine of the Tigers Eye carries all Cat Spirit qualities of Balance, Vision, and Sensitivity. The Medicine of the Cat includes Curiosity that is missing from this stone as it seems to mention the truth that all knowledge lies within Self but you have to look past the Ego layer of Self to see it. You will always land on your feet with this Mineral Spirit stone and the Tigers Eye is always a good gift stone especially to one that is seeking clarity. Tigers Eye is a good stone for the East and Center of the Medicine Wheel and in any Medicine Bag the Tigers Eye or any representative of the Cat is about Balance and Vision. Tigers Eye is very applicable for use in the preparation of potions and teas in the healing way and may be used about the stomach and adrenals in hands on work. The Tigers Eye loves to be worn on rings but is very beneficial in adornments about the neck and becomes very good at helping with issues of expression. Earrings of the Tigers Eye will also effectively support hearing and vision and there is truly no part of the body that will not benefit from the Medicine of this beautiful and enchanting stone.

TOPAZ - *

If a Lapis Lazuli is not at hand, the Topaz is my next favorite stone to represent the Great Spirit Father. Having many color variations, the message of this stone is an ever clear sense of Purpose and Being as a child of the Creator. The Medicine of the Topaz is that of the Source and in my Medicine Bag I use a Blue colored one to represent Wealth. As indeed all is from the Father Creator, the Source, All can Be if we only allow it to ourselves. The Medicine of the Topaz might also be stated as our channel or telephone to the Creator and will enhance the creative force in everyone. Topaz also heightens our listening ability and like Fluorite may be used to heighten our psychic awareness as well. The application of this stone is very effective for enhancing a sense of Well-being and in all applications I prefer to use those stones of the greatest clarity. Topaz is good to use in healing potions and teas and works very well in applications about the head in hands on work. Any color of Topaz is a good Mineral Spirit for use in the North of the Medicine Wheel to represent The Source or Creator, and it is very good in the South as well to represent our Resource, as indeed all comes from Him. The Topaz reminds us of our Wealth Within as well as that we are in constant connection to Him as His children so for obvious reasons is another good gift stone. Topaz wears well in adornments anywhere about the body as it constantly reminds us of who we are.

TOURMALINE - *

The great power stone, Tourmaline is the Mineral Spirit that I call The Stone of Magic in my Medicine Bag. Tourmaline can be found in many color variations from clear, pink, yellow, blue, green, and black and I like them all but seem to be drawn to the one referred as the watermelon. The Plant Spirit known as the Oak or the Tree of Magic works well with the Tourmaline. Some stones may be used as receivers in conjunction with Tourmaline and I will caution against using quartz crystals as one of them but as Tourmaline is of a great linear structure it seems to work best alone. In healing work I mostly use the Tourmaline alone, however it functions well with willow or moss in sucking Medicine applications. Tourmaline has very high receiving and transmitting ability and is more effective than the Quartz Crystal when used this way. It surpasses the Quartz in conductivity and amplification as well. Tourmaline should be used with caution and deserves the highest respect and I Do Not Recommend using Quartz and Tourmaline together, as their combined power potential is that of the Sun! The Tourmaline has a great conscience and softness so is able to operate with great ease at the softer levels as well as in the extremist of the highs and lows. The Medicine of this wonderful stone is indeed that of Magic, as we realize the magic in that truly our prayers are always not only heard but answered as well. Tourmaline works well in any position of the Medicine Wheel and can augment the Medicine of any direction, therefore I personally pay much attention to color in the application of the Tourmaline here. I use the Tourmaline Mineral Spirit as the transmitting and receiving Crystal in the end of my prayer stick, and it is present in or on all of my rattles and it dynamically increases the ability of these prayer tools. The Tourmaline is very good to use in the preparation of potions and teas for obvious reasons, and works well in hands on work, especially about any area of the back. Tourmaline wears well on all parts of the body, but applications about the head and heart should be restricted to short periods, as this is the most powerful of the Mineral Spirits and always has an effect.

TURQUOISE - *

The Turquoise is the Mineral Spirit that I often refer to as the stone of Wealth and the Way of the West or the looking inside place. As indeed if we look inside the Heart of Self, we will find our greatest Wealth there as children of a great and loving Father Creator Great Spirit. The Turquoise also represents the direction that we are continuously seeking on Earthplane in our search of the Fathers Love within, which is represented by the Yellow Ray being combined with the Green and Deep Blue in this softly comforting stone. The Turquoise belongs in the West with the Apache Tear in the Medicine Wheel and represents the Path or Direction of Growth in my Medicine Bag, and no bag should be without this stone as it truly represents the Medicine Way. Turquoise is very effective in potions and teas and may be used about the head and heart in hands on work. The Medicine of the Turquoise is that of the Peace that comes from Knowing the Way, and the Turquoise wears well on all parts of the body.

ADDITIONAL STONES

COPPER - *

The Medicine of Copper is that of Support to Flow and Transference. One might wonder as to why it would be considered to be included here with Mineral Spirits, that is until one remembers that like Gold and Silver, it is a natural mineral form. Copper is also one of the essential minerals that all Beings, animals and plants need to some degree in their physical form to function. So in that sense, one can see how important its Medicine is in the Support of Well-being and Life that could also be considered as the Medicine of Copper. Copper is found in natural formations as well as mixed in smaller amounts of other Mineral Spirits that some call ore. I personally use this wonderful supporting Mineral Spirit in all of my jewelry and much prefer it to that of Silver. I also use it in the making of any Medicine items such as Prayersticks and rattles. Where ever there is a need to support a Union, that is where one will find Copper to be most welcome by all of the elements and Spirits involved. I personally recommend Copper Bracelets to be worn on the left wrist for all health care practitioners as it will reduce the amount of stuff that one will pick up from touching others, yet still not disable one's ability in sensing things. Copper in support to healing is best used in the throat center but is applicable and will support one's efforts anywhere about the body. Copper will also work well with other healing stones and it likes the Amethyst and Rose Quartz the best, just ask it and it will tell you so! Copper is a South oriented Mineral Spirit and therefore is most welcome in that direction as well as Center of any Medicine Wheel. Nuggets of Copper can also be used to represent That which is Coming in a Medicine Bag or for divining purposes. Caution should be taken in using Copper with other elements in potions and teas as it can and will potentially develop toxic effects from use with certain Plant Spirits.

BONE OR IVORY - *

Bone and Ivory have great Memory Medicine and help us to remember how fragile life on the Earthplane is, as well as the structure and foundation of the many dimensions of Self. Bone also may be used to reinforce one's connectiveness to the Spirit plane and has for a long time been used in the calling of Spirits from that place. Ivory has great Memory and can be used to go back in the fabric of time in Vision work and also represents the preciousness of time and place. Ivory can be used in the healing way to aid in calming nervousness and the Bone can be used to enhance Strength. Both Bone and Ivory make good material for use in fetishes and totems for obvious reasons as they remind us of the integration of Mineral Spirit and Spirit in this place called Earthplane. Use in the Medicine Wheel of Bone and Ivory should be in the South and Center and they make good additions to any Medicine Bag representing Power Animals and Memory. Bone and Ivory make good adornments to any part of the body and in the healing way they are most effective for use about the head and spine.

IRON - *

The Medicine of Iron is that of Renewall and Change. One might wonder as to why it would be considered to be included here with Mineral Spirits, that is until one remembers that like Gold and Silver, it is a natural mineral form. Iron is another one of the essential minerals that all Beings, animals and plants need to some degree in their physical form to function. Iron resonates to Will in all Beings and things. So in that sense, one can see how important its Medicine is in The Support of Renewall and Life that could also be considered as being the Medicine of Iron. Iron is found in natural formations as well as mixed in smaller amounts of other Mineral Spirits that some call ore. Wherever there is a need to support Renewall and Life, that is where one will find Iron to be most welcome by all of the elements and Spirits involved. In support to healing, Iron is best used in the heart center, but is applicable and will support one's efforts anywhere about the body. Iron works well with other healing stones and just like Copper it likes the Amethyst and Rose Quartz the best, just ask it and it will tell you so! Iron is a South or West oriented Mineral Spirit and therefore is most welcome in those directions as well as Center of any Medicine Wheel. Nuggets of Iron can also be used to represent one's Desire or Path in a Medicine Bag or for divining purposes. Caution should be taken in using Iron with other elements in potions and teas as it can and will potentially develop toxic effects from use with certain Plant Spirits.

PETRIFIED WOOD - *

Petrified Wood is perhaps the very best grounding stone as it combines both the Spirit of the Plant and Mineral kingdoms. Petrified wood should be used in the South or West of the Medicine Wheel and in Medicine Bags represents Perpetuity of Pattern and Plan as we are ever in a continuum of growth. In the singular word Growth is the Medicine of Petrified Wood. However, it also embraces and represents Renewall as well. The plant Spirit that grew from and was nourished by Mother Earth is now immortalized by her in mineral form. Petrified wood is best in rings, bracelets, and necklaces in adornment and works well in potions and teas in the healing way by adding support to the structure of growth and Renewall.

SALT - *

It took me 30+ years to realize I had omitted what I probably the most common Mineral Spirit that we encounter is some form each & every day of our Lives. Yep, I overlooked SALT! The Medicine of Salt is Embracing and Balancing. The human body can't live without some sodium (Salt). It's needed to transmit nerve impulses, contract and relax muscle fibers (including those in the heart and blood vessels), and maintain a proper fluid balance. Salt plays an important role in most all of my different ceremonies from clearing to healing and witchcraft problem resolution. Salt as well as tobacco may be used in any Medicine Wheel in The Medicine Way.

TEETH - *

Teeth whether fossilized or in natural state have great Protection Medicine and the ability of the Medicine provided by the host animal form. In my Medicine Bag, I have a Sharks tooth that provides Protection and Resource. I also carry a Wolf's tooth that provides support to Earth Wisdom, Family and Protection. Teeth in the Medicine Wheel can be used anywhere, and all parts of the body will be embraced and enhanced by their adornment. Fossilized teeth may be the best for use in healing potions and teas, but any will provide a benefit.

COLOR / RAY MEDICINE

As all Mineral Spirits operate in a radiance of vibration and can be found in different vibrations of color it is given to mention the Medicines of the rays of color here.

Ray	Resonance	Significance
AMBER	ABSORPTION / EMBRACING	PROTECTION
AQUA	UNION / FULFILLMENT	FREEDOM
AUBURN	YIELDING / FLOW	TRANSFERENCE
BEIGE	BALANCE IN GROWTH	WEALTH OF SPIRIT
BLACK	GROWTH / FOCUS	DIRECTION
BLUE	PEACE / FULLNESS	LIMITLESSNESS OF GOD
BRONZE	SUPPORT / CO-OPERATION	UTILITY
BROWN	ABUNDANCE / RICHNESS	FERTILITY
BURGUNDY	CAUSE / REINFORCE	AWARENESS
BUTTERSCOTCH	PURPOSE / COMPLETION	EXPANSION
CANARY	HOPE / ACTUALIZATION	POTENTIAL
CHARCOAL	INNER KNOWING / SUPPLY	DIRECTION WITHIN
CRIMSON	FLOW / CARE	CHANGE
EMERALD	COMMITMENT / HONOR	LOYALTY
GOLD	CALLING / RECEIVING	PRAYER
GRAPE	RELEASE / RENEWALL	REJOICE
GRAY	DEPTH / CONTEMPLATION	UNCERTAINTY / SEEKING
GREEN	SATISFACTION / JOY	LOVE / BALANCE

Ray	Resonance	Significance
ICE BLUE	FREEDOM / LIMITLESSNESS	BIRTH
INDIGO	FLOW / HOPE	INITIATION
IVORY	MEMORY / SUPPORT	RECEIVERSHIP
LAVENDER	LUCK / TRANSFORMATION	GOOD FORTUNE
LILAC	COMFORT / BALANCE	SMOOTHING
LIME GREEN	VOICE / PASSION	FULFILLMENT
MAROON	UNION / INTEGRATION	CAPABILITY
OLIVE	SUPPORT / GROWTH	EXPRESSION
ORANGE	PASSION / EMOTION	WILL
PEACH	CARETAKING / NURTURING	FRUITION
PINK	SENSITIVITY / HARMONY	PHYSICAL
PLUM	RENEWALL / WEALTH	FULFILLMENT
RED	CHANGE / METAMORPHOSIS	PASSION
ROSE	PHYSICAL / SUPPORT	EMBRACING
ROOTBEER	FERTILITY / SUPPLY	OPPORTUNITY
ROYAL BLUE	POTENTIAL / FULFILLMENT	REALIZATION
RUST	MOVEMENT / EMBRACING	TRANSITION
SIENNA	CONSOLIDATION / RENEWALL	CYCLE
SILVER	STEADFASTNESS / EGO	REFLECTION
SKY BLUE	OPENNESS / RESONANCE	ORDINATION
TAN	CAPABILITY / PARTICIPATION	ABILITY
TEAL	OPENNESS / SHARE	LIMITLESS ABUNDANCE
TURQUOISE	WEALTH / WHOLENESS	THE WAY OF MEDICINE & OF SPIRIT

COLOR / RAY MEDICINE - Contd.

Ray	Resonance	Significance
UMBER - BNT	RICHNESS / SUCCESS	ABILITY
UMBER - RAW	POSSIBILITY / ENJOINING	POTENTIAL
VERMILLION	PERSISTENCE / FAITH	CARE
VIOLET	HARMONY / HOPE	CHRIST CONSCIOUSNESS
WHITE	INNOCENSE / TRUTH	SPIRIT
YELLOW	STRENGTH / MAGNETIZING	DESIRE / STIMULATION

****

METAL MEDICINE

Metal	Resonance
GOLD	SECURITY / STABILITY
SILVER	STEADFASTNESS / STRENGTH
COPPER	FLOW / TRANSFERENCE
IRON	RENEWALL / CHANGE
PLATINUM	COURAGE / INNER WEALTH

ELEMENTAL MEDICINE

Element	Resonance
AIR	SUPPORT / EXPRESSION
EARTH	SUPPORT / FERTILITY / PHYSICAL
FIRE	PASSION / CHANGE
WATER	LIFE, FLOW / MOVEMENT
MOUNTAIN	STEADFASTNESS / INNER WEALTH / STRENGTH OF SPIRIT
FOREST	COMMUNITY / SUPPORT
OCEAN	EMBRACING / FULFILLMENT
WIND	SUPPORT / CHANGE
RIVER / STREAM	FLOW / BRINGING FORTH
SNOW	FLOW / RENEWALL / SPIRIT
ICE	FLOW / ONEMENT
RAINBOW	HOPE & HARMONY
STAR	MULTIPLICITY – THAT IS WHY THERE IS SO MANY
SUN	INITIATION / ILLUMINATION / SUPPORT
MOON	REFLECTION / CYCLES
LIGHT	SHARE / ILLUMINATION
LAKE	CONNECTIVITY / SUPPORT

****

STONES BY FUNCTION

The Mineral Spirits listed below are positioned somewhat but not specifically by their relative ability with the strongest being the first in placement as found by my use. It is important to add that any Mineral Spirit may be used for any purpose at any instant and those listed here are not to be considered to be restricted to that. The primary consideration should be as previously described in the discussion about the Medicine of each stone, and remember that truly All Can Be.

ENERGIZING

Primary	*Secondary*	
TOURMALINE	MOONSTONE	OPAL
AMETHYST	CHALCEDONY	MALACHITE
KUNZITE	RUBY	GARNET
QUARTZ CRYSTAL	SAPPHIRE	FLUORITE
ROSE QUARTZ	TOPAZ	CITRINE

INITIATING

Primary	Secondary
TOURMALINE	SAPPHIRE
KUNZITE	RUBY
EMERALD	PEARL
OPAL	MALACHITE
CHALCEDONY	GARNET
MOONSTONE	BLOODSTONE
AVENTURINE	DIAMOND

CALMING

Primary	Secondary
PERIDOT	PEARL
CALCITE	AMETHYST
AQUAMARINE	TURQUOISE
LAPIS LAZULI	RHODOCHROSITE
FLUORITE	JADE
OBSIDIAN	ONYX
TIGERS EYE	CORAL
ABALONE	AGATE

HEALING

Primary	Secondary
AMETHYST	EMERALD
ROSE QUARTZ	RUBY
AMBER	KUNZITE
QUARTZ CRYSTAL	GARNET
TOURMALINE	LAPIS LAZULI
ONYX	OBSIDIAN
CORAL	FLUORITE

PROTECTION

Primary	Secondary
LAPIS LAZULI	GARNET
AMBER	IVORY
ANY TOOTH	BLOODSTONE
ANY BONE	ONYX
AQUAMARINE	JADE
EMERALD	TIGERS EYE
TOPAZ	TOURMALINE
OBSIDIAN	ROSE QUARTZ
RUBY	JASPER

SPIRITUAL DEVELOPMENT

Primary	Secondary
LAPIS LAZULI	QUARTZ CRYSTAL
AMETHYST	GARNET
CITRINE	OBSIDIAN
TOPAZ	PERIDOT
AQUAMARINE	CHALCEDONY
ROSE QUARTZ	PEARL
EMERALD	TIGERS EYE

INCREASED PERCEPTION

Primary	Secondary
AMETHYST	RUBY
FLUORITE	EMERALD
TOPAZ	TIGERS EYE
TOURMALINE	CITRINE
TURQUOISE	SAPPHIRE
ANY BONE OR TOOTH	AQUAMARINE

MANIFESTING

Primary	Secondary
TOURMALINE	RUBY
AMETHYST	AVENTURINE
CITRINE	SAPPHIRE
LAPIS LAZULI	TOPAZ
ANY BONE	ANY TOOTH
QUARTZ CRYSTAL	ROSE QUARTZ
MALACHITE	JADE
OPAL	CORAL
MOONSTONE	DIAMOND

ENLIGHTENING

Primary	Secondary
AMETHYST	TIGERS EYE
LAPIS LAZULI	OBSIDIAN
FLUORITE	TURQUOISE
CITRINE	PEARL
SAPPHIRE	TOURMALINE
TOPAZ	JADE
EMERALD	AVENTURINE

STRENGTHENING

Primary	Secondary
AMETHYST	ANY TOOTH
LAPIS LAZULI	PETRIFIED WOOD
RUBY	QUARTZ CRYSTAL
EMERALD	OBSIDIAN
TOURMALINE	ONYX
KUNZITE	AVENTURINE
JADE	PEARL
ANY BONE	DIAMOND

GROUNDING

Primary	Secondary
LAPIS LAZULI	PEARL
AMETHYST	GARNET
PETRIFIED WOOD	RUBY
TOPAZ	EMERALD
ROSE QUARTZ	JASPER
CITRINE	DIAMOND
CALCITE	ANY BONE OR TOOTH
ANY AGATE	ONYX
BLOODSTONE	OBSIDIAN

FOCUS

Primary	Secondary
TIGERS EYE	LAPIS LAZULI
TOURMALINE	SAPPHIRE
AMETHYST	RUBY
QUARTZ CRYSTAL	AQUAMARINE
FLUORITE	EMERALD
GARNET	OBSIDIAN
TOPAZ	CHALCEDONY
KUNZITE	PERIDOT

****

FINDING THE SPIRIT OF THE STONE

To find the Spirit of a stone it is given to describe a technique which will help the user to sense or "Read" the unique vibration that is the Spirit that is present in any stone. Fundamental to this process is the understanding that All is vibration. As anything that is created by The Great Spirit has Spirit, the Spirit can be sensed, seen, or felt by its unique vibration. Just as some people can see the aura or halo of vibration that exists all about the human form, all can learn to sense the vibration of anything made by Him with the hands.

First in the process is to practice projecting and sensing energy by holding the hands together closely, but not touching, as if one is rolling a small ball between them. Work at sensing and transmitting energy between them as they get closer together, without touching. This energy is a kinetic projection of energy, which we all do, but are usually not conscious of. As you work at this exercise, you might even visually see the waves of energy being compressed and should feel a tingling sensation in one or more area which might be concentrated or compressed into a hot spot. The center of the palm of the hand is usually the area that is most open to this sensation, however the fingertips will often become quickly sensitized as well. Continue to work on this exercise daily and continued improvement of sensitivity will soon be experienced.

For those individuals that might experience trouble at first, it is recommended to place a small Quartz Receiving Crystal, meaning point to the side, in the palm of one hand with the other hand being then placed over it and the exercise continued for improved results. The goal of this exercise is however to develop the feeling senses of the hands without anything between them. For future reference, all stones should be placed in the palm of the left or receiving hand for examination and the right hand placed over it in the sensing process no matter which hand is used in the writing process. However, do whatever works best for you, as there are no absolutes. This is a good exercise to practice at anytime and is a good ability to develop so as to impress small children and large dogs. Not to be taken too lightly, this enhancing exercise will continue to help in hands on healing applications and is a really good one for everyone to use.

Having opened up the sensors of the hands, the next step in the process of finding the Spirit is to learn how to read or sense the different vibrations of the different colors. Take several pieces of plain white un-ruled paper and place a primary color spot or either red, blue, yellow, white, or black upon each piece. The colors needed are at least white, black, red, blue, yellow, green, brown, and violet for the best effect. I use acrylic paint however marks-alot or any other medium will work. I usually make the spot of color about one inch in diameter on a two inch square of paper.

Start with a red and blue colored set at first. Sense the color by placing a hand over it and feeling the vibration that is present. If trouble is encountered in feeling a difference in the vibrations of the two colors I usually place a receiving Crystal over the color spot for amplification. Some people may feel a sensation in different parts of the body from different colors as well as the hand and either or both may be used for identification. I prefer to relate each color to a sound as well, as all vibration has a quality of color and sound and the sound may be an "Aah" or "Eee" or the like. This work at distinguishing the vibrations of the different colors is most important in that it is this color vibration that we need to ignore in finding the Spirit of the stone. This exercise is most important and may enhance other hands on or sensing work as well, so try to develop great proficiency here. During the exercise, you may notice what feels or appears to be humps of energy emitting over some colors, while others appear to draw energy like a sponge.

These are important things to recognize about the Medicine of Color and may be used in every day situations for mood setting and healing work. Of confirmation here is that Yellow, not Red, is the hottest color and projects the highest and strongest vibration with a high "Eee" sound. Red usually is sensed as having a drawing energy with a slow "Aah" sound, and there is really only a slight difference between black and white! Now having mastered color, we are ready to move into the final phase.

The next step is to work with two Citrine stones, which are as close as possible in size, color, and shape. Citrine is chosen as the starter stone in detection both because of its Medicine and color. Place the two stones as far apart as possible in the palm of your left hand. Next hold your right hand over the two stones, moving the hand lengthwise and then side to side and finally in a clockwise motion. Move the right hand closer and then farther away until you detect the pattern that is unique to each. Exclude the vibration of the Yellow Ray, which you previously learned to detect and sense the different pattern of each of the two stones and you will now be in touch with Mineral Spirit. Next hold each stone separately to your cheek next to your ear and you can receive the voice within and receive its message. As you continue to work with Mineral Spirit this way it will enhance your life immeasurably. Next try two Agates and then Crystals of all types and whatever other stones you might choose. As you continue to work with the Mineral Spirit stones this respectful sharing way they will often tell you when they need energizing in the Sun or Moon, go on journey, need cleansing in salt water, or just want to join you for the day.

Many stories have been told about the Medicine Stones that I have given away. Countless other Mineral Spirit stones have enriched the users lives, so help yours best help you by learning its Spirit this way.

SHARING THE SPIRIT

Having learned to isolate the unique vibration of the Spirit of the stone enables communication and thereby relationship with it. It seems too bad that people do not work so easily with each other. Just as in human relationships, the care given in working with Mineral Spirit is returned many-fold. So as we ask our Mineral Spirit Brother or Sister to help us, we can share our thankfulness by our respectful handling and care for them thorough periodic cleansing in salt water and energizing in the light of the Sun or Moon from time to time. Remember, as in all types of relationships, Respect and Communication are the key. From time to time I will change all of the stones in my Medicine Bag so as to allow for a rest period for the ones I had been using there. This allows for others to have the opportunity for serving the Great Spirit this way for a while which is also respectful sharing. So I recommend that you listen often to your stones and allow for a freshening period from time to time and it will make it a better relationship for the both of you.

I have often noticed in Self and others and usually those just starting to learn the way, that there might develop a reddening of the hands in specific areas of use and even some heat sensation or swelling might also occur. Do not be alarmed by this as it will soon pass. Just as an athlete warms up before any test of strength or skill so as not to pull muscles or get cramps, warm up your sensors of the hands with the energy routine described earlier and shake the residual energy from them when through just like the cool down lap for any runner.

The first approach that I personally take to using any stone or crystal is to hold it softly in my left hand and place my right hand over it and send Love energy to it and ask it if it wants to play which is to help with the work. Then if I receive a positive response, I tell it what the purpose of the game is as I have a difficult time of thinking of any Spiritual activity as being any form of work because it always gives me so much pleasure and joy. I might approach many Rose Quartz stones before one feels up to the challenge at hand, but remember that All Can Be. It is always more fun to dance with a willing partner you see.

Crystals such as the Quartz, Tourmaline, Amethyst, and Kunzite have very much energy stored in them and also have a great ability in being able to precisely focus it. A simple test of this ability is to with the right hand hold a crystal at the base steadily over the palm of your left hand for a period of one minute and you will discover what I mean as usually a red spot and some associated heat and pain may be realized in the palm. So when working with the Crystal stones, the movement of them over the affected area is necessary for them to work properly and the greatest benefit to be received.

So having come this far with Mineral Spirit Knowledge, we will next discuss what to do with them or perhaps it might better be expressed as how to allow for them to enrich our lives. As we come into contact with anything that was created by The Great Spirit such as a stone, we are reminded that He made it and that He is the true Source of all things. Perhaps it is this very Essential Nature and Medicine of "Remembering the Source" that is the Medicine of all Mineral Spirits collectively. The Great Spirit Father made all things and each of us as well, therefore whatever substance we come into contact with may be used to reinforce our relationship to Him. Mineral Spirit is a great ally and can be a great helper when used in prayer and contemplation. As we hold in our hand that which is made by The Creator, we share the Spirit of it and thereby realize the Spirit of ourselves as being of, and with, Him. The object then becomes as a telephone line to the Creator and as a loudspeaker to the Universe which is Him also, including all of the forces therein.

In the preparation of teas and potions I will typically use four and sometimes seven Medicine stones. I begin the process by prayer over the stones and asking them for their assistance and then placing them gently in the water at the beginning of the procedure. The Amethyst, Rose Quartz, Citrine, and Tourmaline or Quartz Crystal are always good choices as enablers and others may be added or substituted depending upon the purpose or need. Again I will mention that I always ask first which stones wish to help in this way and allow them to tell me, respectful sharing again you see. As I place them in the pot I say a prayer of thanks and when the process is through, I cleanse them in salt water and thank them again for their help and care. It is always beneficial for the stones to then be placed in the Sun between uses when applied this way. I keep the Mineral Spirits that I use in potions and teas on a ledge in my kitchen window and separate from others as they are constantly bathed in Sun and Moon shine this way and I also have healing plants there and they are very good friends.

Mineral Spirit may also be used in baths to assist in healing therapies and in the cleansing of and Renewall of the energy patterns of the body as well as in energizing the body itself. Again ask which stones wish to do the work and they should be applied as described about the potions and teas. After use special care should be given in the removal of any soaps and oils before placing them in salt water for cleansing and Sunlight for Renewall and energizing. All bath stones should additionally be placed outside under each full Moon and not the new Moon as it lessens their ability in working not only the water of the bath but also the fluid of the body.

Mineral Spirits love to work in necklaces, pendants, and just about any adornment of the body and on ceremonial objects as well. The same periodic cleansing and energy Renewall in the Sun and or the Moon should be applied to these items also. I personally cleanse and renew my necklaces and earrings more often as they are constantly at work about me in the Medicine way and deserve a lot of extra special care. The stones which touched anyone's skin should be cleansed at least monthly as they pick up all of the dynamics of our feelings through our monthly cycle and need to be cleansed more often than those not held so close. Earrings should be cleansed more frequently as they are worn about the head or Mind of one and thereby operate in the highest area of stress about the body. This understanding should help in the selection of Mineral Spirit for this area as well and it obviously is not a good place for Opals.

Mineral Spirits like to be carried about in amulets, Medicine Bags, or in the pocket. I personally carry them in my shirt pocket either loose or in my Medicine Bag as they like to operate about the heart center for me. I use the stones in my Medicine Bag at times for healing work but most often for prayer work and divination. I also have many Medicine stones set up in altars and Medicine Wheels about my home but every home is enhanced by having at least one stone placed in each of the four directions and the center or heart. A general guide is for placement of a Sharks Tooth, Abalone, Coral, or Aventurine in the South. Place an Apache Tear, Turquoise, or Ruby in the West. Place a Lapis Lazuli, Amethyst, or Topaz in the North. And place a Citrine, Wolf's Tooth, Peridot or Tigers Eye in the East with an Amethyst or a stone representing the Medicine of Self in the Center.

Mineral Spirits like to hang around transportation devices also and the Amethyst, Quartz Crystal, and Sharks Tooth will work well here. Often when I go on journey one or more others will often tell me they want to go as well so we share the experience that way. I use Mineral

Spirits on all Prayer Sticks and Rattles but also on my Medicine Drum and Medicine pipe too. One Mineral Spirit used prayerfully in the hand is just as effective as all of these. I even have an Amethyst that sits in the top of my Norfolk Pine Christmas tree and few people can believe how beautiful and quickly this Plant Spirit has grown.

I have seen some situations where some Mineral Spirit stones were placed around pets on collars and the like and it is given to express great caution in their application here as while they might seem cute and represent your Love and care, they might unduly stress the pet and the Mineral Spirit as well. Certain of these applications indeed will prove beneficial but one must really know what they are doing as great harm can also be the result. Of note about stress in Mineral Spirit stone is that the Amethyst and many other stones will fracture or disappear occasionally if proper Respect and Balance in use is not maintained. While some might worry or consider this to be a bad omen consider it a wakeup call to our consciousness and consideration as Mineral Spirit operates only with Love and Nurturing in a positive way as to best assist us in our growth.

Having covered some of the general applications or uses of Mineral Spirit Medicine, I will now elaborate on its use in Meditation. In using Mineral Spirit in the process of Meditation I have found the following procedure to be quite beneficial. In my technique of meditation my goal is to raise my vibration as to resonate with the Violet Ray and go and be with The Great Spirit Father by drawing upon the root center or chakra which I see upon first relaxing as an orangeish-red color. I will usually place a Garnet or Carnelian upon the forehead of the initiate and hold it there until they can feel its vibration resonating and exciting the energy in their root center and also see this color vibration in their third eye center with eyes closed. I will then show them how they can draw this energy up their spine through the drawing in and exhaling of their breath. The Amethyst is usually next applied, however some might wish to work with a separate stone to activate each of the Spiritual Centers. As each stone is applied to the third eye area they are given to take a deep breath and pull the energy up the spine from the root center with a subsequent raising of the vibration through the different colors until the violet color is realized and then the meditation is begun. This exercise not only serves to raise the consciousness and vibration of a person but also serves to clear or identify blocks in the centers of Self as well.

Different techniques may be applied with the Mineral Spirit being placed upon various centers while the person is laying down during meditation as well. As each person as well as Mineral Spirit stone is unique, this is a technique that may be used to discover what works best for you. I sometimes will work with an Amethyst or Fluorite stone placed upon my forehead while laying down and draw through each breath, energy from the universe through my feet in a Renewall process. After only minutes of doing this I often feel as if I just had three days sleep. Often the placement of different Mineral Spirit stones about the head or under the pillow will significantly affect sleep and dream state work.

In working with people's energy fields in healing work or other types of therapies, the Quartz Crystal may be applied. The crystals should be placed with the points placed lengthwise along the spine having a transmitting crystal at the base of the head with the point facing down and hold a receiving crystal at the tailbone area with the point facing up. Use the receiving crystal by slow movement after the connection is felt by moving it up and down the spine and alternately down each leg. As disrupted areas or hot spots are felt use the receiving crystal in a circular motion as if spreading butter over the body zone being aligned or cleared. Progress in this manner using a smoothing motion down the spine and sides, and moving the transmitting crystal through each energy center or chakra until all are cleared this way. Continue this application through the legs and feet. The front of the person may next be applied this way but in most conditions I have found that application to the back to be quite sufficient.

Next move the transmitting crystal back to the original position at the base of the head and position the point so as to face the right shoulder and continue to work the receiving crystal in a circular motion down the right shoulder, arm and hand. Then reverse the position of the crystal so as to face the left shoulder and repeat the process. Now position the transmitting crystal so as to face upwards at the base of the head and use the receiving crystal in a circular motion so as to appear to comb the hair sideways from the center at the top and down each side of the head and then repeating this process down the back and finally down the front. Finish the application with a sweeping movement from the center of the top of the head, straight up and out in a great releasing and drawing motion. In some instances I have found that I have received better effect by swapping the transmitter and receiver crystal positions when working with some people as if their polarity was switched and it is given to express that this is not a harmful condition or one of any concern as it is just a cycle that they are in.

It is important to ask the individual what is being felt by them as you do this application and you will better know which stones to use in what positions and where blocks and improvements are being felt. As communication is the necessary ingredient to all relationships, communicate often with the Mineral Spirit and the special child of the Creator with whom you are working on. If hot spots or pain or humps of energy are felt in specific areas, work in a blending motion from the outside to the center of each location and in these areas it is often recommended to reverse the stones for clearing or easing first and then repeat the procedure with the stones placed the normal way. Often if specific areas such as these are detected, I will replace the clear crystals with the Amethyst as the transmitter and a Rose Quartz as a receiver and repeat the process until release or relief is felt.

In working in this manner it is important to keep a prayerful attitude and be open to what it is that the Mineral Spirit wants to do and try not to get in the way of that, more respectful sharing again you see. With some practice many will not only sense or feel, but will also see the energy fields about the body and know the many patterns and pathways for alignment such as from the left neck to lower right shoulder blade and so forth. Again always communicate with the person to ensure their comfort and enable their participation and the Mineral Spirits will take care of everything else if you are operating this way with the great energy that is the Love from the Heart of Self.

After each use thank each Mineral Spirit and cleanse each with care and place them in the Sun for Renewall and you will have great joy and success working with Mineral Spirit this way.

Remember there are truly no limits and that All Can Be and this is just a brief description of how Mineral Spirit Medicine works for me and I thank you for allowing me to share it with you.

****

Mineral Spirits Index

-A-

Amber	219	Aquamarine	220	Aventurine	220
Amethyst	219	Apache Tear	236	Azurite	221

-B-

Bloodstone	221	Botswana Agate	222	Bone	247

-C-

Calcite	223	Chrysocolla	224	Crystal, Quartz	226
Carnelian	223	Citrine	225	Copper	247
Chalcedony	224	Coral	225		

-Charts-

Color/Ray	250	Focus	259	Manifesting	257
Calming	255	Grounding	259	Metal	252
Elemental	253	Healing	255	Protection	256
Energizing	254	Initiating	254	Spiritual Dev.	256
Enlightening	258	Inc. Perception	257	Strengthening	258

-D-

Diamond - 226

-E-

Emerald - 227

-F-

Fire Agate	228	Flint	228	Fluorite	229

Finding the Spirit of the Stone - 260

-G-

Garnet - 230

-H-

Halite	230	Herkimer	231		

-I-

Ivory	247	Iron	248		

-J-

Jade	231	Jasper	232		

Index - Page 2 of 2

-K-

Kunzite - 232

-L-

Lapis Lazuli - 233

-M-

| Malachite | 233 | Moonstone | 235 | |
| Mica | 234 | Moss Agate | 236 | |

-O-

| Obsidian | 236 | Onyx | 237 | Opal | 237 |

-P-

| Pearl | 238 | Pipestone | 239 | Pyrite | 240 |
| Peridot | 239 | Petrified Wood | 249 | | |

Pain relief - 223, 236, 268

-R-

| Rhodochrosite | 240 | Rose Quartz | 241 | |
| Rhodonite | 241 | Ruby | 242 | |

-S-

| Sapphire | 242 | Sodalite | 243 | |

Sharing the Spirit - 263

-T-

| Teeth | 249 | Topaz | 244 | Turquoise | 246 |
| Tigers Eye | 244 | Tourmaline | 245 | | |

****

Walk in Joy and enjoy your walk upon Earthplane,

and every now and then pick up a stone and talk

to it and all will see much better that way.

May the blessing of

The Great Spirit Father

Be upon

each and every one of you.

WHITE | EAGLE

PLANT SPIRIT

KNOWLEDGE

BY

I ASKED THE GREAT SPIRIT ONE DAY,

FATHER, HOW IS IT BEST FOR ME TO BE?

AND HE TOLD ME.

BE LIKE THE TREE, HE SAID,

AND GROW FROM THE INSIDE OUT.

White Eagle

CONTENTS

Introduction   278

Plant Spirit Medicine   279

The Awakening   280

Talking with Plant Spirits   284

Medicine   288

Potions and Teas   290

Trees   296

Shrubs and Flowers   307

Vines and Berries   316

Cactus and Succulents   321

Reeds and Grasses   325

Mosses and Lichen   328

Ferns and Mushrooms   330

Water Plants and Algae   332

Fruits, Vegetables, Nuts and Herbs   334

Application of Plant Spirit Medicine   364

Index   367

Introduction

This book is but a brief description of how Plant Spirit works for me. I feel that there is an unlimited ability in how they may also help you. It is important therefore to use this book as a guide only in the sense of observing one man's way in working with Plant Spirits. Equally important is to spend time with them so as to develop your own special and unique relationship to and with them.

While the descriptions about the Plant Spirits detailed in this document may or may not agree with some of the many books currently available on the subject, I can only express that this is what was given for me to use in my way. Please remember that All, Can Be, and the joy is in the discovery of it. As the Great Spirit created all things, He embodied us as well as Plant Spirit with unlimited possibility. Therefore it seems obvious that we should easily resonate to the vibrations that are the Plant Spirits in our lives.

The key to working with Plant Spirit as with all others is a condition of Proper Relationship. This proper relationship may better be described as being the condition of respectful sharing in the experience of the expression of growth. As one senses the Love of the Great Spirit in one's Heart, Plant Spirit is an able and most willing partner in the conducting and distribution of this energy to any and all things in the universe. As with all conditions of relationships, the key element for success is communication. So spend some time speaking to and listening to the Plant Spirits that choose to share your Earthwalk journey. I am sure that both your and our lives will be much richer for the experience.

Everything that comes from The Great Spirit has a unique vibration and Spirit. As we learn to resonate with the Spirit of the Plants we find unique partners, teachers, and willing allies in our experience of growth.

PLANT SPIRIT MEDICINE

Of the many things that Plant Spirit can teach us, I feel most important is that about the cycles of life and growth. In my Medicine Wheel way the South direction represents the seed planting time, West represents the sprouting time, North represents the growing time, and East represents the flowering time where the seeds are renewed for the next cycle. In truth the purpose for our being, whether we are in Earth Physical or Spirit planes beyond, all of His creation including ourselves is in a continuous condition of expansion, or growth. Plant Spirit has unlimited ability for teaching and helping us this way. Of the many things that the Plant Spirit provides for all Beings on the Earthplane such as beauty, protection, nourishment, healing Medicine and such, one of the most often overlooked gifts is their great Lesson Giving ability. Even the Water Witch that uses the branch of the Willow to divine or find water, seldom has any idea of the how it works for them this way. This book is not directed at plant identification nor is it a home remedy guide as there is a proliferation of these already available although I have included some of my general tonics and healing aids for use of which some come from other sources but most through channel from my Guides.

In the healing process there are no absolutes and while general tonics work in most cases, each individual is operating at a certain unique rhythm of vibration that may not be affected by something that works well for another. All illness also has a Spiritual component or issue, which allows for the breakdown of the balance of the metabolism thereby allowing for the ever-present viruses (which we all carry in our systems) to attack and grow. We will discuss more about this later but it is given to emphasize here the need to become aware of the Spiritual component of everything. I find it also significant to express the need to develop renewed respect for the role played by our Plant Spirit Brothers and Sisters in our biology and the fragile nature of our environment so as to help them help you. Plant Spirit plays a very fundamental role in the life force upon Mother Earth by cleaning the air and producing the very oxygen that we depend on for life and take so much for granted. Some scientists are finally becoming aware of the enormous pressure on Plant Spirit and the current alarm over the rainforest devastation is indeed most well founded. Yet even this situation has a Spiritual component of Abuse through the Manifestation of Greed and the Lack of Living in Balance and with Harm to No One Being or thing.

It is also significant to mention here that the general color associated with all Plant Spirit is the Green Ray of Love. If one would only think of the colors of things, a great realization of the lesson giving ability of Plant Spirit might be understood. Plant Spirits live in the rich Brown Ray of Abundance, which is the soil of Mother Earth. Their roots connect them to Mother Earth and the All that is, much the same way as our connection and pathway back to the Essential Will and Love of Great Pop. Plant Spirit lives under and reaches up to the Blue Ray color of the sky, which is also the color that represents the Great Spirit Father in my Medicine Wheel Way and indeed the Plant Spirit ever grows up so as to be closer to Him. Plant Spirit uses the Yellow Receiving Ray of the Sun and merges this Yellow Ray with the Blue Ray of the sky into the Green Ray of Love in its leaves to provide for the Renewall of the life forces and resources for the All in the purest example of Respectful sharing and Brotherhood which all people are here on Earthplane to learn in the first place. Very special are these Plant Spirit Brothers and Sisters when we learn to see them this way and what wonderful Medicine they have to give.

THE AWAKENING

Sometimes I will see a tree and go over and talk to it. Some of these trees say they are three or four hundred years old, but then again some think that about me some times. It matters very little about how long in life on Earthplane or what specific experiences are encountered or shared and the least important is longevity. The very most important thing, as I can only speak of such as it is for me, is truly the quality of one's life. Plant Spirit has great lessons to share with us this way. Plant Spirit and specifically that of the tree, knows the importance of the conservation of resources. When the wind blows very hard, Tree Spirit can fight it and break some of its limbs like some of the Oak trees do. Or, the Tree Spirit can embrace the wind and bend with it, as the Willow has learned to do. Some Tree

Spirits like to show and display knowledge about the cycles that we all go through, like the Cherry or Walnut tree. They do such by embracing the new in the time of the spring by budding new branches and leaves, progressing to the flowering time in the summer, bearing its young in the fruit of its seed in the fall, and going south and thereby into the ground for winter as it becomes too cold topside, knowing in faith the spring again will come.

Most important to me perhaps of the many lessons that I get from Tree Spirit might be their teaching about the life experience in the physical Earthplane. The roots of the tree are every growing in the substance of the Mineral Spirit kingdom of Mother Earth and well grounded there with the head and arms of the tree ever reaching to, and growing nearer to, the Great Spirit above. If our roots, which might also be considered our sense of Well-being, begin to outnumber or get larger than our trunk and limbs, which we might see as our Potential or Hope, we will indeed see and feel the imbalance immediately. It is also important to see how all Plant Spirits show us how to grow, which is from the inside or heart outward, in all directions as one. Sometimes, we try to grow from the other way when we put our Ego in charge of who and what we think we are.

If my Ego which I call my Bark on tree, tells me that I am imperfect or incomplete and that I need to be like the person down the street and have what they have and do what they do, usually I will learn lesson in it, as I can never be more or less than the perfect child of The Great Spirit as He created me, just like any plant or tree. When I start to feel something imperfect in the way He made me, I usually go over to a tree and listen as it always tells me a much better way to see myself than others might tell me to be. A tree or any other Plant Spirit lives embracing a perfect balance between heaven and earth, never trying to be more than the fullest expression of growth in the true pattern of itself. At times I will see some Plant Spirits display aggressive Medicine like some people, such as the Tallow tree, and I thank each in showing lessons in willfulness and how I might choose to be, or not to be. Plant Spirit shows us great ability in strength and balance to their conditions and in these cases they sometimes bend around into great shapes and beautiful expressions of themselves for all to see.

Also important in the gift to us from Plant Spirit is that they surround us with the Green Ray of Love and even with their passing or in the changing seasonal cycles, Plant Spirit leaves us with the Golden Ray of Hope. The Plant Spirits which crawl upon the ground often display many beautiful colors to soften our steps in life and those with the prickly needles for defense often compensate for this with precious gifts of the sweet fruit of their berries and great visual effects in their geometry of growth. Outside of their many gifts of beauty, nutrition, housing material, energy, and protection, Plant Spirit also provides us with wonderful aromas that truly must be heaven scent, as well as sent. I do know one or two Plant Spirits that seem to at times come from another place than heaven so to speak, but that too makes them wonderful teachers. I have constantly been using Plant Spirit as a healing ally for a long time and in writing this, I realize even more of the richness of life that they have brought to me. My aboriginal background and Eagle Medicine has helped me to be a keen observer of things, and Plant Spirit would always tell me about droughts or storms to come, the passing by of animals or humans, the condition of Mother Earth or problems with the water or air.

Plant Spirit is important also not only as a filter and provider to the balance of the air and as a food source, but also as a great healing resource. It seems that we are making too much concrete and asphalt folks, and indeed we are making much more desert than fertile ground. Think about it and do something if you can. If people make Plant Spirit an extinct species as seems to be the direction that we are going in certain areas, soon only un-incarnated Spirits will be coming here. I am remembering the time not too long ago when there was plenty of buffalo for everyone, and see what happened to them in such a short period as time goes.

Plant Spirit is unique in the universe in that in every part of itself is a map or guide for growth. The seed of the plant provides us with a reflection of our own beginning and our birthright of Hope and happiness and sense of being a complete Self. The seed is housed in a protective coating or shell, not unlike the Spirit is in the human body form. The seed, like us, has to aspire to a greater expression of itself with hope to emerge past the status quo of its beginning state. The seed just as is each Self, is already complete and perfect just as being that, as matter or Ego in a stable and secure form. Just as all that is created by The Great Spirit has an unlimited potential and opportunity for growth, each has a responsibility to embrace growth in Self and support the growth of all others. The seed is an excellent example of this. It has substance and a beginning pattern of Self, as well as nutrients for growth provided in its formation and a knowledge and consciousness of its potential of growth, past the current idea and dimension of Self. Some variations of this do and will occur, but all have the ability to manifest past their original and current condition of Self, which is also the Ego. As all things made by the Creator are constantly about becoming greater channels of His Light and Love, the process of becoming more than the limited Ego idea of Self is the true definition and condition of the expression of growth.

What better example of the condition of life on Earthplane than a grain of corn or wheat. With a covering hardened not by Fear but with protective care, the seed is supplied with an ample supply of meat to nourish its metamorphosis as well as the knowledge and ability of the direction to the sky and the Great Spirit however it might land upon Mother Earth. The simplest seed personifies our own existence as it knows about the cycles of growth and is conscious of it when it touches, or is embraced by Mother Earth. After getting settled in the embrace of Mother Earth, the seed with timely courage emerges from the cocoon of the shell of Self and begins the process of embracing the opportunity to embrace and express its fullest potential, in whatever condition it finds itself to be in. Like all that is made by the Creator, each seed has a unique vibration or Spirit. Each seed also knows when to break free of its protective shell, and quickly responds to the nutrients and liquid of Mother Earth below. It then stretches itself toward the Sun above, ever seeking the Light of the Creator as to process it in Self in another expression of Love. The great teacher in this seed also shows us in this process of growth, how if it accepts too much of any one thing, which is also a perfect example of not walking in balance, the growth of it is retarded or suppressed.

The seed shows us again that like all things created by Him, that we are to grow from the inside out and this can only happen by the giving way or splitting of the Ego or outer shell of self. The seed must give way its Ego and its limited sense of and comfortable condition of itself and with Faith and Courage, embrace the wake up call and sprout from it shell to experience the full expression of life and itself in the process. Some of the seeds like some people never seem to take that first step of growth and that is okay as well, as in time they will all get another chance. Each seed, like each of us at some point, go through the Awakening as to what we are here upon the Earthplane for, which is to grow so as to become even greater channels of the Great Spirit's Light and Love and to learn the unlimited ways to experience and express Love and Brotherhood.

TALKING WITH THE PLANT SPIRITS

In my Medicine way I often use the Medicine of the Plant Spirits in many ways and the following technique can be used by anyone wanting to learn how to communicate with them. After practicing this exercise, some will be able to talk to the Plant Spirit that made any wood product including their furniture. I like to talk to and touch wood objects and they usually show me where and sometimes when they grew up, and at times I can even see the craftsman working them into their current form. All Plant Spirits have great memory and we can often use this ability to our advantage. I often use Plant Spirit in healing and Tree Spirits are excellent helpers in the process of Renewall or rebirthing, especially for those having holes in their aura or who feel segmented in some way.

While this technique may be applied in various forms to all plants, we will begin by using a large tree. Although they can help us at any time of the year, to start with, it is given to find one that is healthy and awake especially if the time of the year is that of the winter. Pine trees are easy to talk to and pretty much available everywhere so we will use the Pine tree in this simple exercise.

Begin by bringing a gift to the tree and most often Tree Spirits like a gift of tobacco or a small pebble or stone placed at its base and it is given to express that the gift is best placed at the base of the tree in the direction from which you wish to receive help from it. Often there might be a wound spot or hole and these are also good locations in which to place your gift. Listen to the tree and it will tell you where best to place your gift. If no gift is available to you, a simple prayer is sufficient and I will usually make the prayer an askance for the increased Well-being of the tree. I will say this prayer whether a gift is available or not. After placing the gift and expressing the prayer, back away from the tree for a bit and then approach the tree quietly and listen to it. Then express a prayer for guidance and of thanksgiving to the Great Spirit for the blessing from him in the presence of this tree.

Next, touch the trunk of the tree with your hands and feel its outer layer of bark. Let the bark remind you of your own outer side of Self and allow the bark and your outer Self to communicate and integrate in this respectful way. As you look at and feel this bark remember how we too have to keep breaking through our own bark of our Ego limitation of Self and Fear for us to grow or become complete. The Bark of Self is equally as important as the bark of this tree to our individual Well-being. The bark of the Ego of ourselves must keep splitting for us to grow from the inside out just like in this tree, but the bark of our Self is also necessary for the protection that it provides to us in many non-limiting ways. Now examine the trunk of this wonderful tree from all sides. Look at the base of the tree and see how it embraces Mother Earth. Now look up the sides of the tree and notice how the many branches come from the center of it.

As we see the branches about the trunk of this tree we remember the many branches of our own experience and lesson taking in life and each branch can reflect a step taken through a decision or choice about what we desire to experience. Just like some of the branches that never grew very big and died, we see some of our choices as well and better realize that all of our experiences have been good for us if we learn the lesson in them and that not all branches are meant to grow to the fullest of their capacity if we are to keep growing taller like this tree. We realize that all of the branches of our life were necessary for us to be exactly how we are in the pattern of ourselves at this moment in time and it is exactly the same for this tree.

Now look at some of the limbs on these branches of this tree and notice how some may have leaves or needles and others may not. Sometimes we make choices or decisions that really are not good for us and do not walk in Balance and with Harm to No One including Ourselves. Just like some of these branches without leaves, we see that these choices did not have enough Light for us to grow and we see that just as in this tree that is okay because we understand it is much better for us to quit giving so much energy to things that are not productive to our Well-being and growth. We realize that just like in this tree we can at any time redirect our energy to those things in life that receive the most Light and thereby support our growth and Well-being.

As all trees grow in the Round Way from the inside out, we know that we also should follow that pattern of growth in Self. We see also some cases where trees grow in a one-sided way for a while and some even at funny angles to the ground. Then we notice how all of these Plant Spirit Brothers and Sisters, when they can find room and get tall enough and thereby closer to the Great Spirit Father, will grow to their fullest pattern of Self in perfection which is indeed that of the fullest and roundest expression of their Self. Then we realize like these trees, so can we, no matter what our earlier time on Earthplane might have been about and we realize our unlimited potential for Renewall and growth.

Again look at the base of this tree and notice how the trunk and roots are embedded and embraced in Mother Earth for both stability and nourishment. Like this tree we realize that we too, are supported by Mother Earth and the Father above and we realize that all is perfect this way. Now touch the limbs and leaves of this tree and feel the life force there. We can even feel the activity of growth and chemical processes going on there. Ask the tree for a leaf and after removing it caringly, place it to your cheek and feel the force of life in it. Smell the aroma of the leaf and taste of it and you might do the same with a small piece of the bark as well and as you do this begin to feel at one with this Plant Spirit.

Next approach the tree from the direction of choice and for those seeking guidance the directions are as follows:

SOUTH	-	PROTECTION & RESOURCE
WEST	-	RELEASE & UNDERSTANDING
NORTH	-	WISDOM & STRENGTH
EAST	-	REALIZATION & ENLIGHTENMENT

Place both hands around the trunk of the tree about the height of your own heart with the toes of both feet touching the trunk. Now place your forehead against the trunk of the tree and for those not physically able to do this, visualize it while holding any part of the tree. Close your eyes and breathe out real hard to the right and pray with each inhalation to become one with the Spirit of this tree. As you slowly feel drawn inside this tree you will soon see with eyes closed a rich golden brown color and begin to feel the pulsations, which is the heartbeat of the tree.

As you become more at one with the tree you will feel and see the juices flowing through your body and you will feel your feet become the roots of the tree and you become drawn into its heart in the most loving and nurturing of ways. As you continue to breathe and pray this way with eyes closed you begin to feel what it is like to be in any leaf, root, or stem of this Plant Spirit. As you become more centered and get over the initial experience, pray for the Renewall of Self and feel the energy of the Love of the Great Spirit and the Spirit of this tree flow and renew all of the layers of yourself into absolute Balance and Perfection. As you renew yourself this way and become at one with the Great Spirit by being inside this tree, you also become uniquely at one with the Plant Spirit that is this tree. All is Spirit and each Spirit is a direct link to The Father and Universal Knowledge. The Plant Spirit may also help us with questions that we may have as we work together this way so it is a good place to ask any at this time.

After spending as much time as necessary or desired inside this tree, thank it for its Love and return back to the outside of it and then back into your body feeling totally renewed, refreshed, and complete in every way. You may ask the tree for a leaf or a piece of its bark and know that if you are respectful, the tree is most willing to share some of itself with you. As you take this part of the tree with you know that its Spirit walks with you as well. You can call upon the Plant Spirit of this tree now through the holding of this part of it or return here at anytime now with a single thought.

While this exercise is centered around working with a tree variations of it can be successfully applied to any Plant Spirit no matter as to how big or small.

MEDICINE

The medicinal qualities and value of Plant Spirit is wide spread and well known for many centuries. Most druggists and apothecaries use extracts from Plant Spirit Medicine knowledge that has been passed down by the healers since before recorded time. Unlike traditional Western or White thinking, the Medicine of anything made by the Great Spirit is much more valuable than just an extract for a pill to the Shaman or Medicine Man. Application of the Medicine of a Plant Spirit can prevent the individual from falling victim to a disease in the first place. Plant Spirit can also be used to ward off negative thoughts from others and was often used to prepare the warrior for battle and to help make him invisible to his enemy. Plant Spirit is still being used to aid in Vision Quest and Dream Work by many aboriginal people and its curative ability is greatly underestimated by many of these Western cultures that seem to be always walking their Earthwalk at a hurried pace. The Medicines of any specific Plant Spirit is many-fold and to identify each specific one for each plant is not what is given to be presented here. The Medicine for any particular condition of a person from any Plant Spirit will vary with the emotional condition as well as the biological condition that is showing the distress and will vary from Being to Being and time to time, but remember at any specific moment, truly All Can Be. All conditions of infirmity have a specific Spiritual component as well as a physical manifestation and Both need to be examined to provide the greatest benefit from the application of the Medicinal qualities of the Plant Spirit.

The definition of Medicine as it was given to me to be expressed is the Resonance To A Value system, Ability, or Consciousness. Just as the definition implies, Medicine is not so much about the physical sense of one's Being although many people try to restrict its application that way. Medicine is so much more than just being that, as truly Medicine embraces all of the layers and dimensions of one's Being and the conditions or symptoms of the body are just an effect of the condition of the Spirit where ever it might be at. The body is a manifestation of the Mind, Conscience, and most important, the Heart of one. Any problems in the Heart or Conscience or Mind of one will always manifest a physical condition to cause the individual to look inside, and thereby bring Balance and order back into the walk along one's path. As all is Spirit, and, indeed we can realize the importance that Resonance plays in the effects upon one's walk where ever that might be at, whether upon the Earthplane or any of the many other Spirit worlds.

POTIONS AND TEAS

First to be considered is that in the Medicine Way, which can be employed in doing anything in Life is the consciousness that each thing that exists has Spirit and it all comes from The Creator. We really do not make anything, we only facilitate something to have an experience or expression because of our actions, or not. The Wind comes because that is what it chooses to do. If I call it by beseeching its Spirit in a respectful manner, then it is Proper and in the Medicine Way. Also to be considered is the consciousness that in the "making" of anything is a combination of separate entities. Whether an arrow, jewelry, or the simplest of meals, the proper and Medicine Way of it is to see it as a Sacred Union and Marriage of sorts. Likewise, another consciousness to be considered is that whenever two entities are brought together, a third consciousness or Spirit of the group of them is born so to speak. This last consciousness is most important to maintain when making potions and teas, as this overall consciousness is like the Chief of the Tribe of the separate elements. Also to be considered is that in the Medicine Way the Chief is only a spokesperson and representative of the individual elements of the group, not some taskmaster or overlord as some might consider. Therefore in the "making" of or doing anything in the Medicine Way, all of these consciousnesses are embraced and maintained throughout the process. It is also given to add that the asking of anything, is the expression of a Prayer of Desire and it should not be considered as some form of worship or the like. The final consciousness to be considered in this process, is that of Respectful Sharing. In this regard, each and all elements are valued, and one's appreciation is all one can give forth so that one can receive the benefit of their actions and support. Unless one gives something first Proper Receivership will not be realized.

We will next consider the difference between potions and teas. One might best consider potions to be causative in their Medicine and thereby essential nature, and teas to be sustaining or supportive. From this understanding one can see how two separately prepared liquids that contain the same ingredients can actually have two different effects. The difference will be realized in the Prayers that are expressed to each ingredient as well as to the Group Consciousness Spirit of the completed union of them. For instance, a simple composition of water and cinnamon-sticks can yield a curative and purging effect to toxins and irritants in the systems, or it can be an elixir of energizing and hydrating fluid for the body to use. What is the difference? Prayers expressed in the facilitation of such to become, and hence and always, Motive.

It is given to state at this point that the process of combining elements and thereby "Marry" them into a union of sorts is to be considered Sacred, be it in this process or others, like the making of Medicine jewelry. In each case, I will personally take each element into my mouth and "Marry" it first as I know that some of my atoms will join it and some of it will become in me. Each bead or leaf of a plant is treated the same way. I marry the stones that go into the pot as well as the water in this same way, and yes, I have licked quite a few pots, sticks, and all sorts of animals and so forth in respect to this. I do this whether the product of such endeavor is for myself or for others.

I often prepare potions and teas for both curative and preventative medicinal applications. However, teas and potions are also prepared for their Calling Medicine as well as Changing Medicine qualities. I begin the preparation of teas and potions by the cleansing and prayer over the pot that they are prepared in, and then finding and talking to the Mineral Spirit stones that wish to help this way. The Medicine of most of the different stones that I use in potions and teas are listed in the material of Mineral Spirit Knowledge portion of this book. In the preparation of teas and potions I will typically use four and sometimes seven Medicine stones. I begin the process by Prayer over the stones in askance for assistance and then placing them gently in the water. Amethyst, Rose Quartz, Citrine, Tourmaline or Quartz Crystal are always good choices as enablers, and others may be added or substituted depending upon the purpose or need. Again I will mention that I always ask first which stones wish to help in this way and allow them to tell me, Respectful Sharing again you see.

As I place them in the pot I say a Prayer of thanks and then state what I desire specifically from each of them to add to the finished substance. As one might suspect, this process is valid in making anything at all. When the process of their use is completed, I cleanse them in salt water, and thank them again for their help and care. It is always beneficial for the stones to then be placed in the Sun between uses when applied this way. I keep the Mineral Spirits that I use in potions and teas on a ledge in my kitchen window and separate from others. They are constantly bathed in the light and renewing energy of the Sun and Moon this way. I also have healing plants there and they are very good friends.

Next, I carefully place the stones upon the bottom of the pot and add the water to it, also with Prayer for the work that I wish it to do and ask for Harmony of the substances this way. As the heat is applied to the pot, I then pray for the Spirit of Transformation to begin and continue through the life of the potion or tea as I call it. As the water becomes active, I select and say a separate Prayer over each Plant Spirit substance relative to its specific qualities and Medicine and thereby honoring it and its support to the process and product as it is added to the water. I also always add them in the most Caring and Respectful way. After all of the substances are added and the pot is brought to full boil, I say a prayer of Thanksgiving and Release for each element and the All of it to become the fullest expression of its and their, next New Selves and the Sharing and Union of the Love and Medicine of each of the components. It is also at this point that I will honor and express my Prayer of Desire to the Group Consciousness Spirit of the composition of them. In this I am most specific as to what effect is desired upon any physical body part or organ, disease element, pain source, and so forth as well as the overall condition and consciousness of the individual that is to be involved. I always enjoy the music of the stones as they dance upon the bottom of the pot and refreshed by the beautiful aromas that this process makes. After the potion is brought to full boil, typically for five (Fulfillment) to seven (Ordination) minutes, I will remove it from the heat and allow it to sit and relax for a while. Each period of boiling will vary upon the consciousness involved as well as the purpose and intended outcome. Therefore, it is given to include this list of the Medicine of Numbers (from the Book of the same name) as follows:

1 Direction	2 Union	3 Trinity	4 Resonance
5 Fulfillment	6 Passion	7 Ordination	8 Resource
9 Openness	10 Completion	11 Mirroring	12 Ceremony
13 Purpose	14 Metamorphosis	15 Realization	16 Actualization

We will stop here, as any more boiling and one will probably be out of water.

After the potion or tea has cooled but is still warm to some degree, I will strain it into another container. I will also in Prayer, then add either Honey and/or Molasses as is given for each specific use or effect. It is given to mention here that typically honey is given to be added for sweetening but more for its ability in suppressing allergic or sinus reactions in the springtime. The Molasses with its high mineral content helps in the reduction of susceptibility to catching colds in the fall and wintertime. This is because the Molasses helps stabilize the metabolism against the dramatic changes in temperature encountered during these seasons. After all of the components are blended and stabilized, a final prayer for Thankfulness and effectiveness is given to the potion or tea and it is ready to do the work as desired.

The following is what I call a stock Tea or Potion and is pretty much a foundation for most of what is given for me to prepare with usually only a few other ingredients added for their specific Medicine and enhancement. This stock potion is always a good one to use in itself as it has assimilation Medicine and helps in the transfer of fluids between the tissues and cell walls and all membranes such as that. People often remark at how good these potions taste and that is as it should be, because they are made with great Care and Love and that truly is what Plant Spirit is all about.

The Mineral Spirits I will generally use are:

Amethyst, Citrine, Tourmaline, Aventurine

The Plant Spirits are:

2 **Cinnamon Sticks**
1/4 **Nutmeg** - Chipped
1 **Bay Leaf** or **Cherry Laurel** or **Pine Needle** sprout
1 Pinch of **Mugwort** or **Catnip**

If sucking Medicine is desired for removal of toxins add:

1 **Rose Quartz** Mineral Spirit stone
1 **Spanish Moss** fresh clump from the West side of tree

If sucking Medicine is desired for the removal of pain also add to the above:

1 **Willow** twig and 2 leaves

If sucking Medicine is desired to initiate menses add to the above:

2 Pinches additional **Mugwort**

If sucking Medicine is desired for stomach distress, **instead** of the additional **Mugwort** add:

1 **Oak Bark** 3" piece, inner-part of bark is most important
4 **Oak** or **Elm** leaves
1/2 **Vanilla** Bean

While these are a general form of curative potions, a tea that is prepared this way from the initial ingredients of Cinnamon and Nutmeg and consumed on a regular basis will always enhance your

Well-being and life. To that I would only recommend the occasional addition of the Vanilla Bean portion of the rest.

It is important to add here that it is equally important that the receiver of the potion or tea is also of Prayer for its performance and of specific consciousness of the Union that takes place during their consumption and use of such. Being as specific to any ailment or target will always enhance its potential effect. And simply put, that is the Medicine Way of it....

However it is given for us to use, the Medicine of the Plant Spirit is easily assimilated as long as we apply it in a Respectful Sharing and prayerful way whether eaten with the meal or in potions and teas, or in compresses about a wound or ailment, or in a prayer stick for ceremony. As was previously mentioned, each individual case or malady has its own dynamics and it would be much too difficult to expand upon the many Medicines available from all of the Plant Spirits. As they are much too numerous to list, I am given to describe some of those to which I am given most often to use. While there are no specific recipes provided for the use of each plant in any instant, if one is given to address the Spirit of each plant Respectfully I am certain they will work well in any tea or potion.

I am now given to express the Medicines of the Plant Spirits as follows:

TREES

The Medicine of the Tree is indeed many-fold, as they seem to be as good in teaching as they are in doing any other thing. Tree Spirit, more than any other in the Plant Spirit family, not only says **I AM HERE** but more important **I CAN HEAR**. And like any good teacher, Tree Spirit is a great listener. The major Medicine of all Tree Spirits is truly that of Lesson Giving and thereby the support of growth, as only by learning do we grow anyway. The Medicine of the Tree Spirit is also that of Protector, Nurturer, and Pathfinder as well as wherever the Tree Spirit might grow, others will soon follow. The predominant nature of Tree Spirit is Yin or the female expression, and protection is a very Yin thing. The Protector Medicine of the Tree Spirit is not only that of aiding those that might seek refuge from danger, she is very protective of Mother Earth in the stabilizing of the soil, preventing erosion and the destruction of the very face of her. The Nurturing quality of the Medicine of Tree Spirit is not only in the providing of food for all animals including man but through its constant shedding of its outer layer of Ego bark and leaves in a pattern perfect for all to follow. Tree Spirit nurtures the very ground it lives on and provides a much more fertile ground for others to grow. As mentioned before, perhaps a one-word description of Tree Spirit Medicine is Growth.

APPLE

The Medicine of Apple tree is not only about the Fruitfulness in life but also about the softness and beauty that patience brings. The Apple tree might well be said to embrace the fullness of our senses and to see a Springtime in the dawn of each new day. Like its fruit, the Apple tree combines a relatively thin but tough outer layer to secure a sweet and soft inner fiber of its Being and the bark as well as the leaves of this tree have very good sedative and calming ability in potions and teas.

Caution - Large quantities of the seeds are poisonous (arsenic) and should be avoided.

ASH

The Ash tree represents purity in many cultures and its Medicine might best be expressed as Honesty and Trust. The Ash wood has great strength in its fiber and great strength is the obvious result of Honesty and Trust. All Ash trees have winged seeds and remind us in how we should spread our prayer upon the winds for all to share and hear. The bark of the Ash as well as that of the Willow have soothing Medicine and can be added to potions and teas for pain relief.

ASPEN

The Medicine of the Aspen tree speaks of Love and Constancy as even the shape of its leaf is that of a heart and its bark resembles the pattern of an easy flowing river or stream. The Medicine of the Aspen speaks also of Renewall as after a fire or other land-clearing event they are often the first trees to grow. The Medicinal qualities of the leaves are that of a styptic when applied to wounds and the inner bark will aid in problems of the bowel and in digestion.

BEECH

The Medicine of the Beech may easily be thought as the Fruit of One's Prayer in life as evidenced in the formation of its seed nut representing the four directions. The bark of this beautiful Plant Spirit reminds us of the sea of life and its wood also resembles the eddies and currents of the oceans. The leaves, bark and nuts are of calming

Medicine in teas and potions and bring this Medicine to the digestive system and aid in problems of nervousness. Is it any wonder that they would name a chewing gum after it.

BIRCH

The Birch tree is often thought of as a resource to one's journey in life and is it any wonder, as many of the aboriginal people chose to use its bark in the making of canoes. The Medicine of the Birch might best be expressed as Supporting Change and easing the way in the journey of life as the Birch is also one of the trees that first appears after fires or other earth changing events. The leaves and bark have good astringent and diuretic qualities when used in poultices and teas.

CEDAR

The Medicine of the Cedar tree speaks to us about prayer and of everlastingness as the true condition of the Spirit and life. The Cedar and Sage Plant Spirit are those most often chosen to renew Purity and Wholeness through smudging before and after most of the ceremonies of the aboriginal peoples here. Cedar is also often used for its aromatic quality but most often the wood is used in applications where lastingness is sought. The Medicine of the Cedar is that of Life and Prayer and as we send our prayer to the Great Spirit upon the wings or feathers of the birds, or often in smoke, is it any wonder that the greatest medicinal use of the Cedar is in the application of Prayer. Some varieties of this Plant Spirit are referred to as the Tree of Life and is it any wonder as to why that.

CHERRY

The Medicine of the Cherry tree speaks to us about the sweetness in all conditions of life. And as its fruit has different flavors at different times of its growth, we learn from this wonderful Plant Spirit about the sweetness that is truly the condition of life as we realize our lessons in the process of living it. The leaves of some varieties of this tree are toxic and therefore should be avoided in any potions and teas. The inner bark or seed can be used for a styptic and calmative in small quantity by direct application or in potions and teas. The fruit is described later and the Medicine of this wonderful tree is that of Beauty and Sweetness in the lessons and expression of Life.

CHESTNUT

The Medicine of the Chestnut tree speaks to us about the Celebration of Life and like its seeds are often referred to in songs of rejoicing. The Spirit of this tree is indeed that of rejoicing and reminds us of the need to express thanks for that which we receive, and this is why The Great Spirit made the nuts of this tree so darned hard to get into. Constancy is also a part of the Medicine of this Plant Spirit and we are reminded by it, that with the constancy of our endeavor along the chosen direction of our path of life, we also can achieve whatever it might be that is sought. The medicinal qualities as given to express are in the use of the nut in teas, potions, and diet as they are strengtheners and high in the necessary minerals for quickening any recovery.

COTTONWOOD

The Medicine of the Cottonwood tree is Renewall with Purpose and it is used by many of the aboriginal people to represent the Tree of Life. It is also used to represent the Center of some Medicine Wheels and in the ceremony of Renewall that is called the Sun Dance. The Medicine of this Plant Spirit is that of constant Renewall and the strengthening of the fiber of the Spirit as we encounter struggle or strife. It teaches us how to see the value of adversity as well as benefaction in the expression of Growth, which is Life. The leaf of this gracious Plant Spirit is heart shaped reminding us to have Heart in all conditions of life. Its cottony seeds remind us of the softness of our beginning and that at any time we can Renewall aspects of the pattern of the child of The Great Spirit that is the true condition of our Being anyway. The leaves and bark of Cottonwood trees have calming and pain relieving properties in potions and teas as well as styptic qualities in applications to wounds.

CYPRESS

The Medicine of the Cypress tree is that of Adaptation, or learning to walk in Balance wherever one's path might lead. Able to withstand extremes of condition and ever embracing the wind, the Cypress says, I Can Persevere and Achieve. The Medicine of this Plant Spirit might best be expressed as the Strength of Adaptation and Resolve and is a great teacher in finding beauty and balance in any condition. The bark and leaves of this tree are the medicinal parts of this plant, and in potions and teas are effective in the remedy of headaches and allergies as well as problems with the urinary tract and bladder. The sap can be used as an occasional remedy to the itching of chigger bites and that of the mosquito as well. Also the bark and leaves are good for smudging and bringing forth strength and the Renewall of Hope as well as helping us to remember our Ideal, or direction in life.

DOGWOOD

The Dogwood Plant Spirit comes to us in many shapes and sizes and the Medicine of it is Abundance, Purity, and Softness in Life. The Medicinal qualities of this Plant Spirit come primarily from its bark, and its best application is to the outside of the body in poultices as an astringent. Dogwood bark and dried leaves can work well in potions and teas as a tonic and has great calming Medicine when used that way. The Dogwood might well be spoken of as a Plant Spirit that brings forth the condition to one's Being of that of Inner Peace.

ELM

The Elm is another tree that reminds us of the kernel of the seed of life and the power of our prayer. The Medicine of the Elm tree is that of Hope and the empowerment and strength of Prayer. It is not surprising that many people would plant the Elm in their habitat for the shade that this soft living Plant Spirit provides, as in their inner consciousness they resonate to its Medicine of the comfort of knowing that all prayers are answered and they realize Hope. The medicinal quality of this Plant Spirit's bark and leaves is as an astringent or for use in healing most outer body conditions of irritation or disease. In teas and potions the Elm becomes a great enabler in the restoration of balance and soothing in all problems of the dietary tract.

FIR

The Medicine of the Fir is that of Thanksgiving and Joy. Even its seed cones point the way to the Creator in Thankfulness by growing straight up instead of hanging down like other evergreens. It is little wonder that the Fir is the most common Plant Spirit used to celebrate the Yuletide and Christmas. The medicinal qualities of the Fir are from its needles in teas and potions, as they add a great calming affect to any condition of nervousness.

HICKORY

The Hickory tree is a close relative of the Walnut and its Medicine is that of Strength and Resolve. The seedpod or fruit nut of this Plant Spirit also reminds us of the four directions and its message might be expressed as support from above. The medicinal qualities of the Hickory comes from its nuts and leaves which have a purgative and cleansing effect in the removal of toxins from the system.

JUNIPERS

The Medicine of the Juniper is that of Courage and these Plant Spirits grow often where others fear to tread. It is little wonder that the berry of this wonderful tree is often used to give the flavoring to the mineral Spirits called gin. The medicinal qualities of this Plant Spirit comes from the berries and new growth twigs and add a great calming in potions and teas to problems of the digestive tract. Oils from the berry in diluted quantity are also effective in pain relief to joints in epidermal applications.

LAURELS

The Medicine of the Laurels is that of Passion and the beholding of the sweetness in the experience of life. All members of this family of Plant Spirit are very aromatic especially in the crushing of their leaves, which fill the senses with the feeling of richness. The medicinal parts of the Laurel are its berries and leaves which when used in potions and teas can calm and stimulate the digestive process. Plasters of the leaves and berries aid in curing chest colds and oils from the crushed leaves and berries quicken the healing of any condition of the skin.

MAGNOLIA

The Medicine of the Magnolia is that of softness in the Abundance and fullness of life. The medicinal part of this Plant Spirit is in its bark which works well in potions and teas as a calmative for nervousness and fevers. Poultices from its bark are effective in the remedy of many skin diseases. Some people have been cured from the tobacco habit by drinking Magnolia bark tea.

MANGROVE

The Medicine of the Mangrove Plant Spirit is that of Heart and Sharing. Adaptability might also be mentioned about the Spirit of this tree that thrives in saltwater conditions where others would fail. The unusual roots of this wonderful Plant Spirit are the direct cause of the building of new land as they collect the debris and sediment therein. The rooting habits of this tree also provide safe habitat for mollusks and young aquatic life. The medicinal part of this Plant Spirit comes from the stamen and bean and in teas and potions is a good stimulant against lethargy. The bean has much of the same Medicine as that of coffee, so be considerate in its use or nervousness will result.

MAPLE

The Medicine of the Maple is that of The Sweetness of Breath and thereby Prayer in Life. This Medicine also can be considered as being that of Positive and Supportive expression. Is it any wonder that so many Beings and things would enjoy the taste of the Life blood of this most positive tree in the way of its sap, and the maple sugar and syrup that is commonly refined from it? Indeed, it is not only the sap that is the medicinal part of this Plant Spirit with its resources of calcium and iron, or wood in the production of many household items, fine furniture and toys. But also the chewing of its bark, can prevent dehydration. In potions and teas, the bark or sap is very much a sedative and calmative to the stomach, especially in highly stressed individuals.

OAK

The tree of Magic is what I call the mighty Oak and indeed this wonderful Plant Spirit is found in all parts of Mother Earth. As Magic might best be described as prayer answered, is it any wonder that the wood of this Plant Spirit is the most common of those found in places of religious ceremony. The Medicine of the Oak is that of Magic and Prayer Answered and the great strengthening that we receive therein, and the Oak is one of the Plant Spirits that I use in making Prayer Sticks. The medicinal part of the Oak is the bark and the inner bark is preferred for the curing of all problems of balance and digestion in potions and teas.

PALM

The Medicine of the Palm is that of Nurturing, and is it any wonder that if one was situated with only one Plant Spirit available, this one should be it. All varieties of this caring plant Spirit support growth from the pattern of its stalk to the meat of its seed. The voice of this Plant Spirit might best be expressed as to say, I Support Life. All parts of this Plant Spirit are supportive to one's condition in life, from the shelter and utility of things made of its leaves to the variety of foods prepared from its fruit, bark and leaves. The medicinal parts of the Palm are from its bark, leaves, and berries, and used in teas and potions act as a calmative and stops many digestive problems like that of diarrhea. I also use the bark of the Palm as incense to aid in the increase of one's resources in life.

PECAN

The Medicine of the Pecan is that of richness and Wealth in life and this is another Plant Spirit of whose limb I will often use in the making of a Prayer Stick. The medicinal parts of the Pecan are the bark, leaves and nut in potions and teas and aid in the resource of Self in the curative process as they add a strengthening quality therein. The message of this providential Plant Spirit might best be stated as Sure You Can.

PINE

The Medicine of the Pine tree is much about following the straight and narrow to achieve softness in life. I will often ask this wonderfully supportive Plant Spirit to aid in the process of Renewall and in possession clearing and other problems of the Spirit. The Medicine of the Pine might best be expressed as Support and Brotherhood in the walk of life. The needles and bark are the medicinal parts of the Pine tree and in teas and potions they aid in the release of toxins and fevers as well as the strengthening of systems. Pine needle tea taken regularly will aid in the prevention of most colds and also help in problems of allergies.

POPLAR

All Poplar trees have heart shaped leaves and the Medicine of this family of Plant Spirit is Support in the Affairs of the Heart. Indeed the Medicine might best be expressed as to say I Do, and the wood of this tree is of great utility in its ease of conformity to one's desire. The medicinal part of this Plant Spirit is in its bark and buds which have a calming and soothing effect when added to teas and potions. The buds of the Poplar are also very effective in external use in salves to all conditions of the skin.

REDWOOD

The Medicine of the Redwood tree is that of Strength and Perpetuity and they teach us much about Patience and Growth as they reach heights of over three hundred feet as to be closest to the Great Spirit. The Medicine of this Plant Spirit is mostly that of Lesson Giving and Faith. The bark and needles will make the noblest of teas and potions for the enhancement of the Spirit in a direction finding way. For obvious reasons the parts used from these great trees should have been already voluntary shed and will aid in the calming to any condition of the system.

SASSAFRAS

The Medicine of the Sassafras tree is that of the Beauty of Purity and its leaves and berries are very aromatic when crushed or used as incense. The medicinal part of the Sassafras tree is in its bark and the bark of its root and when used in potions and teas is a great purifier of the system. Sassafras tea has great ability in aiding the process of elimination and the aboriginal people used it regularly in bringing down fevers and in pain relief.

SPRUCE

The Medicine of the Spruce tree is that of Sharing and the Collective Will. The medicinal parts of this Plant Spirit are the highly aromatic needles and young shoots used in potions and teas. The Medicinal qualities in teas and potions of the Spruce are that of a calmative and expectorant in aiding in the relief of symptoms of congestion. The shoots and needles of the Spruce added to a hot bath will aid respiratory problems and plasters of the needles have sucking and soothing Medicine when applied to the skin and joints.

SWEETGUM

The Medicine of the Sweetgum tree is that of the Sweetness of the Unusual in Life and the Beauty and Pleasure of Variety. The gum that oozes from the trunk has been used as a chewing gum and for skin disorders and dysentery. The leaves of the Sweetgum tree are very aromatic when crushed and are very good when used as incense. The medicinal parts of the tree are the balsam or gum and the bark. The leaves and roots are effective in the treatment of wounds and the bark and gum in potions and teas for relief of coughs and colds as well as problems in the bowel.

SYCAMORE

The Medicine of the Sycamore is that of Knowing and the Wisdom of Letting Go of that which is no longer of use. The ball shaped fruit of this tree of Knowledge show us how we should grow, which is ever from the inside out in the Round Way and its broad shaped leaf reminds us of the many ways we can accomplish anything. The medicinal part of the Sycamore tree is its bark and is used in poultices for dressing wounds and other problems of the skin.

WILLOW

The Willow tree has great sucking Medicine and is another tree from which I make Prayer Sticks. The Medicine of the Willow is that of Knowing and of embracing change to achieve softness in life. As the Willow always knows where the water is, the water finding knowledge of this tree is why diviners often prefer its use in locating places to drill a well. Simply put, the Medicine of the Willow would be, I Know. The Willow is a very good tree to talk to. It also is a great sharer and of utility in providing for conditions in life from items made from its limbs and branches to the many healing properties of all parts of this tree, it says, I Share. The medicinal parts of the Willow tree are the buds and bark although I will often also add some of the leaves to potions and teas as well. The ability for the Willow bark to relieve pain and reduce fever has been known for thousands of years and added to any potion or tea its great sucking Medicine is beneficial in the relief of all conditions of swelling and problems in the joints as well.

SHRUBS AND FLOWERS

The Medicine of Shrubs and Flowers might best be described as Sharing, which is also representative of the Spirit of the East in the Medicine Wheel. Shrubs and Flowers are representatives of the cycles of growth and like all Plant Spirits are good teachers. Flowers are more focused upon the current cycle as many of these Plant Spirits live for a term of only one year whereas Shrub Spirits are continuously branching out to experience broader horizons. Both of these Plant Spirits provide great beauty and visual effects with the geometry of their design in both in their pattern of growth and in their production of flowers. Shrubs and Flowers also teach us of the beauty in balance and stimulate all with not only the visual spectrum of colors in their flowers and foliage but with wonderful fragrances also.

ALLSPICE

The Allspice Plant Spirit is an evergreen that presents its fruit in a fleshy purple berry that matures from a white flower. The purple of its berry reminds us that All Can Be and its aroma that seems to be a mixture of things is more about that. The Medicine of the Allspice is truly that of reminding us that all prayers are answered and that All Can Be if we truly want it to. The medicinal part of Allspice is the fruit and in potions and teas is a stimulant and in applications to the skin Allspice Plant Spirit has a soothing and anesthetic effect.

BLOODROOT

The Algonquin name for this Plant Spirit is Puccoon and its primary use was a dye, face and body paint and as an insect repellant. The Medicine of the Bloodroot is that of Remembering the Source and our true purpose in being as children of the Great Spirit. As the Red Ray is that of bringing forth change, the Medicine of the Bloodroot can also be expressed as Remembering our goal of growth. The medicinal part of this Plant Spirit is its rootstock and in potions and teas it has bringing forth qualities as a diuretic, stimulant, and expectorant. The Bloodroot works well in poultices for healing sores and conditions of the skin.

Caution is given as very large doses are fatal, but that can be said about most things.

BUCKTHORN

The Buckthorn Plant Spirit with its purplish berries has a Spirit of Peace and seems to say Relax. The Medicine of the Buckthorn is that of Release of Tension and Fear, as even its name seems to imply letting go of fear and to relax. The medicinal parts of the Buckthorn are its bark and berries, which can be used in potions and teas as a tonic or purgative and diuretic. Also, the bark makes a very good laxative.

Use Caution with the berries, as excess doses are poisonous.

CHICKWEED

The Medicine of the Chickweed Plant Spirit is that of Abundance and Hope and is it any wonder that this plant remains available as a food source under the heaviest of snows. In salads this Plant Spirit is a welcome replacement to lettuce and spinach and serves well steamed or boiled in saltwater. The medicinal parts of the plant is its top portion which when added to teas and potions serve well as a laxative or expectorant. The crushed leaves work well in poultices for application to all problems of the skin.

DAISY

The Daisy Plant Spirit is another good one to eat in salads. Its flowers resonate to the inner child in each of us, and remind us of our true condition as a child of a loving Father Creator and to our potential of returning to a state of innocence, purity and truth. The Medicine of the Daisy is that of Purity, Innocence, and Trust and is a welcome addition to any garden or room setting. The medicinal parts of this Plant Spirit come from its leaves and flowers. The Wild Daisy is most often used as a mild laxative and the crushed fresh flowers have soothing Medicine in the application of poultices to the skin, especially those of an inflammatory nature as well as burns. The Daisy in potions and teas is a calmative for intestinal disorders as well as having the properties of an expectorant.

DANDELION

The Dandelion is one of my personal favorites for dealing with swelling and pain and the Spirit of this wonderful plant is that of Nurturing, Release and that All will be Okay. The medicinal parts of this Plant Spirit are seasonal with the use of the whole plant before it blooms, the leaves during flowering, and the root in the fall. The Dandelion Medicine might well be expressed as Cure All, as in potions and teas it works to remove all poisons from the system and is a tonic and stimulant as well. I most often recommend the use of Dandelion tea in the treatment of joint problems such as arthritis and rheumatism and have often been given in channel to use it in potions to aid in the cure of just about anything in the system that needs release. As with Watercress, Dandelion leaves are a great single source for all vitamins and minerals including copper, calcium, potassium, and iron.

GUMWEED

The Medicine of the Gumweed is that of both Expectation and Release and it reminds me of how we have to give away something to make room for that which we wish to receive. Indeed perhaps better said about the Medicine of this Plant Spirit is that of Prayer. The medicinal parts of the Gumweed are its flowers and leaves, and as these have great sucking Medicine they work well in poultices for all conditions of the skin. Aboriginal people boiled the roots and flowers to get the gummy resin for use in treating asthma and conditions of bronchitis and cough, through potions and external poultices. The Gumweed is commercially grown for this extract, which is added to cough remedies even this to day.

Use Caution, as large doses are poisonous.

HAZEL

The Hazel Plant Spirit is that which I refer to as the trumpeter or the calling forth plant. The Medicine of the Hazel is that of Calling and Fruition of one's dreams. Its medicinal parts are its leaves and the covering of its nuts. The fruit of this plant is very tasty and are sought after by all forms of wildlife. The leaves and nuts added to potions and teas act as a tonic and will also enhance the medicine of other additives.

HOLLY

I will often use the Calming Medicine of the Holly Plant Spirit in wreaths for protection and peace of a place and is it any wonder that the Holly would symbolize the Christmas time with its red berries and dark green leaves. The medicinal parts of the Holly are the bark, leaves, and berries. The bark and leaves in potions and teas are an effective stimulant much like coffee and are best when dried or toasted first. They are also good in removing toxins to purify the blood. Holly also works well in poultices as a remedy for skin problems. The berries in small quantity may be added to potions and teas for the release of worms and parasites.

Use with Caution to quantity lest poisoning occurs.

HOREHOUND

The Horehound Plant Spirit was for a long time used in the making of cough remedies and candy but seems harder to find in this time and day. Horehound Plant Spirit has a Medicine that says life is sweet if we can see past the gray. The Medicine of this Plant Spirit might better be expressed as the sweetness that comes from each new Dawn and that All Can Be. The Medicinal parts of the Horehound are the stem and leaves. In teas and potions they are used as a calmative and expectorant as well as a diuretic tea. In a poultice they can improve conditions of the skin, especially sunburns.

LARKSPUR

Larkspur is often referred to by the settlers as locoweed, and produces blue, white, or purple flowers that are similar to an Orchid in appearance. The Aboriginal people of the Hopi extracted a blue dye from the Larkspur and the settlers used it for ink. The Medicine of the Larkspur is that of Communication but more in the sense of that which is everlasting. The medicinal parts are the tops and leaves and Larkspur in potions and teas is a purgative.

Caution should be taken with its use being restricted to mature yet seedless plant tops as the rest are poisonous.

MOTHERWORT

The Medicine of the Motherwort Plant Spirit is that of Angels Wings, Cupid and Affairs of the Heart. The Medicine of the Motherwort might well be considered as that of a Mothers Love. The Medicinal parts of Motherwort are the flowers and leaves. Added to potions and teas this Plant Spirit has a calming effect for heart, digestive and nervous conditions. Motherwort leaves are an excellent astringent and styptic.

Use Caution as this can cause skin irritations.

PLANTAIN

Plantain is a good source of Iron and a richer source of minerals and vitamins than spinach when eaten. The Medicine of the Plantain Plant Spirit is that of Grace and Strength and its graceful flower stalks are a welcome addition to any room although its persistent nature has caused distress to many a gardener. All parts of this plant have medicinal value. The crushed leaves are good in poultices for all skin conditions including bites and hemorrhoids. Potions and teas from the stem and leaves are remedial to gastritis, coughs, and all respiratory problems. More important perhaps is the use of plantain as a blood strengthener when used in teas and Re-establishment is another quality of this most useful plant.

ROSE

The Rose Plant Spirit speaks of Beauty and Independence of space. The medicinal parts of the Rose are the flowers and hips and used in salads, potions and teas are a welcome addition as a tonic for all affairs of the digestion and heart. All infusions to which rosehips are added will be increased with pain relief.

ROSEMARY

The Medicine of the Rosemary Plant Spirit is that of Peace of Place and its presence in any home or garden is truly a symbol of being at rest. Rosemary is an evergreen and this very nature with their delicate appearance speaks also of their great sensitivity of place. The medicinal part of the rosemary is the whole plant and particularly the top flowers and leaves. In potions and teas the Rosemary Plant Spirit is an effective stimulant of the liver and digestive organs and process. The Rosemary is quite effective in poultices for all irritations of the skin.

Caution is given here as to ingesting large amounts of this plant can cause fatal poisoning, however it is a perfect additive in small quantity.

SAGE

Of note here in the beginning as regards Sage, there are many diverse varieties of this Plant Spirit group and all should be considered for use. Certainly those plants with the fleshier leaves will produce more oils and so forth, and hence the drying techniques and requirements might vary. While I will at times use cedar and the bark or leaves of other Plant Spirits, the Sage Plant Spirit is the one that I use most often in smudging for cleansing and clearing. Actually, there are many diverse applications whereby this Plant Spirit group can "Show its Stuff", not the least of which is as an antihydrotic, antispasmodic, and astringent. Also, like cinnamon, it is commonly included in most infusions of potions and teas. The Medicine of Sage is that of Purification and Clarity of Thought and is a welcome addition to most any salad or meal. The medicinal parts of the Sage Plant Spirit are its tops and leaves. Sage added to any potion or tea is a great purifier to all systems, will also stimulate release, and aids in the process of all eliminations. Sage teas are helpful in the reduction of perspiration, and help end fevers and sweats and all conditions of nervousness.

Caution is given as excessive or extended use of Sage can cause symptoms of poisoning.

SARSAPARILLA

The Sarsaparilla Plant Spirit speaks about the spice of variety in life and is it any wonder the tea was the predecessor to the drink known as root beer. The aromatic roots of the Sarsaparilla are the medicinal parts but were used by the aboriginal people as a food source as well, containing high quantities of vitamins and minerals and especially niacin and iron. Sarsaparilla in potions and teas is a good tonic and strengthener of all conditions of the metabolism and skin and helps in purifying the blood as well. It just makes you feel good to drink and smell the aroma of this tea.

SUMAC

Although the Poison variety of the Sumac family of Plant Spirit is a source of discomfort of the skin, the Medicine of the Sumac is that of Embracing Change and Receiving Fruitfulness in life. The Spirit of the Sumac seems to say Of Course I Can. The medicinal parts of the Sumac are its leaves, bark and fruit and in potions and teas are a calmative and have great soothing and clearing properties as well as being a good skin tonic and cleanser. Aboriginal people chewed the root of the Sumac as a cure for gonorrhea with good effect.

SWEETFERN

The Sweetfern Plant Spirit has a Medicine that speaks of Calmness and Softness in the condition of life. The medicinal part of the

Sweetfern is the whole plant although its rootstock is the primary source of its medicinal value in softening all conditions of the dietary tract. Chewing the root is also an effective means of curing the smoking habit as it promotes mild nausea when used in conjunction with tobacco. Sweetfern is useful in potions and teas as well as baths for all conditions of nervousness.

WORMROOT

The Medicine of the Wormroot Plant Spirit is that of Bringing Forth Inner Peace and Harmony to all conditions of life. The medicinal part of this plant is its root. Boiled and used in potions and teas in small amounts it is a purgative and calmative with good effect. Wormroot was used by Aboriginal people to expel worms and parasites from the system.

Caution must be used with wormroot as the difference between poisoning and that of cure is often in the dosage and this plant is no exception.

WORMWOOD

Not to be confused with the root plant, The Medicine of Wormwood is about Bringing Forth Balance in our walk in life. The medicinal parts of the Wormwood plant are in its leaves, flowers, and tops. In potions and teas, Wormwood will stimulate the appetite as well as all conditions of the circulatory system, and aid in all properties of the digestive tract. External application of the potion or tea will act as a pain reliever to muscles and joints.

Caution must be taken when using the pure oil, as it is a poison so use with moderation.

YARROW

The Medicine of the Yarrow Plant Spirit is that of Collective Thought and Co-operation as well as Brotherhood. The medicinal parts of the Yarrow are its leaves, flowers, and seeds. It is an excellent styptic in the dressing of wounds and an excellent addition to other ingredients in potions and teas as it has great enabling ability and speeds the clotting of the blood.

YEW

The Medicine of the Yew is that of the Straight and Narrow in the path of life and is it any wonder that they were often prized for use in arrows and bows. The Yew also speaks the Medicine of Love and Metamorphosis and it is small wonder that its value in cancer fighting is now sought out. Talk especially nice to this Plant Spirit when using it as it is a very powerful one and should be well respected in that, after all, its Medicine is Metamorphosis. The medicinal parts of the Yew are the fruit, needles and tips of branches as well as its inner bark. In potions and teas the Yew is an expectorant and purgative to all conditions and systems.

Caution to its poisonous nature is prescribed.

VINES AND BERRIES

Vines and Berries are constant in their expression of growth as the Ideal for all of us to aspire to. Unlike some of the Flower Spirits, the Medicine of the Vines and Berries is that of Constancy and the statement of I Will Return. No matter what is done to them they always find a way to bounce back even after the hardest freezes of winter or whatever cutting down a man might do. Strength and Tenacity is indeed the Medicine of Vines and Berries but also that of Co-operation and Sharing as they easily mingle with any other plant or structure that is available to experience and express their fullest sense of growth.

BEARBERRY

The Bearberry is a small evergreen with Medicine that speaks of the Sweetness of Breath in Life and works well in potions and teas as an astringent, diuretic, and tonic. The medicinal parts of the Bearberry are in its leaves. Bearberry tea is a good one for use in conditions of uric acid buildup in joints and all conditions of the bladder, including kidney and urinary stones, as it promotes relief and release.

Caution is advised against prolonged use, as a buildup of poisons may occur.

BLACKBERRY

The Medicine of the Blackberry is that of Change and Protection and is it any wonder that this noble provider of wonderful tasting fruit dies off after the production of it. The Blackberry is a willing supporter of all forms of life and its message is to be Fruitful in one's Growth in life. The medicinal parts of the Blackberry are its roots and leaves and the fruit was also used as a source of dyes. The leaves and roots in potions and teas solve problems in elimination such as diarrhea and are an expectorant and astringent as well. Teas made from the leaves are a good tonic for all problems of digestion and chewing them solves disorders of the mouth.

BLUEBERRY

The Medicine of the Blueberry is one that speaks of Peace Of Place and that of being Fulfilled. As with most berries this is another Aboriginal source of dye and Blueberry medicine seems to say that there is permanence here. The berries have for a long time been used in the making of wine and in this capacity the Blueberry reminds us of how sweet life is. The medicinal parts of this Plant Spirit are its berries, stem and leaves, which act as a calmative in potions and teas. The application of crushed leaves to wounds, cuts and sores will quicken healing.

CHOKECHERRY

The Chokecherry has a Medicine that speaks of Beauty in Moderation as in the consumption of its berries one quickly learns that a little goes a long way. The nature of the Medicine of the Chokecherry is indeed that of Temperance. Its berries and leaves in teas and potions should be used in small quantities, as they are a very good stimulant and purgative of toxins in the liver and bloodstream. Chokecherry tea is another good one for Gout.

CRANBERRY

The Medicine of the Cranberry is that of Rejoice and it is little surprise in finding its widespread use in Thanksgiving. The medicinal parts of the Cranberry are its bark, leaf, and fruit and the participation of these in teas and potions is that of a stimulant, therefore add its bark to teas in moderation as the effect is great. The juice of its berry is often used for conditions of the kidney and bladder but there are much better plants for that such as the Currant or Sumac. The crushed leaves are a good styptic.

CURRANT

The berry of the Currant is a welcome addition to any wildlife meal and the Medicine of the Currant is indeed that of Success in one's Endeavor. The medicinal parts of this Plant Spirit are its leaves and berries and when added to potions and teas or chewed whole they have a great calming effect to all systems. The addition of leaves to teas and potions stimulates the kidneys and is a good diuretic, assisting in the release of body fluids and toxins. The berry juice stimulates the appetite and is a quick solution to most problems of digestion.

GRAPE

The Medicine of the Grape in its many various forms is that of Festival and is it any wonder that it is the berry selected mostly in the making of wine. Both a source of food and drink the leaves and stem also have great sucking Medicine when added to potions and teas and aid in the release of toxins from all systems. The crushed leaves are good in poultices in application to the skin.

HONEYSUCKLE

Another of the Plant Spirits that I like to use in the making of wreaths, the Honeysuckle has a Medicine that brings to Earth the Sweetness in Life. Honeysuckle has good Grounding Medicine and brings forth a quality of Peace wherever it finds itself to be at. The medicinal parts of the Honeysuckle are its flowers and leaves and added to potions and teas are a calmative and aid in all conditions of nervousness.

MISTLETOE

Another powerful Plant Spirit when used in the making of wreaths, the Medicine of the Mistletoe is that of I Want To Belong. The parasitic, evergreen Mistletoe most often likes to grow in the tops of the Oak tree, which is the tree of Magic. Mistletoe actually attaches to the Bark on tree of the host plant and works it way inside, thus having to produce no roots of its own. The host plant then naturally produces a bark coating around it, which the embedded Plant Spirit then easily sprouts its way through. In this manner, the Mistletoe then carries some of the Oaks magic with it when found this way. The medicinal parts are the stems and leaves and when used in potions and teas they have a soothing effect to nervousness and conditions of the heart.

Caution must be used with regard to Mistletoe berries. They are poisonous when eaten and can be fatal to children. Aboriginal people used Mistletoe to cause abortion.

MORNING GLORY

The Medicine of the Morning Glory is that of I Supply and the Aboriginal people often survived times of harshness through the eating of its edible tubers gaining both nutrition and moisture from them. Where the Morning Glory grows one is never in need to survive and the sweet potato is a variation of this most providing of the Plant Spirits. The medicinal value of the Morning Glory is in its leaves and when used in poultices are quick relief to all conditions of the skin, particularly in the relief of burns including sunburns.

NIGHTSHADES

The food group of Nightshades gives us potatoes as well as eggplant and has poisonous varieties as well. The Medicine of the Nightshade is that of Release and often in channel this food group is recommended to be eliminated from the diet particularly where joint pains are experienced in conditions of arthritis and bursitis and conditions of back, arm, and leg pain. The medicinal parts of the Nightshades are primarily its stem and leaves, which provide great pain relief and sooth the skin when applied externally in poultices. In teas and potions the leaves and stem are a good purgative, diuretic and causative.

PASSION FLOWER

The Medicine of the Passion Flower is that of Oh Please and the receiving of Pleasure in the walk of life. The fruit of this generous Plant Spirit is an edible, many-seeded berry that is the size of an egg and reminds me of Rhubarb, but that is just my sense of taste. The medicinal parts of the Passion Flower are its leaves and flowers. In potions and teas the effects of the Passion Flower is that of a calmative and sedative to all conditions of nervousness and stress as are many a headache.

CACTUS AND SUCCULENTS

The Medicine of Cactus and Succulents might best be put as not only Conservation, but also Patience and Faith as the Spirits of this wonderful Plant Spirit group know that indeed all they need will be provided by The Great Spirit in time. These Plant Spirits also teach us to work with the cycles of Prosperity and Leanness and to appreciate the conditions at hand whatever they might be. They also do such not with the toughness required by the climbing nature of some of the Vines, but with a softness in the Heart of Self so as to easily receive, store, and channel the greatest amount of the Great Spirit's Light and Love and any other resources it might need. Instead of approaching life in a harsh environment with a thick Ego outer layer of Bark and Fear, these wonderful Plant Spirits teach us that what is important is what is inside.

AGAVE

The Agave has a Medicine of Everlasting Strength and is often referred to as the Century Plant because of its habit in taking long periods to flower. The Agave is a Plant Spirit of great Resource to the Aboriginal people both in the utility in making many things from the fibers in its leaves and as a food and water source as well. Tequila is made from a variety of the Agave and perhaps that is why this brand of firewater makes the user believe they are bullet proof in a way. The medicinal part of the Agave is the whole plant and in potions and teas has a strengthening effect to all systems and is a diuretic and laxative as well. The juice of the Agave is especially antiseptic to conditions of the skin and is effective in poultices and soaps.

ALOE

The Medicine of the Aloe is Of Course I Can Change. The medicinal part of the Aloe is the gelatin in the leaf and is good for any application to problems of the skin and is especially effective in immediate application to burns. Aloe also has good sucking Medicine and when dried and added to teas and potions is a great purgative.

BARREL CACTUS

The Medicine of the Barrel Cactus is Stability and that of Peace in Place and might be best expressed as Absolute Faith and the peace and patience that come from it. The Barrel Cactus has saved many as an emergency water supply by squeezing the pulp inside. The flowers, pulp and skin of the Barrel Cactus are its medicinal parts and all are good styptics and soothers for all conditions of the skin in poultices. In teas and potions the skin and flowers are good strengtheners for all problems of digestion and elimination and a tea from the pulp is effective for headaches and problems of nervousness.

BITTERROOT

The Bitterroot has a Medicine that says Look At Me or perhaps better expressed as Wait and See. The edible root of this succulent Plant Spirit looses its acridity when removed from the husk. The medicinal parts are primarily its leaves and flowers, but can include its root at times as well. These produce an effective tonic when added to potions and teas and are good relievers of conditions of diarrhea, gout, and even some poisons, bites, and venereal diseases.

MILKWORT

The Milkwort has a Medicine of Purity of Thought and that truly All Can Be. The Medicine of the Milkwort is also that of Support and Stimulation and it was often fed to cows and nursing mothers to stimulate their flow of milk. The entire Plant Spirit of Milkwort has medicinal qualities. In potions and teas it can be used as an expectorant to treat congestion and as an aid to stimulate digestion.

PRICKLY PEAR

The Prickly Pear is a Cactus with a Medicine of Fruitful Aggression. The purple fruit of the Prickly Pear are a wonderful source of food and make a dye that is very long lasting. The medicinal parts are its fruit and skin. Poultices and salves of the skins of it leaves are good for all skin conditions as an emollient. In potions and teas the fruit will aid in digestion as well as headaches.

SAGUARO

The Cactus most often visualized as one is the Giant Or Saguaro that reminds us of a man with hands raised. The Medicine of the Saguaro Cactus is that of Reverence and Support to all conditions of Growth in life. Often seen to support many other forms of life, is it any wonder that this most Reverential Plant Spirit might well be thought of as being truly Stately in its presence in the harshness of the desert. All parts of the Saguaro have medicinal qualities and in teas and potions they make an excellent sedative and a tonic to conditions of digestion.

SANDFOOD

The Sandfood looks like a ball that is half buried in the sand and its Medicine is that of Providence and Support. The Yam flavored stems of this parasitic plant were a dietary staple of the western Aboriginal people of the desert. The Medicinal parts of the Sandfood Plant Spirit are its purple flowers and its stem which when added to potions and teas have great sucking Medicine and act as a purgative. Use of the Sandfood stem in poultices against the skin is a good styptic and relieves pain.

STONECROP

The Medicine of the succulent family of Stonecrop is that of Adaptation and a consciousness to Forever. So effective is its ability in conservation of water that the leaves and plants live for extended periods after being picked. The medicinal parts of the Stonecrops are its flowers and leaves which when crushed and used in poultices are effective remedies to any skin condition. When added to potions and teas the flowers of the Stonecrop are diuretic and enable conditions of release.

YUCCA

The Yucca is another Plant Spirit that provided support to the life of Aboriginal people in providing many useful materials as well having an edible core. In fact there is very little about this Plant Spirit that cannot be found to be most useful. The fibers of the leaves as well as trunk can be woven into thread, rope, cloth, and so forth. Outside of their obvious support in making fire, the leaves can be used for shelter as well as to make baskets or mats. This wonderful and most hardy desert Plant Spirit has been a common source for drink to many a thirsty traveler, be they two legged or otherwise. As should be obvious by now, the Medicine of the Yucca is that of Co-operation and Support. The medicinal parts of Yucca are its leaves and flowers which when used in potions and teas are an effective stimulant to digestion and conditions of the blood stream.

REEDS AND GRASSES

The Medicine of the Reeds and Grasses could best be expressed as Rightful Aspiration. All Reeds and Grasses grow as high as possible for their size ever seeking to be closer to the Great Spirit and share their experience of this growth as willing neighbors with whatever might also live close by. All Reeds and Grasses exemplify the Prayer Proper, which is to walk or to grow in Balance and with Harm to No One, including Oneself and all also exhibit the Earthplane experience ideal of Brotherhood and Respectful Sharing. Reeds and Grasses also teach us the benefit of accepting the Winds of Change and to bend with the wind and embrace it instead of fighting it in a Self-destructive way.

CANE

The Medicine of Cane is that of Brotherly Support and is it any wonder it is used in the making of many structures and things. Cane is also edible and the pulp, seeds, and rhizomes may be ground and used in making breads. Sugar Cane is a part of this family that Supports the sweetness of Brotherhood in life. The medicinal parts of Cane are the seeds, leaves and pulp. The leaves when crushed and used in poultices add a calming effect and the seeds, leaves, and pulp together add a strengthening effect.

CATTAIL

The Cattail is another staple in the diet of Aboriginal man as its Rhizomes can be baked like a Yam when peeled, or pounded into flour for bread. All the parts of this most gracious of the Plant Spirits is very tasty at times of the year and the Medicine of the Cattail is that of Support and Balance in Life. The medicinal parts of the Cattail are the leaves and the bud of it stem. When used in poultices the Cattail is highly styptic and its effects are quickly realized. In potions and teas, the buds and leaves are calmative to any conditions of nervousness.

REEDGRASS

The Reedgrass is second in height to the Giant Cane and is quite similar in its utility in the making of things. Having beautiful yet ornamental and often seedless plumes, the Medicine of Reedgrass is that of embracing Strength yet Softness in life. The medicinal part of the Reedgrass is its rootstock and when added to potions and teas, is a diuretic and a good laxative.

RICE

The Plant Spirit called Rice has a Medicine of Harmony and as a food item, Rice goes well with just about everything. Wild rice was a mainstay in the diet of many Aboriginal people and is still one that I favor. The medicinal part of the Rice is in its flower spike and in potions and teas it is a great calmative to the digestive tract.

RUSHES

The Plant Spirit known as the Rush has a Medicine that says I Can, or perhaps better said might be I Know I Can. The Medicine of the Rush speaks of that felling of the Heart and it is indeed the rootstock of the Rush that when used in potions and teas helps in ailments of the heart or bloodstream. The leafy tops are good for weaving and add the quickening effect of a calming force when added to potions and teas.

RYE

and it is small wonder why it is often selected for use in preferred beverages and breads. The medicinal parts of Rye come from its leaves and seed-head. The oils from its seed sooth and heals wounds and burns and slows the aging process upon the skin. In potions and teas Rye is a calmative and soothes all problems of the digestive tract.

SOAP PLANT

The Soap Plant was another of the Plant Spirits of
The Rye Plant Spirit has a Medicine of Grace great use to Aboriginal people and its Medicine is that of Utility and Release. The bulb of the Soap Plant is the medicinal part and its juice when rendered makes a good fixative or glue for attaching things. The juice when used in poultices has good sucking Medicine for rashes and other conditions of discomfort of the skin.

SPIKEGRASS

The Plant Spirit known as Spikegrass or Sea Oats has a Medicine that speaks of Gentleness and Softness. The Medicinal parts of Spikegrass are in its rhizome and seed head and can be added to any tea or potion as a diuretic and calmative to the digestive tract. The rhizome crushed and used in poultices will quicken relief of pain in the skin.

MOSSES AND LICHENS

Mosses and Lichens teach us much in providence and finding resources within. Mosses and Lichen are great conservators and reclaimers of resources and all in this group have great sucking Medicine. These Plant Spirits also remind us of co-operation and the necessity of patience in our endeavors and the attainment of long range goals.

LICHEN

The Medicine of the Lichen is that of the Abundance provided by the Great Spirit and of Hope. The Lichen grows in places and conditions where no other Plant Spirit can. I often use Lichen in combination with Spanish Moss for its sucking and strengthening ability. The Lichen added to potions and teas has a great calming and strengthening effect and is good for any condition of anxiousness and stress. In poultices, the Lichen has a softening effect and is good for the removal of poisons from bites.

SPANISH MOSS

The Medicine of the Spanish Moss is that of Absorption and Peace and Comfort of Place and I often use the Rose Quartz in conjunction with it. The medicinal part of the Spanish Moss is the whole plant and it has great sucking Medicine in external application to the skin. In potions and teas Spanish Moss aids in the removal of toxins from all systems and in poultices it has a soothing quality in addition to its great sucking Medicine.

FERNS AND MUSHROOMS

Ferns and Mushrooms remind us of the ethereal nature of our being on Earthplane and if there is one specific group of Plant Spirits that personify the merging of the Spiritual body with the Physical body, this one is it. The Medicine of Ferns and Mushrooms is that of the Expanded Consciousness in the true nature of our being and reminds us that All Can Be.

FERNS

The Medicine of the Fern is that of Grace and Wholeness as our true condition of being. The medicinal part of the Fern is its rootstock and is boiled for its ingredients to an infusion. In potions and teas the Fern is a good purgative and helps in the removal of worms and parasites from the digestive tract. In poultices, the Fern is a good pain reliever for all conditions of the joints, muscles and skin.

Use <u>Caution</u> with the male plant as when ingested it is poisonous. This is not the case with the female plant.

MUSHROOMS

The Medicine of the Mushroom is Remembering the true Spiritual Nature of things. The Medicinal parts are the tops and like the Fern, it is boiled to obtain its ingredients. In potions and teas, the Mushroom has a stimulant effect and assists in renewing the appetite however, excessive use may cause nervousness and excitability. In poultices the Mushroom has a pain relieving effect to all conditions of the skin.

<u>Caution</u> must be used when choosing Mushrooms as many are poisonous which restricts most varieties except the Chanterelles from most medicinal and other use.

WATER PLANTS AND ALGAE

Water Plants and Algae remind us of the Source and strengthen our link to the Great Spirit. The Medicine of the Water Plants and Algae is that of Inner Peace. As we observe their bounty in the embrace of the water of lake, stream or sea we are brought to an awareness and remembering of who and what we truly are, each of us the children of a caring and loving Great Spirit Father who wishes only the best for us and asks that we willingly open our consciousness to receive.

ALGAE

The Medicine of the Algae is that of Abundance and providence and all forms of this soft Plant Spirit are edible. Many of this variety are being added to commercially prepared foods for their high nutritional value and mineral content. Wherever Algae grows nothing need go hungry. The medicinal parts of this Plant Spirit are the leaves and buds. In potions and teas the Algae is a calmative to all form of intestinal disorder and aids in liver and kidney function. In poultices, Algae is an excellent remedy for burns and irritations to the skin from the wind and sun.

KELP

The Medicine of the Kelp is that of support of Growth and like the Algae is edible and a great source of Iodine if not always so tasty. The medicinal part of the Kelp is its leaf and when boiled in an infusion is also an excellent treatment in poultices to the skin. In teas and potions kelp adds a strengthening effect especially when one is in a weakened state and acts as a calmative to conditions of the bowel and digestive tract.

FRUITS, VEGETABLES
NUTS AND HERBS

The Medicine of the Fruits, Vegetables, Nuts and Herbs Plant Spirit group is that of Fulfillment, Nurturing, Balance, and Care and indeed if one is of such a desire as are some people in today's society, all that is needed to sustain the nutritional requirements to support life on the Earthplane are found here. Inclusive in this group are many Plant Spirits whose Medicine is more for Healing than Nutrition however both have a place in a balanced Earthwalk. The Medicine of this group of Plant Spirits might also be expressed as that of Caretaking and Fulfillment and that we should embrace the spice of life in our expression of our Being in our Earthwalk experience, or Walk in Joy and Enjoy your Walk.

ALMOND

The Medicine of the Almond is that of Courage and Faith and it is small wonder that its application to cancer treatments is finally being expressed. The medicinal applications of this Plant Spirit are varied. When ground the almond can be used in skin emollients, soaps and poultices. When pressed, the oil has sedative properties and can be added to potions and teas to help ease conditions of stress in all systems.

ANGELICA

The Medicine of the Angelica is that of All is Heaven Sent from a loving Creator and reminds us of the Power of Prayer. The medicinal parts of Angelica are its rootstock and seeds. The spicy nature of its rootstock makes Angelica an excellent stimulant in potions and teas and supports overall improvement to the digestive tract. Used in poultices the roots and seeds of Angelica have a soothing quality when applied to the skin.

Caution should be taken as large doses can cause anxiousness and rapid respiration and heartbeat.

ANISE

The Medicine of Anise is that of New Beginnings and Renewall. The medicinal component is best derived from the seeds with alcohol or in boiling in water. Anise is an excellent accelerator and stimulant in potions and teas and makes a good tonic for all conditions of upset. Anise in poultices works well in refreshing the skin and is very soothing to muscle cramps.

ARROWROOT

The Medicine of the Arrowroot plant might best be expressed as Ever To Be Sure. In earlier times many tribes used the Arrowroot as a complete resource plant providing food and weaving materials as well as being a curative. Currently the most used part of this plant is the root in a ground-up state, which makes a beautiful white powder. The very nature of the ground-up white powder is that of Foundation and Stimulation of the Growth of one's Spirit. If one consciousness might be applied to the Medicine of Arrowroot it might be that of Supporting all conditions of Growth, Flow, and Affairs of the Heart. In potions and teas the addition of Arrowroot is truly a wake up message to one's Spirit, which is ever necessary to stimulate Renewall and Growth and thereby one's Well-being. The inclusion of Arrowroot in potions and teas and in the preparation of foods provides a binder upon which other properties and substances can balance upon and increase their individual effect. Arrowroot potions and teas are effective as a stimulant and foundation for bringing forth positive change and are also effective in all conditions where fever is present. Arrowroot can provide a positive remedial effect to problems of the digestive and pulmonary tract and all conditions of the heart. In poultices Arrowroot has good absorptive qualities and is a very effective astringent as well as pain remedy.

ASPARAGUS

The Medicine of Asparagus is Renewall and Growth to attain the sweetness in life. The medicinal parts of Asparagus are the seeds and young shoots, which act as an evacuant and diuretic therefore affecting kidney and bowel function and should not be ingested if problems in the kidneys are present. Asparagus helps in conditions of rheumatism, arthritis and gout and the seed when crushed has a calming effect on the dietary tract.

AVOCADO

The Medicine of the Avocado is that of Wealth and the Seed of Life. The Avocado when ingested is a strengthener to all systems in times of stress and aids in the remission of migraine headaches. Avocado contains no less than fourteen minerals all of which stimulate growth. Included in these are copper, iron, sodium and potassium all of which are good blood strengtheners.

BANANA

The Medicine of the Banana is that of Sunlight as it is a source of natural warmth and energy. The high potassium content of the Banana benefits the muscular system and the meat of the Banana support the bacteria that causes digestion. Bananas are easily digested and are good for enhancing any condition especially that of recovery.

BARLEY

The Medicine of Barley is Settlement and Rest. Un-winnowed barley (that still has the husk on) when boiled is a good purgative and winnowed Barley (with the husks removed) is more astringent and cooling to the dietary tract. Barley in teas and potions aids in conditions of nervousness. The properties of cooked Barley make it useful as a soothing membrane in poultices for tumors and sores.

BASIL

The Medicine of the Basil might be expressed as Twin Lips or perhaps better is To The Lips. Basil is good for improving all conditions of the dietary tract and it makes a good preventative to disorder if ingested regularly. In potions and teas Basil is good for any headache and is a stimulator to the appetite and an antispasmodic for coughs as well.

BAY LEAF

The Medicine of the Bay Leaf is that of A Fresh Start and New Beginnings. Bay Leaf is another name for the Laurel and is commonly used in food preparation as a spice. Because of its tonic and calmative abilities, the bay oil either from boiling or pressed from berries and leaves is an excellent liniment for chest colds and respiratory problems, rheumatism, and skin issues such as bruises and so forth.

BEET

The Medicine of the Beet is that of Seeing Red or Change. As well as being a good source of minerals, Beets help the system assimilate minerals are good for release of acids in the bowel and problems in the Gall Bladder and Liver. The Beet is high in vitamin A and assists with all conditions of the digestive tract.

BROCCOLI

Another of my favorites for helping those with sinus problems and allergies is the Medicine of the Broccoli, which is that of Fruition. Broccoli is high in vitamins A and C and aids all processes of elimination, including that of the sinus. When eaten with protein Broccoli stimulates the acids of the Brain so it is always a smart Plant Spirit to eat.

BURDOCK

The Medicine of Burdock is Co-Operation or better said is To Go With the Flow. The medicinal parts of Burdock are the roots, leaves, and seeds. In teas and potions Burdock is effective for some in easing constipation and for others it reacts just the opposite. Burdock is good for all conditions of intestinal distress and is a good calmative to conditions of nervousness as well. Fresh leaves in potions or teas are good for the relief of liver problems and in poultices work well in calming irritations to the skin.

CABBAGE

The Medicine of Cabbage is that of Stability of Purpose. The medicinal part of Cabbage is its leaf in all varieties and is an excellent laxative. The Juice of the Cabbage is good for accelerating the healing process and is helpful in the remedy of stomach ulcers. Cabbage is rich in minerals and is an especially good source of sulfur and iodine, which enable it to be very effective when used in poultices for conditions of the skin.

CAMOMILE

The medicinal part of the Camomile is the flower and its Medicine is that of Felling Free. The Camomile Plant Spirit in potions and teas is a good stimulant, tonic, and antispasmodic. Camomile is good for the relief of fevers and all conditions of nervousness and problems in the dietary tract. The extract of the oil in poultices aids in the remedy of callouses and painful joints.

CARAWAY

The Medicine of the Caraway Plant Spirit is that of Singleness of Purpose or Staying on Track. The medicinal part of Caraway is the seed and in potions and teas makes a good expectorant as well as a good stimulant to all conditions of the dietary and reproduction systems.

CARROTS

The Medicine of the Carrot is that of Suredness and Focus and being of a Singular Mind. The Carrot is a good Plant Spirit to help in matters of concentration. The tops of the Carrot are very high in Potassium and the root is extremely high in vitamin A, which enhances the eyesight. Carrot in potions and teas is a good diuretic and stimulant and a good remedy for any intestinal disorder.

CATNIP

Catnip is a mint and as the Medicine of it is Playfulness and Joy, no wonder the felines like it so much. The medicinal parts of Catnip are the leaves and tops. In potions it is a good antispasmodic for any condition of the digestive tract and in potions and teas Catnip is a calmative and is good at calming bronchial disorders.

CAULIFLOWER

The Medicine of the Cauliflower is Fruitfulness of Endeavor and the medicinal part of the plant is its leaves, which are high in sulfur and calcium and work well in poultices for dressing wounds and burns. The leaves and florets are good additions to the diet for their strengthening effect.

CAYENNE

The Medicine of the Cayenne is that of Making Change and to the senses this pepper is most hot. The medicinal part of the Cayenne is the fruit and is a general stimulant to all systems. The ingestion of Cayenne in any form is a good preventative and tonic to any onset of a cold and ingesting any amount will stimulate the appetite. The

Cayenne when used in poultices will draw increased blood flow to the area and is good for arthritis and pleurisy, however -

Use <u>Caution</u> in the length of application as skin burns and irritations will occur if left on the skin too long.

CELERY

The Medicine of the Celery is that of Strength of Conviction and the medicinal parts of this Plant Spirit are in its stalk and leaves. Celery when eaten is a good source of sodium, potassium, and magnesium and maintains a condition of wellness in most systems of the body. Celery leaves in juices, potions, and teas aid in digestion and purify the blood and are calming to all conditions of nervousness.

CHIVE

The Medicine of the Chive is that of Sweetness of the Variety in life. The medicinal parts of the Chive are its leaves and flower head. Eaten or used in potions and teas, the Chive is an excellent stimulant to the process of digestion. Chive is high in iron and is a good strengthener to the condition of the bloodstream as well.

CINQUEFOIL

The Medicine of the Plant Spirit known as Cinquefoil is that of Expectation of Good Things to Happen. The medicinal parts of Cinquefoil are the leaves, root, and stems. In potions and teas it is a good antispasmodic so is effective against disorders of the digestive tract including cramps. Other uses are as an astringent, pain remedy and as a calmative. In poultices the root and its bark are effective in the stopping of bleeding.

CLOVE

The Medicine of the Clove is Perpetuity and its medicinal part is the flower buds. Clove oil will stop toothache pain and in potions and teas will relieve pain, nausea and vomiting. Clove is also a great calmative to all parts of the digestive tract and is good in poultices for its pain relieving ability.

CINNAMON

The Medicine of Cinnamon is that of being the Plant Spirit compliment of the Mineral Spirit Citrine. Just as Oak has the same Medicine as Tourmaline in being the tree of Magic which is Prayer answered, Cinnamon has the medicine of Prayer and thereby the magnetism of bringing forth one's desire. I personally use Cinnamon Sticks as the basic starting elements of all of my potions and teas and in such usage it has the property of enabling fluid transfer between the cell walls and therefore is a natural diuretic and will promote fluid movement and passages this way. Cinnamon is also a natural stimulant to the appetite and calmative to all systems.

COMFREY

The Medicine of the Comfrey is that of Let It Be and the Peace that comes from that. The medicinal part of Comfrey is its rootstock and in potions and teas is a good calmative to nervousness in the digestive tract and an anti-inflammatory to all of the digestive system. Comfrey works well in poultices to all conditions of the skin for its healing and renewing ability to cuts, abrasions, and bites.

CORIANDER

The Medicine of the Coriander is that of Softness in One's Step and the medicinal part is the seed. The Coriander in potions and teas is a good calmative to all conditions of the digestion and a stimulant to the appetite as well. In poultices and application to painful joints Coriander has good sucking Medicine in the removal of pain.

CORN

The Medicine of Corn is the Sense of Heartfelt Thankfulness. Maize and Corn have in modern times supplanted Rice and other native grains to the Aboriginal peoples of all of the Americas. Next to Rice, Corn is one of the next easiest foods to digest and is high in roughage for those seeking that in their diet. The Yellow Corn is valued over the White because of its higher phosphorous and magnesium content. Corn in poultices and its oil in liniment have a very softening and soothing effect.

COWSLIP

The Medicine of the Cowslip is that of Good Cheer and Friendliness. The medicinal parts are the leaves and stems of this Plant Spirit and in potions and teas is a calmative, diuretic and expectorant. Cowslip should be dried or cooked before use but can be freshly eaten in the springtime as greens.

CUCUMBER

The Medicine of the Cucumber is that of Safety and Comfort. Cucumber aids digestion and has a purifying effect upon the bowel and bloodstream. Whether used in potions and teas or eaten whole Cucumber is effective in removing toxins and acids from the body through elimination, making a good remedy for heart and kidney problems. Cucumber juice is effective in poultices and lotions to all problems of the skin. Cool as a Cucumber describes its cooling effect upon the blood.

DILL

The Medicine of Dill is that of Bonus or Receiving More Than Expected or as might be said getting an Extra Inch. The medicinal parts of the Dill are the fruit and leaf and in potions and teas it is a calmative and diuretic. Dill is also good for insomnia and stimulating the flow of milk and for calming all conditions of the digestive tract.

DOGBANE

The Medicine of Dogbane is that of Release From Worry and its medicinal part is its rootstock. Dogbane in potions and teas is a good cathartic, expectorant, and stimulant. Dogbane is good for treating constipation, dropsy, gallstones and most conditions of fever. Small doses of Dogbane can be used in poultices for pain relief.

ECHINACEA

The Spirit of the Medicine of the Echinacea is that of Attack and Fortify. The medicinal part is the whole plant though at times the root is preferred. There is a chemical compound in this Purple Coneflower

"Warrior" that the indigenous peoples of North America have been using seemingly forever, to remedy injuries as well as cure any illness. Echinacea can be taken periodically as a Preventative as well as a Curative as it stimulates the immune system and attacks bacteria and viruses. Oftentimes used in conjunction with Goldenseal, Echinacea is truly a "Flower of Life".

ELDERBERRY

The Spirit of the Medicine of the Elderberry is that of Forgiveness. Elderberry juice is a good tonic and purgative in teas and potions. The Wine of the Elderberry is also a good tonic and infusion. When added to poultices, the juice or berry is a good remedy and skin protector.

ERGOT

The Medicine of Ergot is that of Never Ending and reminds us of Perpetuity. Ergot is a fungus that replaces the seeds of the Rye Plant Spirit. Ergot is a source of LSD and works in the manipulation of the vessels of the bloodstream. Ergot is very effective in the constriction of blood vessels in the relief of migraine and other types of headaches and besides its effects of constriction, is very effective in the removal of pain.

While beneficial in the control of hemorrhaging, use with extreme caution in applications to those with Heart conditions.

EUCALYPTUS

The Medicine of Eucalyptus is the benefit of using a sense of Frivolity in obtaining Balance to the Winds of Change. The medicinal part of the Eucalyptus is the oil in its leaves and if eaten in small quantity is a quick remedy to any kind of pain. The leaves when chewed should be quickly expelled as Eucalyptus has an extremely strong stimulant effect. The leaves in potions and teas have a strong energizing effect and work very well in the relief of bronchial congestion. In poultices, Eucalyptus gets to the heart of the problem and expels fluids quickly while greatly relieving pain.

EVERLASTING

The Medicine of the Everlasting is that of Strength of Conviction in walking one's path. The medicinal parts of Everlasting are the leaves and stems, which may be chewed alone or added to salads. In potions and teas Everlasting calms anxiousness and relieves pain. Aboriginal people smoked Everlasting and found it effective against headaches. Everlasting in poultices works well for pain relief and reconditioning of the skin.

FENNEL

The Medicine of Fennel is that of Blowing One's Own Horn or that of Proclamation. The medicinal parts of Fennel are the roots and seeds. Fennel in potions and teas is a stimulant and excellent remedy of all conditions of the digestive tract and increases the appetite as well. The oil boiled from the seed of Fennel is good in poultices when applied to the skin in the removal of pain from joints. When added to water Fennel is an excellent remedy to problems of the eyes and can be used singularly or with Eyebright as an eye-wash or as steam for immediate effect.

FLAX

The Medicine of Flax is Helpfulness and Soft Support to the conditions of life. The Medicinal part of Flax is the seed and in potions and teas is a good purgative to chest, digestive, and urinary disorders. Flax oil is also that called linseed oil and when ingested is a quick remedy for the release of gallstones. Use only mature seeds and when boiled and the residue is used in poultices, Flax is very good for rheumatic complaints.

FOXGLOVE

The Medicine of Foxglove is the Remedy of Waste. The medicinal part of Foxglove is the leaves and is the source of the heart drug digitalis. In potions and teas Foxglove is a powerful stimulant and medical supervision is recommended before its use. Even touching the leaves of this plant has caused rashes and nausea in some people. When used in small quantity or in emergency conditions of stroke or heart attack, Foxglove is a very good one to use. I call it a lifesaver Plant Spirit but I am respectful in its use.

Caution, **this is a poison, do Not use without medical direction**.

GARLIC

The Medicine of the Garlic is that of I Forgive and that of I Believe. The Medicinal qualities of the Garlic has been celebrated since the early times of civilizations and in mineral content it is high in iodine and sulfur which makes it extremely effective chopped and placed in poultices to the skin. The medicinal part is the bulb but I like to include the flower parts in meals as well for their seasoning effect. Garlic eaten and in potions and teas has Great Renewing effect to the pulmonary system and is found to be an effective treatment in problems of asthma and tuberculosis. Garlic in teas and potions is an excellent diuretic, expectorant, digestive, and antispasmodic and if eaten regularly is A good preventive to any distress to any system or onset of a cold. Garlic is good for the returning to balance the condition of any and all systems. Garlic is also a natural preventative and strengthener to all systems and heightens one's metabolism without causing stress or anxiety. Garlic also has good effect in clearing work and ceremony. It is also effective in relationships and situations where one wishes to rid oneself from unwanted witchcraft influences and effects.

GINGER

The Medicine of Ginger is that of Release, therefore Forget and Renewall is often spoken by the Spirit of it. The medicinal parts of Ginger are its leaves and rootstock. Ginger in potions and teas, especially when hot, is an excellent purgative and purifier, which helps release toxins from the system and will stimulate the menstrual cycle as well as perspiration. Ginger teas and potions when taken at the onset of a cold will help in the quick recovery from it, and Ginger is a good stimulant to the appetite as well. The leaves of Ginger when crushed and used in poultices have a stimulating effect in the removal of pain by helping in the increase in circulation to the area.

GINSENG

The Medicine of Ginseng is that of the Orient, or might best be expressed as The Path of the Sun. The medicinal part of Ginseng is the root and it is a strong stimulant when chewed. Ginseng in potions and teas is very effective in purifying the blood and assists in the release and recovery from toxins and poisoning. Because it is a sedative to nerve centers while also increasing blood circulation to the brain, Ginseng in potions and teas is a stimulant while also providing a calming effect in all conditions and systems. Ginseng is especially effective in conditions of stress or hemorrhage. Aboriginal people used Ginseng to calm stomach distress and as a love potion.

GOLDENSEAL

The Medicine of Goldenseal is that of the Removal from Excess. The medicinal parts of Goldenseal are its rootstock, flower, and leaf all of which are effective in poultices for their antiseptic properties. In potions and teas calms the digestive tract and helps with any problems requiring a tonic. Goldenseal rootstock is to be used in potions and teas as a very good douche and will relieve problems in the mucous membranes. It is also an effective eyewash and strengthens the gums.

HELLEBORE

The Medicine of Hellebore is that of Setting Oneself Free. The medicinal part of Hellebore is the rootstock. In potions and teas Hellebore is a stimulant and strong diuretic and acts as a purgative in the release of toxins from all systems. It stimulates the Renewall of balance to the emotional body in problems of mania and depression.

Caution, getting Medical direction in all circumstances is recommended in any use of Hellebore as it has a very strong effect upon the heart.

HOPS

The Medicine of Hops is that of Frivolity and Play in Life. The medicinal parts of Hops are its fruit and leaves. Poultices made with the fruit and leaves sooth and cool sunburn and other skin conditions.

Potions and teas with the fruit of the Hops added will calm nervousness, stimulate the appetite and also act as a diuretic.

Caution, prolonged use of Hop teas can have a negative effect and should be avoided.

HORSERADISH

The Medicine of Horseradish is that of I Can See Clearly. The medicinal part of Horseradish is its root, which is a welcome addition in spicing up any meal especially with beef. In potions and teas, Horseradish is a good tonic and diuretic and is quite effective for gout, bladder infections and any disorder of the intestinal tract. Ground Horseradish used in poultices is a strong stimulant and irritant and thus aids in increasing the blood flow to the effected area as in joint pain or rheumatism.

HYSSOP

The Medicine of Hyssop is That is That and might better be expressed as Completeness or Self-sufficiency. The medicinal parts of Hyssop are its leaves and stems and when crushed in poultices are an effective cure for wounds to the skin due to their astringent effect. Hyssop in teas and potions is a good stimulant, diuretic, expectorant, and general tonic to the digestive system. Hyssop is good to use to correct any problem of internal infection and seems to be good for just about anything just as its Medicine implies. If any Plant Spirit might be considered a Cure All, Hyssop is just about it.

JASMINE

The Medicine of Jasmine is that of Finding the Way. The medicinal part of Jasmine is its flowers. The flowers if eaten in small quantity or used in potions, teas, or poultices are calming and this calming ability is why Jasmine oil is used in the application of massages.

JIMSON WEED

The Medicine of Jimson Weed is that of Great Expectations. The medicinal parts are the seeds and leaves and in poultices have a cooling and astringent effect. Jimson Weed in potions and teas is a strong narcotic and hypnotic and calms coughs and the bronchial tract. Smoking the Jimson Weed has helped some with respiratory problems with some hallucinogenic side effects.

Extreme <u>Caution</u> is to be used with Jimson Weed, as an overdose will be fatal.

KALE

The Medicine of Kale is that of Finding Support from Everything. Kale is high in sulfur, iron, calcium and vitamin A and when added to the diet strengthens bones and teeth. The medicinal part of Kale is its leaf and when used in poultices Kale has a cooling and soothing effect especially to any condition of burn or abrasion. Whether eaten or used in potions and teas, Kale is a good calmative to the digestive and nervous systems.

KNOTWEED

The Medicine of Knotweed is that of Mass Transit or Transportation. The medicinal part of Knotweed is the flower head and in poultices is a good astringent. In teas and potions Knotweed is a diuretic, and calms dysentery, diarrhea and all processes of digestion. Knotweed is a good calmative for breathing and lung problems and works as a coagulant to assist in all forms of internal bleeding, especially those of stomach ulcers.

LEMON

The Medicine of the Lemon is that of: Of Course I Can or it might best be said, A Very Positive Attitude. The medicinal part of the Lemon is its fruit, which is rich in potassium as well vitamins C, B1, and G and being highly alkaline, aids in the prevention and treatment of colds. Lemon is a good enabler and assists other ingredients in doing their work. Lemon juice is a good astringent and eating Lemons or drinking tea with Lemon will aid in purging toxins from the body. In poultices, Lemon juice is good for sunburn, warts, corns, and anomalies to the skin.

LENTIL

The Medicine of the Lentil is that of Calling Forth Renewall to Balance. Lentils have been cultivated for use since before the Bronze Age and are a legume whose protein content is second only to the Soybean. Lentil is high in its mineral content as well and is a good source for phosphorus, calcium, and iron. Eaten whole or used in potions and teas, Lentils are a very good purgative to the muscle acids in the body, strengthen the heart and purify and the bloodstream.

LETTUCE

The Medicine of Lettuce is that of Softness of Flesh or better said, Sensitivity. Leaf Lettuce is what is being described here and in the diet Lettuce is a good source of iron and vitamins A and C. Lettuce looses its medicinal value quickly after being picked and is strongest when allowed to go to seed. The medicinal parts of Lettuce are its juice, leaf, and flower head. In potions and teas Lettuce has a sedative and narcotic effect. It helps induce sleep. In poultices crushed Lettuce has a soothing effect and is good used as a wash after a burn or other issue to the skin. Aboriginal people used Lettuce tea to stimulate the flow of milk.

LIME

The Medicine of the Lime is that of Limitless Hope. Limes are good in the relief of arthritis as they are high in vitamin C and share great alkalizing ability with the Lemon. The medicinal part of the Lime is the fruit. In poultices the crushed skin gives a cooling and soothing effect to burns and abrasions. In potions and teas Limes are good for treating conditions of mental illness, distress and anxiousness. As a drink Lime juice has the ability of increasing blood flow to the brain and will effectively cool any condition of the head and calm the digestive tract.

LOBELIA

The Medicine of Lobelia is that of Peace of Mind and Release of Anxiousness. The medicinal part of Lobelia is the whole plant. In potions and teas Lobelia is a diuretic, purgative, antispasmodic, and expectorant and aids in helping one catch one's breath in cases of asthma and whooping cough and other problems of the chest. In poultices Lobelia's Sucking Medicine is very effective in removing poisons from the skin.

Caution - Overdoses of Lobelia are poisonous.

MANGO

The Medicine of the Mango is that of Lets Dance and the medicinal part is the fruit, which is very high in vitamin A. As the Mango's high sugar content provides quick energy, it has often been recommended in channel to me for helping those with problems of low energy and stress as both a stabilizer and calmative. Mango juice reduces body temperature and is effective in purging toxins from the blood.

MARJORAM

The Medicine of Marjoram is that of Heart Felt, Heart Sent, or simply Thankfulness. The medicinal parts of Marjoram are the leaf and stem. Oil of Marjoram is distilled from fresh and dried leaves, stem and flower tops and is a good toothache remedy. Marjoram in potions and teas is a good tonic, calmative, expectorant, and diuretic, and helps to relieve pain anywhere in the body, especially in the stomach and head. In poultices Marjoram helps to relieve pain with its sucking effect.

MARIJUANA

The Medicine of the Marijuana is that of So What or Perspective. The medicinal part of the plant can be found throughout all parts at specific times of the year. The hemp variety of this plant has been grown for its vast utility for centuries, primarily for its fibers in making things like rope, paper, and cloth products. Now it is being explored as a source for bio-fuels as well as biodegradable plastic products. While oftentimes used recreationally for various reasons, there is documented proof of its effects at blocking pain in some cases as well as calming digestive, neurological, and movement disorders. Marijuana will not relieve pain in the same way that an aspirin will, instead it will alter perspective and move the attention to something other than the pain.

MELON

The Medicine of the Melon is that of Lessening the Overhead or might better be expressed as Getting Rid of Excess Baggage. Melons are high in sodium as well as vitamins A, B, and C, if eaten to the rind. The rind, if juiced, is good for gland and blood building effect. The medicinal value of Melon is as a purgative and aid in alkalinizing the system against disease as well as restoring balance to all aspects of the system by replenishing the water supply and strengthening the bowel.

MILFOIL

The Medicine of Milfoil is that of Socialism or Sociability. The medicinal parts of Milfoil are the leaf and stem. Milfoil in potions and teas is good for any circumstance concerning the bloodstream as well as being an antispasmodic for nervousness and problems of digestion. In poultices Milfoil is a good remedy for any skin pain or discomfort.

MILKWEED

The Medicine of Milkweed is that of Revival or Rejuvenation and the medicinal part is the rootstock. In potions and teas Milkweed is a diuretic and a good purgative for all problems of the kidney or in eliminations. In poultices Milkweed juice is good for warts and other aberrations to the skin.

Caution - in large quantity Milkweed is poisonous, especially to children.

MINT

The Medicine of Mint is Saturation of the Senses or it might be expressed as the Flower of Life. The medicinal part of Mint is the leaf and in poultices Mint has an astringent effect, relieves itchiness and is cooling to irritation. In potions and teas Mint calms all parts of the digestive tract and offers quick relief to pains and cramps as well as nervousness, headaches and problems of the chest.

MUGWORT

The Medicine of Mugwort is that of Forever I Can, or perhaps best stated Realizing the Power of Prayer. Mugwort is often added to the tobacco in my Medicine Pipe and its medicinal parts are the rootstock and herb. Mugwort in teas and potions is a mild purgative, stimulates the appetite, refreshes all conditions of the digestive system, can aid in the regulation of menstruation and assists in the Renewall to balance the condition of all systems. In poultices Mugwort is a good pain remedy and provides relief of itching from poison oak.

MULLEIN

The Medicine of Mullein is that of Sheepskin or better said, Completion. The medicinal parts of Mullein are the leaves and flowers and when used in poultices will quicken the healing process of wounds or skin irritations. In potions and teas Mullein is a diuretic, antispasmodic, and expectorant and helps ease congestion in the chest and dietary tract. The flower of Mullein in tea will relieve pain and help induce sleep as a sedative. Inhaling the steam of the flowers added to boiling water relieves nasal congestion and other respiratory problems.

MUSTARD

The Medicine of Mustard is that of Vexation and the Release of it. The medicinal part of Mustard is the seed. In poultices Mustard is very effective in the removal of pain in the joints and in muscle strain and stimulates blood flow to the affected area. Mustard in potions and teas is a good stimulant to all functions of digestion.

Caution - Do not use the oil upon the skin in an undiluted state as it is a powerful irritant and burning will occur.

NETTLE

Nettle Medicine is that of Catch as Catch Can or Spontaneity. The medicinal part is the whole plant. In teas and potions Nettle is astringent, diuretic, tonic, stimulates the digestive tract and is effective in controlling blood loss and problems of the urinary tract.

Caution – Raw plants are poisonous to the kidney. Steam young Nettle plants before eating.

NUTMEG

The Medicine of the Nutmeg is that of I Will Always Be or simply put Stability. The Medicinal part is the nut. The Nutmeg in teas and potions is aromatic and a stimulant and stimulates digestion. Nutmeg is also hallucinogenic and can be used to stimulate the brain, especially in conditions of lethargy.

Caution - eating just two whole Nutmegs can be fatal.

OAT

The Oat has a Medicine of Substance and the medicinal parts are the grain and straw. In poultices the seed and particularly the straw have good sucking Medicine. The straw may be used in baths and teas for pain relief of muscles, joints, and problems of the chest. The Oat in teas and potions is a nervine, antispasmodic, and stimulant to conditions of the dietary tract.

ONION

The Medicine of the Onion is that of Tomorrow is a New Day or as might best be said, Do Not Worry. The medicinal part of the Onion is the bulb. Onion when eaten, have a high sulfur content and are very good for the heart, liver, and bloodstream. The Onion eaten or in potions and teas is a good purgative and tonic for all respiratory disorders and is a good stimulant to the digestive tract. Onion juice is used most often as a diuretic or expectorant but will serve also as a strengthener to all of the systems. In poultices the Onion is good for bronchial inflammations.

ORANGE

The Medicine of the Orange is that of Bringer of Light in Life. The medicinal parts of the Orange are the rind and flowers. In poultices Orange rind and flowers have good sucking and soothing ability. The Orange in potions and teas is a good purgative, stimulant and general tonic to all systems and its high vitamin C content make the Orange a good food to eat in prevention of disorder to any system.

PARSLEY

The Medicine of the Parsley is Suredness. The medicinal parts of Parsley are the leaf, seeds, and stem. Crushed Parsley leaves in poultices quicken the healing of wounds. In potions and teas, Parsley is a good purgative, blood purifier, expectorant, diuretic, and antispasmodic as well as being an effective remedy to most problems of inflammation including the kidney and digestive tract. Parsley also builds blood and stimulates the brain.

PARSNIP

The Medicine of the Parsnip is Forever More or Great Expectancy. Parsnip when eaten is a good source of minerals especially calcium and phosphorus. The medicinal part of the Parsnip is the root and when ground in poultices, have a stimulating and drawing effect upon pains in the joints. Parsnip is good for the bowel and supports the liver and in teas and potions is a diuretic and purgative of toxins in the blood.

PEA

The Medicine of the Pea is companionship or Lets Hang Together. The Pea when eaten in the pod and especially when steamed is a good source of vitamins A, B1, and C as well as iron and other minerals. The Medicinal parts of the Pea are the pod and seed and when crushed and used in poultices have a good sucking effect in the remedy of poisons and bites. Peas when eaten are diuretic and aid in the removal of acids in the digestive tract.

PEACH

The Medicine of the Peach is that of Joy and Grace of Position of Place in life and the calmness that goes with it. The Peach when eaten is high in vitamin A and easy to digest. The medicinal parts of the plant are the fruit and leaves. Crushed leaves used in poultices have a soft drawing effect useful in burns, bites, sores and wounds. The Peach leaves in potions and teas are a good diuretic, sedative, laxative and purgative for conditions of the chest and digestive tract. Peaches help remove toxins from the system, aid in the recovery from illness and are a great cleanser for the kidneys.

PEAR

The Medicine of the Pear is I Know I Can or the Strength of one's Conviction. Pears are high in vitamin and mineral content and because of their alkaline excess Pears are good energy producers in times of stress. The medicinal parts of the Pear are its leaf and skin, which are very effective in soothing wounds to the skin when applied in poultices. When eaten Pears are good for the digestive and elimination process.

PEONY

The Medicine of the Peony is Message Carrying or the Transportation of Communication. The medicinal part of this Plant Spirit is its rootstock. The Peony root in potions and teas is a diuretic, sedative, and antispasmodic and has good effect upon the organs of elimination, especially the bladder and kidney. The Peony is very effective in assisting in the release of toxins from the system including the bloodstream.
Caution - the flower is extremely poisonous.

PEPPER

The Medicine of the Green or Bell Pepper is that of Wholeness and Space. When eaten the Pepper adds silicon as well as high content of vitamins A, B, and C to the system. The medicinal part of the pepper is the fruit and its influence upon the systems is largely that of a strengthener and preventative.

PERIWINKLE

The Medicine of the Periwinkle is that of I Spy Happiness in Life or it might be expressed as Seeing the Good in Things. The medicinal part of Periwinkle is the herb (the portion above the root) and in potions and teas Periwinkle is a good astringent and sedative that can aid in calming diarrhea, menstruation and hemorrhaging as well as conditions of nervousness and hysteria.

PEYOTE

The Medicine of Peyote is that of Time and Space and a sense of Endlessness or Perpetuity. The medicinal part of this succulent cactus is its fleshy leaf. Peyote in potions and teas is a strong hallucinogenic and narcotic and some Aboriginal peoples still use it to induce visions in a Spiritual way.

Caution - Use Peyote only with supervision.

PLUM

The Medicine of the Plum is Softness in Times of Strife. The medicinal parts of the Plum are the fruit and bark. The dried fruit when eaten is a laxative and high in phosphorous content. Plums in potions and teas are a good purgative to the digestive tract, and adding the bark to teas and potions is good for sores of the mouth and throat. In poultices juice from the fruit is soothing to burns.

POKEWEED

The Medicine of Pokeweed is the High Road in Life and Consciousness. The medicinal parts of Pokeweed are the root, leaves, and fruit. Pokeweed, like the red color found in its stem, is very orientated to the circulatory system and Flow. Oftentimes, I have used a few of the berries or some of the flower head to help induce the moon time process in women that have had difficulty in such. The juice of the fruit has been used in the treatment of everything from cancer to hemorrhoids and tremors. The dried root or leaves in potions and teas is anodyne and cathartic, and is a good laxative as well as remover of pain. In poultices, Pokeweed is good at relieving pain from joints and reducing inflammation.

Caution - In preparation of this Plant Spirit for use in meals such as in Poke Salad, it is recommended boiling the leaves twice, as insufficient cooking of the plant can be poisonous.

POMEGRANATE

The Medicine of the Pomegranate is the Forever Spring or that of Endless Renewall and Joy. The medicinal parts of the Pomegranate are the seeds and rind of the fruit. The seeds in potions and teas are an astringent, causative, and purgative and are one of the oldest recorded cures for tape or other kinds of worms in the system. The rind of the Pomegranate is high in tannin and works well as an astringent whether in poultices to the skin or in potions and teas as well as a douche. The juice of the Pomegranate is also a good purgative and remedy to bladder and kidney problems.

POTATO

The Medicine of the Potato is that of Inner Peace. The Potato is one of the Nightshades discussed earlier and should be avoided in conditions of Gout and Arthritis. The medicinal parts of the potato are the flesh and juice, which work well in poultices for their deep drawing effect of poisons from wounds and bites.

PUMPKIN

The Medicine of the Pumpkin is that of Forever the Clown or experiencing Playfulness in life. Pumpkin when eaten is high in sodium and potassium. The medicinal part of Pumpkin is the seeds and the oil from the seed is especially effective in poultices applied to wounds and burns. The seeds when eaten or used in potions and teas are a good anthelmintic (for the release of worms in the system.)

RADISH

The Medicine of the Radish is that of Spreader of Joy. The medicinal part of the Radish is the root and is a diuretic, astringent, antispasmodic and a calmative to nervous disorders when eaten or used in potions and teas. The Juice of the Radish is a remedy to coughs and problems of the chest as well as that of the gall bladder.

RASPBERRY

The Medicine of Raspberry is Wet and Wild. The Medicinal parts are the leaves and fruit and Raspberry is astringent, cardiac, and calmative. The leaves used in potions for the skin makes a good wash for wounds and sores. In potions and teas Raspberry leaves and juice make a good remedy for diarrhea and the relieve of nausea, stress and pain.

SAFFRON

The Medicine of Saffron is that of Stick-To-It-iveness or might best be said Persistence. The medicinal part is the stigma of the flower, which is why it is quite expensive. In poultices Saffron is good for gout and in potions and teas Saffron is a calmative, sedative, and expectorant which aids in calming coughs and any condition of the chest and helps avert the effects of allergy.

Caution - Use Saffron in small doses as large ones will be fatal.

ST JOHNSWORT

The Medicine of St Johnswort is that of an Informant or a Caution to Betrayal. The medicinal part of St Johnswort is the herb and in poultices is an effective astringent. The oil is very effective in speeding up the healing process of any wound or skin distress. In potions and teas St Johnswort is a nervine, expectorant, and antispasmodic and is an especially good expectorant and calmative to problems of the chest as well as helping with problems of sleep and nervousness.

SANDALWOOD

The Medicine of Sandalwood is that of Fineness of Breath in Speaking of Life or perhaps Better Said. The medicinal part of Sandalwood is the wood from which is Sandalwood oil is extracted. Sandalwood in poultices is antiseptic and disinfectant and good in washes in the treatment of all wounds to the skin. In potions and teas Sandalwood is a good diuretic, expectorant and stimulant and helps relieve problems of the chest and urinary tract.

SENNA

The Medicine of Senna is that Of Helpmate in the Path and the Clearing of Obstacles along it. The Medicinal part of Senna is the leaves and in poultices are a softening irritant to calluses and corns. In potions and teas Senna is a good laxative and diuretic and will remove worms and restore balance to the digestive tract.

SNAKEROOT

The Medicine of Snakeroot is that of Voraciousness, or Large Appetite for Life. The medicinal parts of Snakeroot are the root, leaf and flower head. In poultices, Snakeroot is an irritant and helps draw out poisons from bites and pain from joints. In potions and teas, Snakeroot is a purgative and general tonic for problems of nervousness and distress.

SORREL

The Medicine of Sorrel is that of I will Never Forget and the medicinal part of this Plant Spirit is the whole plant. Sorrel in poultices is good for the treatment of any problem of the skin and in teas and potions Sorrel is a good astringent, diuretic, and laxative, working well with stomach hemorrhaging or excessive menstruation.

Caution – Consuming large quantities of Sorrel is poisonous to the kidneys.

SPINACH

The Medicine of Spinach is that of Wanderlust or Forever On Journey to see what is there. Spinach when eaten fresh is about forty percent potassium and is high in iron, calcium, and vitamins A and C. The medicinal part of Spinach is its leaf and when eaten or used in potions and tea is good for the lymphatic, digestive, and urinary systems.

SQUASH

The Medicine of Squash is that of A Kernel of Knowledge and ever Seeking to Know More. The medicinal parts of Squash are the fruit and leaves. Squash when eaten is high in sodium and potassium and is good for digestion and elimination. Used in poultices Squash effectively sucks poisons from wounds. Squash rind and seeds in potions and teas stimulates the brain, is a slight hallucinogen, aids in the condition of low energy and is a nervine.

STICKELWORT

The Medicine of Sticklewort is that of Seeking Refuge or Getting Out of the Rain. The medicinal part of Sticklewort is the whole plant. In poultices Sticklewort is very good for varicose veins and provides pain relief to conditions of the skin and joints. The root in potions and teas strengthens the liver and the plant in potions and teas is an effective remedy to problems in the gall bladder, kidney, liver, and spleen as well as helping in the removal of toxins from all systems.

STRAWBERRY

The Medicine of the Strawberry is that of To The Point or Directness. The medicinal part of the Strawberry is the fruit and when eaten is a good source of potassium, sodium, vitamin A, and simple, or fruit sugar, which is helpful in energizing and aiding the condition of recovery.

SUMACH / BLUE

The Medicine of Blue Sumach is that of Foretold Knowledge and the Spirit of Wisdom of the Ages. The medicinal parts of Blue Sumach are the bark, leaves, root, and fruit. The Blue Sumach leaves and fruit in poultices are good for the relief of irritations to the skin like that of poison ivy and are also used as a styptic. Aboriginal people chewed the root as a cure of venereal disease. In potions and teas, Blue Sumach is an astringent, tonic, diuretic, and coolant and is good for any conditions of elimination and problems in mucous membranes.

TARRAGON

The Medicine of Tarragon is that of The Stream of Events in the Path of Life or might be said Reflection. The medicinal part of Tarragon is the flowering plant and in poultices is an irritant remedial to painful joints. In potions and teas Tarragon is a diuretic, tonic to the digestive system, hypnotic and calmative and assists with kidney function and any condition of nervousness.

THYME

The Medicine of Thyme is that of Ringing In the New Cycle or Year or more succinctly put, is the Spirit of Renewall. The medicinal part of Thyme is the herb and in poultices it is especially good for rejuvenating the skin and as a local irritant Thyme is good for warts and encourages blood flow to the surface. Thyme baths are good for rheumatic conditions and paralysis as well as bruises, swellings and sprains and a Thyme salve is an effective remedy for shingles. In potions and teas Thyme is a calmative to the digestive tract, an expectorant to conditions of the throat and chest and works as a sedative as well.

TOBACCO

As the Medicine of Tobacco is that of Wealth and Fertility, it is of little wonder or surprise that this is one of the most sacred Plant Spirits to most Native American people and Medicine people in particular. As indigenous peoples, and especially Medicine people, we have been using Plant Spirits for maintaining Well-being and Balance as well as healing since day one, so to speak. Tobacco has been used to cure everything from wounds, snakebites and abdominal distress to skin problems.

TOMATO

The Medicine of the Tomato is that of Chagrin over Fearfulness or that as being The Embarrassing Truth of Love as the Condition of all Things. Tomato is one of the foods often given in channel to restrict in one's diet due to its acid nature and because it is especially effective in worsening problems of the digestive tract, arthritis and pains in the muscles and joints. Tomatoes when eaten with certain other greens as in carrot tops are an effective liver cleanser and remover of toxins and it is given that the Tomato should be eaten mostly baled and skinless to receive its beneficial effects.

TURNIP

The Medicine of the Turnip is that of For Heavens Sake or that of Surprise. The medicinal part of the Turnip is the root or tuber. Eaten raw the Turnip is high in vitamin C and the juice is good for catarrhal conditions (inflammation of mucous membranes, especially the nose and throat). Poultices can be applied to the chest and throat to relieve symptoms of congestion. The Turnip ground in a salve is a good coolant to irritations of the skin.

VANILLA

The Medicine of the Vanilla Bean, which indeed comes from an Orchid plant is that of Hope Prayers come true and reminds that of their everlastingness in our growth. Indeed just as a single Hope Prayer that is realized to oneself in becoming answered by Great Pop, outlasts and outweighs many Fear Prayers is it any wonder that this product of a certain type of Orchid would come from a Plant Spirit type that retains its flowers for months at a time. Yes the Medicine of Vanilla is that of Hope but is also that of everlasting beauty as well and in this can easily positively alter and positively affect one's attitude and mood. I use vanilla in potions and teas as a positive additive supporting extreme conditions and therein it operates both as a blending agent as well as a calmative, sedative, and enhances the digestion process as well as can by itself operate as a dietary aid in reducing one's thirst or appetite.

WATERCRESS

The Medicine of the Watercress is that of Symphony or the Making of Beautiful Music, Together. Watercress is extremely high in mineral content and Vitamins A and C. The medicinal parts of Watercress are the leaves, shoots, and roots. In teas and potions Watercress is an excellent strengthener to all systems, helps purify the blood, is a diuretic, stimulant, purgative, and expectorant and is an aid for serious problems of the respiratory tract such as tuberculosis.

Caution - prolonged use can lead to kidney problems and the juice should always be used with something else for best effect.

WITCH HAZEL

The Medicine of Witch Hazel is that of Where Ever I Can or perhaps better said is Freedom of Expression. The medicinal parts of Witch Hazel are the bark and leaves. In poultices Witch Hazel is effective as an astringent to the skin and has good sucking Medicine in removing pain and poisons from stings and bites. In potions and teas, Witch Hazel is astringent, sedative, and tonic and a good remedy for diarrhea and other maladies of the digestive tract.

WOODRUFF

The Medicine of Woodruff is that of Fighting Back or Vanquishing the Oppressors in Life. The medicinal part of Woodruff is the herb and in poultices is a good irritant in the removing of pain in the joints. In teas and potions Woodruff is a diuretic and calmative and is beneficial for jaundice, migraine, stomach pain and conditions of nervousness.

WOOD SORREL

The Medicine of Wood Sorrel is that Of the Bird In the Bush and the feeling of Free to Rest. The medicinal part of Wood Sorrel is the herb and in poultices is very calming and cooling to the skin. Wood Sorrel in potions and teas is a calmative, diuretic, and anodyne and is good for enhancing the properties of the digestive tract as well as being an effective remedy for problems of the liver and digestion.

YAM

The Medicine of the Yam is that of Sunshine on a Cloudy Day or Sweetness of Breath. The medicinal part of the Yam is the tuber. Yam in the diet is a good source of fiber, niacin and vitamin A and enhances the process of elimination. In poultices the Yam is very effective in the Renewall of the conditions of the skin and is especially effective for all conditions of burns.

APPLICATION

OF

PLANT SPIRIT MEDICINE

In the descriptions previously stated each Plant Spirit was initially described as to its Medicine, its medicinal part or parts and its typical usage in regards to the way I would use it as practicing Medicine Man. Again stated, the definition of Medicine is the Resonance To A Value System, Ability, or Consciousness. Perhaps for some, an easier way of considering Medicine might be the Essential Nature of a thing, and yes everything that is, has Medicine. Each Plant Spirit has a Medicine that is a specialty to the consciousness of its species. Just as the Mineral Spirits all share a Medicine of Support to Prayer and Growth, the Plant Spirits all share a Medicine of Support in the Way of Proper Growth. Mineral Spirit in any form is excellent in the channeling of energy and the transmission of prayer. Yet, some are better specifically than others, much like calling an electrician to fix your faucet. While many might be able to do the work, few of them would be able to do such as easily or as well as a plumber would. The Medicine given for each Plant Spirit is much like that and knowing and giving consideration to such in the selection of which to use in any application, can be used to best effect the desired response with the greatest respect and ease.

The more that one knows about and understands the Medicine of any one thing, the easier it is to work with it in a Respectful Sharing way, which is the definition of Relationship Proper. Great care and Prayerful thanks as well as the bidding of one's desire should be administered to the Plant Spirit in proper preparation for its inclusion into any poultice, tea, or potion. The effects of such will truly be much improved over that done in any other fashion. The easiest way to choose them is to take a small part of each that is being considered for use into one's mouth. Then while sucking on it, become at one with its Spirit by embracing it in one's consciousness and then heart as the meal, potion, or tea is being prepared. In this way, all is done and developed in the manner of a sacred union and marriage. As one thinks about the Medicine of each part of the preparation, including even the stove, pot, utensils and water, all are honored and understood. This coupled with one's particular Prayer of Desire in the use and outcome of the combination of such, will imbue into it a greater enabling and harmony as well as Potential than can be accomplished by any other means, period.

In the removal of a part of or a whole plant living or dead from Mother Earth, a Prayer of Respectful Thanks given to the Great Spirit for providing it and the Plant Spirit for making itself available for use, is always most appropriate. Often I will give the earth or remaining part of the Plant Spirit a token of my appreciation in a gift of a stone or tobacco. The guideline for the selection and removal of a part of a Plant Spirit for use in meals, poultices, potions, and teas is as follows:

SOUTH	-	PROTECTION & RESOURCE
WEST	-	RELEASE & UNDERSTANDING
NORTH	-	WISDOM & STRENGTH
EAST	-	REALIZATION & ENLIGHTENMENT

In the selection of Spanish Moss from trees or Moss on the ground for use in poultices the following guideline is given for use:

SOUTH	-	*EFFECTS OF THE BODY - PHYSICAL* *SUCKING POISONS / RELEASE*
WEST	-	*EFFECTS OF THE HEART - EMOTIONAL* *CALMING ANXIOUSNESS / DIRECTION*
NORTH	-	*EFFECTS OF THE SOUL - SPIRITUAL* *SOUL CLEARING / POSSESSION AND ENTITIES*
EAST	-	*EFFECTS OF THE MIND - MENTAL* *RENEWALL / REVITALIZATION*

For those who might be curious about this differentiation regarding the selection of the Moss, which is really slight in the greater sense, it is that the Moss in itself is a complete Plant Spirit and it chooses most often to hang around this way.

In closing about the Medicine of Plant Spirit is that they each, like us, are a complete and unique creation of the Great Spirit. They choose to incarnate just like us and are provided by Him and themselves in a very loving way to teach us how to Grow. Plant Spirits support us in our experience of Life in this magical garden of Eden that is Mother Earth and the Earthplane.

Have You hugged a tree lately?

May The Great Spirit Keep

Warmth in Your Heart And

Softness in Your Bed,

This And Every Day!

White Eagle

*****

Plant Spirit Medicine Index

-A-

Agave	320	Angelica	333	Asparagus	334
Algea	331	Anise	333	Aspen	295
Allspice	306	Apple	295	Avocado	334
Almond	333	Arrowroot	333		
Aloe	320	Ash	295		

-B-

Banana	334	Beech	295	Blueberry	315
Barley	335	Beet	335	Broccoli	336
Barrel Cactus	320	Birch	296	Buckthorn	306
Basil	335	Bitterroot	324	Burdock	336
Bay Leaf	335	Blackberry	315		
Bearberry	315	Bloodroot	307		

-C-

Cabbage	336	Celery	338	Coriander	339
Camomile	336	Cherry	296	Corn	339
Cane	324	Chestnut	297	Cottonwood	297
Caraway	337	Chickweed	307	Cowslip	340
Carrots	337	Chive	338	Cranberry	316
Catnip	337	Chokecherry	316	Cucumber	340
Cattail	324	Cinnamon	339	Currant	316
Cauliflower	337	Cinquefoil	338	Cypress	297
Cayenne	337	Clove	338		
Cedar	296	Comfrey	339		

-D-

Daisy	307	Dill	340	Dogwood	298
Dandelion	307	Dogbane	340		

Digestion, digestive tract - 299, 312, 324, 325, 325, 331, 333, 335, 337, 338, 339, 340, 342, 344, 347, 350, 351, 352, 353, 354, 356, 359, 361
Direction Charts - 284, 363

-E-

Echinacea	340	Elm	298	Eucalyptus	341
Elderberry	341	Ergot	341	Everlasting	342

-F-

Fennel	342	Fir	298	Foxglove	342
Ferns	329	Flax	342		

-G-

Garlic	343	Ginseng	344	Grape	316
Ginger	343	Goldenseal	344	Gumweed	308

-H-

Hazel	308	Holly	308	Horehound	309
Hellebore	344	Honeysuckle	317	Horseradish	345
Hickory	299	Hops	344	Hyssop	345

Headache - 298, 318, 320, 321, 334, 335, 341, 342, 350

-I-

Itch relief - 298, 349, 350

-J-

Jasmine	345	Jimson Weed	345	Junipers	299

-K-

Kale	346	Kelp	331	Knotweed	346

Kidneys - 315, 316, 331, 334, 340, 349, 351, 352, 353, 355, 357, 358, 360,

-L-

Larkspur	309	Lentil	347	Lime	347
Laurels	299	Lettuce	347	Lobelia	348
Lemon	346	Lichen	327		

-M-

Magnolia	299	Milfoil	349	Motherwort	309
Mango	348	Milkweed	349	Mugwort	350
Mangrove	300	Milkwort	321	Mullein	350
Maple	300	Mint	349	Mushrooms	329
Marijuana	348	Mistletoe	317	Mustard	350
Marjoram	348	Morning Glory	317		
Melon	349	Moss/Spanish	327		

-N-

Nettle	350	Nightshades	318	Nutmeg	351

-O-

Oak	300	Onion	351
Oat	351	Orange	351

-P-

Palm	301	Pecan	301	Plum	354
Parsley	352	Peony	353	Pokeweed	354
Parsnip	352	Pepper	353	Pomegranate	354
Passion Flower	318	Periwinkle	353	Poplar	302
Pea	352	Peyote	354	Potato	355
Peach	352	Pine	301	Prickly Pear	321
Pear	353	Plantain	309	Pumpkin	355

Parasites, removal - 308, 312, 329
Poison, caution - 295, 306, 308, 309, 310, 311, 312, 313, 315, 317, 318, 329, 343, 348, 349, 351, 353, 354, 357
Poison Ivy - 358
Poison Oak - 350
Poison, removal of - 307, 321, 327, 344, 348, 352, 355, 357, 361
Potions, recipe - 292

-R-

Radish	355	Reedgrass	324	Rosemary	310
Raspberry	355	Rice	324	Rushes	325
Redwood	302	Rose	310	Rye	325

-S-

Saffron	356	Snakeroot	357	Sticklewort	358
Sage	310	SoapPlant	325	Stonecrop	322
Saguaro Cactus	321	Sorrel	357	Strawberry	358
Sandalwood	356	Spikegrass	325	Sumac	311
Sandfood	321	Spinach	357	Sumach/Blue	358
Sarsaprarilla	311	Spruce	302	Sweetfern	311
Sassafras	302	Squash	357	Sweetgum	303
Senna	356	St Johnswort	356	Sycamore	303

-T-

Tarragon	358	Tobacco	359	Turnip	359
Thyme	359	Tomato	359		

Teas, recipe - 292

-U-

-V-

Vanilla - 360

-W-

Watercress	360	Woodruff	361	Wormwood	312
Willow	303	Wood Sorrel	361		
Witch Hazel	360	Wormroot	312		

-Y-

Yam	361	Yew	313
Yarrow	312	Yucca	322

*****

ANIMAL SPIRIT

KNOWLEDGE

BY

TO SPIRIT,

MY GREAT EYED WHITE KITTY
            THAT I SO DEARLY LOVE,

I THANK YOU FOR ALWAYS BEING AT MY SIDE,
AND FOR YOUR GREAT LOVE AND CARE
FOR ME AND OTHERS,

INDEED I HAVE LEARNED SO MUCH
ABOUT SPIRIT AND LOVE FROM YOU.

            O HEY ECHI-ANA-NA!

TO SPOT,

SPIRIT'S SPIRITUAL CHOCOLATE SON
THAT I DO SO LOVE TOO,

I THANK YOU FOR BEING MR. SNUGGLES
AND FOR YOUR SWEETNESS AND THE TIMES
THAT YOU DON'T WHINE,

I HAVE LEARNED A LOT ABOUT MYSELF,
 THROUGH YOU.

            ESTE KENNI-WA-HA!

CONTENTS

Nature   374

Medicines   379

Swimmers   382

Walkers   395

Fliers   420

Life   444

Animal Form Medicine Summary   446

Animal Form Cross Reference Index   451

From White Eagle   452

A Prayer to the Two-Leggeds   457

Index   459

NATURE

Today is Friday, the day of the week that seems most comfortable as being my day for ceremony as some might consider church. Upon the completion of my Pipe Ceremony I asked The Great Spirit what it is next for me to do. I had just finished completing several projects when a Butterfly came by and said "Now it is time to write about me and Animal Spirit Medicine".

In considering what the Great Spirit had told me through the Butterfly, I talked to one of my Cats whose name is Spirit and is a great white kitty about eleven years old. He showed me how he would sometimes incarnate as a Wolf or Fox and I began to wonder about such things.

I learned a long time ago about this vibration called Spirit and how all Spirit is vibration and how to see by resonance the vibration of Spirit in all things made by the Great Spirit Creator. It mattered not whether these things made by Him were Mineral, Plant, Animal, or even the Wind or other forces and elements, as I recognized the unique vibration of each that was indeed the Spirit of it. I had accepted that as being the condition of these and all things without giving it too much thought.

I had already learned that Medicine is the resonance to the forces of the vibration of things. The lesson of Butterfly Medicine is that of Metamorphosis or Christ consciousness, whereby the Caterpillar, which used to crawl about and eat the Plant, changes and renews the pattern of Self through the cocoon time or Metamorphosis. This is a process that we also go through periodically. Earlier in life I was given to understand that our Earthwalk is a continuum of Metamorphosis and growth. I began to wonder if I had ever been one of these things such as a Plant, Cat, or Butterfly and so I asked the Great Spirit. His response was simply "NO".

It was then that I began to wonder about the true nature of things and His plan for our growth and I remember what Spirit said to me about being a Wolf and Fox at times. Then I recalled how at times I may change the form of Self so as to help others in dream time whereby I might show up as an Elk, Deer, Wolf, or any of a variety of things that at the time would do the most good. I asked Spirit why he was a Cat this time and he said "So I could be with you again this way", and I had always known this loving vibration had been with me many times before. I seemed to be digging a deep hole thinking about these things so I relaxed from the process a bit. Sometimes it is hard to explain to others what you have always just known.

I then thought about how when I asked the Creator why I was White Eagle, He showed me how and why I was made in the perfect Bird form by Him before the Earthplane was made and the hole got a lot deeper. Then I thought about how I was able to go inside things such as the bodies of others including Plant, Animal and Mineral forms and I then thought this is really getting absurd as the hole was now complete.

Having had many previous experiences in this hole digging process when looking for truthful answers about such things, I knew it was time to go back to the Source.

So then in meditation I asked, "Father, what is the true nature of things"? He laughed and smiled at this great hole that I had dug for myself, saying that I had been very busy it seemed. Then He proceeded to explain it to me this way;

In the beginning of the idea that is what we call the Earthplane, He created the all of it including the galaxies and the stars in the heavens as an idyllic place for growth whereby all present there would serve Him by serving the Him in each other. The Mineral Spirit would serve the Plant Spirit by providing it with a place to grow and food to eat, and the Animal Spirit with the composition of its body. The Plant Spirit would serve the Mineral Spirit by spreading its roots to make room for more to grow and in its death by turning into stone, and serve the Animal Spirit by providing it shelter as well as food to eat and air to breathe. The Animal Spirit would serve the other two by being caretakers of them, spreading the seeds of the plants through foraging and fertilizing the seeds with its droppings and then its body when its Earthwalk journey for that cycle was complete.

In every case and condition, each served for the Well-being and betterment in the condition of the whole, which is the definition of Brotherhood, and all was in a perfect condition of Balance and Brotherhood that way. As the Tree dies when its cycles of growth for an incarnation are through, and thus might provide food and shelter for the Beaver, in its time the Beaver's death may in turn provide that another may eat and this is okay, as the Beaver knows that he may return anyway and the next time he might choose the form of a Mountain Lion if he wished to experience that form for Self. The Great Spirit Father gave free will to all life forms on Earthplane and beyond and each form chooses the form in which they wish to experience the journey. There are however certain conditions to things though and while there might seem to be higher life forms in the structure of Nature on Earthplane, none is any better or more valuable than another to Him, so give thanks and respect to that which you eat.

In the great beginning, life forms on Earthplane were even more diversified with each being anatomically and biologically perfect and complete, and Beings from other worlds would often venture here to study and enjoy the experience of them. Then certain of these Beings joined with the earth forms and great problems began to occur. The problem started when Beings or entities that were following their own plan for growth and operating as pure light forms recanted their commitment to stay in that form of pure light through the complete cycle of the experience of it. These Beings instead began embodying and mating with the various Beings on Earthplane for the sole purpose of self-gratification and were obviously not Walking in Balance and with Harm to No One. Through the fabric of time more and more aberrations occurred resulting in entities becoming entrapped in grotesque and anatomically incorrect body forms which were referred to by many at various times as the Things. If there might be considered anything to be called original sin this might be a whole lot closer to the idea of it than the Apple and Snake story that many are so fond of. However as sin is also an illusion, this event that took long periods of time as we now know or measure it, might indeed best be expressed as the original betrayal of Man to his plan of Self. Either way lessons were learned, perfection again I see.

The Things were continued to be worked upon through the Atlantean and the early Egyptian periods of societies and much documentation still exists about these in myth and legend. These forms were not in such bad condition, but could not achieve the perfect pattern of Self through the normal channels of Renewall. Also note well here, that those Beings that chose to incarnate in the form of a Thing, did so of their own free will for the lesson that could be learned through the experience of it. Therefore, they were not in a condition of punishment by the Great Spirit Creator as some seem to believe, because if He did not will them into that condition in the first place it is most absurd to believe that He would want to keep them that way. Remember, we were all born of a very loving Father.

I then asked the Great Spirit, "What is it about this Animal Spirit Medicine"? I then looked inside and He showed me what appeared to be a printed pattern as one might find to be dyed upon some cloth so as to make a shirt. Each Medicine was one distinct unit of the pattern like the parts of a jigsaw puzzle and at first it was on a blue-black background with each Animal form and its Medicine nestled in neatly next to another. He then took some of them away and I saw how they were connected to each other like the condition of the balls when He showed me that about the All. It was like some perfect merger in as much as it was hard to tell where some began and others left off, with all being in perfect harmony and resonance. I noticed how easily that they all fit together with no hard lines or edges, only a gentle blending with both being supported in the process. I was then shown a yellowish-gold pattern of the Animal forms and their Medicines like the ones before and this time I could see as I took some pieces of it away, as if layer upon layer there would appear masters beneath, like a great framework or support system to the structure of it and I felt so amazingly glad as it indeed was exactly as I had imagined it to be, perfectly uncomplicated. As I noticed the masters beneath and interlaced within the layers of the fabric like reinforcing steel in concrete, I was overcome with an awareness of this being the true condition of all things as made by the Great Spirit Creator if only that we would look inside.

MEDICINE is defined by the Creator as being:

The **RESONANCE** to a value system, ability, or consciousness.

Or might be understood as being *THE ESSENTIAL NATURE* of a thing.

To further understand Animal Spirit Medicine, we must first open the lid upon the well by looking at the Medicines of the Animal Spirits.

I asked The Great Spirit,

"Father, why all of these different kinds of

Medicine"?

He laughed and said,

"To bring color to the fabric of life of course".

Then I understood how truly perfect it is.

White | Eagle

MEDICINES

The **RESONANCE** to a value system, ability, or consciousness is given to best describe what we refer to as Medicine in the Spiritual context. The Animal Spirits, as described before, each have a unique Medicine as well as a unique persona or personality and each Medicine can be learned or shared by another. As the whole Earthwalk experience is about Love and Brotherhood and Brotherhood is best described as the sharing in the betterment in the condition of the All, indeed it is through the expression of each one's unique Medicine that this can be most easily and effectively accomplished. While each Being upon earth and in Spirit planes has a unique pattern that is the Creators original idea of them and may be described as their beginning Medicine, each is obligated to endeavor to keep expanding upon that by adding new Medicines to that originally manifested in them. This is the whole purpose of the process of endless growth. Indeed there are no limits to that which any might expand to embrace within themselves.

For the purposes of this document we will begin by discussing the Medicines in a general sense using broader groupings for ease of presentation. All winged ones be it Bird, Bat or Insect have some of the same Medicines, as each deals with symbiosis and great knowledge of Wind and Air in their movement. As each of these Spirits uses the Spirit of Air and Wind for their mode of transportation they have deep resonance to weather conditions and inherent changes therein, much more so than a Turtle or a Frog would have. In the same way each of the four or two-leggeds share some of the same Medicine as each deals with symbiosis and great knowledge about the earth. Therefore each has greater sensitivity to the inherent changes therein such as eruptions and earthquakes as well as sensitivity to the changes in her vibrations as they use her for nesting and their mode of transportation. Each of the finned ones and those that live in the water have some of the same Medicine as well, all for the same reasons, as each is a specialist in their own environmental element.

So a beginning to the understanding about the Medicines of any Animal Spirit can first be understood by looking at its basic element of environment, Water, Earth, Air, or swimmers, walkers or fliers. I do not know of any that live in Fire, but all thrive from the Medicine of the Sun, hence we have the three major groupings. There is often much misunderstanding or bad publicity about some of our reptile brothers and in particular I speak about the Snake or Serpent. In many cultures he has been made out to be a bad guy or thing to be feared, yet in my aboriginal culture, the Serpent is called the Snake of Knowledge and when one sees a Snake it is a very good sign that one is in the process of beholding a new understanding or experiencing a new step of their growth. And remarkable it is indeed that the Serpent is the one that can swim in the Water, walk on the Earth and fly through the Air from tree to tree, so it seems well stated to call him the Snake of Knowledge as he has Medicine knowledge from all four of the elements and a greater ability of sensing vibrations and changes in them than most others possess.

Understanding the major influence that the element of an Animal Spirit has upon it helps us also realize the Medicine that can be understood and thereby added to that of Self. We will list the most common Animal Spirit Medicines by groupings and it is important to note here that each and every thing created by The Great Spirit has a unique Medicine for us to learn about, so value each and every one however there are way too many to discuss here so we will try to cover as many as we can. It is important to note here also that while we will at best give a brief description about some, it is more important for you meditatively connect with them and The Creator so as to discover what they mean for you, as each is unique and perfect in their own Being.

It is given to relate at this point that any encounter with an Animal form whose Spirit has exited its bodyform and is thereby considered as being dead, does not change the Medicine of its message and should by no means be considered as being a negative message. However if one is thinking about a problem and a lifeless Animal form is presented, one can indeed assume that the potential for one's fulfillment regarding that issue is at that point not available and thereby possible. However one can also correctly assume that one's relative involvement is satisfied and mission complete. It is always recommended to meditate upon the experience of finding or having a lifeless Animal in one's experience or vision and seek guidance from the Creator as to specifically what is being communicated and what to infer from its expression of support. Also note that even the lifeless form is Spirit connected and deserves the greatest of care, value, and respect, as often these wonderful sharing Spirits choose to support us this way not only as food but also as loving allies and support from the other side of the veil.

To begin further discussion we will begin with a broader description of the finned ones:

SWIMMERS

All swimmers or finned ones live in or near the water of course and there is no difference in the Medicine of fresh or salt water in the sense of influence. However there is a major increase in the potency of seawater in the curative process. All swimmers have an affinity and are in Medicine to the water not only for transportation but also as a food source.

Any water or body of water in vision or dream usually signifies the beginning of a change or a journey to a new location or adventure. All water symbolizes Growth and the Abundance within. Falling water represents Receivership and Purification, flowing water represents Abundance and Change, and still water represents Peace and Purity.

ALLIGATORS -

Stealth, Persistence and Patience are the most significant aspects of Alligator Medicine. Alligators have a great sense of smell and smell and sound are part of their Medicine as well.

Alligators live a long time, as once they reach a certain size they do not have any predator to fear except man. All Alligators are nurturing, protective and caring parents. They display great patience and are very territorial. Alligators can move very quickly on land and have a great swimming ability. The Alligator floats real still like a log and allows its prey which is usually Fish, Turtles, Snakes, or Birds to come right up to it and even sit upon it for a while. Then with minimum effort, the Alligator turns its head and swallows whatever it wants to eat whole if it is small enough. Alligators often will store large food in roots under water and let it rot for a while which makes it easier for them to digest.

In vision, dream, or encounter the Alligator always represents a condition or attitude that stifles one's advancement or growth and from which one needs to break free or release. In vision I once saw where this Alligator had me, and the significance of Alligator Medicine in this vision is that of Danger or Entrapment. Alligators also represent fearlessness, especially in hunting or in warfare and are good teachers about Worthiness and Patience. Alligators can also symbolize internal struggles or conflicts.

CLAMS –

Clams and all shellfish represent the Fruitfulness, Industry and Abundance of the Sea. Clam Medicine is that of Inner beauty as well as Patience and a great sense of lower level vibrations or feelings. Clams symbolize Faith that all will be provided by the Great Spirit, as they just sit at the bottom and filter from the water all that they need. Clams have a hard shell for a home and they always decorate it with great beauty inside and after they have outgrown one shell they have no trouble releasing it and moving on to make a new one.

Clams in dreams or visions may represent Abundance or Entrapment generally reflecting conditions of Self about the home. Clams are often used as aphrodisiacs and many cultures have used

Clamshells for their beauty, utility, and even as money. The Abalone shell in my Medicine Bag represents the condition of the home.

CRABS –

Crab Medicine includes Pickiness, as the Crab must tear the food into small pieces with its claws for it to eat. Crabs also have great Tester Medicine but mainly Crab Medicine is about Shedding or giving away its outer shell or Ego, so as to Grow in the Round and Proper Way, from the inside out. Crabs are great swimmers and good weathermen and often before a great storm one will see Crabs swimming in to the protected inlets for safety. Crabs are aggressive hunters and explorers and as scavengers might be considered maids of the water, as they keep the bottom very clean and tidy making sure that nothing is wasted in their search for food.

Most issues relating to Crabs refer to security about the home or occupation so if in vision or dream a Crab was to attack or pinch one, they are merely trying to alert you to some condition and it is indeed a favorable sign. Also in dreams and visions the Crab will test the surety of any decision, goal, movement, or foundation. Like some Snakes, the Crab releases or sheds its shell once a year so as to grow larger, and it seems that both are much wiser for it.

DOLPHINS -

Dolphins or Porpoises have great Hearing Medicine and are often linked to the psychic realms as being able to see with their ears. In one cycle of the Medicine Wheel, I received a Dolphin Guide named Oo-la-hey, and he taught me how to see with my ears the unspoken words that were being expressed by others. Part of Dolphin Medicine is Psychic Ability as well as being very much of the Spirit of the Water, which is always about Flow in some manner. Dolphin Medicine is also about Innocence and Courage and an ever-playful attitude, but in the deeper sense it is about Sensitivity and Compassion for the needs of others. All Dolphin Medicine Beings, including aquatic, two-legged and the four-legged Wolf, are natural partners, parents and nurturers.

The Dolphin is an air-breathing mammal that lives in the sea and like the Whale, has developed great stamina behind this ability. Also like Whales, Dolphins live in family groups called pods, serving both for Protection as well as Companionship, which is one of the needs of this brilliant creature. They are witty and playful, but also very serious about anything that might endanger the pod or family and are extremely courageous and selfless fighters. Dolphins display resourcefulness and have deep knowledge that they sometimes impart to the two-legged Beings.

In encounter, vision, or dreams, the Dolphin is a resource bringer and represents deep and sacred knowledge as well as reminding us of the need for playfulness in our lives. Also in vision Dolphins are often messengers in how to improve relationships and experience the true Spirit of Brotherhood.

EELS –

Adaptability and Strength of Conviction are the primary Medicines of the Eel. Eel Medicine can also be considered as having Tenacity, Trust, Perception and Patience. Eels are very nesting creatures and while they are excellent swimmers, they prefer to stay around the home. They do not have too many predators and like the Alligator are great conservators of energy and will wait until something just swims by to eat. The Eel is quite a timid creature with poor vision, but can be a relentless fighter when it has to. Some fishermen have noticed its refusal to let go, even after its head has been severed from its body symbolizing relentless courage to the end. Like the Crab, the Eel is a good weatherman and knows when the water conditions are about to change.

Eels like to keep their back covered and in dreams or visions usually the message they bring is to keep your back covered as some influence is about you this way. Strength of conviction is also the message that an Eel might bring to dreams or visions.

FISH - SALMON OR TROUT

Fish are excellent swimmers and more important are excellent navigators through the currents of change. Salmon have additional Medicine this way as when it is time to spawn after traveling all over the oceans, always return to the original ground in which they are born. Salmon represent strength of conviction and possess great tenacity and strength, often swimming up waterfalls in their return to spawn. All Fish have good hearing and most have good vision as well as a great sense of balance and rhythm to life that is often seen at the changes of the seasons. Fish have a deep respect for the cycles of life and knowledge of the Abundance that the Great Spirit provides to each of us if only we will see past our egos to embrace it to ourselves. All Fish also possess knowledge about the movement of change and the Balance and Beauty change provides to the condition of growth.

All Fish dreams and visions are about aspects of cycles of growth, the fruitfulness of endeavor to Growth and Abundance in life.

FROGS –

While most often seen as land Animals, Frogs and Toads are best represented here with the swimmers as they are more about the water in their Medicine. As with Butterflies, Frogs go through a Metamorphosis and Metamorphosis is a main ingredient in Frog Medicine, although the Medicines of Patience and Determination are what the Frog can best teach us. Seemingly slow movers whether on water or land, the tenacity and determination of the Frog is very strong and resolute. Frogs use patience in their food gathering and some Frogs go on great journeys for mating. During times of drought some Frogs are indeed able to live for extended periods in hibernation like the Bear and some fishes, by covering their body in a protective film in the mud bottom of a pond and waiting for the water to again come from the sky. There have been stories told that hibernating Frogs have come alive after hundreds of years. All Frogs are excellent swimmers and spend their early life as fish-like tadpoles. With the primary diet being Insects, they are a major influence in keeping the populations in check, so be nice to the Frog brother that keeps the pesky Mosquitoes away. As well as being great communicators and vocalizers, all Frogs blend in well with their habitat, have good hearing, excellent vision and speed of reflex.

Frogs and Toads feed upon Insects and All Insect feeders are natural Protector Spirits and represent the existence or need of such in encounter or vision and dream. All Frog visions and dreams are about Metamorphosis, Resolution, Patience lessons and direction finding and they will always show the way.

JELLYFISH -

Jellyfish are one of the many colonized free-floating creatures of the waters. The major Medicine of Jellyfish is that of Brotherhood and Co-operation. All of the individuals in the colony support the Well-being of each other and are connected by a network of communication nerves and electrical impulses. In the colony that is a Jellyfish, some of the partners serve for defense and protection, others for trapping and food gathering, others for homemaking and distribution of foodstuffs, and still others for transportation. It is in this co-operative effort that the Jellyfish can best teach us specialization and co-operation or better stated, Brotherhood and Respectful Sharing and all conditions of relationship.

In the dark, often I have observed the beautiful light flashes and glows that come from these beautiful creatures through their electrical impulses. While they might appear to aimlessly float about, each knows exactly where they are and where they are going and use the natural resources of the currents and tides to go from place to place using the changing weather to make their pilgrimages across the seas.

In visions and dreams the Jellyfish or Man-o-War signifies the need for caution in travel or is a warning about a coming danger or hazard, hence the stinging portion of some lessons that we receive. The danger message is associated with Jellyfish in groups while in singular form the floating Jellyfish signifies Peace and Grace in the community of life and how effortless and beautiful our journey might truly be.

LOBSTERS - CRAWFISH

Lobster and Crawfish, while they might be biologically associated with Crabs and Shrimp, have a very unique Medicine. The Lobster has great antenna and can sense changes in the rhythm of vibrations in the water with great precision. It is its antenna that differentiates Lobster Medicine from the Crab as the medicine of Lobster and Crayfish is that of Sensitivity to the currents of Change, as well as Providence. The fact that Lobsters and Crayfish both have ten legs adds an additional dynamic to their overall Medicine and that is the Completeness in Self.

Both Lobsters and Crawfish have good vision and possess a great curiosity and sometimes this is what gets them in trouble. Both are essentially solitary creatures but still seem live in colonies. Where there is one there are always more, although you will rarely see them hanging out in large groups except in the mating times. Both are creative homemakers whose homemaking skills are only surpassed by the Octopus. Both are backwards swimmers but will meet any foe head on if confronted by anything that looks like a fair fight. The Lobster and Crawfish both have great claws for defense and the picking apart of their food and they are both pretty constant in their eating habits. Like the Crab, both can regenerate claws that might be lost in conflict.

Lobsters and Crawfish are both considered great food delicacies and in dreams or visions if shown in groups represent Abundance and Wealth to come. In the singular form a Lobster or Crawfish may represent the decision to fight or flight in regards to pending confrontations or decisions and are great teachers of Tenacity and Resource in Self.

OTTERS –

The most important traits of Otter Medicine are their great creativity and playfulness. One might well say that the Medicine of the Otter is that of the gregarious teacher of How to Play and Pray in Life. The Otter is the Coyote of the sea in their Medicine of being great tricksters, ask any fisherman about their penchant for getting a free meal. In naming peoples I will have as much difficulty finding the true form of the Otter as I do with the Coyote, as both will show me many false images before I can discover their true Medicine. All Otters possess great playfulness, tool making and teaching ability and love to share their great discoveries with others. The Otter has excellent vision and hearing as well as a great ability of sensing the lower vibrations. The Otter is a superb swimmer and a very aggressive fighter when he feels threatened or in conflict over territory. These ingenious hunters mate predominantly for life and are seldom seen singularly as they usually are in pairs or larger groups. Otters expend great energy in playing, hunting or loafing and they do everything with gusto.

In visions and dreams the Otter symbolizes the need for creativity in ones industry and many have shown people better ways of doing things. The Otter in vision also reminds us to not take life too seriously and to have fun with and in it.

SEAHORSES -

The Seahorse and Pipefish are perhaps of the most fascinating and delicate creatures of the sea. The female Seahorse passes the eggs to the male's pouch and then he fertilizes and cares for them. Of an almost fanciful appearance, these delicate swimmers of the seas might well surpass the mythical Unicorn as a symbol of Peace and Beauty.
The Medicine of the Seahorse is indeed that of Grace and Peace of Place.
In dreams and visions - The Seahorse signifies the sense of Grace in the conditions about the Self and the home. A Seahorse that is attached to something by its tail signifies the need for holding on to one's dreams or ambitions and one that is releasing signifies the need to let go of the past and / or present goals. A swimming Seahorse signifies ease of transition and the beginning of a new pursuit or cycle. The Seahorse with its mate signifies the condition of Grace soon to come to Self. The Seahorse that is at rest signifies that one's desires will soon come true.

SEA LIONS –

Sea Lions and Seals live in great colonies and are very seldom seen alone. They possess great swimming ability and unlike the Otter, have a very serious demeanor about the business of life. The Sea Lion is much better at moving about the water than land, and has excellent senses of sight and hearing. While some are migratory creatures, most would stay in one place if the weather and food supply would permit. Theirs is a constant cycle of storing up fat reserves to go on long journeys to find more food. When the Sea Lion is in resting mode, little will bother it and often they find themselves with cases of sunburn for their detachment to consciousness. Being herd Animals, Sea Lions might have many mates in a lifetime, and are sometimes poor examples of male aggressiveness and singular focus. However, the Sea Lion has great care and tenacity and will fight to the death if it believes it is in the right.   While this tenacity might be considered as stubbornness or bullheadedness, Great Strength and Courage is Sea Lion Medicine, whom display such with a large amount of race and softness when they are in balance to their elements.   Sea Lions are very vocal possessing great ability in communication once they get started.   The Sea Lion works hard, plays hard, and takes its rest time very seriously as well and is usually at peace with what ever it is doing no matter what it is.   If there might be one message from this Lion of the Sea, it may be to live life with gusto.

In dreams and visions the Sea Lion may represent the need for migration or a change of venue or the great resources that are available to one, including that of Courage.   A swimming Sea Lion will always lead you to Beauty and Abundance.

SERPENTS –

While some Serpents or Snakes live on land, the Medicine of all of them will be discussed with the swimmers.

The Serpent like the tree reminds us that we are to grow from the inside out and so is ever giving his Ego away in the process of constantly shedding his skin.   Those people with Serpent Medicine will often find themselves doing some shedding in cycles, right before changes are made or anticipated.   The Serpent is often called the Snake of Knowledge and Wisdom and they have a great ability in the sensing of things.   The Snake also has a well-developed sense of smell and can often teach us how to see with our tongue.   A Serpent's eyesight and reaction time are acutely sharp and they see in the infrared range like the Cat.   As all Spirits are visible in this range, Serpents and Cats can easily see the Spirit World as well as the physical plane.

Serpents move through the undulations of their body reminding us that vibration is truly the essence of everything.   All Serpents are sensitive to the lower vibrations of Mother Earth and are able to forecast changes in her or the weather, which explains why Serpents will leave an area before an earthquake or any other kind of disturbance.   All Serpents are great conservators of energy and will make food gathering an almost effortless task through camouflage and stillness.   Of all Serpents, the Sea Serpent is the most poisonous variety and great hordes of these have been sighted floating to a new location in groups as large as eight miles wide.   No Serpent deliberately strikes at Man except in a defensive measure and only the water moccasin has been seen to chase after Man although some others may have appeared to do so.

The Serpent is the most significant Animal to see in vision or dreams and always signifies the process of growth and the attainment of a new or deeper understanding or acquisition of a new Medicine to Self. In vision or dreams - a Serpent biting you is a good sign. If biting on the left, it means to open your Self up to receive new understanding. If on the right, it signifies release of retarding worries or fears. A Serpent moving along side of you is a pathfinder and will always show you the right path again; left for receiving and right for manifesting. A Serpent chasing you is helping you to release or move away from a stagnant and unproductive position or relationship. The Serpent will always warn you of danger as well, usually through spoken words.

The Serpent indeed is the best Animal Spirit helper that one can hope for and should be treated respectfully.

SHARKS -

The Shark represents Purity of Form and Purpose and has changed little in the time of the Earthplane. Indeed the Medicine of the Shark is that of Caretaking and Balancing as well as Stamina and Resolve.

Sharks are pretty much community creatures and are often seen to travel in great packs or herds. They like to spend some time alone as well. The Shark is a tenacious swimmer with the ability to swim tirelessly at great speed. The Shark has great vision, smell and hearing ability and a great psychic sense as well. The Shark might well be considered the policeman of the sea or the Great Balancer, as Sharks keep all systems in balance. While at times it might seem in conflict to pods of Whales or Dolphins when attacking them for food, it is acting in Brotherhood by only taking those members that are weak or sick thereby preventing the spread of illness to the rest.

I have a Shark guide that has been with me for a long time. His name is E-Wah-Hey and he often shows me some of the traps or barriers that I build for myself. It was E-Wah-Hey that helped me get rid of an Alligator that had me a few years back and I am still very thankful for that. I also use a Shark's Tooth in my Medicine Bag as it represents Resource and Protection in the physical plane.

The Shark represents the indomitable force of the Will of Self and in vision will help resolve fears about resources or sustenance as they always know where the food is. Any Sharks in encounters or dreams are messengers about dangers or constraints and signify the need and availability of great Strength and Courage and where it should wisely be applied.

SHRIMP -

The Medicine of the Shrimp is Selflessness and Sharing and as they often range in large packs they indeed have much knowledge about Community and Brotherhood. The important part of Shrimp Medicine may well be what it can teach us about its knowledge of the cycle of life, as most varieties live for only one season or year.

The four stages of development of the Shrimp reminds us of the four winds, four elements and pretty much all of the Medicine Wheel can be found in the life of the Shrimp. The Shrimp in its larva form belongs to a group called zooplankton, which forms part of the foundation of the food supply of the sea. Being the sustaining food accommodating the needs of other swimming creatures, the Shrimp is indeed an integral part of everything in the waters. Ever on the move in their various stages of growth Shrimp are excellent swimmers achieving instant speed with a singular flick of the tail. Shrimp can often be seen jumping great distance over the water when chased by other Fish and so it is no wonder that Shrimp represent Grace and Beauty in movement of form, as they are truly one of the Great Acrobats of the sea. The Shrimp readily senses movement through its antennae and the many little hairs about its body and feet.

The Shrimp in dreams or visions represents the Bounty and Wealth of the riches provided to us by the Great Spirit Father and the sweetness of life in the physical form.

SQUID - OCTOPUS

The Medicine of the Squid and the Octopus is about their great Cat-like curiosity and flexibility when ensnared or entrapped. They are jet swimmers in that they propel themselves through the water at great speed by forcing water through an orifice called a funnel or siphon.

Both Squid and Octopus have sucker-equipped tentacles which they use to feel and hold things and can display a great stubbornness when they do not want to release their hold on an object. They share in their eating method using a Parrot-like beak at the center of the tentacles orientated about their head. Squid and Octopus have a great ability at disguise or camouflage, which they use to blend in with their surroundings by changing the color patterns on the surface of their skin. More so than the Squid, the Octopus likes to make unusual and ingenious shelters or homes for itself and has a preoccupation to its nesting or homemaking ability when not in search of food.

In dreams or visions – These creatures foretell of dangers and entrapments that may be going on in one's life, as both are masters of deception and camouflage and possess the ability to escape through the emission of a cloud of ink. It is in this escaping ability that they will often bring their messages in dreams. If entangled in the tentacles it signifies that one will always find the way out of one's current situation through the release of a wrongful goal, ideal or fear. Squid and Octopus in dreams and visions will oftentimes take on the form of the individual that may be causing the problem if you ask them to.

TURTLES -

Turtles may live on land or in water are another Animal that has changed little over the years on Earthplane and so Constancy is indeed part of their Medicine, with the fundamental nature of Turtle Medicine being that of great Heart and Will. In fact aboriginal peoples in certain areas and tribes would oftentimes cut the heart out of a Turtle so as to gain strength of Heart and Will before battle, and even cut in half and swallowed, it would still keep beating in their stomach for up to four hours! Turtles have reasonably good eyesight and a good sense of smell and also have the ability to sense the lower vibrations of Mother Earth and the waters. Turtles may appear deliberate and slow land but these swimmers are very agile and graceful in their water habitat. Wearing their house on their back they are pretty much safe from harm in most conditions and many a Shark or Whale has had trouble cracking the shell on one. Being predominately solitary range Animals they travel great distances over the oceans and like Salmon, always return to their place of birth to lay their eggs. Sea Turtles are docile, timid creatures, have a very independent nature and operate with a great sense of resolve.

In dreams or visions they show us the need for Patience and Commitment in the attainment of our goals. Turtles swimming in dreams or visions are pathfinders and show the need for new direction and Turtles that are closed up in their shell show the need to wait for better opportunity to come before advancing along our path.

WHALES -

Whales are the largest mammal form on the Earthplane and while they may seem like very slow creatures, Whales swim with great speed and display Serenity and Grace in form and movement. Path finding, Leadership and Brotherhood as well as Administration of Resources are the predominate Medicine of the Whale and as this is a composition of Medicines in a Way, so too are Consolidation and Composition a part of the Medicine of these magnificent Animal Spirit Brothers and Sisters.

Whales have great navigation Medicine and like the Turtle they like to journey over great distances in seasonal movement to find food sources. With great eyesight and sense of sound and smell Whales can see with their ears like their Dolphin Brothers.

Being predominately community creatures of a caring nature, Whales have a great sense of Brotherhood and share in the care taking of the young. Whale calves are often nursed and cared for by others than the biological mother.

With their great memory capability Whales are like the Elephant of the sea and while they seem to be mostly of a retiring nature they also possess a great curiosity which in times past almost led to their extinction by Man. Whales have no natural enemies and as mentioned before live in a great symbiotic relationship with their Shark brothers.

In dreams and visions - Whales bring Peace and Brotherhood messages but most often they are pathfinders to hidden resources in the condition of Self. Whales swimming away from one signify a movement of release from current endeavors, and whales swimming up to one signify that new resources or opportunities are soon coming.

WALKERS

All walkers are land based and while the two-legged ones might also be included here, they are omitted as each is in the process of discovery of those very elements of self during their Earthwalk. All walkers live on the surface of Mother Earth and through their legs and sides have a great sensitivity to her deeper vibrations. Walkers also possess great ability of predicting weather changes and changes in the surface of the earth such as tornadoes and earthquakes.

People named with the Medicine of the walkers often tend to feel more in the psychic senses than they might visualize or see. Except for the Cats and Serpents, all Named ones with the Medicine of the walkers also tend to feel the presence of Spirits more than they might see them.

ANTS -

The major Medicine of the Ant is that of Caretaking and Community in life. An Ant colony is a matriarchal society and the Queen and many others have the ability to sprout wings when it is time to fly. Like all hive Animals, Ants are great communicators possessing a sense of dedication to others of the tribe and adhering to a strict social structure. Ants possess great strength and are ever busy in industry for the betterment of the colony. An Ant has large eyes for its size and an excellent sense of smell, hearing, memory and navigation. In addition to these, it uses its small antennae as feelers and to sense the deep vibrations in Mother Earth. It seems these tiny creatures have no underdeveloped senses.

Many of this species of walker are pretty benign in their behavior, while others are extremely aggressive, acting as predators to enslave others in their own species and all Ants are fearless warriors that are not afraid to die. The Fire Ant is perhaps the most aggressive having such a strong bite that it has little to fear from predators. That characteristic, coupled with its great ability in floating upon the currents of water, is mostly why it has expanded so far, so fast in recent times.

The appearance of Ants after the death of a being or thing is the true sign that the Spirit has left the body as they have an extraordinary sense of such things. Ants are truly the cleaner-uppers of all material things, having great mouthparts that can convert even bone and teeth to small particles to be returned to Mother Earth.

The sting substance of most ants is that of folic acid, which it uses in a mostly defensive way and those that receive the bites of ants in the physical plane, are receiving a message for the need to walk more softly and with respect to the conditions of others.

In vision or dreams - All Ant visions and dreams are about the condition of relationship of oneself to others and signify the continuation of life in the Spirit plane. Ants in journey or migrations signify the need for a change in direction and the development of new life or resources to Self. The Ant that is feeding signifies the end of a condition or relationship, and an Ant that is holding or bringing something signifies the need for caretaking about exactly that.

BADGER -

Badger Medicine is about great Sensitivity to Sound, as well as great Strength and Tenacity and Agility. Badger Medicine is also its sensitivity to the deeper vibrations of Mother Earth and his closeness to it through great tunneling ability and creativity.

Badgers are part of the Weasel family but its Medicine is much closer to the Bear as this cave or tunnel maker has extremely strong forearms and great long and sharp front claws. While some will operate in clans, Badgers are predominately solitary Animals. Hunting for small game and rodents primarily at night, this extremely stout and tenacious hunter and fighter fears little, even when confronted by Animals much bigger in size.   A tenacious fighter when confronted or in care of young, like the Bear it prefers to avoid confrontations if possible. The Badger has better smell and hearing than eyesight and being quite fast and agile on the ground is able to dig itself out of trouble and sight very quickly. Badgers are always good Spirit helpers in helping us solve dilemmas.

Badgers in dreams or visions is about tenacity in decision, and the need to use Stamina, Strength, and Courage to leave the old idea of Self and to embrace fully the expression of Growth in Self. Badgers in dreams and visions that are retreating, are showing the need to review or change direction. And Badgers that are burrowing represent the need to dig beneath the surface of illusion to find the truth or source of a dilemma.

BEARS -

The Medicine of the Bear may be considered to be that of Patience and Caretaking as well as the Discovery and the Pursuit of One's Goals. Also, because of their great sensitivity to the cycles of the seasons on the Earthplane, Bear Medicine includes Cycles and the time to feed and the time to rest. The Bear is often referred to as the Healing Bear and therefore Bear Medicine is about Healing as well.

Bears are mostly solitary creatures that usually have little to do with others unless in combat or mating although they might hang around together during feeding times. They are great ranging Animals that cover a large territory in search of food from mid-spring to mid-fall. All Bears are very sensitive to the deeper vibrations of Mother

Earth and some hibernate deep inside her in caves during winter months. The Bear normally is a retiring creature with little to fear in the way of enemies except for other Bears and Man, and usually will evade Man unless surprised or pressured into a confrontation at which time its courage and resolve is indomitable. The Bear exemplifies great strength and courage and the aboriginal people have always held them in great esteem and high regard as a single swipe of the great claws on the front paws of a Bear has laid open the belly of many large Animals including Man. The Bear is a powerful omnivore that has great senses of hearing and smell, although their eyesight is not as sensitive. Varying in size, all are able to move with surprising speed and agility over short distances. Bears are also very curious by nature and this has led to a large depletion of the populations by trappers and the like.

The Bear in visions and dreams signifies the need for Strength and Resolve in the task or direction at hand as well as having Patience and waiting for the right time or cycle to Embrace Change and Growth. An approaching Bear will usually bring a tool or element for use and if it is not carrying something it usually means that the tools are already within your understanding. A Bear running or retreating signifies the need for speed in resolution or the need to seek another plan or direction. A Bear at rest or play signifies the need to put in more time experiencing the joy of life and sharing time with family.

BEAVERS -

The Beaver is well known for his great ability at architecture and industrious nature so it is no wonder that Design and Industry are the major Medicines of the Beaver. It should also be known that the Beaver has great ability in working with Plant Spirit Medicine, especially in Healing.

Beavers are herbivores and have excellent senses of smell, touch and hearing. The Beaver is a monogamous creature that will stay with a mate for life. Adult Beavers are very nurturing caretakers of their young, who usually stay with the adult for at least two years after birth. Being quite dexterous and swift moving upon the land, the Beaver is an excellent and well-adapted swimmer who sees the water not only as a place of which to build its residency but also as a great transportation vehicle, source for foodstuffs and safety. They use their teeth to cut down trees for building and their teeth are in a constant growing state, which is important as they are constantly in the process of rebuilding and storing of foodstuffs. As the Beaver is very conscious of the cycles of life and has great consciousness to the Plant Spirits, the trees that it cuts down are done in a selective process for regeneration. Great at planning, the Beaver often will establish large communities that result in great dam lodgings for many families.

Beaver Named people are constantly in the process of some design and are greatly impacted with the conditions of the home or nest. Beaver people are also great innovators and better administrators and planners although most characteristically have less patience for short-term projects preferring to be involved in large ones.

Just as the Beaver's pelt is highly prized for its durability as well as its lushness and beauty, better it were that the Beaver be prized for its industry and tenacity as it never quits a project once begun no matter what happens. In dreams and visions the Beaver is often about the planning of long-range goals and sealing with the cycles of growth. The Beaver in dreams and visions also may signify the need for establishing direction or goals for the growing experience of life as well as the need for planning and nurturing of Self and others. Most of all the Beaver in vision and dreams is that about Softness and Persistence in the walk of life.

BEETLES -

The Beetle is perhaps one of the best examples of Animal Spirit adaptability as it sure looks like it is much too heavy to fly. All Beetles have hard outer shells that cover wings but not all Beetles can fly. Beetles are very deliberate walkers and exhibit great strength in their legs as well as jaws, enabling them to carry large objects for great distances on the ground. It is due to this image of them that we choose to discuss the Medicine of the Spirit of the Beetle with the walkers instead of the fliers, as it is more about their Medicine on the Earth than in the Air that we speak of.

The Beetle like the Butterfly is one of the Animal Spirits that undergoes a complete Metamorphosis and Metamorphosis is one of the major Medicines of the Beetle. While some of the Beetle family have seemingly destructive tendencies, the Dung Beetle has great ability in its endeavor to convert much waste material into a food source and indeed Conversion is another Beetle Medicine. Beauty and Balance are also part of the Medicine of the Beetle as even though their sense of Beauty is often strange and grotesque, all will admire the beautiful and sometimes iridescent colors of their shells, and in their aspect to the condition of things they bring Balance through their house cleaning and scavenging of Mother Earth. If Persistence can best be exemplified it truly is that in the Spirit of the Beetle and while some might be considered as pests to the gardener, all can be respected for their persistent endeavors.

The Beetle in vision or dream is almost always a signal of caution, sometimes warning of the pending predation of others on Self and can may also be bringing a message as to the need for greater conservation of resources. It can also be a signal to the need for a change in direction or to bring more balance to the objectives in life and to see the beauty and perfection in any and every circumstance.

BUFFALO -

The major Medicines of the Buffalo are Strength and Courage and they are also associated with the Wisdom of the Spirit of the North in the Medicine Wheel. Buffalo Medicine might well be put as Reverence and Respectful Sharing in the Abundance of Life.

The Buffalo is probably considered to be the single most sacred of all of the walkers by the aboriginal people of the Americas as it was the greatest provider of the people in that it provided food, clothing, tools from its bones, housing from its hide and in some cultures even boats were made from its skin. If such a magnificent Animal might have a flaw it might be having some of the stubbornness more commonly associated with its Goat brother.

Buffalo senses are about feeling or sensing from the body and like most four-leggeds, have great sensitivity to the deeper vibrations of Mother Earth and to Earth changes. Their sense of hearing and smell are much better than their eyesight. A symbol of great Courage, the Buffalo was never one to run from a fight and often was the aggressor in any chance encounter. Existing on the North American continent for hundreds of years with little change and able to withstand extreme changes in climate from deep cold to times of great heat, it has survived an ice age but nearly did not survive the abusive nature of Man. For this reason, the status of the Buffalo might well be a barometer to the consciousness of the Spirit of Man.

The Buffalo is a herd Animal and likes living in large groups that used to number in the tens of thousands. Before the White Man brought horses over to this continent the aboriginal peoples often hunted them. By exciting one to run, the rest would blindly follow and large numbers of them could be directed to fall off of shear cliffs to their deaths. In later times many a horse and rider was killed in the hunt by the mighty Buffalo as the Buffalo against a rider with spear was a pretty even match.

Buffalo dreams and visions are about Truth and Purity, Consciousness, Courage and Resource and the Buffalo in dreams or vision will always show the way as a pathfinder of Spirit.

CATS -

While there are many species like the Bob Cat, Lynx, and Jaguar the Cats we will discuss are those aboriginal species of the North Americas, predominately that of the Mountain Lion, sometimes called the Cougar or Puma. The Cat family like the Bears operate pretty much the same in their Medicine and Cat Medicine might be best expressed as Balance, Sensitivity, and Curiosity. Extremely Sensitive might well be included in describing the Medicine of the Cat however their Tenacity, Courage and Perception should never be overlooked. Their great sense of Balance can only be augmented with their regal-like ability at aloofness and independence. I asked The Great Spirit Father one day what He might choose to be if He were on the Earthplane and he showed me this great Lion and I understood.

Even though Cats are long sleepers and seem to do little else between eating and sleeping they are wonderful creatures, full of surprises. Cats are enormously good teachers and parents and are greatly sensitive to deeper vibrations and Mother Earth changes. With their infra-red vision they can see Spirit forms in or out of body and enjoy a keen sense of smell and hearing as well. Cats have great ingenuity and are very dexterous with their paws, are great runners and have the ability to change direction instantaneously.

As Cats are extremely territorial and range over wide expanses they will fight quickly and to the death for mating rights or ranging areas. All Cats can and often do take down prey that is much greater than themselves and as they are also great conservators of energy, will often leave the chase if the prospects look in doubt for quick success. Having only Man for an enemy the Cat is perhaps the purest of the predators or hunters and often the Lion will lick in the most appreciative and loving of ways the prey it has just killed.

The Cat in one's dreams or visions is about Balance and Provider-ship in one's life path. A Cat yelling is saying to listen to the truth and not what you want to hear, as one is probably trying to deceive you. A Cat running signifies the need to pursue one's direction or goal with greater endeavor and the Cat resting signifies the need for pacing, patience, or the necessity to review or examine the cycle of growth that you are in. An attacking Cat signifies the need for protection or more aggression and courage in ones endeavors and the Cat at play signifies the need for play and relaxation in the current events. The Cat nursing, feeding or caring for young signifies the provider-ship of the Great Spirit and the abundance in ones life.

CHIPMUNKS –

The Medicine of the Chipmunk is that of The Pleasure in the Chase or might better be expressed the Joy of the Pursuit of one's next fulfillment. Chipmunks are highly social and interactive ground dwelling members of the squirrel family and both share some of the same Medicine especially with regard to resources and softness in life. The Chipmunk is playful and has very good vision and hearing augmented with a great sense of Balance and Curiosity.

In dreams and visions the Chipmunk signifies one's own condition to one's personal pursuit or goals as well as both Hope and Renewall and is often a forecaster of good things to come. A Chipmunk in visions and dreams will often tell specifically what it is for you to know. The Chipmunk that is running with tail up signifies that one's desire is soon to be realized or close at hand, while when running with tail down signifies the need for caution in continuing one's pursuit, as safety or caution is more important at this time. The Chipmunk that is emerging from its community hole signifies the need for more exposure or to communicate more broadly or openly one's prayer of desire and the opposite is true if going down its hole. A Chipmunk that is sitting still or stops in its path signifies the need to do the same in one's own expression of pursuit, and more than one Chipmunk or Chipmunks in play signifies the need to join others in one's pursuit.

COYOTES -

The Coyote is a member of the Wolf family that is spoken of separately as its Medicine is quite specialized and separate. The Medicine of the Coyote is that of being a consummate and Caring Observer of its environment and will easily leave a territory for a more productive one. Coyote Medicine is also that of being a great Professor of the Lessons of Growth and Balance in Life and while it possesses great Stealth it also possesses great Humor.

The Coyote is perhaps one of the most adaptable of the four-leggeds and is often called the great trickster by the aboriginal people. The people used to follow the Wolf to food and water and knowing this, the coyote would go to the horizon where he would look like the Wolf and make Wolf sounds until the people would leave the camp to see where the new food was at. While the people were looking where the Coyote was at he would double back to the camp and steal the food they already had. While this seems to be mean or harmful behavior, all may learn lesson and a great part of Coyote Medicine is about lesson giving and teaching. Many of the people that I have Named as being of Coyote Medicine are illustrators, artists, musicians, photographers, newsmen, and teachers.

The Coyote is monogamous and is usually seen by itself or with its mate, unlike the Wolf that is more like the herd Animals that hunt and live in packs. Coyotes make wonderful and caring parents and are greatly resourceful hunters. The Coyote is very psychic and has great ability in knowing of weather changes as well as dangers from fires and earthquakes and easily feels and senses the deeper vibrations of Mother Earth. The Coyote has good eyesight and very good senses of smell and hearing and will often bypass traps and poisoned meats as if it were watching the preparation of such, although many are taken this way. The Coyote is also given to great curiosity and it is on many occasions that I have been fishing in some stream in the woods that I would look around to see a pair just sitting there watching me. The Coyote is very intelligent and even with the great slaughter by irate farmers and ranchers, has developed a great ability to co-exist with the ever-expanding settlements of Man. Sadly, often in journey I would see where farmers and ranchers would hang the bodies of slain Coyotes on fences to keep others in the area away.

The message of the Coyote might well be not to take any situation too seriously but always seek the lesson in it. Any Coyote dream or vision is a good one although some may be danger warnings. The Coyote in dreams is close to that of the Serpent in that you are approaching a new understanding and gaining Wisdom and Knowledge. In dreams and visions the Coyote also represents the need for looking for alternate methods and the use of all of one's abilities in solving dilemma. The Coyote will often tell you specifically that which it wishes you to know and playing is about the need to lighten the load of Self that we all need to do at times.

DEER - ELK

The Deer family includes the Elk, Buffalo, Antelope, Caribou, Moose and Gazelle and in general the Medicine of them as a group is to be given here. While there are specific differences in the Medicine between each of these species, especially when one is being named, there is much to be found in the Group Consciousness of them as well and as these are all herd Animals, it seems appropriate to Understand what the Medicine is that makes them of that Nature. As one might easily guess, the primary Medicine of this group Consciousness is that of Cooperation, Support, Brotherhood, and Share. We will specifically describe aspects of one of them being that of the Deer and begin with the two-legged group who have been Named with Deer.

The great herd Animals are all consummate grazers and Deer people often are given to appear to be constantly feeding on something especially late at night in the refrigerator. Deer people are also extremely social, and can often be seen to drive in close groups down the highway while not necessarily realizing it. They also are the ones that do not mind crowded conditions and the bigger the party group the better for them, no matter how crowded it might seem. Like all herds Deer people are seldom monogamous and will usually have many mates during a lifetime and seldom seem to continue any relationship once the kids are grown. Deer people also are constantly searching for greener grasses and often will change careers and homes if for no other reason than needing the change. All Deer people will usually sense the presence of something through their body, before they will actually see it.

Deer have a great sense of smell and hearing as well as good eyesight and are consummate observers of things of interest. The Deer if not eating or in search of food or mate, will spend much time nesting or laying down as it is also a great conservator of energy. All

Deer are given to rapid and spontaneous movement with great strength and agility. Tall fences are but small hurdles for most Deer. The Deer or Elk that wants something on the other side of anything will just bow its head and crash right through to it with no care for anything that it might step on in the process, and while they most often are not purposely trying to hurt anything, the goal attainment is more important than how it gets there. All Deer Animals and Named people have a great sensitivity to the deeper currents of Mother Earth and most like running or dancing. After the Buffalo, the Elk and Deer are the greatest source of food and clothing to the aboriginal people and all in this family are held in high regard for their Medicine of Swiftness and Alertness as well as their sensitivity and knowing where the resources are located.

The Deer in dreams and visions is about resources; running signifies the pursuit of goals, standing signifies that what is desired is already under foot, laying down or eating is about the nesting and nurturing the needs of Self.

FOXES -

While the Fox is part of the Wolf family, its Medicine is quite unique and deserves separate mention here. The Fox, known worldwide for its cunning and great ability at escape, is an avid participant in the dance of life and is the consummate parent and caretaker of others. The Fox seems to play as much as work in its effort of life and the Medicine of the Fox might well be put not to take it all so seriously. The serious side of the Fox is that it is a great defender of family and a great Provider and Nurturer. Foxes possess highly developed senses of hearing, sight, and smell and have great perception including the psychic sense. Most Foxes live in dens and burrows in Mother Earth and are highly sensitive to her deeper vibrations. While the Fox might resemble a small dog it far surpasses even the Wolf in its Adaptability, Independence, and Creativity in developing resources for Self. While the Medicine of the Fox is about Adaptability, it is equally about Balance as well as Family and Ingenuity. Having shared my home with a Fox before, I found that it is a most entertaining Animal brother with extremely high energy and resourcefulness.

The great adaptability of the shy as well as sly Fox has given it the ability to co-exist with the ever-increasing encroachments of Man as it is able to flourish in the inner cities of metropolitan areas of some countries and achieves almost a domestic status. Few other Animals besides Raccoons and Mice have been able to withstand the pressure of the two-leggeds with so much ease and grace. Foxes have great playfulness and an ever-expanding curiosity with a great ability in innovation in getting what they want. Generally night hunters and experts at stealth the Fox seems dauntless and might well walk right up to the chicken who would not believe he just stole the eggs right beneath where she sat. The Fox seems like the constant joker and entertainer in life with a ready laugh and smile and always you wonder what it is going to do next. Foxes are great homemakers and extremely good parents and while they mate for a while they do not often make lifetime commitments except to the family at hand. A Fox parent will often surrender itself for the continuation of its young and is also a great nurturing and teaching parent. Many a Fox has been seen to climb trees and little seems to daunt this great explorer of life.

The Fox in dreams and visions is about the lessons in life and that we should walk our path of life in joy and enjoy our walk. The Fox in dreams is also about relationships and the caring for Self and others. The Fox that is hunting signifies our need to develop new resources, while the Fox at play or rest is about the need to lighten up and realize the joy of life. Foxes also will often bring the message that they want you to know.

HORSES -

As the very nature of the Horse is that of being a Free Spirit and great wanderer and explorer, the Medicine of the Horse is predominantly that of Romance and Journey.

The Horse has great hearing and a pretty good sense of smell and sight and is also a very adaptable herbivore but unlike the Buffalo is rarely equipped to handle extreme changes in the weather or environment. While Horses like many of the Animals commonly found on the North American continent are not aboriginal but were introduced species brought over from Europe by the White Man like the pig, chicken and cow, the Horse deserves special mention as it has had a major impact upon the lifestyle of many tribes of the aboriginal people here. The Horse is singularly responsible for the taking over of this country by the white man and is greatly responsible for the subsequent changes of the topography by what can be called the sodbusters and fencers. Horses meant a new mode of transportation and greatly enhanced the lives of people who previously relied upon their feet or the waterways to explore their territory in hunting efforts whether against enemies or for food. Aboriginal people greatly prized the Horse and quickly became better riders than the white people, as the natives appreciated and talked to the Spirit of the Animal and learned and respected the Medicine of it. The Horse is one of the most romantic of the Animal Spirits and will often act in extremely selfless ways to each other and Man. Much like the Wolf the Horse likes to live in packs with a predominant pair in charge and when the packs become seemingly large, the young will spin off new packs as the drive for dominant positions is expressed.

In dreams and visions Horses signify the coming of Resource and Travel. A running Horse signifies great change in conditions where a standing Horse signifies the coming of increase and options in the condition of Self. Playing Horses or groups of Horses signify consciousness to family and joy in life.

LIZARDS -

The Lizard is another Animal that has seen need to change very little in their time on the Earthplane and one of the Medicines about the Lizard is that of Constancy. This great consumer of pesky insects and flies has great Evasion Medicine and many will quickly release its tail in order to survive. All Lizards are adept runners and often great burrowers as well but the major Medicine of the Lizard is that of Patience and Observation as they will lay in still wait for long periods for food to come by. The Lizard is extremely adaptable and is also a great conservator of energy often wearing many colors to blend into its surroundings and the ones known as the Chameleon or Anole are the ones that often come to mind as they will easily change their skin color to blend in with their surroundings.

In dreams and visions the Lizard is indeed signifying the need for exerting Patience and Faith in the achievement of goals and a Lizard that is running away signifies the need for evasion in the current conditions to overcome strife. An approaching Lizard in dreams and vision is also an adept message carrier and usually it is about the abundance of variety in life.

MICE -

Sensitivity to All is the major Medicine of Mice as well as Co-operation and Share. The Mouse and any of its variety of family is often a symbol of the South in the Medicine Wheel. Mice are voracious feeders and are extremely prolific in their breeding habits. The Mouse typically is a nocturnal feeder and based upon its family the diet varies usually between insects and grain. Mice are very close to Mother Earth and have great sensitive whiskers and a sensitive and soft nose. The greatest sensitivity of the Mouse is that of hearing and smell although their eyesight is adequate. Mice will sense the vibrations of Mother Earth and can feel footsteps from long away. The Mouse is a great explorer and investigator and a very acrobatic and agile runner. Mice in vision and dreams signify the Sensitivity to Softness in Life as well as Abundance and Variety that exists. Unlike what most people think, the Mouse is only faintly related to the Rat.

MUSKRAT -

Despite the continuing destruction of natural habitat by Man especially the wetlands that support the very Renewall and continuance of most aquatic life forms, the versatile and immensely adaptable Muskrat continues on. The Medicine of the Muskrat is indeed that of Sensitivity, Care, and Adaptability as well as Prosperity, Softness, and Passion in Love and Life. On seeing my first Muskrat, I was captivated by the gentleness and ease with which it moved about the swamp that I was living upon. Although it prefers aquatic plant life the Muskrat will make a meal on clams and shellfish as well as an occasional fish, frog, or crustacean. The Muskrat most often lives in aquatic dens and nests that are similar to that of the Beaver's yet smaller in size. Producing several litters of young with up to eleven members in each, this prolific breeder has weathered the trapping pressure of Man seeking its fine pelt like that of the Beaver. Indeed the Medicine of the Muskrat might be considered in the simplest manner as being that of Adaptability and Renewall in Love and Softness in Life.

These wonderful shy and quiet mammals in vision or encounter reflect one's condition in relationship to one's family, particularly children as well as home and life in general. In vision, dream or encounter if the Muskrat is moving away from oneself then that is the condition that is in process or will be soon to consider. A single Muskrat in pursuit of anything such as a food source, one should consider changes in one's own current endeavor particularly regarding occupation. If the Muskrat is playing with another in their natural way of courtship then one is soon to find a new relationship and mate and a Muskrat with its children suggests that one might consider such to be the case for oneself in the near future as well.

OPOSSUM -

The great acrobat of the trees, the Opossum is North America's answer to the Kangaroo and Koala Bear, being also a marsupial or pouch bearer. The major Medicine of the Opossum is Safety and a sense of Abundance, Home, Family, and Softness in Life. The Opossum has adequate vision with an enhanced sense of smell and good hearing. The Opossum is perhaps the greatest traveling band as the family of young, or kits, usually numbers as many as fourteen and the parents are often seen carrying these youngsters upon their backs in their nocturnal journeys in search of food. Basically omnivorous, the Opossum still prefers the sweets of fruits and grubs and has a great and sensitive nose for finding any of these. While quite strong and agile climbers of trees the Opossum is much less agile on land and developed its habit of playing dead by rolling over upon its back in times of imminent danger. Often it is the case where one of the parents will use this ploy to protect the other and the young by distracting the danger to Self. Having the most teeth of the land mammals at fifty, the Opossum finds very little during its nocturnal foraging that it cannot use as food or cannot get into in search of it, much to the chagrin of many campers.

In vision or dreams the Opossum signifies the coming of Abundance and Comfort in life. An Opossum carrying young signifies the need for consciousness in family needs or matters, while the single Opossum signifies the establishment of rest and home. The Opossum playing dead is a warning of impending danger and the need for caution in one's steps.

PORCUPINE –

The Medicine of the Porcupine is that of Caution and Defense against adversaries and now the major predator of this Animal are the traps of Man. The Porcupine is perhaps only bested by the Beaver in its love for the flesh of the trees. This nocturnal feeder is an agile climber and has a voracious appetite for the buds, twigs and bark of northern and western trees. Porcupines spend most of the day nesting high in the trees like the Squirrel and have always been seen as a great resource to the aboriginal people that used its meat, skin and most important quills. The double pointed quills are used by the people both as tools, points for darts, needles, and are often flattened and dyed and used in decoration of clothing and other items. When accosted by any predator the Porcupine will turn its back to the enemy and raise and strike with its tail or roll up into a tight ball like the Armadillo and become a most prickly adversary. The Porcupine is an agile climber and has good eyesight and hearing with an adequate sense of smell.

The Porcupine in dreams or vision is indeed that of a warning that one might truly be in a sticky or dangerous situation and to be cautious of deceptions by others. The Porcupine in journey signifies the need for Caution in Travel and a feeding Porcupine signifies the Need for Conservation of Resources. All Porcupine visions and dreams are warnings and sometimes they will tell you specifically what they are.

RABBITS -

The Medicine of the Rabbit is that of Softness, Environmental Sensitivity and Abundance in Life. This is the significant message as well when seen in dreams and visions, and this cuddly creature has often been the gift item to a child at the Easter time. Indeed the Rabbit is one of the most prolific breeders and provides for the food needs of most of the predators on the North American continent and was often the food staple for aboriginal people when bigger game was not close at hand. Often hunted with bow and arrow, it was most often the snare that enabled them to secure this tasty food source as their speed and ability at instantaneous changes of direction make the Rabbit extremely difficult to pursue. Many a Cat would stop in its tracks, if the chase would begin to look anywhere near an even condition. Rabbits with their large ears have extremely good hearing as well as vision and as they are a burrowing creature, they also have a great sensitivity to the deeper vibrations of Mother Earth. The sense of smell of the Rabbit is also excellent and it is this sense that enables it to find food even in deep snow. Highly adaptable, The Rabbit also has a great psychic sense and it perhaps is because of this that the Rabbit or Rabbit's foot symbolizes good fortune, however it seems like it was not so fortunate for the Rabbit that lost his foot. Rabbit fur is still highly prized for its softness and luxury, and this might well be the best statement about Rabbit Medicine which is Softness and Comfort in Life. Although they are prolific breeders, the Rabbit is predominately a solitary Animal that spends most of its time alone. A Rabbit also knows when to stand real still so as not to be noticed.

In vision and dreams the Rabbit signifies the condition of Comfort and Stability in Life. A Rabbit eating signifies the need to nourish the future of Self or signifies the time to start a new endeavor. A dead Rabbit in dreams or vision signifies a change in condition and often is the forecast of a pending loss of a loved one or friend. In dreams a running Rabbit is a sign of caution and may also signify the need to examine direction

RACCOON -

The wary Raccoon is indeed a prolific thief as befits its masked appearance, ask any camper. Strength of Will and great Innocence are qualities of the Medicine of the Raccoon as well as its ability to stand its own ground in seemingly insurmountable odds. Raccoon Medicine is also that of great Sensitivity, Nurturing, Care and Curiosity. Of a great inquisitive nature Raccoons will often get into quite humorous conditions and circumstances and are often found to make very entertaining and good pets. Being of a tenacious and yet noble character the Raccoon is also a brave and honorable hunter, fighter and protector of its young. At home in the trees as well as on land the Raccoon is also an ardent swimmer and no ground or place is unattainable to the Raccoon that sets its mind to be there. With a great sense of smell, balance, agility, strength, and sensitivity as well as good hearing and eyesight, the Raccoon is an extremely intelligent Animal that can easily foil the hunter as well as those thinking their possessions are well out of sight. The Raccoon knows when it is outmatched in a fight and shares a lot of its hunting and fleeing skills with its Bear brother. Basically omnivores, Raccoons prefer the flesh of aquatic finds but will truly eat most anything. While seemingly solitary hunters, the Raccoon does intend to mate for life and is a great caretaker and teacher of its young and prefers the family life. When seen in groups, it is not due to a herd or pack nature, it is its benefactor nature to share with others its good find. All Raccoons know when and where others are in its territory and if they are not family, they will put up a good fight to protect it. Very clean by nature, the often coveted tail is used as a balancing tool and they tend to caretake of their pelt more for camouflaging their scent than for cleanliness sake. The Raccoon has adapted well to the encroachments of the settlements of Man but has suffered often to the blinding nature of his headlights.

Raccoons in dreams and visions signify the search and acquisition of treasures and the coming appearance of great finds. The Raccoon on the ground standing still signifies the need to begin the search and if it is eating or washing signifies the coming appearance of the Wind of Change. A Raccoon scampering away is a warning of the need of flight or the presence of deceit or a danger. The Raccoon often will bring a symbol or totem in dreams and visions and it is always good to pay attention to these consummate messengers and go-betweens to the Spirit World.

RATS –

The Rat is the one walker that is often seen with fear and disgust and it is ironic because Rat Medicine is about being the Fearless Waste Disposal and Caretaker of the environment. While both Mice and Rats reproduce in numbers reflective to the available resources of food, the Rat is more competitive and thereby less social or communal than the Mouse. Unlike what most people might think this Balancing of their Populations to the available resources at hand is a common Medicine between them. The Rat gets its negative reputation because of its Fearless nature in its house cleaning of debris and feeding upon whatever is available. The Rat has become the great waste disposal animal of the waste of man, causing it to be seen with contempt and regard which is reflective of the behavior of many if not most of the people in the Prevalent Culture. Because of this habit, the Rat becomes the disease carrier and as it is also a carrion feeder has caused great plagues amongst peoples. It is also ironic that the Rat that causes most of this disruptive behavior in most city environments is actually an introduced species brought over in ships by the White Man. In most cases the Mice and Rats found in the country environments are not of this kind and of these there is little to fear however rabies, another White Man's disease, can sometimes be found. This danger can exist in almost any Animal around the populations of people and their poor handling of their immense production of waste. It is the Fearless part of its Medicine that the Rat signifies in vision, dream and encounter and signifies a need to take charge of one's resources in Self as well as material things in ways that Walk in Balance and With Harm to No One Being or thing!

SKUNKS -

The Skunk, most often noted for its personal protection or defense mechanism, is really a very beautiful, sensitive Animal form as well as a very good and kind parent. The Skunk dens up in the winter and emerges in good weather to forage for food and if seen doing such foraging one can be sure that good weather is at hand. Basically an omnivore, the diet of these quiet Animal forms varies with the seasons. The Skunk population is very important in maintaining the balance of insect and rodents in any region, and the major predator upon these most noble Animals is that of the Serpent and Owl. This predator and prey relationship also speaks well of the nature and Medicine of the Skunk as both of these predators have an insatiable appetite for Knowledge and Wisdom as well as what is sacred. One can easily understand the Why of this when one realizes that the Medicine of the Skunk is that of The Wisdom of Expressing Balance and Care in ones Walk in Life. Indeed, even the stripes of White, being that of Spirit and the Black of Direction on its coat speaks of this Medicine and value. Certainly no Being or thing has ever experienced the spray of one of these sensitive messengers if they operate in accord to its Medicine and message.

The Skunk in encounter, vision or dreams - always relates to one's personal trust and safety issues. The Skunk is a great communicator as well as making an excellent pet and will often tell specific information if asked. The Skunk that is eating signifies the condition of safety and surplus being at hand, while the skunk that is defending itself signifies the need to isolate oneself from one's adversaries in one's current pursuit. Any group of Skunks relate to family and communal issues and pairs of Skunks reflect one's condition to one's mate or partners be it a potential or current relationship. An attacking Skunk signifies the need to withdraw and any journeying Skunk signifies the need to relocate to safer or more productive conditions.

SPIDERS -

The Spider is nature's consummate Architect and Engineer. Ever weaving webs, the Spider wonders often why and mostly thinks others seeming to be less industrious to be lazy. People with Spider Medicine generally exhibit great Tenacity and Attention to Detail but like the Spider they also often exhibit a false sense of aloofness and often bring upon themselves conditions to bring themselves down to earth, usually through cowardly behavior. Spider people often make busy work for themselves and do so only for the sake of appearance as Spider Medicine is much about the Art of Deception. Often the Spider will weave a strange symbol or design in its web as a lure to curious prey. The Trapdoor Spider weaves pebbles and sticks into a door over a tunnel that it has dug from the earth. This species waits with the door closed for its prey to come by, then at the right moment springs the door open and pounces upon its prey, which can sometimes be of formidable size. One of the largest Spiders most often seen is the Tarantula, which is a ground dweller that ranges long distances at night in search of its next meal. Spiders of the Brown Recluse, Tarantula, and Black Widow varieties will inject their victims with a paralyzing venom that can be harmful to humans. After injecting the prey the Spider will often weave a cocoon-like fabric over its prey as it may take several victims at a time before feeding from them. It is indeed the very nature of its feeding habit, which is that of sucking the juices from its victims that is the rest of the Medicine of the Spider in that they all have great Sucking Medicine. The Medicine of the Spider might best be put as that of great Sucking, Deception and Ensnaring with immense intricacy of design.

The Spider still depends mostly upon its sense of feel through its eight legs, even though most also have eight eyes and like all ground dwellers is very sensitive to vibrations including the deeper vibrations of Mother Earth. All Spiders are consummate weathermen and always seek a safe place before a storm occurs. While the Spider might portray great sensitivity it is only in pursuit of what it wants for itself as the Spider is truly a solitary creature that is interested in serving no other. This is clearly shown by the Black Widow who gets its name from killing its mate. While no one has been Named a Spider by me there are those that have been seen as exhibiting the Medicine of it.

The Spider in vision or dreams is that of an obvious warning for Caution and to be aware of Deception by those people or conditions around one. The Spider weaving its web is often a sign of industry that may or may not be of benefit to Self and may represent the need to exert one's own energy in productive efforts, but always with caution to the balances involved lest you get trapped in a web of your own design. False prophets are a prime example of Spider Medicine as well as scammers and con artists. The appearance of the Spider in one's home is often favored by many as they will keep the other insects at bay, however a home that is resonating in the higher vibrations of Light will seldom have the need of nature's insect parasite.

SQUIRRELS -

The Squirrel is one of the favorite foods of the aboriginal peoples of the North American continent and is still often hunted by Man. One of the Medicines of the Squirrel is indeed that of Adaptability as they have suffered little because of the encroachments of Man and it is partly because of his incessant eradication of the populations of the predators that now has the Squirrel populations extremely dense even in the inner cities. Being a highly vocal Communicator, this aspect of Squirrel Medicine is only surpassed by its consummate efforts at storing away food supplies for the needs of the winter and the Tree Spirits are quite thankful as the Squirrel often forgets where he has put some of these and so is singularly responsible for the planting of the seeds of most trees, especially the mighty Oak. The Squirrel represents Softness, Abundance and Industry in life and most important a sense of the future as the Squirrel is always planning ahead. The Medicine of the Squirrel is that of Communication, Saving for the future and a sense of home and Softness and Comfort in life. Highly prolific in breeding, the Squirrel is equally at home in trees or upon the ground and can move about each with great speed and agility. While some have made pets of these consummate nibblers, none that have done so have escaped their propensity to bite with their ever-growing teeth. The Flying Squirrel has flaps of skin upon its sides that it expands on outstretched legs as it leaps from treetops and branches to glide in the air to another location. The

Squirrel has a soft, fine fur and its very good vision and hearing are augmented with a great sense of Balance and Curiosity. The Squirrels Agility and Balance come from its large and bushy tail. A herbivore that prefers Acorns and nuts from most any tree, the Squirrel will most commonly make its nest in the tops of the tallest of these, although attics of homes are another favorite place, much warmer there to raise its two litters of young a year.

In vision and dreams the Squirrel being the consummate Communicator will often tell specifically what it is for you to know and signifies both Hope and Renewall. It is often a forecaster of good things to come about the home or nest of Self or conditions about these things and also signifies the need for thrift and communication. A Squirrel that is running away is a sign of danger or the need for relocation or journey, and the Squirrel at rest or play is saying to be about just that. If a Squirrel is bringing or carrying some item it is a hidden resource to Self and it is wise to pay good attention to these.

WEASEL - ERMINE

The Weasel family includes Mink, Ermine and Marten and while the size and colors may vary slightly with diet, their basic habits and Medicines are predominately the same. The Medicine of the Weasel is that of Ardent Aggression and Tenacity and might best be expressed as to Live Life Fully From the Heart. Being almost singularly responsible for keeping the rodent populations in check including that of the Squirrel, the Weasel will often eat the birds from nests and has been known to also eat a Snake or two. As all of this family live near the water and are ardent and most skillful in aquatic sports, their diet includes the fish as well. The Weasel likes to play and is often seen in pairs but hunts alone over quite a large territory. With its long and slender body the Weasel is a great tunnel explorer and its hunting habit might well be called tenaciously aggressive, as it gets what it puts its mind to and it is extremely intelligent. An extremely ferocious fighter, the Weasel also knows when it is outmatched and is a master of evasion and escape. Its great playfulness and curiosity has led to its decline to the traps of Man, however the Weasel is most elusive in any manner of chase as it seems to somehow suddenly evaporate from sight. Weasels are agile climbers as well as swimmers and burrowers and there is little about the Weasel's environment that can truly be considered a safe place for its prey. Prized for its soft and fine pelts this beautiful creature has great sensitivity to the deeper vibrations of Mother Earth and often will be seen playing in swimming pools immediately after a storm has passed, and indeed these are one of nature's very best weathermen. Having extremely fine eyesight and hearing as well as sense of smell and agility very little was overlooked when the senses were given out by the Great Spirit.

The Weasel in dreams and vision is always one of Prosperity. An escaping Weasel is a sign to examine the safety of one's resources, while the Weasel at play is signifying the need for recreation and ease of stress. The Weasel fighting is a direct warning of a pending conflict and the Weasel that is showing its prey signifies the pending success of one's endeavors and to not give up yet. If in a trap, the Weasel signifies the need to examine the safety of one's resources and one's current direction. The Weasel with young signifies the resources of the family and to value the lesson giving and nurturing of and to others.

WOODCHUCK / GROUNDHOG -

The Medicine of the Woodchuck, often called the Groundhog is that of Sweetness, Sensitivity, and the Good Life. These gentle sensitive creatures are consummate Providers and natural Safe-keepers as well as parents and I have often thought that I would love to have one as a pet at times. Male Woodchucks will do battle much like the Seal or Elk for mating rights however they do not seriously injure each other as those other Animal forms do. This behavior is just another example of Woodchuck Medicine as it shares the example of what the Woodchuck desires to Safe-keep. Safekeeping and attention to Safety and Resources are also part of Woodchuck Medicine.

In vision and dreams as well as encounter the Woodchuck signifies the need to take inventory as to what is precious to oneself as well as to insure in the safety of that which one has already attained. The Woodchuck that is feeding signifies the need to store up more reserves and the Woodchuck that is still signifies the need for caution. A Woodchuck that is moving signifies the need for the same in the life of oneself and if the Woodchuck is defending or attacking it signifies the condition of danger or jeopardy in one's current relationships or pursuits.

WOLVES –

The Medicine of the Wolf is about Earth Wisdom, Resource, Protection and Family. One of the main Medicines of the Wolf is that of Teacher and the tribal way of the aboriginal peoples are direct patterns of social structure copied by the societies in all cultures

Wolves have good eyesight, hearing and a keen sense of smell as well as heightened communicative and social skills. The Wolf is a Gatherer and Bringer forth of Knowledge about Family and Brotherhood to the people and like the Buffalo is held in high esteem and as a sacred symbol in vision and dreams by the aboriginal peoples. A large carnivore that preys predominately upon much larger game, the Wolf lives in a pack with a chief or dominant male. Respectful Sharing are the key words of Relationship Proper and this is quite evident in a Wolf pack. All members of the pack share in all aspects of life including the care, discipline and well-being of old and young as well as hunting, defending its members and protecting territory. As the definition of Brotherhood is Sharing in the Well-being of the condition of the all, it seems well that we see the Wolf as the great Teacher of how to live in a society that benefits all. The Wolf is a carnivore and extremely intelligent hunter and often aboriginal peoples have followed the packs of Wolves to resources of food and water. Many clans of tribes were named after the Wolf and it is still held to be a most sacred Brother in the Animal kingdom in both the Physical and Spiritual plane. Long periods of predation by Man have left the Wolf in almost an extinct status with the Red variety almost eradicated in the south.

While the Medicine of the Wolf might well be that of Teacher, the Wolf in visions and dreams usually relates to Relationships, Sensitivity and most often Resource. In vision or dreams - the Wolf often will tell its own lesson or message as it is the most adept communicator. The Wolf that is walking or running signifies the need for direction or a change in the current goals of ideals for growth. A Wolf that is bringing something to you signifies to accept that condition or resource to Self. A Pair of Wolves signifies a condition about a relationship or mate and the action of the pair will speak for itself. Wolves in a pack relate to family or relationships such as business groups. A hunting Wolf or hungry Wolf signifies the need to expand upon the resources for Self and can signify to be of caution of a possible betrayal by a close friend or ally. A Wolf bringing food will signify the potential of and closeness of success in an endeavor. A Wolf at play or rest signifies the need to do that as well. A howling Wolf signifies the need to communicate with others about a deep disturbance or condition of unrest. A crying Wolf signifies an impending death. My Wolf Spirit guide is a young white female named Kikiyaya and she has taught me very much about Relationships and Love.

WOLVERINE -

Wolverine Medicine is about Adaptability, Inner Fortitude, great Strength, Stamina, Tenacity and Self-Reliance. While it has similar Medicine to that of the Badger, the Wolverine is much more solitary and independent by Nature. The Wolverine (*Gulo gulo*), also referred to as a glutton and occasionally as a Carcajou, Skunk Bear, Quickhatch, or Gulon, is the largest land-dwelling species of the Weasel family. The Wolverine is a stocky and muscular carnivore, more closely resembling a small Bear than other mustelids (Weasels). The Wolverine has a reputation for ferocity and strength out of proportion to its size, with the documented ability to kill prey many times its size. The Wolverine is distributed primarily in remote reaches of the Northern boriel forests and subarctic and alpine of the Northern hemisphere, with the greatest numbers in Alaska, Canada, the Nordic countries of Europe and throughout western Russia and Siberia. Wolverine populations have experienced a steady decline since the 19th century in the face of trapping, range reduction and loss of habitat, such that they are essentially absent in the southern end of their European range and are quite rare in the continental United States. Wolverines are always good Spirit helpers in helping us solve dilemmas as well as being great Guides and Protectors.

In dreams or visions the Wolverine is about Tenacity in decision, and the need to use Stamina, Strength, and Courage to leave the old idea of Self and to embrace fully the expression of growth in Self. Wolverines that are retreating are showing the need to review or change direction in one's current pursuits. Wolverines that are burrowing represent the need to dig beneath the surface of illusion to find the truth or source of a dilemma or discover a hidden resource in oneself. A standing or sitting Wolverine is telling us to hold our ground, as well as letting us know of some present threat

FLIERS

All Fliers are in touch with the Spirit of the land, water and air and are often given to guidance in dreams and visions because of it. As all Fliers are aware of the constantly changing nature of the currents of the Wind they also are very much in tune with the cycles and rhythms of the Force of Change itself. While some like to effortlessly soar aloft, other Fliers are quite happy in their very energetic form of flight and have modified their metabolism to accommodate it. All Fliers also possess good vision Medicine and are quite adept at it in visions and dreams, however the communicative skills of some fliers are not as developed as others.

People Named with the Medicine of the Fliers often tend to see more in the psychic senses than they might feel. All Named ones with the Medicine of the Fliers also tend to see the presence of Spirits or the condition of auras and have the capacity to develop a sense of feel. Some of the Fliers such as the Owl have a more developed sense of hearing, but not very many of the Fliers seem to have a great sense of smell. If there is one quality shared by all Fliers it is their inherit ability to accept the Condition of Change and thereby, Grow.

BATS -

The Bat is one of natures most unusual Fliers in that it is a mammal and its wings are made of skin. The Medicine of the Bat is that of Caretaking and Community. Bats usually roost during the day in large numbers and share the herd Medicine with many of the walkers. The Bat typically is a night predator, preying upon all flying insects and plays a major role in containing and depleting the hordes of Mosquitoes that develop after each rainfall. The eyesight of this nocturnal hunter is good but their ability of echolocation lends an even greater sense to that of vision. In flight the Bat will echolocate its prey and swoop down upon it often catching it in the membrane between its hind feet like a baseball player catches the ball in his glove. Having caught the prey this way the Bat will adeptly and with great dexterity remove it and eat it in flight with one swift move of its head. The Bat is often seen as having very large ears and their sense of hearing is extremely good. Of all of the fliers they might have the best sense of smell however this might be hard to imagine if you have ever spent some time in the caves in which they dwell. Bats are communal by nature and great caretakers and nurturers of their young.

The Bat in dreams and visions signifies the need for Change and new direction in growth. The single Bat winging its way signifies the need for journey and if flying in groups it signifies the need and value to community or working in groups. The Bat that is flying toward one signifies the challenging and need to release one's fears and the Bat that is eating signifies the need for rest and sustenance.

BLUEBIRDS -

As Blue is the color of the Creator is it any wonder that the Bluebird would be referred to in song and image as the Bluebird of Happiness? The Medicine of the Bluebird be it of either the eastern or western variety is that of Hope Everlasting and Fulfillment of Desire. These sensitive and gracious fliers live primarily on flying insects and as these often represent negative Consciousnesses when in Vision to me, I consider the Bluebirds as well as the Frogs and Lizards as being great Balancers or Custodians in the energies and thoughts or expressions in the universe. The Bluebird is a very accommodating and thereby also passive Life form and because of this was in decline due to the introduction of other species especially from the Europeans such as the Sparrow and Starling.

The Bluebird in encounter or dreams and visions always relates to issues of desire and the Heart, and thereby one's true Hope prayers. The single Bluebird represents one's life expressions. In pairs or groups, represents one's relationships whether actual or potential. The Bluebird that is singing signifies the need to be outwardly expressive of one's Hopes, Feelings, or Desires, and the bluebird that is feeding signifies the need to be more physically expressive of one's thoughts and feelings. A Bluebird that is flying towards oneself signifies that one's desire is soon to be realized. If flying away from oneself it signifies the need to relocate. All fliers that are passing in front of oneself from left to right relate to future conditions and a positive result, while the opposite is true if flying from right to left and thereby referencing the past.

BLUE JAYS -

One of my personal favorites is the Tattletale bird or Blue Jay. Whenever I see this flier, I tell it my greatest wish and prayer and know well it will tell it to everyone else on the Earth and Spirit planes. The Medicine of the Blue Jay might well be put as Lesson Giving and Aggressive Communication as this beautiful bird is a consummate Communicator that can keep no secret. An ardent parent, this rascal is also an adept nest robber that will let little get in the way of caretaking of itself and its young. The Blue Jay also is a great Teacher and we would do well to learn from its lessons about growth. It often will land at the base of a tree and then move from branch to branch to its final destination at the very top and then repeat this process of evidencing the right path of growth. Typical of most omnivores there is little that the Blue Jay will not eat and in this way it shows us of the abundance provided to us by the Great Spirit in life. This beautiful Flier has keen eyesight and a loud and varied vocal ability with good hearing as well. The Blue Jay is a highly active bird, a great protector of nest and territory and has often been seen to chase away a Hawk or a Cat or two.

In visions and dreams the Blue Jay signifies the power of prayer and our link to the Great Spirit and His constant care and attentive ear. The Blue Jay flying signifies the need for a change of direction, and the feeding Blue Jay signifies approaching Providence and Prosperity.

A singing Blue Jay signifies the value and need for prayer and to receive Joy and Happiness as your birthright. A flock Of Blue Jays signifies the support to and from your community and family.

BUTTERFLIES -

The four wings of the Butterfly represent the four winds or directions and the three body segments remind us of the master number seven of vibration on the Earthplane. A powerful symbol in aboriginal cultures, the Butterfly is truly the symbol for Metamorphosis and the Christ consciousness and the child of the Great Spirit Father that is within each and all of His creation. The major Medicine of the Butterfly is indeed that of both Transformation and Metamorphosis and might well also be expressed as the potential to return to the Beauty and Purity that is the true essence of the Spirit of each of us. The strongest Medicine of the Butterfly is the power to accept and Embrace the Condition of Change and make things better for Self and others in the process. The Butterfly also has great Sucking Medicine and those working in the healing way have great need to purge and spit away the negative energies and wrongful thinking that they easily absorb from others. All people named with the Medicine of the Butterfly share a great penchant for things of Beauty. While the hearing of the Butterfly is adequate and it has good vision, it has an even greater sense of feeling and touch and a nose that easily finds things that are sweet to smell. The Butterfly's antenna enables it to sense the vibration of change in the wind and Sensitivity is indeed the major sense of this beautiful Messenger, Sharer and Caretaker of the Great Spirit's beautiful things. The Monarch is one of the most famous of this species and after Metamorphosis into the Butterfly, this great adventurer will store up energy and fly for thousands of miles to distant places often over large expanses of water to rendezvous with countless others to winter at a secret and sacred place. Then when weather conditions again improve they will return to northern places to assist in the pollination work that they have chosen to do. The Monarch Butterfly has great adaptability and has developed a defence from attack by birds by eating certain plant types when in the Caterpillar form that gives it a toxic and bitter taste. Other species of the Butterfly have often taken on similar appearances to the Monarch so as to share in this protection from predation.

The Butterfly in dreams and visions signifies Metamorphosis and the embracing and nearness of the true sweetness in life through the continuum of growth. The Butterfly that is flying represents the need to change direction or location and the Butterfly that is sitting signifies the need for looking inside to see the true condition of Self. A Butterfly upon a flower or a nest signifies the coming of Peace and Prosperity as relates to the condition of Self and home. Butterflies in groups signify the need to share and be about the Well-being of Self through others. Any Caterpillar in vision or dreams signifies the need and potential for Transformation and is usually a warning of a condition of abuse. The caterpillar also signifies the destructive nature of immaturity.

BUZZARDS -

The Buzzard is a great caretaker of Mother Earth and cleaner upper of things and so may be thought of as the Ant of the bird family in life. The California Condor is the largest of this species and will grow to the wing span of ten feet. Often mistaken for the Eagle, the "Thunderbird" is indeed truly the Condor as it will often fly high up the mountainside and fold its wings up just so, and dive leaving its wing tips exposed so as to make a cracking sound much like that of a whip as it dives toward Mother Earth making a thunderous roar all the way. The Thunderbird or Buzzard represents Change and Transformation. The Buzzard is a predator as well as carrion feeder and is often depicted as a symbol of doom or death as it can be seen patiently waiting until the prey is dead or near death. The unusual adaptation to its work of cleaning up the remains upon Mother Earth has left the Buzzard with a strangely grotesque beauty with the strongest example of this being its adaptation to carrion feeding by having no feathers upon its head to collect debris and thereby promote bacteria and disease. Letting little go to waste, this great conservator of energy applies this trait in its technique of flight as well as it prefers effortless flight by surfing upon the waves of the currents aloft and little passes by the excellent eyesight of this lofty bird. Often seen in groups the Buzzard is indeed a great communicator yet prone to petty squabbles over little things. Just as it is often hard to pass by the auto wreck without staring, the Buzzard truly symbolizes much about out mistaken fears and mystery about the process known as death. The

Medicine of the Buzzard is not about death nor symbolizes death, but is that of Transformation and that truly ALL CAN BE.

The Buzzard in vision or dreams represents impending Change and Transition. In almost any case, the Buzzard in visions and dreams relates to the condition of goals and thereby growth. The single Buzzard not in flight, signifies the need for Faith and Patience in one's pursuit of the current goal while the Buzzard in any group signifies the need for the application of collective resources to realize the current goal. A Buzzard in flight going in any direction signifies the need to change agendas or goals, preferably for those with loftier ideals. A feeding Buzzard signifies that Success or Transformation is indeed close at hand and the need for replacement or release. The final message given to state is this about the message of the Medicine of the Buzzard; it is not about Death for heavens sake, it is about Life and to live it fully and with Passion and not to worry about the next mistake, all will ultimately be forgiven anyway if you try as best you can in life.

CARDINALS -

This beautiful songbird of the Red Ray is also a Messenger of Change. The Medicine of the Cardinal is about Change and how to approach it with Softness, Beauty and Balance. Often in many areas the harbinger of Spring, the Cardinal seems to usher in the change of the seasons so very well. This beautiful communicator with its variety of whistles and calls could well best be described as nature's wake up call as it readily ushers in the changes of the seasons. Liking to stay close to Mother Earth in the tree or the bush this endeavorous feeder passes on many seeds that help the Plant Spirits migrate along their path as well and helps all things grow this way. While often only the bright red male is easily visible and might well be seen upon the smallest of twigs it is seldom far from its mate. Both are ardent parents in the care of their young and the good eyesight of this tree dweller is only exceeded by its great balancing ability.

All Cardinal visions and dreams relate to change and as the Cardinal is an avid communicator it will often show or draw your attention to what it is that it wants for you to know or change. Often the Cardinal is about a forecast of change in the condition of occupation or the need for relocation about the nest. A flying

Cardinal is showing the need to journey or relocate and the Cardinal about the nest with its mate is about matters of the home or family.

CRANES -

The Medicine of the Crane is that of Softness, Comfort and Grace of place and when one appears it signifies that indeed the place is of Balance and Peace. Another good way to describe the Medicine of this beautiful bird is Grace in the Quest for Knowledge on the Path of Growth. The message of the Crane might well be to enjoy the dance of life and to see the great beauty in it as all Cranes are spectacular dancers. The Crane family includes the Blue Heron, Heron and Egret as well as the Stork. Mostly quiet and shy, Cranes are truly one of the great explorers of the Animal world and prefer solitary expeditions of exploration at times but also the comfort and safety of the flock. Cranes make caring and nurturing parents, are highly communicative and vocal and enjoy good hearing and eyesight. Birds in the Crane family have long legs and bills with large bodies as well as wings and all but the shortest of the species is quite long of neck. Ever picking the bottoms of shallow bodies of water in search for morsels of food these large birds are sure of foot as well as being extremely agile and graceful in flight.

The Crane in vision and dreams most often signifies the condition of the home or environment. A Crane that is flying signifies that a new direction or exploration is in the agenda of Self. A Crane with its mate signifies that condition soon to Self. Cranes flying in formation or a group signal the need for reunion or relocation. If the group is at rest, a message of the need to do group work or communications with others is at hand. A single Crane is about the condition of Self and symbolizes most often a condition of softness in life. A Crane that is feeding signifies that the fruit of one's endeavor is soon at hand, and any of these birds in this family will often show you specifically what it wants you to know in dreams and visions as they all are truly great communicators.

DIVING BIRDS - KINGFISHER

The Diving Birds include the Kingfisher, Cormorant, Coot, Loon, Plover, Tern, and Pelican and whatever else might be in your specific area. If one word might describe the Medicine of this family of fliers it might well be Pluck or Spunk or even Dauntless, as they seem to defy the belief of 'No, it cannot be done.' The Medicine of these adventurers includes that of Ardent Endeavor and to never give up. As adept below the surface of the water as they are in the air, there is very little about the elements of Mother Earth that surpasses or escapes their abilities. Expert fishermen and swimmers this family is sometimes much more at home in the water than on land and being extremely hard-headed is another trait of this magnificent family of birds with some of them able to dive to depths of over one hundred feet. Ever able to see the Abundance provided by the Great Spirit is another aspect of this Bird family and it truly symbolizes Grace and Ease. A Kingfisher will often hover like a Hummingbird holding steady over a spot until it sees what it wants and then drop like a rock beneath the surface of the water usually returning with a tasty morsel in its mouth. All Diving Birds have developed special adaptations, be it the placement of their feet, their lung size, beak shape or size, or structure of bones in the head and these are part of their Medicine as well.

All dreams and visions about Diving Birds relate to Resources and the Attainment of Goals and the Abundance in Life. In visions or dreams Diving Birds represent the need for applying one's Will as to come from the Heart in the achievement of the present goals and the application of Adaptability and Determination in the pursuit of them. The Diving Bird will usually appear as a solitary hunter however when they appear in groups the message is to include or embrace the resources of others and to work in the collective way, respectfully sharing of course. The solitary Bird with its prize catch in its mouth or feeding signifies the nearness of Achievement and the Abundance in Life. A Diving Bird with its young signifies the teaching and sharing process to others. Diving Birds that are flying represent the need to find new goals and resources or examine the validity of the ones at hand. Any Bird on its nest signifies the conditions about the home and these wonderful Birds are also great communicators and will often tell or show you specifically what it is that they want you to know.

DOVES - PIGEON-

The Dove or Pigeon is used in many cultures to symbolize Peace and Love. The Medicine of the Pigeon and Dove is that of Softness in Life and Undying Love. The most often seen representative of this family is the Pigeon that has adapted so well to the city life and has such great homemaking skills in Trees, buildings, bridges and even signs. The Morning Dove is the favorite of most with its wonderful voice and repetitious song that has lulled many to sleep under a hot summers sun. These peaceful singers of songs of Softness in Life and Love are at home on the ground as well as in the Trees and air. Often seen in groups and in pairs these creatures of softness are nurturing parents that will mate for life, however most do not as they are great journeyers in life sharing their messages with many everywhere. Doves and Pigeons are swift and ardent fliers and a favorite of the hunter as well as of Birds of prey and are quite resourceful in their ability of camouflage when need be. These seed feeders are partners to the Plants and Trees as they provide the locomotion of the seeds of these rather than just waiting for a fair wind to blow.

In visions and dreams the Dove and Pigeon like the Butterfly, represent the Christ consciousness in Self and are about Love and Softness in Life. Whether it is in a group or flying, the Dove in visions or dreams is about sharing the message and resources of Self to and with others in community. The Dove in its nest or with mate or family signifies the condition of the home and the center of Self and security. The Pigeon or Dove that is feeding represents the resources at hand and the peaceful condition in and of it. A Dove in a tree signifies the condition of peace in place wherever it might be. The Pigeon or Dove that is carrying something wants to show you just that, as this is the only manner that they might speak of such things.

DRAGONFLIES

The Dragonfly might well be called the helicopter of the insect world with its great hovering and backwards flying ability that of the Fliers is only shared with the Hummingbird. This graceful Flier even mates in the air but is also one of the great predators of the Mosquito at whatever stage in its life. Of often iridescent but always beautiful colors, the Dragonfly will often catch mosquitoes on the fly and then holding them in its legs, consume them in flight.

Of great and a very specialized design, the Medicine of this adept and graceful Flier is that of Gracefulness, Specialization, and Adaptability. The Dragonfly in visions and dreams is that of being a harbinger of changes to come and signifies the need to approach them with grace and poise. The Dragonfly in visions and dreams that is at rest, often delicately balanced upon a seemingly too small reed or blade of grass, signifies the need to reestablish balance to ones goals and aspirations in life and the Dragonfly hovering signifies the need for patience in the pursuit of ones goals. The Dragonfly feeding signifies the nearness of completion or attainment and the Dragonfly buzzing is a warning of a pending condition of strife.

DUCKS - GEESE

The Medicine that best describes that of Ducks and Geese is that of Renewall and of Hope. The Duck or Goose is another of the favorite food fare of many of the aboriginal people of the North American continent. The feathers of these beautiful birds have for centuries been used to bring Softness to Man in life whether to stuff a pillow or a bed or blanket and such and were often used in adornment and for beautification. Basically herd Animals that are prone to long migrations these beautiful creatures are as graceful and adapted to aquatic feats as well as very long journeys of flight. Highly vocal and of good eyesight these noisy ones have excellent hearing as well. Being omnivorous they will often be seen to feed upon any aquatic form of life as well as the seeds and grasses that we know so well especially those of rice. Duck and Geese also have great sensitivity not only to the deeper vibrations of Mother Earth but to the Winds of Change as well. Prolific breeders, the male of these species will often unintentionally drown its mate by holding her head under water too long while in the process of copulation and as with most herd Animals a single Animal will usually have many mates in life.

The Duck and Goose in dreams and visions always relates to one's goals and comfort and signifies Softness and Abundance in Life. A Duck or Goose in flight signifies the need to seek out that which one wishes to achieve outside the current sphere of influence or location. The single Duck or Goose at rest on the ground or water signifies the need for Patience for a favorable wind in the pursuit of the current goal. A Duck or Goose that is making noise represents the need to share your vision or needs with others so that they may support your journey in life. The Duck or Goose also will often present its message to you personally in visions and dreams as they are sharers and great communicators and believe in team play.

EAGLES –

The Eagle in aboriginal societies has often held the position of the highest ranking as it flies to the highest position in the skies and therefore reaches the closest position to the Great Spirit Father there. Of extremely good eyesight and speech with good hearing as well, the Eagle is another of the Fliers that mates in mid-air. The Eagle typically will mate for life and is a great nest builder and care-provider for its young. Possessing great strength the Eagle has been known to take a young Goat or Deer straight up off a rocky ledge. All Eagles are excellent fishermen as well as they seem to psychically know where the fish are at as they sweep down over the water without looking down, and in a single motion snatch large fish from the depths and carry these away with such grace and ease. Ask any Eagle and they know where everything is at and usually without looking for it. The Osprey, or Fishing Eagle, being of smaller size but ever an Eagle and of great intellect, will most often turn its prize fish as to be head first in flight back to its nest as it knows all about aerodynamics as well. Little goes by unnoticed from any Eagle and often they will sit for long periods just watching the goings on as well as be constant observers in flight.

Being a migratory bird the Eagle develops a great cognizance of a very large territory. The Eagle alone or in society is a dauntless bird as it lives its experience pretty much on the edge. Some may view it as all seeing and knowing and in the aboriginal way I think better said might be all feeling, as this is what comes through channel as most to be said. Perhaps that is why in this time, past the encroachments by Man, the Eagle has fallen victim to the very poisons of mankind and its society as they reject any idea of the Great Spirit Father or any that can fly so high as to be with and hear the words of Him. Aboriginal Man on this part of Mother Earth as well as others never feared the Eagle but always held the pattern of it in the deeper recesses of the Heart, as all know that where the Eagle flies, so do they. So high sometimes as to only be seen by air machines and other birds most

Eagles live a very solitary life. Even though they are thought to be the top of the food chain by certain biologists the Eagle at best represents the consciousness of Man. The aboriginal society and peoples that my bloodline are from held the Eagle as a precious Spirit and totem and often wore the feathers of one in honor of its highest ideal as Strength and Courage in Self.

There used to be in my societies of aboriginal peoples, those called Eagle catchers in which a brave young Man would seek out and raid, as you would have it, one of its young. In truth, the first born from the usual clutch of two eggs would through its Greed or Strength as might be seen that way, at time of fledgling, kick the other smaller one out of the nest or kill it in some way as to be the only one. In the society of some of the peoples that I come from, the Eagle catcher, by the way of centuries of knowledge of the sacred nature of all things on Mother Earth, would brave the relentless attacks and sometimes even the death of Self in order to retrieve one of the two birds in the nest. This feat was usually preformed in a very precarious place and then the young Bird would be raised to maturity on top of a special lodge or place. Through the obvious taking of one the other Eagle was sure to survive to adulthood. The one taken was held in the highest honor and often the Eagle catcher, which always took the Bird by hand, took the young child from that place and would individually raise and care for it to maturity. Then with a great ceremony and with great Grace, the Eagle that was caught and raised would be fed a final meal and then the ceremony would be embraced in its passing again to the Spirit world which we all come from. Finally, every part of the Bird and especially the feathers would be shared or adorned and put in a very high place so as the keep the vision and Spirit of it alive. Seems brutal to some, but might it not be better to be of respect and service than be abused by anyone.

The Eagle, in my Red Man's society or in almost any culture most often represents Strength and Courage. In any society since the recordings of such by Man, the Eagle has represented the pinnacle of its search of ideal as all beings intuitively feel its closeness to the Great Spirit, wherever and when. Eagles can be found on most continents but it seems they are all suffering not just from the predations of Man but purely from the imbalance of his Fear and Greed. A pure symbol of Strength and Vision, it almost seems proper that this magnificent species might fall to extinction by the lack of vision which is one of the highlights of the senses of this truly most splendid Animal. The Eagle has suffered its decline by the stupidity and greed as well as poisoning of Mother Earth which is all of our habitat. Listen to the silence of this very vocal Bird and hear the shame of Selfishness, Wantonness, and Greed. Where an Eagle can fly no more, there are those that do not believe in Beauty, Balance, and what most call GOD, much less the truth of the ALL THAT CAN BE.

The Medicine of the Eagle is that of being a Resource finder, Pathfinder, The Way finder, Knowledge, Truth, Strength, and most of all, Loyalty, Integrity, and Honor. Not because it is part of my Name, but more important to understand is that most of this is through channel, the Medicine of the Eagle is to be said that which is past all understanding. The Eagle is the Path or Way finder, the Light Bringer to Understanding, Strength and Courage are only sometimes necessary tools in the walking of the path. The Eagle does not make the path or even say what you should see there, but most often it has seen it and might merely say, I know. Know well sure that the Eagle lives with great passion and feeling about the condition of all things and a great sensitivity to such. The Eagle has not just Knowing Medicine but also a strong dedication to Truth and Sharing. Just as the Fluorite is the companion Stone to the Dolphin, the Emerald is that of the Eagle as it personifies its Medicine of Loyalty, Commitment, Honor, and Trust. The Eagle not only has extremely great eyesight, but also from its highest flights can make noises that truly all of Mother Earth and those upon it can hear.

The Eagle is not a warrior for warrior sake like some cultures have led us to believe, but a compassionate caring species that lives its life in a very passionate way. Fearless and Dauntless, the Eagle fears not even the predations of the Snake upon its nest and often will allow a Snake to take one of the early eggs as it knows that in time, the Snake will also make a good meal for one that develops. This culture and those of this time that we live in might all do well to listen to the call of the wild, or better said messages from the non-polluted ones wherever we might yet find one in any species that might remember how things are supposed to be. As the Eagle goes, so do the Hopes and Truth of the ideal.

The Medicine of the Eagle is also that of Strength and Purity in an ever knowing way. The best that can be said about the Eagle and its Medicine is Vision and that All Can Be. Ever knowing where things might be as well as where they are at, the Eagle might well be called an inventory of where the resources are located. I asked the Great Spirit this day, "What about Eagles and that part of me?" and He showed me an old kind of brass lamp. In the lamp I saw great function and beauty but then I thought what if the lamp runs out of fuel or such and where am I, wanting to do as much as I can. He told me "You are an Eagle, a lamp and vessel of Light to show the way for others." And then I worried about running out of wax, oil or Light. He told me that cannot happen, "You are the lamp and I am ever the Light" and I understood. The Medicine of the Eagle is also that of 'whichever you might choose in it to be', as the Eagle is ever in service to The Great Spirit.

In dreams and visions the Eagle is the Way Finder. More important than the idea of Strength and Courage that the Eagle truly represents as well, in dreams and visions the Eagle represents the Path. An Eagle flying signifies Growth to Truth. An Eagle sitting still signifies to stand your own ground, no matter what others might think or say. An Eagle with its wings outstretched signifies that an arduous task is at hand, but also to have the Strength of Courage in your convictions, and an Eagle flying and screaming signifies that change and better is coming immediately for you, although not always, but sometimes through conflict. An Eagle with its mate or young signifies pleasantness in the rest of your life and an Eagle bearing a gift or sign is exactly about that. All Eagles in visions and dreams will tell you what they want you to know as they, of almost all of the Animal Spirits, are the most consummate communicators to the Great Spirit that lives in each of you. Always in the Eagle, you will see the Truth in the best and least of you, as they are the mirror of everyone's soul. I truly believe all people are children of the Great Spirit and can be Eagles of some sort. If only one thing might be expressed about the Medicine of the Eagle it is that it is a Pathfinder to the Great Spirit.

HAWKS -

The Hawk family includes the Harrier, Falcon, and Kestrel. Like sports car racers these Fliers love to perform at great speed and make sharp turns in the air as well as many other acrobatic flying feats. Quite vocal and being of keen vision, very little escapes unnoticed by this often impatient predator of the sky. Primarily feeding upon other Bird species that it often takes in great diving feats from high in the sky, the Hawk is also a consummate carnivore as they truly will attack and eat anything that moves including Insects, Amphibians, Fish and Reptiles. Although being considerably smaller than the Eagle the Hawk is often mistaken for it in the skies as it likes to take advantage of free rides upon the thermals there. The Hawk that zooms so well all over the skies also has pinpoint or crystal vision as its prey never leaves the focus of its eyes. Unlike the Eagle that can snatch its fish way behind the position of its head as it flies over the water, the Hawk only sees that which is its target well out in front or as to say, dead ahead. This has sometimes gotten many of these high speed racers of the skies in trouble as they slam into wires and even parts of Mother Earth at times of the chase. This crystal or highly focused vision is a part of the Medicine of this mostly solitary Bird of prey.

The Medicine of the members of this group can best be expressed as being that of Crystal and Target Vision. Although some of this species migrate in groups most often they are seen in their solitary way of hunting. Unlike the Eagle most of this species are not much in the way of nest building and some will often just lay their eggs on a rocky ledge or in the crotch of a tree or often in the nest of another type of Bird. Both male and female share in raising the young and good parenting skills are exemplified by this species, as they teach the young to hunt and fly and are ardent Protectors and Providers to the needs of them. Part of the Medicine of this highly vocal and Communicative bird is that of Sharing The Vision with others of that which it can see, or perhaps more simply put, Nurturing in a visionary way. More about the Medicine of the Hawk is that about ardent Focus and Swiftness in the pursuit of a goal. My guide in the Medicine Wheel way at the time of the writing of this is a Hawk and his name is Illeyeaha. He is of the Red-tailed kind in vision but all kinds in Spirit. Hawk Medicine is about Sharpness and Clarity of Vision and the Pursuit of One's Goals.

All Hawk visions and dreams are about value systems and goals. Hawks in dreams and visions that are circling or soaring signify the need to redefine Direction and assess the validity of the current path of pursuit or goal. The single Hawk in vision being also a great communicator, will most often tell you specifically what it is for you to know. Two or more Hawks in flight signify the need for new Support or Direction, while a single one flying signifies the need for constancy in your pursuit. A Hawk that is feeding or has caught its prey signifies the condition that success is near at hand and the Hawk sitting or in a Tree signifies the need for Patience and a more favorable wind. A mated pair of Hawks with young represents the need to resolve some issues, usually in communication with other members in the condition of relationship or family.

HUMMINGBIRDS -

The Humming Bird is a species of the Fliers that is unique to the New World. There are approximately fifteen species of the Hummingbird that nest north of Mexico and some of this species may be found as far north as Alaska at certain times of the year. The Hummingbird is perhaps the most skilled of the Fliers as it can fly forward and also backwards and sideways, hover, and fly straight up and straight down. This species has been seen as high as thirteen thousand feet above sea level in some mountains and have been recorded flying at speeds over twenty-five miles per hour which they can maintain over great distances. Like the Monarch Butterfly most Hummingbirds migrate to Mexico and Central America and can fly long distances non-stop over bodies of water. The Hummingbird is an ardent and fearless aviator and has even been seen to attack Hawks in flight.

Fearing little about predators when reaching adult size due mainly to its great speed and agility in flight, the Hummingbird does watch out for the occasional nest robbing Snake. While some of this species nest in colonies, most nest alone. The female does the raising of the usual clutch of two young and feeds them a mixture of Tree sap, Insects, and nectar until they are ready to venture out on their own. The Hummingbird's metabolic rate is extremely high in both the respiration and heart cycles and the age of this species has been found to average approximately twenty-five years largely due to the lack of predation. It is truly amazing that this seemingly fragile and delicate creature has survived so well while many others have suffered under the influence of Man and part of this is from the major Medicine of this Bird, which is Courage, Strength, Adaptability, and Specialization.

Of incredible strength for its size and weight the Hummingbird also has keen eyesight as well as perhaps the best sense of smell of all Birds. Another part of the Medicine of this most beautiful species of the Bird family is that of Heart. The Hummingbird shows us that indeed All can Be if we only put our Heart into it.

The Hummingbird in visions and dreams that is feeding upon the nectar of the flower represents the sweetness in life and usually a need to inventory your blessings, but it also can foretell of a wish to soon come true. The Hummingbird that is flying in groups signifies the need to Change or alter the current goal or Direction and reminds us of the ever changing cycles of life. A Hummingbird that is about its nest or caretaking of its young signifies the need of focus to the family matters of Self and to take Courage in them. A Hummingbird that is sitting still signifies the need for Rest and Restoration of one's energy in the pursuit of one's goals. All Hummingbird dreams and visions relate in some sense to the pursuit of one's goals and to take a heartfelt attitude in all conditions of life.

MOTHS -

The Medicine of the Moth might well be said to be that of Renewall, as the adult cycle is about That Which is to Come and Moth Medicine could also be well expressed as being quite Reclusive at most times. The Moth is best distinguished from the Butterfly by the characteristics of their antennae as the antennae of the Moth is much fuzzier or feathery as well as having some of the same fuzziness on parts of their bodies. Like the Butterfly Moths go through a complete cycle of Metamorphosis and indeed Metamorphosis is part of Moth Medicine. Unlike the Butterfly most Moths are active primarily at night and do without food during their adult life. The Moth also has to fly by very rapid wing strokes just to support its much greater body size in flight. Most Moths spend their earlier stages in and about the Trees and indeed Tree knowledge and Growth is very much also part of the Medicine of this Flier. Most of the Caterpillars of Moths live in communal societies and all are very adept at silk spinning whether for a web or cocoon and are of great enterprise, even if it might seem as a destructive endeavor. All Life Named Moth people are very adept with the use of threads and in skills that require the use of the hands. Moths do not see well and are constantly drawn to and blinded by bright lights. Like the Butterfly, Moths have an extended sense of feel or touch. The Moth in its adult stage is usually a solitary creature that likes long rests between periods of flight.

In dreams and visions the Moth represents the cycles in life and relates to periods of Renewall. A flying Moth signifies the need to evaluate current Goals and Challenges and to possibly seek new Direction and a resting Moth signifies the need to include Softness and Rest in the current cycle of Self. The Moth that is about the light signifies the need to assess the current situation as all is not as it seems and there might be something of deception or that might be harmful that is of current attraction to Self. All Moth dreams and visions relate to cycles as well as goals.

OWLS -

The Owl is the great information seeker of all of the Fliers. Constantly attentive and alert the Owl can rotate its head almost all the way around just to see what might be going on back there. Predominately nocturnal fliers and hunters, there are some of this species that are quite active by day as well. Most Owls live in trees or roost in buildings and some live in burrows underground. Owl Named people are constant data collectors, ever watchful of the goings on and as most are as comfortable just watching an event as participating in it they make excellent score keepers and referees as little escapes their watchful eye. Owls are very nurturing parents and the nest and condition of it are very important to them. While the Owl is not given to flights of great distances or heights, it most skillfully maneuvers upon silent wings and is able to operate under the canopy of Trees and Brush with great dexterity.

While its eyesight is good the hearing of the Owl is highly specialized and the feather pattern that is often mistaken as an adornment of the eyes is actually an enhancement to the ears. Some experiments have shown that the Owl needs only its hearing to successfully locate and capture its prey which can include Birds, Snakes and Frogs as well as Insects and Rodents, all of which it typically swallows whole with a single great gulp. Specialization and Information Gathering are some of the Medicines of the Owl, which is a great Communicator as well. The species possesses a variety of screeches and calls but they all seem to personify the question of ' Who?', as they are ever seeking more input to their knowledge banks. Often used by various cultures as a symbol of Wisdom the Owl in my Medicine Wheel is a totem of the North. Being the "Go-Between" of the physical and Spiritual realms, the Medicine of the Owl is about Knowing and Knowledge but is also about the Communication of it.

The Owl in visions and dreams that is flying signifies the need to expand the Resources or the arena of one's Resources of and to Self, the message might well be said to 'Keep looking farther for what it is that you seek.' An Owl that is sitting in the Tree signifies is telling one to be Patient in one's endeavors. If it is looking in any direction other than straight ahead it is showing the need to review and make an internal assessment of that what is sought and also a review of one's direction is indicated. The Owl that is feeding indicates that an Achievement or Accomplishment is near and an Owl in or about its nest represents the need for Care or Consideration about the condition of family and most often that of the home. A screeching Owl signifies the need for Self-expression. As mentioned, one of the highlights of this beautiful Bird is its Communicative ability and its Medicine is often used to Communicate between the Physical and the Spirit world. In dreams and vision the Owl will often tell or show you exactly and most precisely what it is for you to know.

QUAIL – BOBWHITE

The Medicine of the Quail or Bobwhite is that of Joy, Softness and Pleasure in Brotherhood or as might be considered that of sharing the best in life such as to Love to Love and be Loved. These highly social birds roost on the ground and at night often form a circle with bodies touching and heads facing outward. This arrangement representing the sacred circle also serves them for protection as well as warmth even when covered with snow. I have a Quail Spirit Guide and friend named Ooo-coo-wah whom has taught me much about Sensitivity and Joy in life. All Quail and Bobwhites are more prone to run than fly and many a person has been startled by their "Whirring" sound when surprisingly bringing these loving Animals to flight. All Quail in visions and dreams are excellent communicators, so ask them whatever you desire to know. Any Quail or Bobwhite in encounter, vision or dream signifies that good things are coming and one's desires are soon to be fulfilled.

RAVENS - ANY BLACK BIRD

The Raven, Magpie, Crow or any Black Bird is a Path or Direction finder and that is the Medicine of this group as a whole. Is it any wonder that the needles used to indicate direction or anything else on most indicative devices and gauges would most often be black like the Pathfinder Bird? The Black Bird or Raven has been the center or focal point of countless stories in the aboriginal teaching and societies of North America. All of the Ravens and Black Birds are great Communicators and some seem almost to be able to imitate the voice of one at times. Often one will hear the sound, usually loud as well as unusual, of one of these Fliers long before one will finally spot the location of it.

By some considered to be the most intelligent of the Bird species and having the ability to learn to count as well as repeat certain tasks the Raven and Crow have a complex language as well as developed social structures. The great intelligence of these Birds has often been to the disadvantage of many gardeners and farmers who have often put a bounty upon this sly Fox of the Bird species. More clever at getting into things than any Raccoon or Fox the Spirit of these pathfinders might well be put as extremely bold. Boldness is indeed perhaps the most significant part of the Medicine of the Raven or Crow. What better to serve as a Pathfinder than a fearless as well as extremely intelligent explorer. Just as I tell the tattletale Blue Jay the prayer I want all to hear, upon sighting any of these Birds in flight after a prayer for Direction, I know where to find that which I seek. The feathers found of these wonderful Birds are also of great value and the direction that it is pointing from the quill is important to note as well. The direction the quill is pointing at the time of picking up the feather?

All of these great communicators operate well alone or in a large or small group and Resource Sharing is indeed some of the Medicine of all of them. This consciousness to Resources combined with their high intellect however gives cause to associate all encounters with the Crow especially to that of Witches and Witchcraft. The reason for this is that like the Self-serving way of the Witch, which is predominately associated with willfulness and operating more from the Mind than Heart, the Crow also operates from the ideology of having the end justifying any means necessary for its own advantage or Self-fulfillment. So as one can now understand, any vision or encounter with a Crow or Black Bird such as the Raven is most often a great signifier that one is under the pressure of a Witch's desire or influence of some sort. Of course this is not to imply that this is bad, only a warning from these most specific and capable communicators and direction pointers. While felt by some societies to be of darkness or mystery, these wonderful communicators represent the true Light that lives in each of us which is the Spirit of Self. Any Raven or Black Bird whether in the awakened state or in dreams or visions is always a good sign as they confirm our communications channel to the Great Spirit and the Spirit world is well and open.

The Raven in dreams and visions will most often tell you specifically what it is for you to know and will often be found or seen to be bearing a item that is of significance to you. Any of these Birds in flight are pointing the path or way and a single Bird that is perched indicates the need for Rest and to start fresh on your pursuit of that which you seek. Often enlightenment is shown to one in dreams and visions within the conscious or telepathic ability of these great communicators. The Black Birds in groups indicate the need to share one's needs or aspirations with others and to develop support in one's immediate society. A nesting Black Bird or one with young usually represents the need for home repairs or improvements to the condition of home or family and the Black Bird feeding usually signifies the need for improved diet or that a new Resource or Direction is soon at hand.

ROBINS -

The Robin as well as the rest of its family of Thrushes have a great Medicine of Family and Community, as well as working well together in one's endeavors in life. The Robin and other members of the Thrush family are very often found in the society of Mankind living and nesting in the middle of cities and suburbs alike. Robins are often seen as the first active thing after a period of rain as they are ever showing that the storm has passed as they easily feast upon the Worms, Grubs, and Insects flushed by the cleansing waters of the storms and showers. Certainly the message of the Robin or Thrush might well be stated upon observing this beautiful Bird in its effortless endeavor of gathering up the harvest in Peaceful and Trusting foraging, is that the storm is indeed over and that one's needs are every provided in the easiest way by trusting in the Abundance provided by the Creator if one will only pray and be Patient and of Faith. The Medicine of the Robin or Thrush is that of showing us the Peaceful way of living life on Earth in the Community and Brotherhood Way of coexistence with others, and the Force of Change by Prayer and Faith. The Medicine of the Robin is indeed that of the Peace that comes from Trust and Faith in the Creator.

In dreams and visions a Robin or Thrush that is feeding in any way is a messenger that one's true wishes are close at hand. If the Robin is on the ground during its feed is a message to increase one's endeavor. A Robin sitting on a branch is a message that Patience will soon provide a windfall and not to disrupt the flow of one's benefaction through acting in impatience, which will only be an expression of Fear thus pushing one's benefaction away. Robins and Thrushes in pairs are a message to share and communicate with one's partner or mate the endeavors or desires of oneself or both in bringing forth that desired by each and to be more about the co-operative way of goal attainment. While a Robin or Thrush alone is a message to work independently for one's goals, one should also seek support from others as well. Robins or Thrushes in visions or dreams that appear in groups is a message to seek support from family or community for one's Aspirations or way of service or Share. And any Robin or Thrush that is landing on Earth is a message to soon rest one's endeavor or that one's efforts are soon complete. Any Robin or Thrush flying in any manner is a message to seek more fruitful ground for Self-attainment. As the Robin has its Red breast in the male, it is to remind us to keep Heart with Change providing a betterment in the condition of Self and be of Trust and Faith.

SEA GULLS -

The Sea Gull and its family of Skimmers and Terns are given special mention here as they have specialized Medicine that relates to Peace and Well-being during the discovery and journey along one's path of life. Ever-present along the shorelines these graceful Fliers are often seen far inland and may well be the best weathercaster of all of the Fliers. Adaptability is one of the great senses of this Communal and Communicative Bird and they are also of great Grace as well as skill on the water and in the air. With a varied diet that includes Insects and Grubs as well as Crabs, Clams and fishes of the sea this family of Birds is mostly responsible for picking our beaches clean. Ever-present in flight before and after any storm when these vocal birds return be well sure that the storm is gone. Ardent adventurers and travelers in groups or alone the range of this species is quite large and most always seems settled. Often seen squabbling over a morsel or two during beach encounters Sea Gulls are great caretakers of their young but may prey on the young of other species to feed the voracious appetites of their own. Good eyesight and hearing are two of the senses of this Bird and Adaptability to Change is part of the Medicines of this Flier as well as that of Great Balance. The Medicine of the Sea Gull might well be expressed in one word and that being Grace.

The Sea Gull in dreams and visions is often that of being a Provider and usually identifies a hidden desire or goal. The Sea Gull signifies the need to journey or to wait for that which is sought and the Gull at rest upon the water represents that the path is straight and keep Patience. A Gull sitting on any structure signifies the need for Balance in one's walk in life and the Gull sitting on land signifies the need to pace oneself or to find a resting place. The Sea Gull with others in dreams and visions shows the need to Balance oneself to the competitive Spirit and a Sea Gull with family or feeding signifies substance and Well-being are at hand and to have Grace. Often the Sea Gull will speak out its message in dreams or visions, as it too is a very expressive Bird.

TURKEYS -

The major Medicine of this Bird might well be put as Abundance and Beauty of Life.

The Turkey was one of the favorite game Birds sought by aboriginal North American Man and many a hungry Man left well-fed by the taking of one. It seems fitting that this Flier is now used to celebrate a holiday as often it was a great celebration after the sighting and taking of one. Many a young boy learned to call this most vocal and inquisitive Bird and as a resource the Turkey provided much to aboriginal society. It's meat was often smoked or dried into jerky and pemmican, its bones were used for needles and whistles and its splendid feathers, claws, and beak were used for ornamental wear. While the Owl might well be expressed as an ardent pursuer of information, it pales in respect to the curiosity of this great sized Bird. Able to fly short distances the Turkey often prefers to run and it runs well in the most maneuverable of ways. Turkeys most often roost in Trees and feed on Insects, berries, and seeds.   Given to splendid mating dances the Turkey is a very territorial bird that likes a clutch of family members for company. The nest might indeed include up to as many as twenty young, which is taken care of by the female as like most herd species most males are about defending their territory. The Turkey will often distract predators from the whereabouts of the young by playing the injured bird routine and the adults are most wary of the presence of one including Man. Quite vocal and keen of sight this bird also has good hearing and a keen sense of smell often used in its constant search for food.

In dreams and visions the Turkey represents Abundance and Pleasure and that one's goals are indeed at hand. The Turkey that is sitting signifies the need for Patience and a Turkey that is flying away shows the need to strengthen one's endeavor or pursuit. The Turkey that is coming toward one in vision or dreams signifies that success is imminent. A Turkey that is calling represents the need to enlist the support of others or to communicate one's desires. If the Turkey is on the nest it signifies Comfort and Peace of place about the family or home or the need to establish a better condition of one's presence there.

WOODPECKERS -

While the Woodpecker and its family might be often thought of for its hardheadedness, it should be best appreciated for its industry. Indeed Tenacity is one of the Medicines of this industrious bird that in its variety also shares a varied diet as well from seeds to insects. The Acorn Woodpecker stores acorns in holes drilled in trees for later use and most of this species raise four young in nests in holes dug in the sides of trees by these great insect destroyers. Although most of this species live a solitary life the Northern Flicker travels in loose flocks and the Acorn variety nests in colonies and shares in the caretaking of young. The Woodpecker has good eyesight as well as keen hearing and smell and its Medicine might well be put as Adaptability, Industry and Tenacity. The condition of the nest is as important to the Woodpecker as it is to the Owl and sometimes the same nests have been used by both.

In visions and dreams the Woodpecker relates to goals and ideals and signifies the condition of the ideal of Self. The Woodpecker that is busy at work signifies the need for both tenacity and continued endeavor while the Woodpecker in flight signifies the need for restructuring or re-establishment of goals or ideals. A resting Woodpecker signifies the presence of a rest cycle and the Woodpecker about any condition of the nest signifies the same condition or consideration for Self.

LIFE

I start this part after talking about the Medicine of the Animal Spirits, because the Tree Spirit that has been steadily growing next to me said, "Wait, now it is time to write this". The caring fronds of this tree of life said "See not the differences in the separate as you call species, but truly the oneness and Spirit of life. Love the mole or scab and scar on the face of each other as you can only see truly that in Self. See and hear the life force in Self and take responsibility to Self and thereby each other. Give up falseness and Fear in the idea of the Creator and the question as to the biological idea of or the true nature in the origin of Self for the freedom of the truth which is the absolute beauty of the Spirit of Self".

About Animal Spirit, none but the two-leggeds, Man, would maliciously or egocentrically hurt another. Indeed it is only the two-legged that kills, not for food or defense of territory, but purely for killings sake. In the true Spirit of Relationship Proper, both predator and prey share respectful sharing of the environment and the experience of life with each other. In the Animal kingdom there are no losers or winners in the big picture. There are only Spirits that incarnate into one of the many Life form and lifestyle offerings and fulfill, or not, their own personal Life Plans. And of course they too are here learning to do so in ways that Walk in Balance and with Harm to No One including Oneself. It seems odd that I was given to talk about the only other species here and it is chosen to not to discuss much about the most out of balance, destructive, self effacing, and ignorant of all of the Animal species and this truly is the two-leggeds known as mankind. The very name of Mankind is a major misnomer as Mankind is in its present idea of Self anything but kind, to Self, the environment, or any other. Mankind is a product of his own separation from not his nature, but from his truth of his condition of being Spirit. The only things that are no longer useable or renewable come from the byproducts of Man. The only things that are not of biological origin or beneficial to the betterment to the condition of the ALL are manufactured by Man and surely the only things on the face of Mother

Earth that are not only harmful to others but also Self are only those of and by Man. If there is one species that is not in accord to the balance and Well-being and the betterment in the condition of the All and needs to learn and grow the most, it is truly Man. It was given to me to understand about what is called by some in the Spirit world as to be the Earthplane experiment, that this most beautiful environment began as a garden of Eden but unfortunately many of us here do not hear or remember that the garden is about the experience and expression of growth.

ANIMAL FORM MEDICINE SUMMARY

Listed below is the Medicine of the Animal forms that are possible in Named Beings

1. BEAR -

The Sensitivity to Balance in Growth and Well-being in the Cycles of Life as well as The Integration of Consciousness to the Physical and Spirit in All that the Creator has Made.

2. BEAVER -

The Creative Passion of Influence and Sensitivity to Design, Balance and Utility in the Continuous Process of Growth and Caretaking.

3. BUFFALO -

The Stalwart Leader and Provider of Physical and Spiritual Resources and Justice to All of Creation and The Passionate Warrior for the Betterment in the Condition of Creation, Mother Earth, and the Human Experience.

4. BUTTERFLY -

The Stimulation and Exemplification of the Cycles of Change that are Necessary to Support Well-being and Growth and The Exemplification Of the Christ Consciousness and God Awareness in all Beings and things.

5. CARIBOU -

The Harmonious Sharing in The Bounty and Beauty of Life and the Support of Brotherhood and Well-being as well as Growth of All of Creation.

6. CAT / LION -

The Curiosity, Balance, and Sensitivity of All things of Creation in both the Physical and Spiritual Realms, Sensing and Valuing the Spirit in everything in a most Nurturing Way as well as Patience, Harmony, and Gentle Stealth in the Expression of Desire and Pursuit of Goals in a Way of Innocence and Sensitivity.

7. CRANE / HERON

The Gentle Bringing Forth of Balance, Dignity, Grace and Peace of Place as well as The Patience and Inner Knowing that comes with True Faith and Trust.

8. COYOTE -

The Teaching Through Illustration of How to Find Joy, Humor, and the Positive in anything in the Process of Growth as well as the Sensitive Challenging of the Limits of Oneself in the Process of the Pursuit of Desire.

9. DEER -

The Sensitive Enjoining of others into the Brotherhood Way of Personal Expression, and The Sensitive Support and Sharing of Resources for the Growth and Well-being of All of Creation.

10. DOLPHIN -

The Creative, Sensitive and Playful Teaching and Nurturing of All things of Creation and The Naturally Perceptive and Passionate Parent, Caretaker, and Entertainer of all of Creation.

11. EAGLE -

The Spiritual Leader and Loyal and Trusting Way-finder to the Source, His Light, Love, and Benefactions supporting the Brotherhood, Growth, and Well-being of all Creation and The dauntless Warrior and Advocate of Truth, Honor, Integrity, and support to the Balance, Dignity and Way of Brotherhood in the Condition of All Things in Creation.

12. ELK -

The Tenacious Location of Resources and the Facilitation of Endeavors Supporting the Growth and Well-being of All of Creation, as well as The Conscientious Leader, Guide, and Coordinator Supporting Those both the Physical and Spiritual Realms.

13. FALCON / HAWK -

The Self Sufficient and Keen Eyed Observer and Pursuer of Goals and Objectives as well as The Crystal Focused Visionary and Communicator of the Physical or Spiritual Realms.

14. FOX -

The Clever, Free, and Sensitive Resource Gatherer and Illustrator of How Any and All Things Can Be Possible as well as The Sure-footed and Agile Expression of Playful Curiosity in a Sensitive, Teaching, and Nurturing Way.

15. HUMMINGBIRD -

The Ardent Pursuer of Goals and Desires in a Supporting Way to the Growth and Betterment of All of Creation in the Process of Them as well as The Dedicated Partner and Teacher of Brotherhood and Sharing in the Way.

16. MARTEN -

The Continuous Discovery and Persistent Search for Positive Expressions and Greater Utility of Resources and then Sharing That Knowledge with others of that which it can see, hear, or know in some way.

17. OTTER -

The Creative Teacher of Playfulness in Being, and Teacher of Balance and Industry in Life as well as The Inventive Practitioner of Making the Best of Conditions and Utility of Everything in Creation.

18. OWL -

The Steadfast Observer, Teacher, and Communicator Between the Physical and Spiritual Realms as well as The Sensitive Caretaker and Nurturer of All Beings and things in all Realms.

19. RACCOON -

The Sensitive and Playful Discoverer of Ways and Means to Share Light and Love in the Experience of Growth as well as The Tenacious and Passionate Caretaker and Free Expression of Passion.

20. SEA LION -

The Ardent and Jovial Discoverer and Creator of New Perspectives, Approaches and Utility, reminding All that Any and All Things Can Be as well as The Passionate Pursuer of Dreams and Ardent Expression of Hope.

21. SERPENT -

The Dedicated Pursuer of Truth, Trust and Knowledge, as well as The Sensitive Teacher and Provider of Respectful Sharing and Brotherhood.

22. TURTLE -

The Tenacious and Courageous Pursuer of Discovery of New and Everlasting Truths as well as The Personification of Persistence and Exemplification of the Unlimited Potential of Expressions of Care and Heart.

23. WHALE -

The Steadfast Champion of Brotherhood, Community and Common Goals and Causes, as well as the Ardent Pursuer of Goals and Dreams in the Ways of Balance and Utility.

24. WOLF -

The Personification and Exemplification of Brotherhood, Respectful Sharing and Cooperation as well as The Exhibition and Illustration of Nobility, Sensitivity, and Society.

ANIMAL FORM
CROSS REFERENCE INDEX

AMERICA	ASIA	AFRICA	AUSTRALIA
BEAR	Panda	Lemur	Koala
BEAVER		Hippo.	Platypus
BUFFALO	Elephant	Elephant	
BUTTERFLY	Butterfly	Butterfly	Butterfly
CARIBOU	Reindeer	Rhino.	
CAT	Tiger	Lion	
COYOTE		Hyena	Tasm. Tiger
CRANE	Crane	Flamingo	Crane
DEER	Deer	Gazelle	Kangaroo
DOLPHIN	Dolphin	Dolphin	Dolphin
EAGLE	Eagle	Eagle	Eagle
FALCON	Falcon	Falcon	Falcon
FOX	Fox	Fox	Fox
HUMMINGBIRD			Kiwi
MARTEN	Ermine		Tasm. Devil
OTTER	Otter		
OWL	Owl		
RACCOON			
SEA LION		Sea Lion	Sea Lion
SERPENT	Serpent	Serpent	Serpent
TURTLE	Sloth	Turtle	Turtle
WHALE	Whale	Whale	Whale
WOLF	Monkey	Gorilla	Dingo

FROM WHITE EAGLE

NOT SO VERY LONG AGO SOME ONE SAID TO
ME,

YOU DO NOT LOOK LIKE AN INDIAN,

I ONLY SAID THIS,

I SEE WHERE YOU ARE COMING FROM.

Quie nee no lokai

****

ON EARTHPLANE,

UNLIKE WHAT OTHERS WOULD HAVE FOR
THEM TO BE,

THE WATERS AND SANDS DO NOT MAKE MUD,
OR THRONES,

THEY ONLY SHARE THE ELEMENTS,
WITH TIME.

I ASKED THE GREAT SPIRIT
ABOUT MULTIDIMENSIONALITY
AND THE MANY LAYERS OF BEING.

HE GAVE ME A MIRROR AND SET ME WITH MY
BACK TO ANOTHER WITH IT IN FRONT OF ME AND
SAID "NOW LOOK THROUGH THE ONE IN FRONT AT
THE ONE BEHIND AND IN THE FARTHEST MIRROR
YOU CAN FIND, YOU AT BEST CAN ONLY SEE A
LITTLE PART OF YOURSELF, AND ME".

I LOOKED IN THE MIRROR,
AND AS I GAVE AWAY THE IMAGE OF ME,

I TRULY SAW HIM,
EVEN IN EVERY PART OF THE GLASS YOU SEE.

IT IS ONLY BY GIVING UP THE IMAGE OF SELF,
THAT WE TRULY CAN HAVE AND BE ONE.

I PRAY TO LEAVE NO FOOTPRINT IN THE SAND,
THEN ONLY CAN I HAVE, AND BE, ONE.

WHITE EAGLE

ONLY THE TWO-LEGGEDS ARE AT ODDS WITH THE SPIRIT OF MOTHER EARTH AND THEIR RELATIONSHIP WITH THE GREAT SPIRIT CREATOR, AND TRULY ARE THE ONLY ANIMAL THAT CAN DESTROY HER AND ONESELF.

THAT IS NOT POWER, OR EVOLUTION, BUT ONLY STUPIDITY. ANIMAL AS WELL AS PLANT AND MINERAL IS MADE BY THE GREAT SPIRIT AS ARE THE TWO-LEGGEDS ALSO.

ONLY BY OVERCOMING THE DENIAL OF, AND THROUGH THE ACCEPTANCE OF THE SPIRIT OF SELF AND THE TRUE SPIRIT OF THE NATURE OF THINGS ON EARTHPLANE, CAN THE TWO-LEGGEDS KNOWN AS MANKIND SURVIVE THEIR OWN LESSONS OF NATURE AND THEREBY THEMSELVES.

THE ONLY ANIMAL THAT CREATES ITS OWN CONDITION OF FEAR AND SUFFERS ABUSE TO SELF AND OTHERS IS TWO-LEGGED.

THE TWO-LEGGEDS SHOULD DO AT LEAST AS WELL AS THE SNAIL. IF THE WEAKNESS IN THE CONDITION OF THE EGO OF ONE HAS NEED OF SUCH, THEN LEAVE AN OBVIOUS TRAIL OF YOUR PATH IN LIFE SO ANOTHER WILL NOT FOLLOW.

BUT JUST AS THE SNAIL CARRIES HIS HOUSE ON HIS BACK, REMEMBER TRULY WHOSE HOME THE EARTH PLANE IS AND BEGIN TO BE...

PROPER AND RESPONSIBLE VISITORS AND GUESTS.

WHITE EAGLE

I AWOKE ONE MORNING AND I FOUND MYSELF STILL
HERE ON EARTHPLANE, AND I WONDERED WHY AS OFTEN I
AM PRONE TO DO.

I THEN REMEMBERED THE TRUE SOURCE OF ALL THINGS,

THE GREAT SPIRIT FATHER CREATOR.

SO I LOOKED DEEP INSIDE WHERE I KNOW TO FIND HIM
IN ME AS WELL AS IN ALL THINGS AND I ASKED:

"FATHER, WHY AM I STILL HERE?"

AND HE TOLD ME.

BECAUSE I CHOSE TO, AND I HAVE GOOD WORK TO DO.

SO I NOW MUST TAKE RESPONSIBILITY TO AND FOR,
THAT. I THOUGHT ABOUT THIS FOR SOME TIME AND AS
USUAL WHEN HE SPEAKS TO ME, I LEARN MORE TO SEE
FULLY HIS MULTIDIMENSIONALITY OF ME.

IT IS GOOD SOMETIMES TO BE,
A TWO-LEGGED JUST LIKE YOU AND I WILL KEEP TRYING
TO BE THE BEST ONE I CAN.

THIS DOES SEEM IMPORTANT TO ME, BUT BETTER YET, I
STILL HAVE MUCH TO LEARN AND SHARE IN THE LEARNING
OF THE MEDICINES OF ALL OTHERS.

YES, I AM A MEDICINE MAN.

THE TRUTHFUL CONDITION OF ALL BEINGS IN SPIRIT AND EARTHPLANE IS THAT OF GROWTH IN LEARNING THE UNLIMITED WAYS TO EXPRESS LOVE AND LIFE. THIS IS NOT A TANGIBLE GOAL THAT I SEEK TO ACHIEVE IN THE PATH OF LIFE, BUT TO EXPERIENCE AND EXPRESS THE BEAUTY AND JOY IN THE EXPRESSION OF THE BECOMING OF IT.

AS A POHTIKAWAH AND MEDICINE MAN I HAVE LEARNED IF NOTHING ELSE, THAT MORE IMPORTANT THAN THE CONTINUUM OF GROWTH IS THE PROCESS OF LIFE THAT WE SEEK TO EXPERIENCE AND SHARE.

I THANK YOU FOR LISTENING TO THAT WHICH COMES FROM THE CHANNEL OF THE LIGHT AND LOVE OF THE GREAT SPIRIT AND HIS EMISSARIES IN AND THROUGH ME. PLEASE, OH PLEASE, DO TAKE THESE WORDS NOT TO MIND BUT TO HEART. AS IN EACH OF YOU, KNOW THAT THE TRUTH LIVES IN EVERY ONE OF US THERE. BE OF JOY IN LIFE AND LIVE IT IN CREATIVE, CARETAKING, SHARING, AND THE MOST EXPRESSIVE OF WAYS AND PERHAPS MOSTLY, IN AND WITH A GREAT PASSION.

PLEASE LIVE IT IN BALANCE AND WITH HARM TO NO ONE BEING OR THING, INCLUDING ONESELF AND ALL OF THE OTHER ANIMAL SPIRITS.

ELLIAKKE NOATEYHAYA

A PRAYER TO THE TWO-LEGGEDS

THE WANTON DESTRUCTION OF ANYTHING ON EARTHPLANE WHETHER IT IS AN ANIMAL, A STONE, HILL, OR A TREE, IS REMOVING THE OPPORTUNITY AND PLEASURE OF THE EXPERIENCE OF IT IN ITSELF, IT'S GREAT GRANDCHILDREN AND ONCE AGAIN SOMETIME ME AND POSSIBLY YOU. QUIT IT, NOW!!! MAKE NO MORE BYPRODUCTS OR WASTE THAT AN ANT OR BUZZARD CAN NOT EAT, MUCH LESS ANYTHING THAT WILL KILL THEM AND US FOR THE NEXT THREE DAYS MUCH LESS THAN FOR HUNDREDS AND THOUSANDS OF YEARS.

THE GREAT SPIRIT CREATOR HAS GIVEN US MANY THINGS, INCLUDING THE VERY BEING OF OUR SELVES AND THE RESPONSIBILITY OF HAVING FREE WILL AND THEREFORE SELF-DETERMINATION. HOWEVER, HE HAS ALSO GIVEN US THE CONSEQUENCES OF OUR CHOICES AND ACTIONS BOTH INDIVIDUALLY AND COLLECTIVELY. THE CREATOR HAS GIVEN US THE ELEMENT OF BARK ON TREE OR WHAT SOME CALL EGO AS WELL AS THE ESSENCE OF FEAR TO USE WITH IT TO PROTECT NOT ONLY THE PHYSICAL FORM OF ONESELF, BUT ALSO THE FUTURE FOR NOT ONLY ONESELF BUT ALSO THAT OF ALL OF THOSE YET TO COME IN THE FUTURE, WHICH MAY BE THAT OF AGAIN ONESELF. HOWEVER, EVEN AS PRECIOUS AS EACH OF THESE GIFTS ARE, HE HAS ALSO GIVEN US THE PRAYER PROPER WHICH CAN AND SHOULD BE USED IN MAKING ANY AND ALL CHOICES OF ACTION AND EXPRESSION WHIS IS THE QUESTION OF:

DOES IT WALK IN BALANCE AND WITH HARM TO NO ONE BEING OR THING OF CREATION, INCLUDING THAT OF ONESELF?

I PRAY FOR THE WELL-BEING IN THE CONDITION OF THE ALL AND THAT INCLUDES ALL OF THE GREAT SPIRIT FATHER'S CREATION INCLUDING EACH AND EVERY ONE OF YOU. I PRAY FOR YOUR WELL-BEING AND GROWTH, YOUR UNDERSTANDING, AND MOST IMPORTANT, YOUR RESONANCE TO THE ALL THAT IS IN AND OF, THE GREAT SPIRIT THAT LIVES IN AND THROUGH EACH AND EVERY ONE OF US. I PRAY FOR PEACE AND HUMANITY, AND THE RELIEF OF SUFFERING THAT USUALLY COMES FROM GREED IN LIFE. MOST OF ALL I PRAY FOR THE WELL-BEING AND HAPPINESS THAT IS THE BIRTHRIGHT OF ALL OF HIS KINGDOM, NOT JUST THE TWO - LEGGED BEINGS BUT ALSO EACH AND EVERY MINERAL SPIRIT, PLANT SPIRIT, ANIMAL SPIRIT, AS WELL AS MOTHER EARTH, FATHER SKY, AND THE HIM IN EVERYTHING.

AND EVER I TRULY PRAY FOR HIS BLESSING UPON THE SPECIAL ONE THAT IS YOU.

White | Eagle

Pusch Na Tu Ku Oayte

(I Love You Great Pop With All of My Being and Heart)

Animal Spirit Medicine Index

-A-

Acorn Wdpecker	441	Anole	405	Ants	394
Alligators	381	Antelope	402		

-B-

Badger	395	Blackbird	436	Bobwhite	436
Bats	419	Bluebirds	419	Buffalo	398
Bears	395	Blue Heron	424	Buffalo	402
Beavers	396	Blue Jays	420	Butterflies	421
Beetles	397	Bob Cat	399	Buzzards	422

-C-

Cardinals	423	Chipmunks	400	Coyotes	401
Caribou	402	Clams	381	Crabs	382
Caribou	444	Condor	422	Crane	424
Cat	399	Coot	424	Crane	447
Cat	445	Cormorant	424	Crawfish	385
Chameleon	405	Coyote	447	Crow	436

-D-

Deer	447	Dolphin	447	Dragonflies	426
Deer	402	Dolphins	382		
Diving Birds	424	Doves	426		

-E-

Eagle	447	Egret	424	Elk	402
Eagles	428	Elk	446	Ermine	414
Eels	383				

-F-

Falcon	431	Flicker	441	Frogs	384
Falcon	446	Fox	403		
Fish	384	Fox	446		

-G-

Gazelle	402	Geese	427	Groundhog	415

-H-

Harrier	431	Heron	424	Hummingbirds	433
Hawk	431	Heron	445	Hummingbird	446
Hawk	446	Horses	404		

-J-

Jaguar	399	Jellyfish	385		

-K-

Kestrel	431	Kingfisher	424		

-L-

Lion	445	Loon	424	Lynx	399
Lizards	405	Lobsters	385		

-M-

Magpie	436	Mice	406	Moths	434
Marten	414	Mink	414	Muskrat	406
Marten	446	Moose	402		

-O-

Octopus	390	Otters	386	Owls	447
Opossum	407	Otters	446		
Osprey	428	Owls	435		

-P-

Pelican	424	Pipefish	387	Porcupine	408
Pigeon	426	Plover	424	Porpoises	382

-Q-

Quail	436				

-R-

Rabbits	408	Raccoon	447	Ravens	436
Raccoon	409	Rats	410	Robins	438

Index - Page 3 of 3

-S-

Salmon	384	Serpents	388	Squid	390
Sea Gulls	439	Serpent	447	Squirrels	413
Sea Horse	387	Sharks	389	Spiders	412
Seals	387	Shrimp	390	Stork	424
Sea Lion	387	Skimmers	439		
Sea Lion	447	Skunk	411		

-Summaries-

Bear	444	Dolphin	445	Marten	446
Beaver	444	Eagle	445	Otter	446
Buffalo	444	Elk	446	Owl	447
Butterfly	444	Falcon	446	Raccoon	447
Caribou	444	Fox	446	Sea Lion	447
Cat	445	Hawk	446	Serpent	447
Coyote	445	Heron	445	Turtle	447
Crane	445	Hummingbird	446	Whale	447
Deer	445	Lion	445	Wolf	447

-T-

Trout	384	Terns	439	Turtles	391
Tattletale	420	Thrushes	438	Turtle	447
Tattletale	437	Thunderbird	422		
Terns	424	Turkeys	440		

-W-

Weasel	414	Woodchuck	415	Wolf	447
Whales	392	Woodpeckers	441	Wolverine	417
Whale	447	Wolves	416		

****

OTHER BOOKS
BY
WHITE EAGLE

While this was the very first book that Great Pop would have me write, it certainly would not be the last as I was to find out when it was first completed. At this time there are also the following:

The Proper Way
The Medicine in Names
The Medicine of Numbers

Origins -
Volume 1 - The Very Beginning
Volume 2 - The Beginning of Life
Volume 3 - Being Human
Volume 4 - The Future

The Medicine of Selves –
Volume 1 - How to realize Real Success in Life
Volume 2 - Tribes
Volume 3 – Life & Survivor's Guilt

How To Make –
My Medicine Pipe
The Beaded Medicine Wheel
The Crystal Dew Claw Rattle

About –
Great Pop
Possession
Dancing With The Boogie-Man
About – 2012

****

****

I close with a special Thank You
To Susan "Speaking Wolf" McLellan
For her editorial support of this material,
And to You for reading it.

****

Great Pop has gifted and blessed me with so very much and in so
very many ways including being able to Name people.

Naming lets one know what one's Medicine is and thereby what
is uniquely perfect about oneself and Why one likes
or does things a certain way which is invaluable.

To be Named please visit

ASpiritWalker.com

And click on About Names

WHITE EAGLE

CPSIA information can be obtained
at www.ICGtesting.com
Printed in the USA
LVHW041229010320
648602LV00004B/45